Messages, ~~Signs~~, and Meanings

MW01194225

Messages, Signs, and Meanings

A Basic Textbook in Semiotics and Communication

3rd edition

Volume 1 in the series
Studies in Linguistic and Cultural Anthropology

Series Editor:
Marcel Danesi, University of Toronto

Canadian Scholars' Press Inc.
Toronto

Messages, Signs, and Meanings: A Basic Textbook in Semiotics and Communication Theory,
3rd Edition
by Marcel Danesi

First published in 2004 by
Canadian Scholars' Press Inc.
180 Bloor Street West, Suite 801
Toronto, Ontario
M5S 2V6

www.cspi.org

Copyright © 2004 Marcel Danesi and Canadian Scholars' Press Inc. All rights reserved. No part of this publication may be photocopied, reproduced, stored in a retrieval system, or transmitted, in any form or by any means, electronic, mechanical or otherwise, without the written permission of Canadian Scholars' Press Inc., except for brief passages quoted for review purposes. In the case of photocopying, a licence may be obtained from Access Copyright: One Yonge Street, Suite 1900, Toronto, Ontario, M5E 1E5, (416) 868-1620, fax (416) 868-1621, toll-free 1-800-893-5777, www.accesscopyright.ca.

Every reasonable effort has been made to identify copyright holders. CSPI would be pleased to have any errors or omissions brought to its attention.

CSPI gratefully acknowledges financial support for our publishing activities from the Government of Canada through the Book Publishing Industry Development Program (BPIDP).

National Library of Canada Cataloguing in Publication

Danesi, Marcel, 1946-
    Messages and meanings : an introduction to semiotics / by Marcel Danesi.
— [3rd ed.]

(Studies in linguistic and cultural anthropology)
Previously titled: Messages and meanings : sign, thought and culture.
Includes bibliographical references and index.
ISBN 978-1-55130-250-8

    1. Semiotics. I. Title. II. Series.

P99.D26 2004   302.2   C2003-907010-7

Cover design by Hothouse Canada
Page design and layout by Brad Horning

08   09   10   11   12   5   4   3

Printed and bound in Canada by Marquis Book Printing Inc.

All royalties from the sale of this book will be donated to St. Jude Children's Research Hospital.

Table of Contents

PART II: Messages and Meanings

Preface

With *Messages and Meanings: An Introduction to Semiotics,* published by Canadian Scholars' Press in 1994, and its second edition, retitled *Sign, Thought, and Culture*, published in 1998, my aim was to provide my own students at the University of Toronto, and students anywhere else, with a basic textbook in semiotics and communication theory that would explain and illustrate the technical and often abstruse subject matter of these fascinating interrelated fields in practical ways, with plenty of applications to contemporary culture. Starting with the first edition, I envisaged preparing a book that would be not too technical, yet not too watered down, so that students and interested general readers could get a comprehensive look at what semiotics and communication theory were all about.

As it turned out, the book struck a resonating chord with that very audience, as instructors at other universities who adopted it (in either or both of its two previous editions) have often told me. They have been both its staunchest supporters and its most constructive critics. The suggestions and commentaries that they have passed on to me have guided every stage in the preparation of this updated and enlarged third edition, titled *Messages, Signs, and Meanings*. I sincerely hope that it will truly reflect both what they and my own students have told me would be even more useful to them. I feel truly fortunate and privileged to have had the opportunity to share my views with so many over the years. I thank one and all from the bottom of my heart. Readers may contact me at my e-mail address any time they so wish: marcel.danesi@utoronto.ca.

Marcel Danesi
University of Toronto, 2004

Acknowledgments

First and foremost, I wish to thank the editorial staff at Canadian Scholars' Press for all the advice, support, and expert help they have given me over the years. I am especially indebted to Jack Wayne and Althea Prince — it is a delight to work with both of them. My appreciation also goes to copyeditor Alban Harvey for his skilled work on the manuscript.

I must also thank Victoria College for having afforded me the privilege of teaching semiotics and of coordinating its Program in Semiotics and Communication Theory since 1987 (if memory serves me right). In that regard, I would especially like to mention Dr. Roseanne Runte, Dr. Eva Kushner, and Dr. Paul Gooch, the presidents under whom I have worked, and Dr. Alexandra Johnston, Dr. William Callahan, Dr. Brian Merrilees, and Dr. David Cook, the Principals of the College with whom I have had the pleasure of coordinating the Program. I am also thankful to Lynn Welsh, Barbara Kinton, Susan McDonald, and Joe Lumley for their constant help and their patience with me over the years.

A third debt of gratitude goes out to the many students I have taught over the years. Their insights and enthusiasm have made my job simply wonderful! They are the impetus for this book. I would especially like to thank the following students for having provided me with valuable information that I was able to use for this edition of the book. Amanda Hare gave me information on writing systems (chapter 5); Carolyn Johnston on elephant tool-use (chapter 11); Catherine Hayday on the origin of the Ronald McDonald character (chapter 10); and Jamon Camisso on the notion of cognitive compression effect (chapter 13).

Finally, I really must thank my family for all the forbearance and tolerance they have had with me over the years. I dedicate this book to them: Alexander, Sarah, Danila, Chris, Lucy, and Danilo.

Introduction

The human species is consumed by a need to unravel the reason for its existence on this planet. This has led it to create "signs" and "sign systems," such as languages, myths, art forms, sciences, and the like, to help it do exactly that. The study of these and the laws that govern them in cultures throughout the world comes under the rubric of semiotics.

This is a basic textbook in semiotics. It has been designed specifically for use by students taking introductory courses in semiotics, communications, media, or culture studies. It can be used, additionally, by those taking courses in cognate disciplines (psychology, mythology, education, literary studies, anthropology, linguistics) as a complementary or supplementary text. Its organization and contents are based on a first-year course in semiotics and communication theory I have been teaching at Victoria College of the University of Toronto since 1987. I have composed it so that a broad audience can appreciate the fascinating and vital work going on in this relatively unknown area of scientific-philosophical inquiry, most of which is often too technical for general consumption. I have thus made every attempt possible to build upon what the reader already knows intuitively about signs. Nevertheless, the style is not so diluted as to make it a popular "all-you-wanted-to-know-about-semiotics-but-were-afraid-to-ask" book. Some effort to understand the subject matter of each chapter on the part of readers will be required.

Since the focus of this book is practical, the usual critical apparatus of references to the technical literature is kept to a minimum. I have also provided opportunities for readers to do "hands-on" semiotics through the exercises and questions for discussion that accompany each chapter. These are found in Appendix A at the back. Biographical sketches of a few major figures in the field are also included in Appendix B. There is also a convenient glossary of technical terms.

The overall plan of the book is as follows. Part I *(Signs)* consists of six chapters dealing with the basic semiotic notions and techniques. The first two introduce the foundational concepts of the discipline, and may require more effort to grasp than all subsequent chapters. Chapter 3 discusses nonverbal signs, chapter four visual signs, chapter five verbal signs, and chapter six metaphorical signs. The topics dealt with in Part II *(Messages and Meanings)* constitute areas of application—myth and narrative, art, clothing, food, space, television, advertising, communication, and media. In other words, the nine chapters that make up this part are meant to illustrate how message-making and meaning-making can be studied from the specific vantage point of the discipline of semiotics.

I must warn the reader, however, that the topics chosen for treatment, as well as the specific contents of each chapter, reflect my own particular approach to the teaching of semiotics. The presence of the "author in the text" is inevitable. But whether the reader agrees or disagrees with any of the comments made throughout the book, it is my sincere hope that he or she will nevertheless be stimulated enough to know more about the interrelation of signs, messages, and meanings in human life. That and that alone will have made the writing of this book worthwhile.

Signs

What Is Semiotics?

A science that studies the life of signs within society is conceivable. It would be part of social psychology and consequently of general psychology. I shall call it *semiology* (from Greek *semeion* "sign"). Semiology would show what constitutes signs, what laws govern them.

Ferdinand de Saussure (1857–1913)

PRELIMINARY REMARKS

Semiotics is the science that attempts to answer the following question: What does X mean? The X can be anything from a single word or gesture, to an entire musical composition or film. The "magnitude" of X may vary, but the basic nature of the inquiry does not. If we represent the meaning (or meanings) that X encodes with the letter Y, then the central task of semiotic analysis can be reduced, essentially, to determining the nature of the relation $X = Y$. Let's take, as a first case-in-point, the meaning of *red*. In this case, our X constitutes an English color term. As it turns out, there is hardly just one answer to the question of what it means. At a basic level, it refers of course to a primary color located at the lower end of the visible spectrum. However, that very color can have a host of other meanings. Here are few of them:

- If it appears as a traffic signal, it means "stop" to anyone facing the signal at an intersection.
- If it is the armband color worn by someone at a political rally, then the wearer is perceived to be an individual who espouses a particular kind of political ideology, often labeled as "left-wing" or "radical."

- If it is the color of the flag used by someone at a construction site, then it is a signal of "danger."
- If it is used in an expression such as "turning red," then it is a figure of speech that allows people to refer to emotional states without naming them precisely.

In sum, *red* is an example of a *sign*. It is something, *X* (a color), that stands for something else, *Y* (a traffic signal, a political ideology and so on). Describing and investigating the nature of the *X* = *Y* relation constitutes, *tout court,* the subject matter of semiotics. The distinguishing characteristic of our species is its remarkable ability to portray the world in this way—that is, to use *X*'s such as colors, pictures, vocal sounds, hand gestures, and the like to refer to things. This ability is the reason why, over time, the human species has come to be regulated not by force of natural selection, but by "force of history," that is, by the accumulated meanings that previous generations have captured, preserved, and passed on in the form of signs. As opposed to Nature, Culture is everywhere "meaningful," everywhere the result of an innate need to seek meaning to existence.

Since the middle part of the twentieth century, semiotics has grown into a truly enormous field of study, encompassing, among other endeavors, the study of body language, art forms, rhetorical discourse, visual communication, media, myths, narratives, language, artifacts, gesture, eye contact, clothing, advertising, cuisine, rituals—in a phrase, anything that is used, invented, or adopted by human beings to produce meaning. The purpose of this chapter is to sketch a general picture of what semiotics is and purports to do, introducing its fundamental notions and principles.

SIGNS

A sign is anything—a color, a gesture, a wink, an object, a mathematical equation, etc.—that stands for something other than itself. The word *red*, as we saw, qualifies as a sign because it does not stand for the sounds *r-e-d* that comprise it, but rather for a certain kind of color and other things.

Actually, the term *semeiotics* (spelled in this way) was coined by Hippocrates (460–377 BC), the founder of Western medical science, as the science of symptoms. The symptom, Hippocrates claimed, was a *semeion*— the Greek word for a physical "mark" or "sign." Unraveling *what* a symptom stands for, *how* it manifests itself physically, and *why* it is indicative of certain ailments or conditions is the essence of medical diagnosis. Now, while the goal of semiotics today is to investigate something quite different (a sign such as *red*), it nevertheless has retained the same basic method of inquiry. As a case in point, observe the following figure:

What does it mean? The answer is "a bright idea." How does it present this meaning? It does so by showing a light bulb inside a bubble. Why is it indicative of this meaning? Answering this last question entails unraveling the cultural roots of each component of the sign. The use of light in the sign is consistent with the general view in our culture of light as an analogue for intellect and intelligence. This can be seen, for instance, in such expressions as "to become *enlightened*," "to shed *light* on something," and so on. The use of a "bubble" to enclose the light bulb (the source of light) is derived from the comic book tradition of putting words and thoughts into bubbles. This simple example illustrates the sum and substance of semiotic method. The same triad of questions is used to understand everything from a simple visual figure (such as the one above) to a complex narrative or scientific theory.

The thing to which a sign refers is known, logically, as the *referent*. There are two kinds of referents: (1) a concrete referent, such as the animal designated by the word *cat*, and (2) an abstract referent, such as the "bright idea" concept designated by the light bulb figure above. The former is something that can be shown to exist in the real world—e.g., a "cat" can be indicated by simply pointing to one. The latter is imaginary and cannot be indicated by simply pointing to it—how would you point to a "bright idea" inside the brain? Signs allow us to refer to things and ideas, even though they might not be physically present for our senses to perceive. When we say or hear the word *cat* the image of the animal in question comes instantly to mind, even if the actual animal is not around for us to perceive with our senses.

The image itself is called a *concept*. There are three types of concepts. Consider the word *cat* again. If one were to ask you what kind of animal it is, you might answer that it is a type of *feline*, as is a *lion* or a *tiger*. If one were to ask you to specify the type of cat, you might say that it was a *Siamese* or a *Persian* cat. The word *feline* encodes what is known today in psychology as a *superordinate* concept. Such a concept has a general classificatory function. The word *cat* encodes instead a *basic* or *prototypical* concept. Cats, lions, and tigers are examples of basic (feline) concepts. Finally, the word *Siamese* encodes a *subordinate* concept. This is a subtype of cat. The three kinds of concepts can be shown in relation to each other as follows:

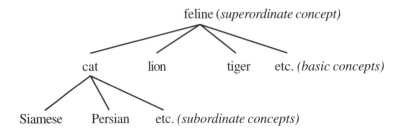

After determining what kind of concept a sign elicits, the semiotician then focuses on the concept itself, attempting to unravel what it entails culturally and personally. In our own culture, the concept that *cat* elicits is that of an animal that we have domesticated as a household companion. But in other cultures, it may elicit instead the concept of a sacred animal, of a scavenger, or of edible meat.

From the foregoing discussion it can be seen that there are three dimensions to a sign: (1) a physical, such as the sequence of sounds *c-a-t*, which (2) elicits a concept ("a type of feline"), which (3) is given culturally conditioned form ("a household companion," "a scared animal," etc.). A sign can now be defined, more precisely, as *something that stands to somebody for something else in some respect or capacity*.

Incidentally, *sign* was a word slow to enter the English language. It came into usage in the thirteenth century, referring at first to a gesture or motion, and by the end of the century to either the sign of the cross or a figure on a banner or shield. As early as the 1390s English merchants were required to label their premises with "signs." By the sixteenth century, there emerged a tradition throughout Europe of placing a sign over the door of a house bearing the owner's name. Such "place signs" have since become common.

AN HISTORICAL SKETCH

As mentioned, in its oldest usage the term *semiotics* meant essentially medical diagnosis. The term was not applied, as far as I know, to the study of the relation between human symbols and reality. It was Plato (c. 428–c. 347 BC) who indirectly dismissed such study because he argued that human forms were deceptive things that did not stand for reality directly, but rather as mental idealizations of it. As an example of what Plato meant, consider the geometric figure called the *circle*. Circles do not really exist in Nature. They are human constructs. When geometers define a circle as a series of points equidistant from a given point (called the center), they are referring to an idealized form. They are not referring to actual physical points. Objects existing in the physical world are called "circles" insofar as they resemble or approximate the geometric form. Thus, the concept encoded by the word *circle* is unlikely to have been pried out of Nature directly. Unconvinced by his teacher's particular perspective, Plato's illustrious pupil Aristotle (384–322 BC) took it upon himself to investigate the relation between forms and reality more closely. He pointed out that words, for instance, do indeed refer to real things, allowing us at the same time to classify the world into real categories—e.g., *plants* vs. *animals* vs. *objects*, and so on.

The first true sign theory is due to St. Augustine (AD 354–430), who did not, however, use the term *semiotics* to identify it. He defined a *natural sign* as one that is found, literally, in Nature. Bodily symptoms, the rustling of leaves, the colors of plants, etc., are all natural signs, as are the signals that animals emit in response to physical and emotional states. He distinguished this type of sign from a *conventional sign*, which is a sign made by humans. Words, gestures, and symbols are examples of conventional signs. In modern-day semiotic theory, these are divided into *verbal* and *nonverbal*—words and other linguistic structures (expressions, phrases, etc.) are examples of *verbal signs*; drawings and gestures are examples of *nonverbal signs*. As St. Augustine emphasized, conventional signs serve a fundamental psychological need—they allow humans to encode and, thus, remember the world. They make thinking and recognition fluid and routine. Finally, St, Augustine defined *sacred signs*, such as miracles, as signs containing messages from God. These can only be understood on faith. He also emphasized that the whole process of understanding what signs mean is partly based on social conventions and partly on individual reactions to them. This idea was consistent with the hermeneutic tradition that had already been established by Clement of Alexandria (AD 150?–215?), the Greek theologian and early Father of the Church. *Hermeneutics* was (and continues to be) the study of texts by taking into account their linguistic features and the historical contexts in which they were written.

St. Augustine's views lay largely unknown until the eleventh century, when interest in human signs was rekindled by traveling Arab scholars, who had translated the works of Plato, Aristotle, and other Greek thinkers. The result was the movement known as *Scholasticism*. Using Aristotle as their inspiration, the Scholastics asserted that signs captured truths, not constructed them. But within this movement there were some—the so-called *nominalists*—who argued that "truth" was a matter of subjective opinion and that signs captured, at best, only illusory and highly variable human versions of it. John Duns Scotus (c. 1266–1308) and William of Ockham (c. 1285–c. 1349), for instance, stressed that signs only referred to other signs, rather than to actual things. The great theologian St. Thomas Aquinas (1225–1274) countered, however, that signs referred to real things, since they were derived from sense impressions. But, like St. Augustine, he asserted that sacred signs revealed truths that were beyond rational comprehension and, therefore, had to be accepted on faith.

Almost four centuries later, the British philosopher John Locke (1632–1704) finally introduced the formal study of signs into philosophy in his *Essay Concerning Human Understanding* (1690), calling it *semeiotics* for the first time (at least to the best of my knowledge). Locke clearly anticipated that it would allow philosophers to study the relation between concepts and reality much more precisely. But the task he laid out for philosophy remained virtually unnoticed until the late nineteenth century, when the ideas of the Swiss linguist Ferdinand de Saussure (1857–1913) and the American philosopher Charles S. Peirce (1839–1914) became the platform on which an autonomous field of inquiry was gradually constructed in the twentieth century. In his *Cours de linguistique générale* (1916), a textbook put together after his death by two of his previous university students, Saussure used the term *semiology* to designate the field. He coined it in obvious analogy to other scientific terms ending in –*logy*, such as *psychology, biology, anthropology,* (from Greek *logos* "word," "study"). Saussure's term betrayed a belief in the supremacy of language among sign systems. Here is what he had to say about it:

> Language is a system of signs that expresses ideas, and is therefore comparable to a system of writing, the alphabet of deaf-mutes, symbolic rites, polite formulas, military signals, etc. But it is the most important of all these systems (Saussure 1916: 16).

Nowadays, the term *semiotics* is the preferred one, and it is the one that will be used throughout this text. This is probably due to the strong influence of Charles Peirce on modern-day theory and practice. Peirce reintroduced Locke's term because he saw it as being consistent with previous traditions. My own sense is that those who prefer to use *semiology* perceive the discipline as similar in overall method to other sciences such as psychology; while those who use *semiotics* perceive it as a more philosophically oriented form of inquiry. My view is that both are complementary perspectives that can easily be integrated into an overall "science of the sign," however we wish to name it. Incidentally, Peirce also provided the most comprehensive typology of signs so far devised. He identified 66 species of signs, according to their function. For example, he defined a *qualisign* as a sign that draws attention to some quality of its referent. In language, an adjective is a qualisign since it draws attention to the qualities (color, shape, size, etc.) of objects. In nonverbal domains, qualisigns include the colors used by painters and the harmonies and tones used by composers.

Semiotic method includes both the *synchronic* and the *diachronic* study of signs—terms introduced by Saussure. The former refers to the study of signs at a given point in time, normally the present, and the latter to the study of how signs change, in form and meaning, over time. As a case in point, consider the word *person*. Today, we use it to refer to any human being. But a diachronic analysis reveals that this was not its original meaning. In ancient Greece, the word *persona* signified a "mask" worn by an actor on stage. Subsequently, it came to have the meaning of "the character of the mask-wearer." This meaning can still be found in the theater term *dramatis personae* "cast of characters" (literally "the persons of the drama"). Eventually, the word came to have its present meaning, probably because of the perceived importance of the theater in Western society in portraying human character. This is why we still say that people "play roles in life," "interact," "act out their feelings," "put on a proper face [mask]," and so on.

In the twentieth century, a number of key figures developed semiotics into the discipline it has become today. Only a few will be mentioned here. The American semiotician Charles Morris (1901–1979) divided semiotic method into: (1) the study of the relations between a sign and other signs, which he called *syntactics*; (2) the study of the relations between signs and their basic meanings, which he called *semantics*; and (3) the study of the relations between signs and their users, which he called *pragmatics*. The Russian-born American semiotician Roman Jakobson (1896–1982) put forward the pivotal notion of "motivated signs," which he defined as the tendency to make signs represent the world through simulation. The French semiotician Roland Barthes (1915– 1980) illustrated the power of using semiotics to unravel the meaning structures hidden in everyday spectacles, performances, and common concepts. French semiotician Algirdas J. Greimas (1917–1992) developed the branch of semiotics known as *narratology*, which he defined as the study of how human beings in different cultures invent similar kinds of narratives (myths, tales, etc.) with virtually the same stock of characters, motifs, themes, and plots. Greimas also characterized the sign as a four-component relational structure, whereby we purportedly come to understand the meaning of a specific sign (e.g., *rich*) by relating it to its contradictory (*not rich*), its contrary (*poor*), and its contradictory (*not poor*). Thomas A. Sebeok (1920–2001) was influential in expanding the semiotic paradigm to include the study of animal signaling systems, which he termed *zoosemiotics*, and the comparative study of symptoms, signals and signs in all living things, which he called *biosemiotics*. He also stressed that semiotic method should always unfold in an interdisciplinary fashion. The interweaving and blending of ideas, findings, and scientific discourses from different disciplinary domains was, Sebeok claimed, the distinguishing feature of the semiotic approach. Finally, Italian semiotician Umberto Eco (1932–) has contributed significantly to our understanding of the relation between signs and reality. He has also single-handedly put "semiotics" on the map of contemporary pop culture, so to speak, with his best-selling 1982 novel, *The Name of the Rose*, which became a major movie shortly thereafter.

Semiotics is often confused with communication science. Although the two fields share much of the same theoretical and methodological territory, the latter focuses more on the technical study of how messages are transmitted (vocally, electronically, etc.) and on the mathematical and psychological laws governing the transmission, reception, and processing of information. Semiotics pays more attention to *what* messages mean, and on *how* they have been put together with signs. This is why it also includes the study of purely fanciful, misleading, or deceitful signs and messages. The capacity for artifice, as Eco argues, is a powerful one indeed, allowing us to conjure up nonexistent referents. When we use words such as *unicorn, mermaid,* and *elf*, for example, we are doing exactly this. We can also get people to act dangerously by misusing signs—we can cause serious problems on the road by intentionally wiring the traffic lights to flash green on all sides at once; we can incite people to hate others by telling them deceitful lies; and so on. As Prometheus stated in Aeschylus' (525?–456 BC) great ancient drama *Prometheus Bound*, the capacity for lying with signs has ensured that "rulers would conquer and control not by strength, nor by violence, but by cunning."

The term *communication theory*, as used in this book, refers to the study of how messages are put together so that they can be exchanged effectively. In effect, it is an extension of semiotics proper, since it deals with the "negotiation" of meaning in specific ways. It is based on Jakobson's idea that communication is regulated by personal, social, and purely semiotic factors.

SIGNIFICATION

Semioticians seek answers to the *what*, the *how*, and the *why* of meaning. But what is *meaning*? In their 1923 work, titled appropriately *The Meaning of Meaning*, Ogden and Richards came up with 23 meanings of the word *meaning*, showing how problematic a term it is. Here are some of them:

She *means* to watch that show	=	"intends"
A red light *means* stop	=	"indicates"
Happiness *means* everything	=	"has importance"
His look was full of *meaning*	=	"special import"
Does life have a *meaning*?	=	"purpose"
What does love *mean* to you?	=	"convey"

Compounding the problem is the fact that when we try to "define" the meaning of something, we invariably end up going around in circles. Take the dictionary definition of *cat* as "a small carnivorous mammal domesticated since early times as a catcher of rats and mice and as a pet and existing in several distinctive breeds and varieties." The first problem that emerges with this definition is the use of *mammal* to define *cat*. In effect, the dictionary has made the unwarranted assumption that we are familiar with the meaning of this term. So, what does the dictionary have to say about the meaning of *mammal*? A mammal, it states, is "any of various warm-blooded vertebrate animals of the class Mammalia." But this definition now assumes that we already know the meaning of *animal*. So what does the dictionary have to say about the meaning of that term? It defines an *animal* as an *organism*, which it defines, in turn, as an individual form of *life*, which it defines, in turn, as the property that distinguishes living *organisms*. Alas, at that point the dictionary has gone into a loop, since it has employed an already-used concept, *organism*, to define *life*.

This looping pattern surfaces with all definitions. It arises because words are used to define other words. So, like the axioms of arithmetic or geometry, the notion of *meaning* is best left undefined. It is something of which everyone has an intuitive understanding, but which virtually no one can really explain. On the other hand, the term *signification* has a specific meaning in semiotics, even though the terms *meaning* and *signification* are often used interchangeably by semioticians (as will be done in this book as well). Essentially, *signification* is what happens in our mind when we use or interpret a sign. The process of signification is, thus, the relation $X = Y$ itself. It unfolds in one of two ways, known as *denotation* and *connotation*. Take, for example, the word *house*. This elicits in our mind an image that can be characterized as a "structure for human habitation." The evocation of this type of basic image is known as *denotation*. It allows us to determine if a specific real or imaginary object *(Y)* to be labeled *house* is, in its basic outline, a "structure for human habitation," no matter what its dimensions are, what specific shape it has, and so on. Similarly, the word *square* denotes a figure consisting of "four equal straight lines that meet at right angles." It is irrelevant if the lines are thick, dotted, 2 meters long, 80 feet long, or whatever. If the figure has "four equal straight lines meeting at right angles," it is identifiable denotatively as a *square*.

Now, the word *house* can be extended to encompass a whole range of other referents. This extensive process is called *connotation*. Here are just three examples of the connotative uses of *house*:

The *house* is in session	=	"legislative assembly, quorum"
The *house* roared with laughter	=	"audience in a theater"
They sleep at one of the *houses* at Harvard	=	"dormitory"

Note, however, that the basic concept of "structure for human habitation" is either implied or suggested in all three uses—a legislative assembly, a theater audience, and a dormitory imply "structures" of certain kinds that "humans" can be seen to "inhabit" in some way. Connotation allows humans to expand the application of signs creatively. It is, in fact, the operative mode of signification in the construction and interpretation of all creative texts—poems, novels, musical compositions, art works, and the like. And, any interpretation of culture-specific concepts, such as *motherhood, masculinity, friendship,* and *justice*, invariably involve connotation. In 1957, Osgood, Suci, and Tannenbaum invented an interesting technique for fleshing out the connotations that such concepts entail, known as the *semantic differential*. It consists in posing a series of questions to subjects about a specific concept, using opposites—*Is it good or bad? weak or strong?* etc.—as seven-point scales, with the opposites at each end. The answers are then analyzed statistically in order to sift out any general pattern. Suppose that subjects are asked to evaluate the concept *President* in terms of the following scales:

Young	_	_	_	_	_	_	_	*Old*
	1	2	3	4	5	6	7	

Practical	_	_	_	_	_	_	_	*Idealistic*
	1	2	3	4	5	6	7	

Modern	_	_	_	_	_	_	_	*Traditional*
	1	2	3	4	5	6	7	

Attractive	_	_	_	_	_	_	_	*Bland*
	1	2	3	4	5	6	7	

Friendly	_	_	_	_	_	_	_	*Stern*
	1	2	3	4	5	6	7	

A subject who feels that a *President* should be more youngish than oldish would place a mark towards the *young* end of the top scale. One who feels that a *President* should be bland, would place a mark towards the *bland* end of the *attractive-bland* scale, and so on. If a large number of subjects were asked to rate *President* in this way, we would get a "culture-specific profile" of the *presidency* in terms of the statistically significant variations in connotation that the concept evokes.

Interestingly, research utilizing the semantic differential has shown that, while the meanings of most concepts are subject to personal interpretation and subjective feelings, the range of variation is not simply a matter of randomness, but forms a socially based pattern. In other words, the experiments have shown that the connotations of many (if not most) concepts are constrained by culture: e.g., the word *noise* turns out to be a highly emotional concept for the Japanese, who rate it consistently at the ends of the scales presented to them; whereas it is a fairly neutral concept for Americans, who tend to rate it on average in the mid-ranges of the scales.

The study of connotation constitutes the core of contemporary semiotics. This is because most of the meanings that signs bear in cultural settings are connotative. Rarely is denotation evoked in the interpretation of signs in such settings, as will become obvious throughout this book. In a fundamental sense, culture can be characterized as a huge system of connotative meanings that cohere into an associative "macro-code" that allows members of the culture to interact purposefully and to represent and think about the world in specific ways. This is why some semioticians prefer to call it the *semiosphere*. In biology, a region that sustains life is called the *biosphere*. By analogy, the semiosphere is the region of social life that sustains knowledge-making and representational activities.

STRUCTURE, TEXT, AND MESSAGE

In order to extract meaning from a form X, one must be able to recognize it as a sign in the first place. This means that signs have *structure*. Specifically, a form X is a sign if: (1) it is distinctive; and (2) it is constructed in a predictable way. The former is called, more specifically, *paradigmatic* and the latter *syntagmatic* structure. For instance, what keeps the words *cat* and *rat* recognizably distinct? It is, of course, the initial sound. The articulatory difference between c (= /k/) and r (= /r/) is, in fact, what allows us to recognize that the two words are different signs. Paradigmatic structure is a feature of all types of signs, not just words. In music, a major and minor chord of the same key are perceivable as distinct on account of a half tone difference in the middle note of the chord; the left and right shoes of a pair are identifiable as different in terms of the orientation of each shoe; raising the index and middle fingers in a vertical orientation can mean "victory," "peace" (among other meanings), but aiming the same two fingers in a horizontal way at someone would be interpreted instead as a threat, and so on.

Now, note that the words *cat* and *rat* are legitimate signs, not only because they are recognizable as different in a specific way, but also because the combination of sounds with which they are constructed is consistent with English syllable structure. On the other hand, *pfat* would not be recognized as a legitimate word in English because it violates an aspect of such structure— English words cannot start with the cluster *pf*. Syllable structure is an example of *syntagmatic* structure. Syntagmatic structure too is found in the composition of all kinds of signs. In music, for instance, a melody is recognizable as such only if the notes follow each other in a certain way (e.g., according to the rules of harmony); two shoes are considered to form a pair if they are of the same size, style, and color, and so on.

Something is a sign if it has both a discernible (repeatable and predictable) form and if it is constructed in a definable (patterned) way. Signs are comparable to the pieces of a jigsaw puzzle. These have visual features on their "faces" that keep them distinct from each other, as well as differently shaped "edges" that make it possible to join them together in specific ways to complete the overall picture.

Because of the predictability of their structure, some signs can replace each other—a relation known as *analogy*. For example, European cards can replace American cards for playing solitaire, because a structural match can be easily made between European and American suits. Analogy constitutes a force of change in sign systems. Words are often re-formed or created on the model of existing patterns in a language. For example, in Old English the plural of *name* was *naman*. This was changed over time to *names* on the model of nouns like *stone—stones*. Analogy is the operative force when children utter a form like *goed*, rather than *went*. This is created in analogy with forms like *played, stayed*, etc.

The X part of a sign can take any form, or "size," we desire to give it, as long as it does not violate paradigmatic and syntagmatic structure, and it assumes signification $(X = Y)$ in some way. It can thus be something "small," such as a word or two fingers raised in a vertical way; or it can be something much "larger," such as a mathematical equation or a narrative. If we ask a mathematician what $c^2 = a^2 + b^2$ means, he or she would instantly recognize it as an $X = Y$ relation, namely as an equation standing for the Pythagorean Theorem ("the square on the hypotenuse of a right-angled triangle is equal to the sum of the squares on the other two sides"). If we ask someone who has just read a novel what he or she got out of it, we would receive an answer that reveals a perception of the novel as an $X = Y$ structure—that is, as something containing a message.

In contemporary semiotic theory, such "larger X's" are called *texts*, rather than simply signs; and the meanings, or "larger Y's" that they encode are called *messages*. The term *text* embraces such things as conversations, letters, speeches, poems, myths, novels, television programs, paintings, scientific theories, musical compositions, and so on. A novel, for instance, is a verbal text constructed with language signs ("smaller X's) in order to communicate some overarching message (the "larger Y"). Texts are composite phenomena—they are not interpreted in terms of their constituent parts (the smaller X's), but holistically as single signs—as $X = Y$. This is why when we ask someone what a novel means, he or she couches the answer in terms of the message he or she extracts from it: e.g., "The novel *Crime and Punishment* paints a grim portrait of the human psyche."

The term *message* is not synonymous with meaning. Consider a simple greeting such as "Nice day, today!" It encodes, of course, a simple message. However, the meaning of that message can be literal, whereby the speaker is acknowledging the kind of day it is simply to make contact; on the other hand, it could be ironic, if uttered on a rainy and miserable day. As this example shows, a message can have more than one meaning, and several messages can have the same meaning. In the mass media, as in art, it is often the case that many layers of meanings are built into the same message. These can only be determined or deciphered in reference to other meanings. Needless to say, this creates problems of interpretation and comprehension of various sorts. To avoid such problems, semioticians often employ the technique of *binary opposition* to flesh out what something means in relation to something else. This approach assumes that meaning is something that cannot be determined in the absolute, but only in relation to other signs: e.g., *cat* vs. *dog*; *cat* vs. *bird*; etc. From such oppositions we can see, one or two features at a time, what makes a *cat* unique among animals. In effect, such oppositions cumulatively allow us to pinpoint what *cat* means by virtue of how it is different from other animals.

SEMIOSIS, REPRESENTATION, AND INTERPRETATION

The brain's capacity to produce and understand signs is called *semiosis*, while the knowledge-making activity this capacity allows all human beings to carry out is known as *representation*. The latter can be defined more precisely as the use of signs (pictures, sounds, etc.) to relate, depict, portray, or reproduce something perceived, sensed, imagined, or felt in some physical form. It is, in other words, the process itself of putting X's and Y's together. Figuring out the meaning of $X = Y$ is not, however, a simple task. The intent of the form-maker, the historical and social contexts in which the representation was made, the purpose for which it was made, and so on and so forth, are complex factors that enter into the picture. One of the main objectives of semiotics is, in fact, to study those very factors. Charles Peirce called the actual physical form of a representation, X, the *representamen* (literally, "that which does the representing"); he termed the Y to which it calls attention, the *object* of the representation; and the meaning or meanings that can potentially be extracted from the representation ($X = Y$), the *interpretant*. The whole process of deciding the meaning of the representamen is, of course, called *interpretation*.

As an example of what representation entails, consider *sex*, as an object. This is something that exists in the world as a biological and emotional phenomenon. Now, as an object, it can be represented (literally "presented again") in some physical form. For example, in our culture, common representations of *sex* include: (1) a photograph of two people engaged in kissing romantically; (2) a poem describing the various emotional aspects of sex; or (3) an erotic movie depicting the more physical aspects of sex. Each of these constitutes a specific kind of representamen. The meanings that each captures are built into each representamen not only by its maker, but also by certain preexisting notions relative to the culture in which the representamen was made. Representations of sex in, say, Paris are thus going to be different from representations of the same object that are made, for instance, in Bombay or San Francisco. Moreover, the type of representamen used to portray the object also shapes the meaning. Photographs can show fairly limited views of sexual activities, whereas movies can provide much more graphic detail. Finally, the ways in which people living in Paris, Bombay, or San Francisco will derive meaning from the representations will vary widely. This is because they have become accustomed in their specific cultures to different perceptions of what sex is.

Interpretation is a crucial aspect of the human condition. The instant children start to interpret the world with signs, they make a vital psychosocial connection between their developing bodies and conscious thoughts to that world. To put it figuratively, signs constitute the "conceptual glue" that interconnects their body, their mind, and the world around them in a holistic fashion. Once the child discovers that signs are effective tools for thinking, planning, and negotiating meaning with others in certain situations, he or she gains access to the knowledge domain of his or her culture. At first, the child will compare his or her own attempts at interpreting the world against the signs he or she is exposed to in specific contexts. But through protracted usage, the signs acquired in such contexts will become cognitively dominant in the child, and eventually mediate and regulate her or his thoughts, actions, and behaviors. Most of the raw, unorganized sensory information that comes from seeing, hearing, and the other senses is organized into meaningful wholes by signs. Our understanding of the world is thus not a direct sensory one. It is mediated by signs and, thus, by the images that they elicit within our mind-space.

The semiotic interconnection between the body, the mind, and culture can be shown graphically as follows:

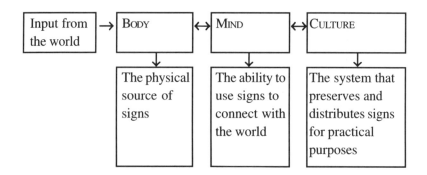

Charles Peirce referred to these three dimensions as *firstness*, *secondness*, and *thirdness*. A sign starts out as a sensory structure, that is, as something that has been made to simulate an object in terms of its sensory properties. It is then used by the sign-user to establish a connection to the object, even if the actual object is not present for the senses to perceive (= secondness). Finally, the sign itself becomes a source of knowledge about the world, once it enters the world of culture and distributed for general usage (= thirdness). Cultures are, essentially, "sign-preserving" systems that distribute signs to people for various kinds of practical purposes.

The research of the Swiss psychologist Jean Piaget (1896–1980) and the Russian psychologist L. S. Vygotsky (1896–1934) on the nature of the child's mind has largely confirmed this three-dimensional model of human development. Piaget's research showed that children progress from a sensory and concrete stage of mind to a reflective and abstract one. Around the age of two, they develop representational abilities derived from constant exposure to words and symbols in cultural context. As these become more dynamic, they prepare the child for more abstract thinking. Vygotsky showed that human development goes from an unconscious "feeling" that the world has meaning to a cogitation of the world with the resources of language ("thinking in words"). This is why he defined speech as a "microcosm of consciousness."

CODE

The signs that we use to make messages are not randomly chosen structures. When we enter into a conversation, for example, we will be able to encode and decode messages only if we know the language used. Language is a system that provides the structures and specifies the relations that these bear to each other for the purpose of making messages. But messages can also be made with music, painting, and other kinds of nonverbal systems. The term used in semiotics to refer to all such systems is *code*. Language, dress, music, and gesture are examples of codes. These can be defined as systems of signs (verbal, visual, gestural, etc.) that have specific properties and, thus, can be used over and over to encode and decode texts and their messages. Indeed, the words *encode* and *decode* reveal, by themselves, that the making and interpreting of messages involves use of a code.

A simple example of a code is the type used in secret communications. Take the following combination of letters:

JGNNQ

If told that each letter represents another letter of the alphabet and that the combination stands for an actual word, then it is easy to see that the actual English word is *Hello*, and thus that the code used consists in replacing each letter with the second letter after it in the normal alphabetic sequence: hence, H = J, E = G, L = N (twice), and O = Q.

There are many kinds of codes used by human beings, each with a specific kind of function. For example, *intellectual codes* allow for representational and message-making activities of a logical, mathematical, scientific, or philosophical nature, providing the appropriate resources (numerical, geometrical, etc.) to represent certain kinds of objects. A perfect example of an intellectual code is trigonometry, which is based on the relations between the sides of a triangle. The six trigonometric functions are defined in terms of a given acute angle in a right triangle:

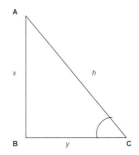

The *sine* (sin) of the angle at **C** is the ratio of the opposite side to the hypotenuse, x/h; the *cosine* (cos) is the ratio of the adjacent side to the hypotenuse, y/h; the *tangent* (tan) is the ratio of the opposite side to the adjacent side, x/y; the *cotangent* (cot) is the ratio of the adjacent to the opposite side, y/x, the *secant* (sec) is the ratio of the hypotenuse to the adjacent side, h/y, and the *cosecant* is the ratio of the hypotenuse to the opposite side, h/x. For any angle the numerical values of the trigonometric ratios can be easily approximated by drawing the angle, measuring, and then calculating the ratios. While this code appears to have little relevance to real-world situations, the remarkable thing is that it can be applied to solve real-world problems. By envisioning an unmeasurable distance as one side of a triangle, measuring other sides or angles of the triangle, and applying the appropriate trigonometric ratios, the distance can be easily determined.

Another type of code is called a *social code* (dress, gender, food, space, etc.). Such codes provide the structures for making messages about oneself in socially appropriate ways and for regulating interpersonal activities. We will discuss social codes in more detail in Part II of this book. Food codes, for example, underlie how people prepare food and when and how they eat it. Many Christians say grace before starting a meal together; Jews say special prayers before partaking of wine and bread. At a formal meal, the order in which dishes are presented, what combinations can be served in tandem, how the foods are to be placed on the table, who has preference in being served, who must show deference, who does the speaking and who the listening, who sits where, and what topics of conversation are appropriate are all based on an appropriate food code, steeped in cultural history and tradition. All cultures, moreover, have a discrete set of table rituals and manners that are inculcated into the members of the culture from birth. If one does not know the *table-manner code*, then he or she will have to learn it in order to continue living in the culture without censure and disapprobation.

While intellectual codes tend to be more or less stable and fixed (e.g., mathematical theorems vary very little over time, if at all), social codes are adaptive and can be recycled in various ways. For example, the "mythic code of the hero," which was embodied in ancient world figures such as Achilles, Prometheus, Samson, and many others is recycled by contemporary pop culture into comic book or movie heroes. Such heroes must be strong, superhuman, have a tragic flaw, etc., just like their mythic predecessors. For example, the comic book and movie Superman comes from another world (the planet Krypton); he has come to help humanity overcome its weaknesses; he has a tragic flaw (exposure to the fictitious substance known as kryptonite takes away his power), and so on. In the figure of Superman, thus, the code of the mythic hero reverberates in modern guise.

Codes guide interpretation in a *context*. In semiotics, the term *context* is defined as the environment, situation, or process—physical, psychological, and social—in which interpretation unfolds. Consider a discarded and damaged beer can. If you were to come across this item on a sidewalk on a city street, you would no doubt view it as a piece of garbage or rubbish. But if you saw the very same object on a pedestal, displayed in an art gallery, "signed" by some artist, and given a title such as "Waste," then you would be inclined to interpret it in a vastly different way. You would, in fact, be predisposed to interpret it as an artistic text, descrying a throw-away or materialistic society. Clearly, the can's physical context of occurrence and social frame of reference— its location on a sidewalk vs. its display in an art gallery—will determine how you will interpret it. The art gallery is, in effect, a social code. This is why we interpret anything that is put on display within it as "art," rather than as something else.

The network of interconnected meanings that constitute a culture is configured with codes. These can be characterized as "organizational grids" within the network. Utilization of the codes for various representational reasons will, of course, vary, but the basic structure of the code will remain intact and be recognizable. As a concrete example, take 1950s rock and roll music. This constitutes a specific type of musical code, providing a system of musical structures with which songs can be composed. Differences in the actual songs composed are attributable to differences in *style*, that is, to the peculiar way in which a particular song has been composed. Thus, one can talk of an "Elvis Presley style" or a "Little Richard style," which are characteristic uses of the same musical code by particular artists. Nevertheless, all 1950s songs retain an essential recognizable form because they are based on the same musical code.

CONCLUDING REMARKS

A sign selects what is to be known and memorized from the infinite variety of things that are in the world. Although we create new signs to help us gain new knowledge and modify previous knowledge—that is what artists, scientists, writers, for instance, are always doing—by and large, we literally let our culture "do the understanding" for us. We are born into an already-fixed semiosphere that will largely determine how we view the world around us. Only if, hypothetically, all our knowledge (which is maintained in the form of codes) were somehow erased from the face of the earth would we need to rely once again on our instinctive meaning-making tendencies to represent the world all over again.

As an example, consider the concept of health. Although this might at first appear to capture a universally shared meaning, in actual fact what is considered to be "naturally healthy" in one culture may not coincide with views of health in another. Health cannot be defined ahistorically, aculturally, or in purely absolute terms. This does not deny the existence of events and states in the body that will lead to disease or illness. All organisms have a species-specific bodily warning system that alerts them to dangerous changes in bodily states. But in the human species bodily states are interpreted in culture-specific ways. This is why in American culture today a "healthy body" is considered to be one that is lean and muscular. Conversely, in others it is one that Americans would consider too plump and rotund. A "healthy lifestyle" might be seen by some cultures to inhere in rigorous physical activity, while in others it might be envisaged as inhering in a more leisurely and sedentary lifestyle.

Moreover, as the writer Susan Sontag cogently argued in her compelling 1978 book *Illness as Metaphor*, the semiosphere predisposes people to think of specific illnesses in certain ways. Using the example of cancer, Sontag pointed out that in the not-too-distant past the very word *cancer* was said to have killed some patients who would not have necessarily succumbed to the malignancy from which they suffered: "As long as a particular disease is treated as an evil, invincible predator, not just a disease, most people with cancer will indeed be demoralized by learning what disease they have" (Sontag 1978: 7). Sontag's point that people suffer more from interpreting their disease in cultural terms than from the disease itself is, indeed, a well-taken and instructive one.

Medical practitioners too are not immune from the influence of cultural symbolism. The body, as we shall see in chapter 4, is as much a source of symbolism as it is organic substance. Several decades ago, Hudson (1972) showed how this affects medical practices. He found that medical specialists trained in private British schools were more likely to achieve distinction and prominence by working on the head as opposed to the lower part of the body, on the surface as opposed to the inside of the body, and on the male as opposed to the female body. Hudson suggested that the only way to interpret such behaviors was in cultural terms: that is, parts of the body, evidently, possessed a symbolic significance that influenced the decisions taken by medical students: "students from an upper-middle-class background are more likely than those from a lower-middle-class background to find their way into specialties that are seen for symbolic reasons as desirable" (Hudson 1972: 25).

Basic Sign Theory

The basic tool for the manipulation of reality is the manipulation of words. If you can control the meaning of words, you can control the people who must use the words.

Philip K. Dick (1928–1982)

PRELIMINARY REMARKS

Human intellectual and social life is based on the production, use, and exchange of signs. When we gesture, talk, write, read, watch a TV program, listen to music, look at a painting, we are engaged in using and interpreting signs. As Charles Peirce aptly remarked, human life is characterized by a "perfusion of signs." The primary task of semiotics is to identify, document, and classify the main types of signs and how they are used in representational activities. Since they vary from culture to culture, signs constitute mental templates that invariably condition the worldview people come to have. The study of signs thus reveals that the age-old idea of an "objectively knowable reality" is something that may be elusive. This chapter will introduce basic sign theory, and end with a discussion of culture as a system of signs that invariably shapes perception of reality.

DESCRIBING THE SIGN

As stated in the previous chapter, Ferdinand de Saussure and Charles S. Peirce are the founders of contemporary semiotic theory and practice. Their ideas make up the basic framework for describing and classifying signs, as well as for applying semiotics to the study of knowledge and culture systems.

Saussure was born in Geneva in 1857. He attended science classes at the University of Geneva before turning to language studies at the University of Leipzig in 1876. As a student he published his only book, *Mémoire sur le système primitif des voyelles dans les langues indo-européennes* ("Memoir on the Original Vowel System in the Indo-European Languages," 1879), an important work on the vowel system of Proto-Indo-European, considered the parent language from which the Indo-European languages descended. Saussure taught at the École des Hautes Études in Paris from 1881 to 1891 and then became a professor of Sanskrit and Comparative Grammar at the University of Geneva. Although he never wrote another book, his teaching proved to be highly influential. After his death, two of his students compiled their lecture notes and other materials, writing the seminal work, *Cours de linguistique générale* (1916), that bears his name.

In the *Cours*, Saussure described the sign as a binary structure, that is, as a structure made up of two parts: (1) a physical part, which he termed the *signifier*, and (2) a conceptual part, which he called the *signified*. In terms of the $X = Y$ relation discussed in the previous chapter, the signifier corresponds to the X and the signified to the Y:

NAMING THE PARTS OF THE SIGN
$X = Y$

X = *signifier* (= the physical part)
Y = *signified* (= the conceptual part)

Saussure considered the link between the signifier and the signified, $X = Y$, to be an arbitrary one established over time for some specific social purpose. To make his point, he noted that there was no evident reason for using, say, *tree* or *arbre* (French) to designate "an arboreal plant." Indeed, any well-formed signifier could have been used in either language—*tree* is a well-formed word signifier in English; *tbky* is not. Saussure did admit, however, that there were some signs fashioned so as to make the signifier imitate some sensory or perceivable property of the signified. Onomatopoeic words (*drip*, *plop*, *whack*, etc.), he granted, did indeed mirror real physical sounds. But Saussure maintained that this was the exception, not the rule. Moreover, the highly variable nature of onomatopoeia across languages showed that it was itself an arbitrary phenomenon. For instance, the word used to refer to the sounds made by a rooster is *cock-a-doodle-do* in English, but *chicchirichí* (pronounced "keekkeereekee") in Italian; the word employed to refer to the barking of a dog is *bow-wow* in English, but *ouaoua* (pronounced *wawa*) in French; and the list could go on and on.

But Saussure may not have noticed that the sounds in a language are themselves suggestive of actual sounds, and that many words are "latently onomatopoeic," so to speak. Consider the word *duck*. The combination of sounds used to construct this signifier is indeed one of an infinite number of permissible combinations that can be envisioned in English, as Saussure would have it. But the final /k/ sound suggests that it has something sonorous in common with *quack*—the actual onomatopoeic word used to represent the sounds made by the animal in question. The use of linguistic sounds to model sonorous referents is called *sound symbolism* in both linguistics and semiotics. Here are few examples of the sound symbolism of English consonants that, when used to make actual words, suggest or model specific types of real sounds:

Consonant Sound	Examples	Type of Sound Modeled
/p/	dip, rip, sip, …	a quick abbreviated explosive sound
/k/	crack, click, creak, …	a sharp abbreviated guttural sound
/b/	rub, jab, blob, …	an abrupt explosive sound
/l/	rustle, bustle, trickle, …	a lingering liquid sound
/z/	ooze, wheeze, squeeze, …	a smooth hissing type of sound
/f/	puff, huff, cough, …	a constricted type of sound

In line with this kind of reasoning, it can now be suggested that the signifier *duck* was probably constructed with /k/ rather than some other final consonant (*dup, dut, dun,* etc.) in order to call attention to the actual sounds emitted by a duck—a feature captured more explicitly by the word *quack*. Although we probably do not experience the signifier consciously as sound symbolic, we certainly seem to feel (unconsciously) that it is better suited to represent the animal than alternative candidates that could in theory have been chosen arbitrarily (e.g. *glop, jurp, flim,* etc.).

Charles Peirce argued that a phenomenon such as sound symbolism revealed, in actual fact, a fundamental unconscious tendency in sign creation; namely, a tendency to make the *X* part of any type of sign—verbal or nonverbal—imitate the concept or object it stood for in some way, to lesser or greater degrees. Thus, while Saussure viewed the sign as an arbitrarily devised structure, Peirce saw it instead as a structure that tended to be "motivated" by some form of simulation.

Peirce was born in Cambridge, Massachusetts, in 1839. He was educated at Harvard University, and lectured on logic and philosophy at Johns Hopkins and Harvard universities. He conducted experiments to determine the density and shape of the earth and expanded the system of logic created by the British mathematician George Boole (1815–1864). But Peirce is best known for his philosophical system, later called *pragmatism*, which maintains that the significance of any theory or model lies in the practical effects of its application. His model of the sign has become highly influential, shaping a large portion of contemporary work in contemporary semiotics.

As discussed in the previous chapter, Peirce called the sign a *representamen* and the concept, things, idea, etc., to which it refers the *object*. He termed the meaning (impression, cogitation, sense, etc.) that we get from a sign the *interpretant*. These three dimensions are always present in signification. Thus, the Peircean viewed the sign as a triadic, rather than binary, structure:

THE "PEIRCEAN" SIGN

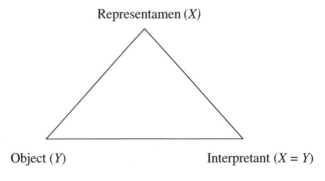

Representamen (*X*)

Object (*Y*)   Interpretant (*X* = *Y*)

He also identified 66 different types of signs, of which three are used commonly in all kinds of semiotic work today. They are called *icons, indexes,* and *symbols.* An icon is a sign that stands for a referent through some form of replication, simulation, imitation, or resemblance. Sound symbolism is an example of iconicity in language, as is onomatopoeia. But iconicity is found as well in the domain of nonverbal representation—a photo resembles its referent visually, as does a painting of a natural scene. An index is a sign that stands for a referent by pointing to it or by relating it (explicitly or implicitly) to other referents. Manifestations of indexicality include a pointing index finger, adverbs such as *here* and *there*, and diagrams known as maps. A symbol is a sign that stands for its object by convention or agreement in specific contexts. For example, a *rose* is a symbol of love in some cultures; the letter ð stands, by agreement among mathematicians of the world, for the number 3.14; and so on. Iconicity constitutes an attempt to simulate the sensory properties perceived in things. Indexicality constitutes a strategy for referring to the existence and location of objects in time-space. And symbolism is the result of historical and social conventions, agreements, or pacts:

Sign Type	Relation between the Sign and Its Referent	Examples
icon	the sign is designed to represent a referent by simulation or resemblance (i.e., the referent can be reseen, reheard, etc., in the icon)	drawings of all kinds (charts, diagrams, etc.), photos, onomatopoeic words, etc.
index	the sign is designed to indicate a referent or to put referents in relation to each other	the pointing index finger, adverbs such as *here, there,* pronouns such as *I, you, he,* etc.
symbol	the sign is designed to encode a referent by convention or agreement	social symbols such as the rose, math symbols, etc.

ICONICITY

Iconicity abounds in all domains of human representation. Photographs, portraits, maps, Roman numerals such as I, II, and III are iconic forms designed or created to resemble their referents in a visual way. Onomatopoeic words such as *drip, plop, bang, screech* are vocal icons simulating the sounds that certain things, actions, or movements are perceived to make. Perfumes are olfactory icons imitating natural scents. Chemical food additives are gustatory icons simulating the taste of natural foods. A block with a letter of the alphabet carved into it is a tactile icon allowing the user to figure out the letter's shape by touch. Peirce called the object of an icon the "immediate" object. He termed the actual referent, which lies outside the sign and may be represented in an infinite number of ways the "dynamical" object.

It is relevant to note that, before Peirce's use of the term to refer to a specific type of sign, icon was used in art to refer to the image of a religious figure or event. The word is still used with this meaning today. The icon is believed to be sacred in itself and, thus, to aid believers in contacting the represented figure. Few early painted icons survive, but a small group of sixth- and seventh-century encaustic paintings on wooden panels, from the Monastery of Saint Catherine on Mount Sinai, remains. Beginning in the eighth century, *iconoclasm*, a movement that condemned the worship of icons as idolatrous, contributed to the destruction of much religious art throughout the Byzantine Christian world. It was not until the next century that making of icons was restored to its former position of honor in religious observance.

Iconicity is evidence that human perception is highly attentive to recurrent patterns of color, shape, dimension, movement, sound, taste, etc. The first inscriptions, cave drawings, and pictographic signs of humanity indicate that iconicity has always played an important role in human development. The imitative hand movements used to portray shapes were transferred to a cave wall or to an object by means of some sharp cutting tool, constituting our first genuine works of art. The earliest of these goes back some 30,000 years. They took two main forms: (1) the vivid carvings of animals that cover the roofs and walls of caves, such as those at Lascaux in France and Altamira in Spain; and (2) the small sculptures and relief carvings of animals and female figures found in caves throughout Europe. As the hand movements used to make such works of art became more abbreviated, the figures became more condensed and abstract. This led to the invention of writing. The earliest form of writing was, thus, vastly different from the alphabetic or syllabic writing systems that we use today. The work of Schmandt-Besserat (1992) has shown, in fact, that the earliest precursors of modern writing systems were pattern-making forms, such as those found on clay tokens discovered in western Asia from the Neolithic era. The tokens were used as image-making objects.

Iconicity is also evident in childhood development. The relevant scientific literature makes it saliently obvious that children invariably pass through an initial stage of gesticulation and vocal sound imitation before they develop full language. Gestures are used for practical purposes (e.g., pointing to something desired) and are probably reinforced by osmosis with adult gestures. It is relevant to note that, although vocal language eventually becomes the dominant form of communication among human beings, the gestural modality does not vanish completely. It remains a functional subsystem of human communication that can always be utilized as a more generic form when vocal interaction is impossible or limited. This happens typically when two interlocutors speak different languages. And, of course, for individuals with impaired vocal organs, gesture constitutes the only possible mode of communication.

Iconicity also shows up in the tendency of children to make scribbles and elemental drawings at about the same time that they utter their first words. If given drawing materials around the age of two or three, young children instinctively start scribbling on the drawing surface. As time passes, their scrawls become more and more controlled; geometrical shapes such as crude circles, crosses, and rectangles, at first accidentally produced, are repeated and gradually perfected. Although children, with adult prompting, may learn to label circles as "suns" or "faces," they do not seem inclined at first to draw anything in particular. The act of making shapes appears to be pleasurable and satisfying in itself. Of course, shapes eventually suggest "things" to the child as his or her ability to use language for naming purposes develops, but in the beginning, the child seems to engage in drawing solely for the pleasure of it, without attaching explicit associations of meaning to it. It is truly an example of "art for art's sake."

In the adult world, icons serve a vast range of social functions. They are found on posters, on toilet doors indicating "male" and "female," and so on. In our digital world, the very term icon is used to designate a tiny picture on a computer screen. Each icon represents a command. The system of icons, pointer, and mouse is known as a graphical user interface (GUI), a system that provides a user-friendly way of interacting with a computer. Users can usually tell by the icons how to get the computer to do what they want. Without a GUI, the computer screen is black, and the only way to tell the computer what to do is to type in commands. There is little doubt that GUIs contributed to the rise of the personal computer in the mid-1980s, starting in 1984 when the

Apple Computer company introduced the Macintosh, the first personal computer to include a GUI. Because they make computers easy to use, GUI's quickly became standard throughout the computer industry. Today, most users encounter only GUI-based programs and never have to type in commands to control their computers.

INDEXICALITY

Indexicality manifests itself in all kinds of representational behaviors. Its most typical manifestation can be seen in the pointing index finger, which humans the world over use instinctively to point out and locate things, people, and events in the world. Many words, too, have been devised as indexes—for example, *here*, *there*, *up*, *down* allow speakers of English to refer to the relative location of things when speaking about them.

There are three basic types of indexes:

- *Spatial Indexes*. These refer to the spatial locations of objects, beings, and events in relation to the sign-user. Manual signs like the pointing index finger, demonstrative words such as *this* or *that*, adverbs like *here* or *there*, and figures such as arrows are all examples of spatial indexes.
- *Temporal Indexes*. These relate things to each other in terms of time. Adverbs such as *before*, *after*, *now*, or *then*, timeline graphs representing points in time as located to the left and right of each other, and dates on calendars are all examples of temporal indexes.
- *Person Indexes*. These relate the participants taking part in a situation to each other. A personal pronoun such as *I, you, he, she* or an indefinite pronoun such as *the one, the other* are examples of person indexes.

Indexicality is evidence that human consciousness is not only attentive to patterns of color, shape, etc., resulting in iconic signs, but also to the recurrent relational and cause and effect patterns that are contingent on time and space. In this case, Peirce referred to the object of the sign as a "reagent," since it constitutes a reaction to an agent that allows us to infer its whereabouts, its relation to other objects, and so on.

Incidentally, the word index is used commonly and appropriately to refer to classification and referential practices. For example, an index at the end of a book is an alphabetized list of names, places, and subjects treated in a printed work, giving the page or pages on which each item is mentioned. In mathematics, an index is a number or symbol, often written as a subscript or superscript to a mathematical expression that indicates an operation to be performed, an ordering relation, or the use of an associated expression. And to help users find the appropriate information on a computer, search engines have been designed so that indexes can be accessed to summarize the contents of the Internet. The user begins by entering a series of words, called a string, to tell the search engine what to look for. The search engine then tries to match the string to the available indexes. For example, a user who wanted to learn about semiotics might begin by entering the word *semiotics* itself. But this search would return thousands of matches, many of which the user would not want. If the user added *Peircean theory* to the string, far fewer matches would result, and these would probably contain relevant information.

SYMBOLISM

A symbol stands for its referent in a conventional way. Words in general are symbols. But any signifier—an object, a sound, a figure, etc.—can be symbolic. A cross figure can stand for the concept "Christianity;" a V-sign made with the index and middle fingers can stand for "peace;" *white* can stand for "cleanliness," "purity," "innocence," and *dark* for "uncleanness," "impurity," "corruption," and the list could go on and on. These meanings are all established by social convention or through the channel of historical tradition.

Iconic, indexical, and symbolic modes of representation often converge in the creation of a sign or text. As an example, consider the common traffic sign standing for a crossroad:

The signifier of this sign consists of two straight lines intersecting at right angles. The vertical line has an arrowhead. This cross figure is, clearly, iconic because its shape visually resembles a "crossroads." But since the cross figure could easily be used to represent a "church" or a "hospital" in other situations (without the arrowhead of course), it is also symbolic insofar as we need to know that it has been chosen, by convention, to constitute a particular type of traffic sign. Finally, the sign is also an index because when it is placed near an actual crossroads it indicates that one is about to reach it physically, as indicated by the arrowhead.

Nowhere has symbolism borne more remarkable fruits than in mathematics and science. The science of geometry, for instance, has helped human beings solve engineering dilemmas since ancient times. Here is a simple demonstration of this. Suppose that a tunnel is to be dug right through the middle of a mountain. Since the length of the tunnel cannot be measured directly, the Pythagorean Theorem suggests a plan for doing so without direct measurement. A point A on one side of the boulder and another point B on the other are chosen such that both points remain visible from a point C to the right. C is chosen so that angle ACB is a right angle (90^0). Then, by aligning A with A' (the entrance to the mountain on one side) and B with B' (the entrance to the mountain on the other side) the required and "unmeasurable" length can be seen to be $A'B'$:

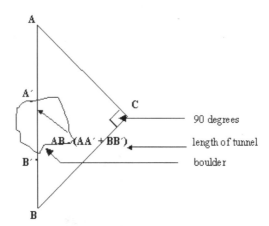

How can $A'B'$ be determined without actual measurement? First, we measure AC and BC. We plug the values into the equation $AB^2 = AC^2 + BC^2$, the relevant Pythagorean equation in this case. This yields a measure for AB. Next we measure the distances AA' and BB'. When we subtract these two distances from **AB** we get the length of **A´B´**: **AB** − (**AA´** + **BB´**) = **A´B´**. That is the length required to dig a tunnel through the mountain.

It is important to note, however, that even though the symbols used to represent the whole situation were based largely on conventional practices, the use of a diagram reveals a need to supplement symbolic reasoning with iconicity. Knowledge of how to represent a real-life physical situation in a symbolic way is a truly remarkable achievement of the human mind. It allows us to eliminate physical intervention through representations of the real world by means of symbols and diagrams that allow us, in turn, to experiment mentally with that very world to see what they yield.

Symbolism is everywhere. It plays, for instance, an important part in religious life—the cross symbolizes Christ's death and all Christian beliefs; the Star of David represents Jewish teachings, and so on. People throughout the world have agreed on certain symbols to serve as a shorthand system for recording and recalling information. Every branch of science has its own system—astronomy uses a set of ancient symbols to identify the sun, the moon, the planets, and the stars; in mathematics, Greek letters and other symbols make up an abbreviated language; and so on and so forth. Specific kinds of symbols appear in such fields as commerce, engineering, medicine, packaging, and transportation. The chart on page 34 shows some common visual symbols used in various fields of human endeavor and enterprise:

All countries have official or unofficial national symbols. A flag or an anthem may symbolize a nation. Familiar symbols of the United States include Uncle Sam and the Statue of Liberty. Symbols for other countries include the maple leaf for Canada, John Bull for England, and the *fleur-de-lis* for France. Political parties also use symbols for identification. In the United States, a donkey symbolizes the Democratic Party, and an elephant represents the Republican Party. Throughout early history, many people considered the swastika a good luck charm. But in 1920, the Nazi Party of Germany adopted it as its symbol. The swastika came to represent the Nazi attempt to conquer Europe. Today, it ranks as one of the most hated symbols of history.

CULTURE

The emergence of culture onto the evolutionary scene can be traced originally to the development within the human species of an extremely large brain, averaging 1400 cc/85.4 cu. in., more than 2 million years ago. Humankind's ability and disposition to think and plan consciously, to transmit learned skills

Table of Symbols and Signs

The following symbols and signs are among the most commonly used.
The designations are also those most commonly used, and do not exhaust the meanings that may be attached to the symbols.
Symbols consisting of letters of the alphabet are entered in the regular alphabetical sequence of entries.
See also symbols in tables at *particle* and *proofread*, and foreign letters at *alphabet*.

ASTRONOMY
- ☉ or ☀ sun
- ● or 🌑 new moon
- ☽ first quarter
- ○ or 🌕 full moon
- ☾ last quarter
- ☿ Mercury
- ♀ Venus
- ⊕ or ♁ Earth
- ♂ Mars
- ♃ Jupiter
- ♄ Saturn
- ♅ Uranus
- ♆ Neptune
- ♇ Pluto
- ♈ Aries
- ♉ Taurus
- ♊ Gemini
- ♋ Cancer
- ♌ Leo
- ♍ Virgo
- ♎ Libra
- ♏ Scorpio
- ♐ Sagittarius
- ♑ Capricorn
- ♒ Aquarius
- ♓ Pisces
- ☌ conjunction
- ☍ opposition
- △ trine
- □ quadrature
- ⚹ sextile
- ☊ ascending node
- ☋ descending node

BIOLOGY
- ☉ or ① annual
- ☉ or ② biennial
- ♃ perennial
- δ or ♂ male
- ♀ female
- □ male (in charts)
- ○ female (in charts)

CHEMISTRY
- ⬡ benzene ring
- → reaction direction

- → reaction direction
- ⇌ reversible reaction
- ↓ precipitate
- ↑ gas
- ‰ salinity

DIACRITICS
- ´ acute
- ` grave
- ~ tilde
- ˆ circumflex
- ¯ macron
- ˘ breve
- ¨ dieresis
- ¸ cedilla

MATHEMATICS
- $+$ plus
- $-$ minus
- $\pm$ plus or minus
- $\mp$ minus or plus
- $\times$ multiplied by
- $\div$ divided by
- $=$ equal to
- $\neq$ not equal to
- $\approx$ or $\cong$ approximately equal to
- $\equiv$ identical with
- $\not\equiv$ not identical with
- ≎ equivalent
- $\cong$ congruent to
- $>$ greater than
- $\not>$ not greater than
- $<$ less than
- $\not<$ not less than
- $\geq$ greater than or equal to
- $\leq$ less than or equal to
- $| \; |$ absolute value
- ≐ approaches
- → approaches
- $\propto$ proportional to; varies as
- $\parallel$ parallel
- $\perp$ perpendicular
- $\angle$ angle
- L right angle
- $\triangle$ triangle
- $\square$ square
- ▭ rectangle

- ▱ parallelogram
- ○ circle
- ⌒ arc of circle
- ⊥ equilateral
- △ equiangular
- $\sqrt{\;}$ radical; root; square root
- $\sqrt[3]{\;}$ cube root
- $\sqrt[4]{\;}$ fourth root
- Σ sum
- $!$ or L factorial product
- ∞ infinity
- $\int$ integral
- f function
- ∂ or δ differential; variation
- π pi
- $\cup$ logical sum or union
- $\cap$ logical product or intersection
- $\subset$ is contained in
- $\supset$ implication
- $\in$ is a member of; mean error
- $:$ is to; ratio
- $::$ as; proportion
- $\therefore$ therefore
- $\because$ because
- $\sim$ difference

METEOROLOGY
- ⦶ rain
- ✳ snow
- ⊠ snow on ground
- ← ice crystals
- △ hail
- ▽ sleet
- V frostwork
- ⊔ hoarfrost
- ≡ fog
- ∞ haze; dust haze
- T thunder
- ≴ lightning
- ⊙ solar corona
- ⊕ solar halo
- ⎚ thunderstorm
- ⬉ direction

PHARMACOLOGY
- ℞ take (from Latin *recipe*)
- āā, ā, or āā of each

- ℔ pound
- ℥ ounce
- ʒ dram
- ℈ scruple
- ƒℨ fluid ounce
- fℨ fluid dram
- ♏ minim

PHYSICS
- ° degree
- ′ minute
- ″ second
- Δ increment, change
- ω angular frequency; solid angle
- Ω ohm
- $\mu\Omega$ microhm
- $M\Omega$ megohm
- Φ magnetic flux
- Ψ dielectric flux; electrostatic flux
- Λ equivalent conductivity
- → direction of flow
- ⇌ electric current
- R reluctance
- ρ resistivity

TYPOGRAPHY
- [ ] brackets
- { } braces
- ¯ vinculum (above letter)
- ( ) parentheses
- & or & and; ampersand
- # number
- / virgule; slash; solidus; shilling
- © copyright
- % per cent
- ℅ care of
- ℀ account of
- @ at
- * asterisk
- † dagger
- ‡ double dagger
- § section
- ☞ index
- ^ caret
- ℔ per

to subsequent generations knowingly, to establish social relationships, and to modify the environment creatively are the felicitous consequences of that momentous evolutionary event. The brain's great size, complexity, and slow rate of maturation, with connections among its nerve cells being added through the pre-pubescent years of life, has made it possible for *Homo sapiens* to step outside the slow forces of biological evolution and to meet new environmental demands by means of conscious rapid adjustments, rather than by force of genetic adaptation: that is, it has bestowed upon the human species the ability to survive through intelligent activities in a wide range of habitats and in extreme environmental conditions without further species differentiation. However, in balance, the prolonged juvenile stage of brain and skull development in relation to the time required to reach sexual maturity has exposed neonatal human beings to unparalleled risks among primates. Each new infant is born with relatively few innate traits yet with a vast number of potential behaviors, and therefore must be reared in a cultural setting so that it can achieve its biological potential. In a phrase, Culture has taken over from Nature in guaranteeing the survival of the human species and in charting its future evolution.

Evidence from the field of *paleontology*, the science of fossil interpretation, suggests that cultures have ancient origins. The fashioning of tools, the earmark of early cultures, was accomplished at least 2.5 million years ago, as was, probably, the use of gesture for communication. Gradually, planned hunting, fire-making, the weaving of cloth, and the ritualized burial of the dead became well-established characteristics of hominid groups. By about 100,000 years ago, the making of art, communication by means of vocal language, and communally established systems of ethics became the distinctive attributes of the first human tribes. Since then Culture, in the sense of individuals living together, thinking and planning consciously, transmitting skills and systems of social relationships to each other through language, and working together to modify the environment, has become *the* defining attribute of the human species. Simply put, without culture human beings would have great difficulty surviving. Anthropologist Clifford Geertz (1973: 23) has perhaps best expressed the paradox of the human condition by stating wryly that without culture human beings would be "unworkable monstrosities, with few useful instincts, few recognizable sentiments, and no intellect."

So, the question of what is culture is hardly a trivial one. To understand human nature is to unravel the *raison d'être* of culture. Although interest in culture is as old as human history, the first scientific definition of culture had to await the nineteenth century, when the British anthropologist Edward B. Tylor (1832–1917) defined it in his 1871 book *Primitive Culture* as "a complex whole including knowledge, belief, art, morals, law, custom, and any other capability or habit acquired by human beings as members of society." Tylor's definition was also one of the first ever to differentiate qualitatively between *culture* and *society*. Although these terms continue to be used commonly as synonyms in many languages, in actual fact they refer to different things. Within a social collectivity, there can, and frequently does, exist more than one culture. In an opposite manner, several societies can be thought of as belonging to the same general culture—for example, European culture, Asian culture, African culture, etc. Societies are simultaneously the geographical and historical "reifications" (manifestations) of cultures: that is, they have existence in time and space.

General philosophical interest in the phenomenon of culture is as old as civilization itself. It can be seen, for instance, in the written descriptions of the first travelers of the ancient world who were captivated by the behavioral diversity that they saw among the peoples they visited. Those who have made it their objective to study culture have tended to do so by means of an essentially descriptive, or so-called *ethnographic*, method. This consists in chronicling first-hand the characteristics of each culture's language, artifacts, modes of dress, rites of passage, religious and mythological systems of belief, rituals, ceremonies, and indigenous art forms. The starting point for the study of culture is the Greek historian Herodotus (c. 484–425 BC), who spent a large part of his life traveling through Asia, Babylon, Egypt, and Greece, noting and recording for posterity the differences he perceived (with respect to Athenian culture) in the language, dress, food, etiquette, legends, and rituals of the people he came across. The annotations he made constitute the first significant accounts of the cultures of virtually the entire ancient Middle East, including those of the Scythians, Medes, Persians, Assyrians, and Egyptians. Inspired by Herodotus, other ancient historians, like the Roman Tacitus (c. AD 55–117), also made it a point to describe systematically and comparatively the languages, character, manners, and geographical distribution of the peoples they visited.

In the nineteenth century, German social theorist Karl Marx (1818–1883) argued that new forms of culture emerged not as reflexes of genetic adaptations, but as consequences of individuals struggling to gain control over their personal and social lives. At the turn of the twentieth century, the American anthropologist Franz Boas (1858–1942) argued that culture was so powerful that it shaped worldview. Boas's account came shortly thereafter to be known as *cultural relativism*. Among Boas's students at Columbia University in the 1920s and 1930s, Edward Sapir (1884–1939), Margaret Mead (1901–1978), and Ruth Benedict (1887–1948) became well-known cultural relativists. Sapir (1921) devoted his career to determining the extent to which the language of a culture shaped the thought patterns of its users. Mead (1939, 1950) sought to unravel how child-rearing practices influenced the behavior and temperament of the maturing individual. Benedict (1934) was fascinated by the fact that every culture developed its own particular canons of morality and lifestyle that largely determined the choices individuals made throughout their life cycle. From the moment of birth the customs into which an individual is born shape his or her behavior and worldview. By the time the child can talk, he or she has become a creature of his or her culture—its habits are his or her habits, its beliefs his or her beliefs, its challenges his or her challenges.

The Polish-born British anthropologist Bronislaw Malinowski (1884–1942) argued that cultures came about so that the human species could solve similar basic physical and moral problems the world over. Malinowski claimed that the symbols, codes, rituals, and institutions that humans created, no matter how strange they might at first seem, had universal structural properties that allowed people everywhere to solve similar life problems. The British anthropologist Alfred Radcliffe-Brown (1881–1955) similarly noted that in a specific cultural context even a physical response like weeping could hardly be explained in purely biological terms. Among the Andaman Islanders, in the east Bay of Bengal, he found that it was not primarily an expression of joy or sorrow, but rather a response to social situations characterizing such meaningful events as peace-making, marriage, and the reunion of long-separated intimates. In crying together, the people renewed their ties of solidarity.

The basic question of the relation between Nature and Culture continues to bog down a lot of scholarship to this day. On the side of Nature today are so-called sociobiologists, who claim that Nature has Culture on a leash. The emergence of culture, sociobiologists assert, has taken place as a survival strategy—the body's survival mechanisms have been gradually replaced by the survival formats provided by culture.

The sociobiological perspective has gained widespread popularity beyond academia in large part as a result of the publication of accessibly written books such as those by the contemporary British biologist Richard Dawkins—e.g., *The Selfish Gene* (1976), *The Blind Watchmaker* (1987), *River Out of Eden* (1995). With great rhetorical deftness and aplomb, Dawkins portrays cultures as collective adaptive systems that emerged in the human species to enhance its survivability and future progress by replacing the functions of genes with those of cultural units that he calls *memes*—a word he coined in direct imitation of the word *genes*. Dawkins defines memes as replicating patterns of information (ideas, laws, clothing fashions, art works, etc.) and of behavior (marriage rites, love rituals, religious ceremonies, etc.) that people inherit directly from their cultures. Like genes, memes involve no intentionality on the part of the receiving human organism. Being part of culture, the human being takes them in unreflectively from birth, and then becomes part of a collective system that passes them on just as unreflectively to subsequent generations, which improve adaptively over preceding generations. The *memetic code* is thus responsible for cultural progress, advancement, and betterment, having become the primary agent in the human species' evolutionary thrust forward. Dawkins's clever proposal poses an obvious challenge to virtually everything that has been written in traditional philosophy, theology, and the social sciences on human nature. If Dawkins is correct, then the search for meaning to existence beyond physical survival is essentially over. Any attempt to seek metaphysical meaning to life would be explained as one of the intellectual effects of culturally inherited memes such as *soul*, *God*, and *afterlife*. To sociobiologists, memes have arisen simply to help human beings cope with their particular form of consciousness, thus enhancing their collective survivability as a species—no more, no less.

In my opinion, Dawkins's case is, at its core, a deceptive metaphorical one. Genes can be identified and separated from organisms, and then studied, altered, and even cloned physically. All this is scientific fact. Memes, on the other hand, are figments of Dawkins's imagination. Only in a technological society that is being constantly exposed to the convincing discourse of evolutionary biology, to advancements in cloning and genetic engineering, is the portrayal of human ideas, information, and behavioral patterns as if they were genes a believable one. Indeed, even before Dawkins put forward his meme theory, the parallelism between ideas and genes was already a firmly entrenched one.

The key figure behind sociobiological theory and research is the American biologist E. O. Wilson (1929–), known for his work on the effects of natural selection on insects. Since the mid-1950s, Wilson has constantly maintained that the psychological capacities and social behaviors that humans manifest are genetically based, enhancing reproductive success and survival. Thus, characteristics such as heroism and altruism, for instance, should be understood as evolutionary outcomes, not as the result of the particular psychic nature of humanity. Moreover, he sees the creative capacities undergirding language, art, scientific thinking, etc., as originating in the same pool of genetic responses that have helped the human organism solve physical problems of survival and species continuity. But so far, all Wilson has produced is a theory. He has not produced any empirical evidence to substantiate any of his claims. Moreover, one can legitimately ask: What do such things as paintings, musical compositions, marriage rites, burial rites have to do with survival or reproductive success? To paraphrase the French philosopher Michel Foucault (1926–1984), human beings have, since their origins, sought to understand and define their identities and their states of consciousness. They have done so by ascribing them to Nature, human effort, or God. As others have done in the past, Wilson has simply placed most of his bets on Nature.

Finding hard scientific evidence to explain why culture emerged from the course of human evolution has proved to be a monumental challenge. So, scholars have understandably resorted to speculating or reasoning inferentially. What would happen if modern human beings were somehow forced to survive without culture? The best examples of this form of inferential thinking have, actually, come not from scientists or philosophers, but from writers of fiction—Daniel Defoe's novel *Robinson Crusoe* (1719) and William Golding's *Lord of the Flies* (1954), for instance, deal with intriguing fictional "test cases" of people forced to live outside of a cultural ambiance, inferring what would happen to them because of it and how they would respond to it. In all such "cases" a tribal-like form of living is the one that is assumed to be the default one. And indeed tribalism has hardly disappeared from contemporary cultures. In complex city-societies, where various cultures, subcultures, countercultures, and parallel cultures exist in constant competition with each other, where the shared territory is so large that it constitutes a mere abstraction, the tendency for individuals to relate to tribal-type groupings that exist within the larger societal context manifests itself regularly. People continue to perceive their membership in smaller groups as more directly meaningful to their lives than allegiance to the larger society and/or nation. This inclination towards tribalism, as the great Canadian communications theorist Marshall McLuhan (1911–1980) emphasized, reverberates constantly within modern-day humans, and may be the source of the angst and sense of alienation that many city-dwelling individuals feel, living as they do in large, impersonal social systems.

THE SEMIOSPHERE

The semiosphere—a concept originating in the work of the great Estonian semiotician Jurij Lotman (1922–1993)—is the term used in semiotics, as indicated in the previous chapter, to refer to culture as a system of signs. The semiosphere, like the biosphere, regulates human behavior and shapes evolution. But although they can do little about the biosphere, humans have the ability to reshape the semiosphere any time they want. This is why cultures are both restrictive and liberating. They are restrictive in that they impose upon individuals born into them an already-fixed system of signification. This system will largely determine how people come to understand the world around them—in terms of the language, music, myths, rituals, technological systems, and other codes that they learn in social context. But cultures are also liberating because paradoxically they provide the textual resources by which individuals can seek new meanings on their own. The artistic, religious, scientific, and philosophical texts to which individuals are exposed in social contexts, moreover, open up the mind, stimulate creativity, and engender freedom of thought. As a result, human beings tend to become restless for new meanings, new messages. For this reason, codes are constantly being modified by new generations of artists, scientists, philosophers, and others to meet new demands, new ideas, new challenges.

Leaving aside this knack for creativity for the moment, the fact remains that cultures influence beliefs, attitudes, worldview, and even sensory perception to varying degrees. As a concrete example, the reader should look at the following classic visual illusion. As he or she can confirm for himself or herself, the line **AB** appears to be longer than line **CD**:

In actual fact the lines are equal in length, but the orientation of the arrowheads fools the Western eye into seeing **AB** as longer than **CD**. In other areas of the world, on the other hand, psychologists have found that people see the lines as equal in length. The factor behind this illusion is cultural, not biological—Western individuals are accustomed to seeing drawings in *perspective*. The arrowheads "add" or "subtract," according to their orientation, to the length of the line. This forces the eye to make an adjustment accordingly. In painting, this is the technique of creating an illusion of depth or length in two-dimensional surface drawings. As a historical footnote, it should be noted that the craft of perspective drawing dates back to the Renaissance, after the Italian artist Filippo Brunelleschi (1377–1446) discovered and then entrenched this technique in Western painting. Visual illusions provide strong evidence to support the notion that signs mediate perception. The great Swiss psychologist Carl Jung (1875–1961) was fond of recounting how visual perception was intrinsically intertwined with representational practices. During a visit to an island tribal culture that had never been exposed to illustrated magazines, he found that the people of that culture were unable to recognize the photographs in the magazines as visual representations of human beings. To his amazement, he discovered that they perceived them, rather, as smudges on the paper. Jung understood perfectly well, however, that their erroneous interpretation of the photographs was not due to defects of intelligence or eyesight; on the contrary, the tribal members were clear-sighted and highly intelligent. Jung perceptively understood that their primary assumptions were different from his own and from those of individuals living in Western culture, because they had acquired a different system of signs that blocked them from perceiving the pictures as visual signs.

The semiosphere always leaves gaps, offering up only a portion of what is potentially knowable in the world. Indeed, an infinite number of signifiers could be created without any signifieds attached to them. This is exactly what young children do when they make up "nonsense words," creating them seemingly only for the pleasure of making imitative, pleasant, or humorous sound effects. The great British writer of children's books Lewis Carroll (1832–1898) invented his own nonsense language, in his poem *Jabberwocky,* to show that the English language as constituted does not tell all there is to tell about reality. Using signifiers such as *brillig, slithy, tove, wabe* and others (from *Through the Looking Glass,* 1871: 126–129), Carroll showed that it is an easy thing to make up legitimate words that seem to beg for legitimate meanings:

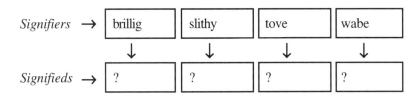

In effect, Carroll had coined signifiers without signifieds; that is, words that suggested ideas by virtue of the fact that they were structured like English words. Actually, Carroll provided his own signifieds for the words as follows to make his point even stronger:

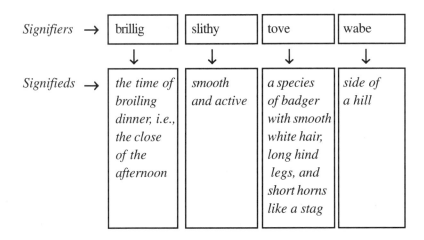

Analogously, there are infinitely many potential signifieds that are not captured by a specific language such as English. Indeed, there are still no words in English for "side of a hill," "smooth and active," and other such concepts. Here are a few other examples of potential signifieds not captured by existing English words:

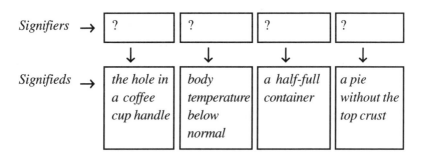

However, even though gaps exist in a cultural system, humans have the ability to fill them any time they wish. They do this typically by inventing new signs, altering already-existing ones to meet new demands, borrowing signs from other cultures, and so on. One can always find ways to refer, for instance, to the above signifieds by paraphrase or some other verbal strategy—e.g., *a pie without the top crust = a top-crustless pie.* But the lack of signifiers to enshrine these concepts in a direct way implies that they will not be anticipated by speakers of English within the scheme of things.

The foregoing discussion in no way purports to lay out a theory of mind or of culture; it simply acknowledges that the semiosphere shapes human thinking. In actual fact, there are creative forces constantly at work in individual human beings. The Neapolitan philosopher Giambattista Vico (1688–1744) termed these the *fantasia* and the *ingegno.* The former is the capacity that allows human beings to imagine literally anything they desire freely and independently of biological or cultural processes; it is the creative force behind new thoughts, new ideas, new art, new science, and so on. The latter is the capacity to convert new thoughts and ideas into representational structures—metaphors, stories, works of art, scientific theories, etc. So, although human beings are indeed shaped by the cultural system in which they are reared, they are also endowed with creative faculties that allow them to change that very system.

Culture can be compared to the default mode of computer software. A computer is formatted in a way that is known as its default mode. This format can, of course, be changed intentionally by a human programmer. But if there are no changes made, the computer will automatically operate according to its original format. Analogously, culture is the human being's default mode for knowing the world. But in the same way that a human programmer can always choose to change a computer's format, so too, the individual human being can always decide to alter his or her own "format" at any time. Indeed, therein lies the paradox of the human condition—throughout the life cycle, there is an unexplainable need within each person to transcend the categories of knowing provided by existing sign systems. Changes to the format, in fact, are what lead cumulatively to cultural change and evolution. Sign systems are products of human intelligence and, therefore, subject to being changed constantly by them to suit any new need or demand. As the philosopher of science Jacob Bronowski (1977: 25) remarked, this is the feature of the human mind that makes it unique among all species:

> The images play out for us events which are not present to our senses, and thereby guard the past and create the future—a future that does not yet exist, and may never come to exist in that form. By contrast, the lack of symbolic ideas, or their rudimentary poverty, cuts off an animal from the past and the future alike, and imprisons it in the present. Of all the distinctions between man and animal, the characteristic gift which makes us human is the power to work with symbolic images.

CONCLUDING REMARKS

Signs allow us to represent the world in various ways—by simulation, indication, and conventional agreements. In a sense, they allow humans to imprint their own mark on Nature. At the same time, they serendipitously unravel patterns within Nature itself. The invention of the mathematical ratio π (= approximately 3.14) was motivated by the need to calculate the area of a circle. But, as it turns out, this very same ratio appears to be an unexpected "descriptor" of such physical phenomena as the motion of a pendulum or the vibration of a string. This synergy between the semiosphere and the biosphere is a remarkable one indeed.

From the dawn of civilization to the present age, it has always been felt that there is an intrinsic connection between the two. The *raison d'être* of semiotics is, arguably, to investigate whether or not reality can exist independently of the signs that human beings create to represent and think about it. Is the physical universe a great machine operating according to natural laws that may be discovered by human reason? Or, on the other hand, is everything "out there" no more than a construction of the human mind deriving its categories from the world of sensations and perceptions? Although an answer to this fundamental question will clearly never be possible, one of the important offshoots of the search for an answer has been a systematic form of inquiry into how the mind's products and the body's natural processes are interrelated.

Body Signs

For male and female alike, the bodies of the other sex are messages signaling what we must do—they are glowing signifiers of our own necessities.

John Updike (1932–)

PRELIMINARY REMARKS

Humans convey over two-thirds of their messages through the body, producing up to 700,000 physical signs, of which 1000 are different bodily postures, 5000 are hand gestures, and 250,000 are facial expressions (Morris et al. 1979). The body is, in a phrase, a primary source of signification. Studying the signs that are produced with, through, or on the body is a central objective of semiotics. Technically speaking, the study of these signs falls under the rubric of *nonverbal semiotics.*

Body signs generally have a social function, regulating Self-Other relations. They ensure that the ways in which people interact in their cultural spheres, and in society generally, are regular and fluid. Consider the following typical, but hardly trivial, vignette that illustrates how Self-Other relations are regulated by the "signifying body":

- An individual in the United States or Canada is about to step into an elevator of a skyscraper on the ground floor. Inside, he or she sees three people, all obvious strangers to each other.
- The individual knows this because the people in the elevator are near or leaning against separate corners of the elevator, facing the door or looking down at the ground, and silent.

- Once inside, the individual knows that he or she is expected to go near the fourth corner and assume a similar posture; namely, to face the door or look down at the floor to avoid eye contact with the others and, of course, to maintain silence.
- In short, if he or she is an active participant in North American culture, he or she instinctively knows the appropriate *elevator code*.

If the individual decides to act in some other way—to face the others and/ or to look straight at them—the others would become uneasy or angry, because they would interpret his or her behavior as either conflictual or disturbed. To cope with the transgressor's breach of the elevator code, they would more than likely ignore his or her actions completely, as if they hadn't occurred. This chapter will deal with such patterns of behavior, with their meanings, and with the kinds of typical messages that are made with them.

NONVERBAL SEMIOTICS

Across cultures, the body signs and the codes that regulate nonverbal behaviors are the result of a perception of the body as something more than physical substance. Winks, hand gestures, facial expressions, postures, and other bodily actions all communicate something culturally relevant in particular social situations.

As mentioned in the opening chapter, the semiotician is guided by three basic questions in his or her search to understand such behaviors: (1) *What* does a certain nonverbal sign, code, or text mean? (2) *How* does it mean what it means? (3) *Why* does it mean what it means? The semiotician seeks answers to these questions essentially by observing people being themselves in their social ambiances. The activities of the semiotician-as-people-watcher, however, are not random. They are guided by five specific goals:

- identifying the basic sign properties behind the observed behaviors (iconicity, indexicality, etc.);
- relating these to the culture in question;
- documenting and explaining the effects that bodily codes have on individuals;
- investigating how these codes are interconnected throughout the semiosphere;

- utilizing the findings or techniques of any cognate discipline (anthropology, psychology, etc.) that are applicable to the situation at hand.

Nonverbal behaviors seem "natural" because they are acquired osmotically (unreflectively) in cultural context. In reality, they are largely a matter of historically based conventions, not of naturalness or lack thereof. Consider the behaviors that we associate with *gender* as a case in point. Humans, like other animals, sense and respond instinctively to the sex (male or female) of another human being. Across the animal realm, such responses are elicited by sexual signals emitted during estrus (going into heat). From an evolutionary perspective, however, the human species has evolved a sexuality independent of estrus. Other animals experience chemical and physical changes in the body during estrus, which stimulate desire. People are the reverse. We normally experience desire through the mind first. This then produces changes in the body. Thus, sex is literally in the mind of the beholder.

But the human story of sex does not end there. Throughout the world, certain behaviors are perceived as constituting appropriate manifestations of male and female sexuality. These are the result of *gender codes* that define "masculinity" and "femininity" within a tribe or society. This is why sexual behaviors and practices vary considerably: for example, in Western society, men are often expected to be the "sex-seekers," to initiate courtship, and to show an aggressive interest in sex; but among the Zuñi people of New Mexico, these very same actions and passions are expected of the women.

Note that if a person alters his or her biological sex, by surgery and hormone treatment, then that person's gender behavior will change accordingly. This shows the power of codes in human behavior. Because of their social value, the types of messages made with nonverbal signs invariably involve connotation, that is, they are rarely interpreted as being purely physical signals. Most of the body signs discussed in this chapter thus entail a connotative interpretation. So, unless otherwise indicated, when the word "meaning" is used below it will refer to "connotative meaning."

SIGNALS

Body signals are of two types—witting (emitted on purpose) or unwitting (emitted instinctively by the body). All animals are endowed with the capacity to emit and respond to species-specific signals for survival. Birds, for instance, are born with the capacity to produce a particular type of coo, and no amount of exposure to the songs of other species, or the absence of their own, has any effect on their cooing. A bird reared in isolation, in fact, will sing a very simple outline of the sort of song that would develop naturally in that bird born in the wild. This does not mean, however, that animal signaling is not subject to environmental or adaptational factors. Many bird species have also developed regional cooing "dialects" by apparently imitating each other. Vervet monkeys, too, are born with the usual set of instinctive signals to express emotional states and social needs, but they also have developed a particular predator signaling system—a specific call alerting the group to eagles, one to four-legged predators such as leopards, another to snakes, and one to other primates. The calls and referents they represent seem innate, but in actual fact the young of the species learn them only by observing older monkeys and by trial and error. An infant vervet may at first use an aerial alarm to signal a vulture, a stork, or even a falling leaf, but eventually comes to ignore everything airborne except the eagle.

Most animals emit signals unwittingly in response to specific types of stimuli and affective states. The research in ethology has documented that animals use them for survival, social interaction, and all kinds of pragmatic activities. And because manifestations of signals are truly remarkable, it is little wonder that they often trick people into seeing much more in them than may be actually there. A well-known example of how easily people are duped by animal signaling is the case of Clever Hans. Clever Hans was heralded the world over as a German "talking horse" in 1904 who appeared to understand human language and communicate human answers to questions by tapping the alphabet with his front hoof—one tap for **A**, two taps for **B**, three taps for **C**, and so on. A panel of scientists ruled out deception and unintentional communication by the horse's owner. The horse, it was claimed, could talk! Clever Hans was awarded honors and proclaimed an important scientific discovery. Eventually, however, an astute member of the scientific committee that was examining the horse, the Dutch psychologist Oskar Pfungst, noticed that Clever Hans would not tap his hoof without *observing* his questioner. The horse, he suspected, had obviously figured out—as most horses can—what the signals that his owner was unwittingly transmitting meant. The horse tapped his hoof only in response to inadvertent cues from his human handler, who would visibly relax when the horse had tapped the proper number of times. To show this, Pfungst simply blindfolded Clever Hans who, as a consequence, ceased to be so clever. The "Clever Hans phenomenon," as it has come to be known in the annals of psychology, has been demonstrated over and over with other animals as well (a dog will bark in lieu of the horse's taps in response to signals unwittingly emitted by people).

The way in which Clever Hans learned to do what he did is called *programmed learning*. This is defined as the process by which animals learn particular things in specific ways at predictable times in their lives. A large amount of bodily communication among humans also unfolds in the form of unwitting signals. It has been shown, for example, that men are sexually attracted to women with large pupils, which signal unconsciously a strong and sexually tinged interest, as well as making females look younger (Sebeok 1994). This would explain the cosmetic vogue in central Europe during the 1920s and 1930s of women using a crystalline alkaloid eye-drop liquid derived from *belladonna* ("beautiful woman" in Italian). The women of the day bought the liquid because they believed—and correctly so, it would appear—that it would enhance facial appearance and sexual attractiveness by dilating the pupils.

But humans are capable as well of deploying witting signals for a vast range of intentional purposes—nodding, winking, glancing, looking, nudging, kicking, head tilting, and so on and so forth. As the linguist Karl Bühler (1934: 28) aptly observed, such signals act like regulators, eliciting or inhibiting some action or reaction. Mechanical and artificial signaling systems have also been invented by people for conventional social purposes. The list of such systems is extensive, and includes: railway signals, smoke signals, semaphores, telegraph signals, warning lights, flares, beacons, balefires, red flags, warning lights, traffic lights, alarms, distress signals, danger signals, whistles, sirens, bleepers, buzzers, knocking, gongs, bells, and drums—among many others!

FACIAL EXPRESSION

Facial expressions in human beings can also be witting and unwitting. The former types of expressions are, in effect, special types of signals. In 1963, psychologist Paul Ekman established the Human Interaction Laboratory in the Department of Psychiatry at the University of California at San Francisco for the purpose of studying such facial signals. He was joined by Wallace V. Friesen in 1965 and Maureen O'Sullivan in 1974. Over the years, Ekman and his team have established specific facial expressions as universal signs of specific emotions. They have shown this by breaking down facial expressions into characteristic components—eyebrow position, eye shape, mouth shape, nostril size, etc.—which in various combinations determine the form, X, and meaning, Y, of the expression. Ekman found very little variation across cultures in the nature of the components and in their combinations. Indeed, he has shown that it is possible to write a "grammar" of the face that shows less cross-cultural variation than do language grammars. The following four sketches of facial expressions show how we interpret facial components in emotional terms:

amusement   anger   surprise   sadness

The reason why we perceive the top left face as expressing *amusement*, the one to its right anger, the second from the right one *surprise*, and the last one *sadness* is because of how the eyes, the eyebrows, and the mouth are oriented with respect to each other. These are, in effect, universal unwitting signifiers that constitute the facial signs of amusement, anger, surprise, and sadness. Similar patterns have been found in other species. Dogs, for example, prick their ears during an alert mode; lynxes twitch them in conflictual or agitated modes; and cats flatten them when they are in the protective mode. These same animals stare during an alert mode or frown during a protective mode. They also gape and pout in order to convey hostility, aggression, or amicability.

But the semiotic story of the human face does not stop at a study of such biologically programmed signals. There is in fact an important connotative chapter to that story. Above all else, the face is perceived the world over as a sign of Selfhood. This is why we tend to evaluate a stranger's personality on the basis of his or her facial appearance. And, of course, we judge the "beauty," or lack thereof, of a person on the basis of how that person "looks." This is why facial decorations and alterations constitute critical Self-representational props and activities that reach back into the origins of culture. The cosmetic make-up that we use today has a long and unbroken connection to ancient courtship practices. The alterations made to the face and the props used to embellish it during courtship are all latent sexual signifiers. Red lipstick, for example, connotes the redness associated with female fertility; the wearing of mustaches by males connotes virility; and the list could go on and on. From the beginning of time, human beings have made up their faces to convey sexual and gender identity as well as images of attractiveness. As the anthropologist Helen Fisher (1992: 272–273) has aptly remarked, the available archeological evidence suggests, in fact, that the sexually constructed face is a characteristic Self-representational phenomenon that goes right back to our Cro-Magnon ancestors, who spent hours decorating themselves, plaiting their hair, and donning garlands of flowers to show off for one another around the fire's glow. The contemporary cosmetic and jewelry industries are modern-day versions of these age-old traditions.

Interestingly, psychologists have found that specific individuals are responsive romantically to certain particular kinds of faces and not to others from puberty onwards. One explanation as to why such preferences surface at puberty is the presence of what the psychologist Money (1986) calls "lovemaps" in the mind. He defines these as mental images that determine the specific kinds of features of the face that will evoke sexual arousal and love moods (such as infatuation) in an individual. Lovemaps are developed during childhood in response to various environmental experiences and influences. At adolescence, they unconsciously generate an image of what the ideal "sweetheart" should be like, becoming quite specific as to details of the physiognomy of the ideal lover, as well as to his or her general demeanor.

The perception of the face as a purveyor of Selfhood or *persona*, as it is sometimes called, permeates the semiosphere across the planet. This is why we use connotative expressions that reinforce the perception that the face is a sign representing the person behind it:

- We argued *face* to *face*.
- Don't show your *face* on my property again.
- He criticized the supervisor to her *face*.
- Put on a happy *face*.
- You wear your feelings on your *face*.
- You can see his hypocrisy on his *face*.
- He's just another pretty *face*.

This perception underlies the practice of portraiture. A portrait is a visual representation of a subject whose facial appearance, as depicted by the artist, is typically interpreted by viewers as a signifier of the Self—a sign that we interpret as betraying the subject's character, social position, profession, etc. A portrait is a probe of human character.

EYE CONTACT

Eye contact is, of course, not unique to the human species. A dog uses a direct stare as a threat or challenge. The dog will break eye contact as a sign of surrender to a more dominant (powerful) dog or person. Incidentally, people can avoid dog bites by not staring directly into the dog's eyes because it may consider the stare a threat and attack the looker. One should avoid eye contact and slowly back away.

Such eye contact patterns are unwitting. However, in human cultures across the world many patterns transcend biological processes, reflecting cultural meanings and fitting in with social interaction patterns. Consider the following facts as cases in point:

- Across cultures, the length of time involved in eye contact conveys what kinds of relationships people have with each other.
- Staring is often interpreted as a challenge; *making eyes* at someone is normally interpreted as flirtation.
- In many cultures there exists the concept of an *evil eye*, which is perceived to be a certain kind of stare that is purported to have the power to harm or bewitch someone.
- Making eye contact early or late during a verbal exchange will indicate the kind of relationship one wishes to have with the interlocutor.
- When the pupils contract during excited states, they tend to elicit a sexual response in an observer.
- Narrow eyelids communicate pensiveness across cultures.
- Making the eyebrows come nearer together communicates thoughtfulness universally; when they rise they convey surprise.
- Southern Europeans will tend to look more into each other's eyes during conversation than do North Americans; in some cultures males do not look into female eyes unless they are married or members of the same family.

Looking patterns convey specific meanings in specific contexts. For example, in our own culture, gazing is interpreted as indicative of sexual wonder, fascination, awe, or admiration; staring as sexual curiosity, boldness, insolence, or stupidity; peering as looking narrowly, searchingly, and seemingly with difficulty; ogling as staring in an amorous, usually impertinent manner; and the list could go on and on. Incidentally, until recently, Western cultural tradition has dictated that men should be the "lookers" and women the ones "looked at." Although this has been changing radically, the semiotic remnants of this tradition are still found throughout the semiosphere—in language, courtship behaviors, artistic practices, etc.

BODY LANGUAGE

Body language is the general term used to indicate communication by means of gestures, postures, and other witting and unwitting body signals and signs. It also includes grooming habits, hair and clothing styles, and such practices as tattooing and body piercing. Body language communicates unspoken information about people's identity, relationships, and thoughts, as well as moods, motivation, and attitudes. It plays a critical role in interpersonal relationships. The scientific study of body language is called *kinesics*. Kinesics was developed by the American anthropologist Ray L. Birdwhistell, who used slow-motion films of conversations to analyze speakers' behaviors. He borrowed many terms and techniques from linguistics to characterize the basic motions that made up meaningful body language. He reported the results of his findings in two classic books, titled *Introduction to Kinesics* (1952) and *Kinesics and Context* (1970).

Kinesic signals can be inborn (unwitting), learned (witting), or a mixture of the two. Blinking the eyes, clearing the throat, and facial flushing are innate (inborn) signals. These are often involuntary, as are, for example, facial expressions of happiness, surprise, anger, disgust, and other basic emotions understood by people in all cultures. Laughing, crying, and shrugging the shoulders are examples of mixed signals. They may originate as innate actions, but cultural rules shape their timing and use. Gestures, such as a wink of the eye, a thumbs up, or a military salute, are learned signals. The meanings of such signs vary among different cultures. Messages made with body language can give a look and feel to a conversation remembered long after spoken words fade away. Body language can also be structured to lie or conceal something. For example, pressing the lips together may indicate disagreement or doubt, even if the person's verbal statements convey agreement. When verbal statements and body language conflict, listeners will more likely believe the latter more.

Kinesic signs cohere into *kinesic codes* that regulate how people behave in certain social situations. They are a product of cultural history, and thus largely conventional in nature. Recall the elevator vignette described above. This time, imagine that the stomach of one of the passengers sends out one of those uncontrollable growls that result from hunger, digestion, or some other bodily process. Undoubtedly, the person will feel embarrassed or uneasy, even with the knowledge that he or she has no control over a sound emitted naturally by the body. This is because the *kinesic code* that applies to the "elevator situation" does not permit any sound to break the measured silence in the cubicle. So, as a socially redeeming strategy the individual might either excuse himself or herself, make a facetious remark about the sound, attempt to hide it by making some more kinesically acceptable noise (like clearing his or her throat), or ignore it completely as if it hadn't occurred.

The sounds made by the body—sneezing, coughing, burping, etc.—and the fluids that issue forth from it are similarly interpreted in terms of the kinesic codes that regulate a specific situation. These codes prescribe what body image is socially acceptable. In contemporary Western society, for instance, the "slim, lean look" is a requisite for both males and females who desire to be perceived as attractive. The margin of flexibility from any idealized thinness model is larger for males than it is for females, but males must additionally strive to develop a muscular look.

Body language is especially powerful in courtship displays. In our culture, when strangers are attracted to each other, the male attempts typically to look "virile" by cocking his head, assuming an exaggerated tone of voice, and displaying a pseudo-nonchalant attitude towards the female suitor, as he casts glances towards her. The female, on the other hand, will typically tilt her head down and to the side as she looks away. Raising her shoulder, arching her back, tossing her head in one sweeping motion, and playing with her hair are other unwitting female signifiers in such situations. A female might also tuck her hair behind her ear (if she wears longer hair) to expose her neck, an alluring erogenous zone for the males. Males tend to react to such signals by engaging in exaggerated movements—linking their hands behind the head with the chest out, laughing loudly, swaying markedly, etc. Similar "coded behaviors" exist across cultures. The specific manifestations will vary highly, but their courtship or romantic functions will be identical or similar.

Courtship displays may look comical or absurd to outsiders. But to the members of a society or group they constitute a crucial kinesic mode of communication at a key stage in the enactment of reproductive urges. They make sense only if the appropriate physical and social contexts are present during flirtation. So, while human kinesic codes may be residues of some ancient animal signaling mechanism, as some sociobiologists suggest, the great diversity that is evident in them across cultures suggests that they are not mere contemporary versions of instinctual mating behaviors. Rather, they are shaped in large part by human notions of gender and romance and are, therefore, constantly inclined to change. In the human species, courtship is not only a reflex of biology, but also a product of history and tradition. It is the outcome of Nature and Culture cooperating in a type of partnership that is found nowhere else in the animal realm.

Kinesic codes also mediate people's perception of which bodily parts or zones are erogenous. The semiotician Michel Foucault (1926–1984) argued persuasively that the "sins of the flesh" are hardly universal. They must be defined culturally. The Puritans of England, for instance, saw any form of sexual contact or gazing in a marriage situation as a kind of "necessary sin." "Sexual temptation" is still felt by some people to be "sinful." On the other hand, the many "hedonistic" rites and practices of our own and other cultures exalt and glorify the eroticism of the human body. Obviously, what is "obscene" behavior to some is "natural" behavior to others. While sexual urges are based in biology, perceptions of what is or is not erotic, sinful, or obscene are ensconced in cultural traditions and habits.

TOUCH

In most cultures, a basic form of greeting involves handshaking, which is a perfect example of a social behavior regulated by a *tactile code*, that is, by a code that governs the patterns of touch in interpersonal situations. The study of touch goes under the rubric of *haptics*. The zoologist Desmond Morris (1969) claims that the Western form of handshaking may have started as a way to show that neither person was holding a weapon. It thus became a "tie sign," because of the bond it was designed to create. Throughout the centuries, the sign became a symbol of equality among individuals, being used to seal agreements of all kinds. Indeed, refusing to shake someone's outstretched hand continues, to this day, to be interpreted as a "counter-sign" of aggressiveness or as a challenge. Predictably, this form of greeting reveals a high degree of cross-cultural variation. People can squeeze the hand (as Europeans and North Americans do), shake the other's hand with both hands, shake the hand and then pat the other's back or hug him or her, lean forward or stand straight while shaking, and so on. Haptic communication is not limited, of course, just to handshake greetings. Other forms include patting someone on the arm, shoulder, or back to indicate agreement or to compliment; linking arms to indicate companionship; putting one's arm around the shoulder to indicate friendship or intimacy; holding hands with family members or a lover to express intimacy; hugging to convey happiness at seeing a friend or a family member; and so on.

Anthropologists are unclear as to why tactile and haptic codes vary so much across cultures. But throughout the world the skin is perceived to be a surface "sheath" and the body a "container" of sorts. Some people seem to think of themselves as "contained" in their skin. The zones of privacy that define Self-space in these cultures, therefore, include the clothes that cover the skin. Others feel instead that the Self is located within the body shell, resulting in a totally different perception of haptic behaviors. People in such cultures are in general more tolerant of crowds, of noise levels, of the touching of hands, of eye contact, and of body odors than most North Americans are (Hall 1966).

One aspect of tactile behavior that is shrouded in evolutionary mystery is "lip touching" or osculation in the human species, known, of course, more commonly as *kissing*. When the lips of both people touch, the kissing act is perceived normally as an erotic one. But not all kissing is erotic. It can be a way of showing affection to children, friends, pets, etc. But erotic kissing is particularly interesting as an evolutionary and cultural phenomenon, because it seems to be a kind of mock-suckling or mock-feeding of the sexual partner, implying vulnerability, closeness, and sensuality. This is perhaps why prostitutes may be willing to perform a variety of sexual acts for hire, but generally draw the line at kissing. However, erotic and/or romantic kissing is not universal. It is not common in China or Japan, for instance; and it is completely unknown in many African societies. Traditional Inuit and Laplander societies are more inclined to rub noses than to kiss.

GESTURE

Gesture can be defined simply as the use of the hands, the arms, and to a lesser extent, the head to make signs. Although there are cross-cultural similarities in gesture, substantial differences also exist both in the extent to which gesture is used and in the interpretations given to its particular uses. For example, the head gestures for "yes" and "no" used in the Balkans seem inverted to other Europeans. In 1979, Desmond Morris, together with several of his associates at Oxford University, examined 20 gestures in 40 different areas of Europe. The research team found some rather fascinating things. For instance, they discovered that many of the gestures had several meanings, depending on culture—a tap on the side of the head can indicate completely opposite things, "stupidity" or "intelligence," according to cultural context. Morris also found that most of the gestural signifiers were used in many countries.

Gesture is also found in primates. Chimpanzees raise their arms in the air as a signal that they want to be groomed; they stretch out their arms to beg or invite; and they have the ability to point to things (Beaken 1996: 51). These gestures are, evidently, purposeful and regulatory of the actions of other chimps. But the number of gestural forms of which chimpanzees are capable is limited. Human gesturing, on the other hand, is productive and varied. It encompasses, for instance, the many sign languages used in communities of the hearing-impaired, the alternative sign languages used by religious groups during periods of imposed silence, the hand signals used by traffic personnel, and the hand and arm movements used to conduct an orchestra. Some gestures can have quite specific meanings, such as those for saying good-bye; for asking someone to approach, the clenched fist of anger, the raised palm of peace, the "V" for victory or for peace, the "thumbs down" for disapproval, and the gesture for hitchhiking.

Many semioticians and linguists consider gesture to be a more fundamental form of communication than vocal language. A pragmatic confirmation of this is obtained when one doesn't speak the language of the people of a country one is visiting. In order to communicate with the people on the street, in a hotel, or in a store one instinctively resorts to gesture in order to get a message across or to negotiate meaning. For example, if one were to describe an automobile to someone, one would instinctively use the hands to iconically portray a steering wheel and the motion used to steer a car, accompanying this gesture, perhaps, with an imitative sound of a motor. This anecdotal scenario not only suggests that gesture is a fundamental mode of communication, but also that its essentially iconic modality makes it a much more universal, and less culture-dependent, mode of message-making than vocal language.

Gesture spans the entire range of signification. Using the index finger is the most common manifestation of indexical pointing, although any body part that can be moved directionally (lips, nose, tongue, etc.) can also be used to point out referents in the immediate environment, to indicate directions, etc. Iconic gestures are employed commonly to represent the shape of objects: for example, to refer to a round object people the world over tend to use both hands together moving in opposite—clockwise (the right hand) and counter-clockwise (the left hand)—directions. Such a gesture is characterizable as a kind of spatial drawing technique. And indeed, if the movements of the hands during gesture are transferred by some drawing instrument onto some surface such as paper, the referent of the gesture will be transferred to the paper as a rudimentary figure. Fingers can also be used to represent symbols (by portraying the outline of the symbol). The most common use of this kind of gesturing is in the sign languages for the hearing-impaired. Lastly, symbolic gestures are often used to stand conventionally for social functions or for carrying out interactional protocols such as greeting, affirmation, negation, etc. So-called "obscene gestures" are also culture-specific symbolic gestures.

Theories connecting gesture to vocal language abound. Most posit that the use of gesture to refer to objects was the proto-form of communication. The transfer of gestural signifiers to the vocal channel is explained by some theorists in terms of an imitation and substitution process, whereby the hand signs were mimed osmotically by the organs of the vocal apparatus. The version of gesture theory that has become a point of departure for all subsequent ones was formulated by the philosopher Jean Jacques Rousseau (1712–1778) in the middle part of the eighteenth century. Rousseau became intrigued by the question of the origins of language and by early humans, whom he called "noble savages." Rousseau proposed that the cries of nature that early humans must have shared with the animals, and the gestures that they must have used simultaneously, led to the invention of vocal language. He explained the evolutionary transition by positing that when the accompanying gestures proved to be too cumbersome, their corresponding cries were used to replace them completely. Needless to say, he could not provide any empirical evidence linking the two.

In the early twentieth century, Richard Paget (1931) suggested that the manual positions and movements were copied unconsciously by the lips and the tongue in tandem, thus vocalizing them. The continual apposition of the two led eventually to the replacement of the manual ones by the vocal counterparts. Paget's account is interesting because it can be shown to be compatible with the recent research on brain and vocal tract evolution. Nevertheless, gestural theories raise a whole range of rudimentary questions that they seem incapable of answering: What made the transition from gestures to vocal signs attainable and even desirable? Why has gesture survived as a communicative system? The child developmental literature has documented, moreover, that children invariably pass through an initial stage of pointing and iconic gesturing before they develop vocal language. They use gestures for practical purposes (for example, pointing to something desired), and these remain as forms in a functional subsystem that can always be utilized throughout life as a more generic mode of communication when a vocal interaction is impossible. This happens typically, as mentioned above, when two interlocutors speak different languages. And, of course, in individuals with impaired vocal organs, gesture constitutes the only possible mode of communication.

Some truly fascinating research by the linguist David McNeill (1992) shows, moreover, that gesture is a complement of vocal language, not its alternative or substitute. McNeill videotaped a large number of people as they spoke, gathering a substantial amount of data on how gesture complements vocal language. The gestures that accompany speech are known as *gesticulants*. McNeill's findings suggest that gesticulants are complementary components of vocal communication—exhibiting images that cannot be shown overtly in speech, as well as images of what the speaker is thinking about. Speech and gesticulation constitute a single integrated communication system in which both cooperate to express the person's meanings.

On the basis of his findings, McNeill was able to classify gesticulants into five main categories. First, there are *iconic* gesticulants, which, as their name suggests, bear a close resemblance to the referent or referential domain of an utterance: e.g., when describing a scene from a story in which a character bends a tree to the ground, a speaker observed by McNeill appeared to grip something and pull it back. His gesture was, in effect, a visual icon of the action talked about, revealing both his memory image and his point of view (he could have taken the part of the character or the tree instead).

Second, there are *metaphoric* gesticulants. These are also pictorial, but their content is abstract, rather than strictly iconic of a referent. For example, McNeill observed a male speaker announcing that what he had just seen was a cartoon, simultaneously raising up his hands as if offering his listener a kind of object. He was obviously not referring to the cartoon itself, but to the "genre" of the cartoon. His gesture created and displayed this genre as if it were an object, placing it into an act of offering to the listener. This type of gesticulant typically accompanies utterances that contain expressions such as *presenting an idea, putting forth an idea, offering advice*, and so on.

Third, there are *beat* gesticulants. These resemble the beating of musical tempo. The speaker's hand moves along with the rhythmic pulsation of speech, in the form of a simple flick of the hand or fingers up and down, or back and forth. Beats are indexes, marking the introduction of new characters, summarizing the action, introducing new themes, etc., during the utterance.

Fourth, there are *cohesive* gesticulants. These serve to show how separate parts of an utterance are supposed to hold together. Beats emphasize sequentiality, cohesives globality. Cohesives can take iconic, metaphoric, or beat form. They unfold through a repetition of the same gesticulant form, movement, or location in the gesture space. It is the repetition that is meant to convey cohesiveness.

Fifth, there are *deictic* gesticulants. Deixis is the term used to designate all kinds of pointing or indicating signs. Deictic gesticulants are aimed not at an existing physical place, but at an abstract concept that had occurred earlier in the conversation. These reveal that we perceive concepts as having a physical location in space.

McNeill's work gives us a good idea of how gesture and language suggest each other in normal discourse. As Frutiger (1989: 112) has also observed, accompanying gestures reveal an inner need to support what one is saying orally: "If on a beach, for example, we can hardly resist drawing with the finger on the smooth surface of the sand as a means of clarifying what we are talking about." McNeill's gesticulant categories are actually subtypes of the more generic category of gesture known as an *illustrator*. Other categories are *emblems, affect displays, regulators,* and *adaptors:*

- *Illustrators:* As just discussed, these literally illustrate vocal utterances. Examples are the circular hand movements when talking of a circle; moving the hands far apart when talking of something large; moving both the head and hands in an upward direction when saying *Let's go up.*
- *Emblems:* These directly translate words or phrases. Examples are the *Okay* sign, the *Come here* sign, the hitchhiking sign, waving, and obscene gestures.
- *Affect Displays:* These communicate emotional meaning. Examples are the typical hand movements that accompany states and expressions of happiness, surprise, fear, anger, sadness, contempt, disgust, etc.
- *Regulators:* These monitor, maintain, or control the speech of someone else. Examples include the hand movements for *Keep going, Slow down, What else happened?*
- *Adaptors:* These are used to satisfy some need. Examples include scratching one's head when puzzled, rubbing one's forehead when worried, and so on.

Many societies have developed "gesture languages" for the use of hearing- or speech-impaired individuals. These are known generally as *sign languages*— the term *sign* being used as a synonym for *gesture*. These share many structural and semantic features with vocal languages. The spatial and orientational use of hand movements, as well as facial expressions and body movements, make up the grammar and lexicon of sign languages. In American Sign Language (ASL), for instance, the sign for "catch" is formed with one hand (in the role of agent) moving across the body (an action) to grasp the forefinger of the other hand (the patient). ASL signifiers are made by one or both hands, which assume distinctive shapes and movements. A number of manual communication systems use the sign vocabulary of ASL in combination with other hand movements to approximate the syntax of English.

Sign languages are also used by hearing peoples for various purposes. One of the best-known examples is the sign language developed by the Plains people of North America as a means of communication between tribes with different vocal languages. The manual signs represent things in nature, ideas, emotions, and sensations. For example, the sign for a white person is made by drawing the fingers across the forehead, indicating a hat. Special signs exist also for each tribe and for particular rivers, mountains, and other natural features. The sensation of cold is indicated by a shivering motion of the hands in front of the body; and the same sign is used for "winter" and for "year," because the Plains peoples count years in terms of winters. Slowly turning the hand, relaxed at the wrist, means vacillation, doubt, or possibility; a modification of this sign, with a quicker movement, is the question sign. The sign language is so elaborate that a detailed conversation is possible using the gestures alone (Mallery 1972).

Gestures may also be used for sacred symbolic purposes, revealing the ancientness and thus "mythic symbolism" of the hands. For example, in Christianity the "sign of the cross" is a gesture that aims to recreate the central event of Christianity—the Crucifixion. In Buddhism, the gestures known as *Mudras* are used during ceremonies to represent meditation, reasoning, doctrine, protection and request, enlightenment, unification of matter, and spirit. The "devil's hand," with the index and little finger raised, on the other hand, belongs to the domain of superstition, symbolizing, in some cultures, a horned figure intended to ward off the evil eye and in others a sign of "cuckoldry."

DANCING

Dancing is common to all peoples and cultures. It is a body art based on rhythm, movement, and gesture connected to each other through pattern and musical ideas. Dance serves five main functions in human life:

- It can be a form of aesthetic communication, expressing emotions, moods, or ideas, or telling a story. Classical Western ballet is an example of aesthetic dance.

- It can be a part of ritual, serving communal functions. In Java, for example, spirit-possession dances remain a part of village life. Sub-Saharan African societies engage in masked dances to exorcise spirits.
- It can be a form of recreation, serving various physical, psychological, and social needs, or simply as an experience that is pleasurable in itself.
- It plays an important role in social functions. All societies have characteristic forms of dance, which take place at ceremonial occasions or at informal gatherings. Like traditional foods and costumes, dance helps members of a nation or ethnic group recognize their connection to one another and to their ancestors. By dancing together, members of a group express their sense of common identity or belonging.
- Dance is especially important during courtship, which is the reason why it is so popular among young people. People dance as a way of attracting mates by displaying their beauty, grace, and vitality.

Evolutionary psychologists see dancing as a residue of movement for survival—it is harder to attack moving prey. This animal mechanism might explain why it is virtually impossible to remain motionless for any protracted period of time. When we are forced to do so by the situation, our body reacts against it. There is, of course, some truth to this theory. During the public performance of a lengthy slow movement of a classical piano sonata, for example, it is almost impossible for audience members to keep perfectly still or not to cough or make some other kind of vocal sound. These involuntary reactions result in all likelihood from a latent need for movement. But why this need was converted in early cultural contexts into dancing defies such facile explanation. The reason behind the origin of dance as *art* remains a mystery. Throughout the world dance, like all art, serves a spiritual need—a need to seek meaning to life.

The best known form of "artistic" dancing is *ballet*, which originated in the courts of Italy and France during the Renaissance, becoming primarily a professional discipline shortly thereafter. The basis of ballet is a turned-out position of the legs and feet with corresponding arm positions. Certain relationships of the arms, legs, head, and torso produce an aesthetic, harmonious effect. A ballet may be choreographed either to music especially composed for it or to music already existing. The plot of a ballet is called its *libretto* or *scenario*. Ballet choreographers may use narratives from literature, drama, and films. Ballets not based on any story, on the other hand, are intended to create a mood, interpret a musical composition, or celebrate dancing for its own sake.

Early precursors to ballets were the lavish court dances of Renaissance Italy. Professional ballet dancers first appeared in the mid-1600s, with the art form being developed extensively during the reign of Louis XIV of France (1643–1715). Louis established the Académie Royale de Danse, a professional organization for dancing masters. At first dancers were men; professional female dancers appeared in 1681. During the second half of the eighteenth century the Paris Opéra was still dominated by male dancers. By the end of the century, and by the time of the romantic nineteenth century, ballet came to be dominated by women.

In the 1920s and 1930s popular dance forms, such as jazz, enriched ballet's form and stylistic range. Two great American ballet companies were founded in New York City in the 1940s: the American Ballet Theater and the New York City Ballet. Since the mid-twentieth century, ballet companies have been established in many cities throughout the United States and Canada. Beginning in 1956, Russian ballet companies such as the Bolshoi Ballet and the Saint Petersburg Ballet began performing in the West.

In sum, dance is an intrinsic activity of human life. People frequent discos, take dance lessons, and enroll their children in ballet school because they feel that dance is linked with something basic about us as human beings. Dancing is an attempt to involve the entire body in a search for meaning to life. As the American philosopher, Susanne K. Langer (1895–1985) suggested, art forms are *presentational* forms, which allow for a variety of interpretations, unlike the *discursive* forms found in science and ordinary language, which have dictionary meanings. Beautiful movements in dance have no specific purpose, claimed Langer, other than to elicit our instinctive sense of beauty and of the sublime—both of which are universal. Paradoxically, art can accomplish one thing Nature cannot. It can offer ugliness and beauty in one object—a fine painting of an ugly face is still beautiful aesthetically!

CONCLUDING REMARKS

The body is a primary source of signification, and a vehicle for understanding the connection between Nature and Culture in human life. The universal, cross-cultural facial expressions that are programmed into us by Nature are being constantly converted into signifying forms in culture-specific ways. We use the body, the face, the hands, and other parts of the body to represent and communicate intentions, roles, impressions, needs, etc., not only to signal biological states. To understand bodily semiosis is to unlock one of the primary modes of message- and meaning-making in the human species. Discoveries in neuroscience have shown that nonverbal signs are produced and processed differently from words. Spoken language is processed in the cerebral cortex, a more developed area of the brain that is unique to human beings. In contrast, nonverbal cues—such as smiling, staring, and clenching the fists—are processed in lower, more primitive areas such as the limbic system. People often produce and receive nonverbal cues without conscious awareness of doing so.

Visual Signs

If only we could pull out our brain and use only our eyes.
Pablo Picasso (1881–1973)

PRELIMINARY REMARKS

Visual signs are all around us. From graffiti on city walls to traffic signals, they serve many social functions and send out many different kinds of messages. As mentioned in previous chapters, the visual art going back some 30,000 years was probably the result of "iconic gesturing" being transferred by means of some sharp cutting tool to a cave wall—producing the vivid images of animals that cover the roofs and walls of caves all over the world—or to an object—producing the small sculptures of animals and female figures found at archeological sites. As the hand movements used to make such representations by our sapient ancestors became more abbreviated, they evolved into more condensed and abstract visual symbols. This led eventually to communication by means of pictures.

The study of visual signs falls under the rubric of *visual semiotics*. Visual signs can be defined simply as signs that are constructed with a visual signifier, that is, with a signifier that can be seen (rather than heard, touched, tasted, or smelled). Like all other types of signs, they can be fashioned iconically (the faces drawn in the previous chapter), indexically (figures of arrows showing direction), and symbolically (advertising logos).

This chapter deals with how we represent the world through eyesight. It is about pictures, drawings, and all the other visual signs and texts we constantly use and interpret in daily life.

MENTAL IMAGERY

Before discussing visual signs, it is necessary to digress briefly and discuss mental imagery. Images of sensations, sights, sounds, tastes, smells, ideas, and so on are being constantly manufactured by the human brain. These allow us to generate hypothetical scenarios of situations or conditions that we may not even have actually experienced. Mental images are substitutes for real things, allowing a person to plan and predict things.

People differ widely in their abilities and tendencies to use different aspects of imagery. For example, some people are better than others at moving objects around in their heads. They can visualize, say, an *N* changing into a *Z* when rotated to a certain point. In addition, some people are better than others at picturing more objects in their minds or at creating new images of objects.

Images are hardly free of cultural conditioning. To see what this means in concrete terms, imagine a triangle first and then a cat. What *kind* of triangle did you see in your mind? What *kind* of cat did you see? People living in the same culture would come up with very similar mental pictures of the two referents, known as "cultural prototypes." The triangle you pictured in your mind was, in all likelihood, an equilateral triangle, because that is the type of triangle that is perceived as the ideal form in Western culture, that is, the one that is thought to be exemplary or representative of all triangles:

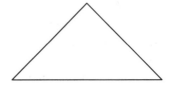

Equilateral triangle = Prototypical triangle

Similarly, the image of the cat that probably came to your mind was that of a common house cat, because that is the kind considered to represent all cats:

Common household cat = Prototypical cat

Such visual images show that we tend to look at things in culture-specific ways. Mental images are not exclusively visual. Think of: (1) the sound of thunder, (2) the feel of wet grass, (3) the smell of fish, (4) the taste of toothpaste, (5) the sensation of being uncomfortably cold, (6) the sensation of extreme happiness. The image that came to your mind in the case of (1) has an auditory quality instead, (2) a tactile one, (3) an olfactory one, (4) a gustatory one (5) a kinesic one, (6) an emotional one. A mental image, obviously, is a conceptual version of some physical or emotional sensation. Moreover, images need not only be sensory in nature; they can be abstract, fictitious, or narrative. As an example of an abstract image, think of *love*. The image that this concept evokes is certainly different from that of a triangle. But whatever the image is, there is no doubt that you were able to conjure up something in your mind that stands for the concept (a face, a vignette, etc.). Images can also be elicited by fictitious or imaginary referents. Think of a "winged table." Although no such thing exists in real life, you undoubtedly had no trouble imagining it. Finally, a narrative image is one that unfolds within mind-space like a story. Think, for instance, of an encounter you had recently with someone from start to finish. The sequence of images generated in your mind in this case is narrative in nature, in that the different images represent the different episodes of your encounter in a story-like fashion.

The topic of imagery has a long history in psychology. Individual differences in the ability to experience imagery had been documented in the nineteenth century. The research that shows how mental imagery can be elicited is actually straightforward and, in my view, uncontroversial. People can imagine faces and voices accurately and quickly, rotate objects in their heads, locate imaginary places, scan game boards (like a checker board) in their minds, and so on with no difficulty whatsoever. While researchers might disagree on exactly what it is that their subjects conjure up in their minds, there is general agreement that something is "going on." Stephen Kosslyn (e.g., 1983), who is well known for having investigated empirically how the brain's imagery system might work, has conducted a series of ingenious experiments that show how subjects can easily form images in their mind to help them carry out tasks, such as arranging furniture in a room, designing a blueprint, and so on.

Saussure used the word *image* to fashion his theory of the sign. He defined a word signifier, in fact, as a "sound image" and its signified as the "image" of the referent it simultaneously calls to mind. However, Saussure never went into the specifics of what he meant by the term. This is perhaps why semioticians and linguists have shied away from using it until recently with the development of *image schema* theory by the American linguist George Lakoff and the American philosopher Mark Johnson (Lakoff and Johnson 1980, 1999, Lakoff 1987, Johnson 1987). Image schemas are defined as largely unconscious mental outlines of recurrent shapes, actions, dimensions, etc., that derive from perception and sensation. Image schemas are largely unconscious. But they can always be elicited easily. If someone were to ask you to explain the expression "I'm feeling *up* today," you would not likely have a conscious image schema involving an upward orientation. However, if that same person were to ask you the following questions—"How far *up* do you feel?" "What do you mean by *up*?" etc.—then you would no doubt start to visualize the schema in question.

According to Lakoff and Johnson, such schemas guide the formation of common concepts. As an example, consider the image schema of an *impediment*. An impediment is something, such as a wall, a boulder, another person, etc., that blocks our movement forward. Familiarity with such impediments produces a mental outline that can be shown somewhat as follows:

Impediment Image Schema

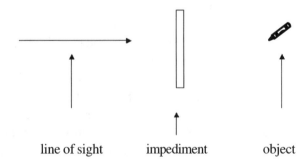

line of sight   impediment   object

As we also know from experience, we can go *around* an impediment, *over* it, *under* it, *through* it, or else *remove* it and continue on towards the object. On the other hand, the impediment could successfully impede us, so that we would have to *stop* at the impediment and *turn back*. All of these actions can be easily seen within mind-space. These are derivatives of the basic impediment schema. Now, as Lakoff and Johnson have persuasively argued, the image schema itself is used to understand the nature of a host of abstract ideas. This is why we say such things as: "We *got through* that difficult time"; "Jim felt better after he *got over* his cold"; "You want to *steer clear of* financial debt"; "With the bulk of the work *out of the way*, he was able to call it a day"; "The rain *stopped* us from enjoying our picnic"; "You cannot *go* any *further* with that idea; you'll just have to *turn back*"; and so on and so forth. More will be said about this in chapter 6. Suffice it to say here that the connection between mental imagery and sign-making is an intrinsic one indeed, as image schema theory makes clear.

Incidentally, images have been shown by psychologists to aid memory and recall. A mental picture can be provided, for example, by the so-called *key-word method*, which is particularly useful for learning foreign words. Suppose you want to remember that the German word *Gabel* means "fork." First, you think of a key word in English that sounds like the foreign word— for example, *gobble*. Next, you connect the two words through a mental image, such as that of a person gobbling food with a fork. From then on, to recall the meaning of *Gabel*, you would remember *gobble* and the stored image linking it to *fork*. Mental images can also be used to remember names. When you meet a person for the first time, pick out a physical feature of the individual and relate it to his or her name. For example, if you meet a very tall man named Mr. Shackley, imagine his bumping his head on the roof of a shack. Subsequently, this image will help you remember his name when you see or think of him.

COLOR

The ability to perceive color in various forms is the basis of many sign-making and sign-using activities across the world. At a denotative level, we interpret colors as gradations of hue on the light spectrum. Hue is the property that leads us to give a color its name—for example, *red, orange, yellow, green, blue,* or *violet*. But the naming process is hardly free of personal and cultural factors. The color terms we use in English predispose us to see "differential categories" of hue. Experts estimate that we can distinguish perhaps as many as 10 million colors. Obviously, then, our limited number of color terms is far too inexact to describe accurately all the colors we are potentially capable of seeing. The restrictions imposed on color perception by color vocabularies is the reason why people often have difficulty trying to describe or match a certain color.

To overcome problems in describing and matching colors, experts have developed various systems of classifying colors. Two widely used ones are: (1) the Munsell Color System, and (2) the CIE System of Color Specification. The former is one of the most popular and useful systems for classifying colors used today. It was developed in the early 1900s by Albert H. Munsell, an American portrait painter. It classifies colors according to basic characteristics of hue. To match a particular color, one must find that color among the samples provided. However, the number of samples in such systems cannot approach the number of colors we are able to distinguish. For this reason, it is sometimes impossible to find an exact match. The CIE System of Color Specification is used by manufacturers of such products as foods, paints, paper, plastics, and textiles who must often match colors precisely. But because of the nature of color, all such systems turn out to be highly limited. The CIE System simply provides a more refined color nomenclature by using metaphorical expressions ("sea green," "sky blue"). CIE stands for Commission Internationale de l'Eclairage (International Commission on Illumination), an international organization that establishes standards for measuring color.

In a real sense, color is what our terms say it is. Consider what you would see if you were to put a finger at any point on the spectrum. You would perceive only a negligible difference in gradation in the hues immediately adjacent to your finger at either side. Depending on where you put it, however, your perception of the difference will vary. This is because you have become accustomed to "seeing" the spectrum in terms of English color terms. But there is nothing inherently "natural" about our organizational scheme; it is a reflex of English vocabulary, not of Nature. By contrast, speakers of other languages are predisposed to see other color categories on the very same spectrum. Speakers of Shona, an indigenous African language, for instance, divide it up into *cipswuka, citema, cicena,* and *cipswuka* (again), and speakers of Bassa, a language of Liberia, segment it into just two categories, *hui* and *ziza.* The relative proportional widths of the gradations that these color categories represent vis-à-vis the English categories can be shown graphically as follows:

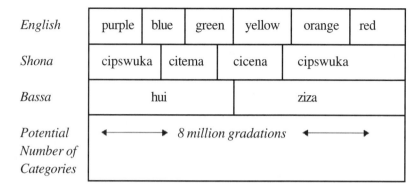

English	purple	blue	green	yellow	orange	red
Shona	cipswuka	citema	cicena	cipswuka		
Bassa	hui			ziza		
Potential Number of Categories	← → 8 million gradations ← →					

So, when an English speaker refers to something as *blue,* a Shona speaker might refer to it as either *cipswuka* or *citema,* and a Bassa speaker as *hui.* If we refer to something as *yellow, orange* or *red*, the Bassa speaker would see it as *ziza*, and so on. In this case, "reality" is exactly what different people "say" that it is. But this does not mean that the use of a specific set of color terms blocks people from seeing reality as others do. The specific color categories one has acquired in cultural context in no way preclude the ability to perceive the color categories used in other cultures. This is, indeed, what a learner of another language ends up doing when he or she studies the new color system. The student must learn how to reclassify the content of the spectrum in terms of new lexical categories. Moreover, in all languages there exist signifying resources for referring to more specific gradations on the spectrum if the situation should require it. In English the words *crimson, scarlet, vermilion,* for instance, make it possible to refer to gradations of *red.* But these are still felt by speakers to be subcategories of *red*, not distinct color categories on their own.

In 1969, the linguists Berlin and Kay argued, moreover, that differences in color terms are only superficial matters that conceal general underlying principles of color perception. Using the judgments of the native speakers of twenty widely divergent languages, they came to the conclusion that there were "focal points" in basic (single-term) color systems that clustered and evolved in certain predictable ways. They identified eleven focal points that corresponded to the English words *red, pink, orange, yellow, brown, green, blue, purple, black, white,* and *gray.* Not all the languages they investigated had separate words for each of these colors, but there emerged a pattern that suggested to them the existence of a fixed way of perceiving color across cultures. If a language had two colors, then they were equivalents of English *black* and *white.* If it had three, then the third one corresponded to *red.* A four-term system had either *yellow* or *green*; while a five-term system had both of these. A six-term system included *blue*; a seven-term system had *brown.* Finally, terms for *purple, pink, orange,* and *gray* were found to occur in any combination in languages which had the previous focal colors. Berlin and Kay found that languages with, say, a four-term system consisting of *black, white, red*, and *brown* did not exist. Berlin and Kay represented the *universal color system* they had apparently discovered as follows:

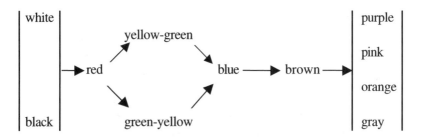

Examples of languages possessing from two to eleven focal terms are given in the following chart:

Number	Terms	Example of Language
two	white, black	Jale (New Guinea), Ngombe (Africa)
three	white, black, red	Arawak (Caribbean), Swahili (southern Africa)
four	white, black, red, yellow/green	Ibo (Nigeria), Tongan (Polynesia)
five	white, black, red, yellow, green	Tarascan (Mexico), !Kung (southern Africa)
six	white, black, red, yellow, green, blue	Tamil (India, Sri Lanka), Mandarin (China)
seven	white, black, red, yellow, green, blue, brown	Nez Percé (Montana), Javanese
eight-eleven	white, black, red, yellow green, blue, brown, purple/pink/orange/gray	English, Zuñi (New Mexico), Dinka (Sudan), Tagalog (Philippines)

In 1975, Kay revised the universal color system in order to account for the fact that certain languages—such as Japanese—encode a color that can only be termed in English as "green-blue," which may occur before the labeling of *yellow*. Kay called this category GRUE and placed it either preceding or following *yellow* in the original sequence:

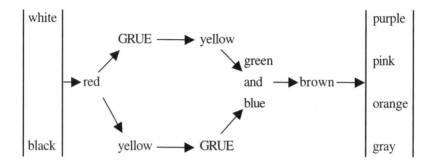

Since then it has been found that further modification is required because Russian and Italian do not have a single color for *blue*, but rather distinguish "light blue" and "dark blue" as focal colors.

The intriguing implications of Berlin and Kay's research were pursued vigorously in the 1970s by many linguists and psychologists. Eleanor Rosch (e.g., 1975a, 1975b), for instance, demonstrated that the Dani people of West Irian, who have a two-color system similar to the Bassa system described above, were able to discriminate easily eight focal colors. Using a recognition-memory experiment, Rosch found that the Dani recognized focal colors better than non-focal ones. She also found that they learned new colors more easily when the color names were paired with focal colors. Such findings suggested to Rosch that languages provided a guide to the interpretation of color, but they do not affect its perception in any way.

But many problems remain to this day with the conclusions reached by such color researchers. For one thing, the fact that the eleven focal colors posited by Berlin and Kay corresponded to the color terms of their own language (English) is suspicious. Could the researchers have been predisposed by their own language to gloss all other terms according to the English categories? Many of the terms Berlin and Kay listed, some critics have also pointed out, turn out to be borrowings (color terms taken and/or adapted from other languages), which would greatly undermine their theory. The focal points of Berlin and Kay's theory would seem to be no more than the points on the color spectrum categorized by the language to which they had become accustomed.

Semiotically speaking, color terms are verbal signifiers that predispose people to attend primarily to the hues they encode. This is a practical strategy; otherwise, millions of terms would need to be invented to classify the spectrum accurately. But the semiotic story of color does not stop there. Throughout the world colors are used for connotative purposes. The archeological record strongly suggests, in fact, that sensory and emotional meanings attached to colors may even have been the source for the color terms themselves (Wescott 1980). In Hittite, for instance, words for colors initially designated plant and tree names such as *poplar*, *elm*, *cherry*, *oak*, etc.; in Hebrew, the name of the first man, *Adam*, meant "red" and "alive," and still today, in many languages, *red* signifies "living" and "beautiful."

The use of colour terms in connotative ways is more widespread than one may at first think. Here are some examples in English of three colors—red, blue, and green—used to refer to various concepts by connotation:

red
- *red* carpet treatment ("preferential treatment")
- into the *red* ("in debt")
- *red* herring ("something used to draw attention away from the real issue")
- *red* light district ("area of a city with sexual activities and places such as brothels")
- *red* tape ("overly bureaucratic")

blue
- the *blues* ("type of music")
- once in a *blue* moon ("rarely")
- true *blue* ("loyal")
- *blue* funk ("a state of dejection or depression")

green
- *green* envy ("great envy")
- *green* horn ("inexperienced person")
- *green* thumb ("having the ability to grow things in a garden")

Such expressions reveal that we perceive color as much more than a phenomenon involving pure visual perception. In all societies, colors play a critical function in the realm of symbolism. The Navajo of North America, for instance, allocate to colors a hierarchy of symbolic importance—blue is "good" and red "bad"; nation societies perceive great significance in the colors of flags and national emblems, and the list could go on and on.

VISUAL REPRESENTATION

Colors are, in effect, signs that we can use to represent whatever we deem appropriate. Visual representation is so common and all-encompassing that we hardly ever realize what it involves. To grasp how it unfolds, draw a happy face with pen or pencil on a piece of paper. Now, how did you do it? Or, more precisely, what visual signifiers did you employ to create the image of a "happy face?"

You drew the face, of course, with *points, lines,* and *shapes.* These are the visual signifiers, or minimal forms of visual representation, that can be combined in various ways to represent the human face. They can be straight, round, curved, etc., and used in various combinations. In the face above, the mouth was represented with a U-shaped signifier, and the eyes with two points.

Now, consider what can be done with three straight lines. Among other representations, they can be joined up to represent a triangle, the letter *H*, or a picnic table iconically:

Lines and arrowheads can be used indexically to represent movement and direction, as follows:

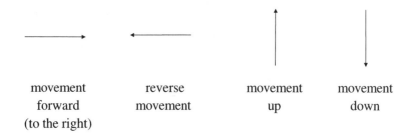

movement   reverse   movement   movement

forward   movement   up   down

(to the right)

Visual signifiers designed to show an outline of something are known as *shapes*. Virtually everything we see can be represented by a combination of lines and shapes: for example, a cloud is a shape, a horizon is a line. Other elements include *value*, *color*, and *texture*. Value refers to the darkness or lightness of a line or shape. It plays an important role in portraying dark and light contrasts. Color conveys mood, feeling, atmosphere. This is why we speak of "warm," "soft," "cold," "harsh" colors. As we saw above, connotatively, color has culture-specific symbolic value—in our culture *yellow* connotes cowardice, in China it connotes royalty. Texture refers to the sensation of touch evoked imagistically when we look at some surface. Observe how differently you react when looking at wavy lines vs. angular zigzag lines:

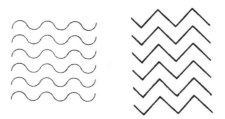

The wavy lines produce a much more pleasant sensation in us than do the angular ones. By increasing the number of edges, the unpleasant gnawing sensation one feels by looking at the latter increases proportionately. Try this out on your own. It is amazing to contemplate how a simple visual signifier such as a zigzag line can evoke a tactile sensation. This is strong evidence that semiosis is intermodal, involving more than one sensory modality at once. The term that is used to characterize this phenomenon is *synesthesia*. The above sensations associated with touch, but evoked by visual signs, are examples of synesthetic reactions. Incidentally, the term *aesthesia* is commonly used to refer instead to the activation of all the sensory modalities in a holistic way. When we call the appreciation of a work of art an "aesthetic experience," we literally mean that we sense and feel the meaning of a work of art as a whole. The aesthetic experience can also be evoked by the specific shape and dimensions of simple figures. For example, it is a documented fact by psychology that people tend to perceive a rectangle whose sides are in the so-called "golden ratio" (which is 5:8) as aesthetically pleasing. Of the following rectangles, **E** is the one constructed with the golden ratio:

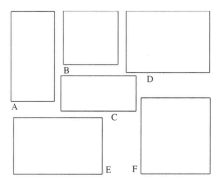

Lines and shapes can also be combined to create an illusion of depth. In the following plane figure there are 12 lines. The way they are put together, however, makes us believe that they represent a three-dimensional box:

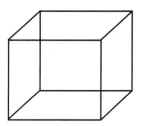

The figure has been drawn with straight lines drawn on a two-dimensional surface (the page). Yet we cannot help but interpret it as a three-dimensional box. This is because we "see" the parts of the diagram in a three-dimensional relation to each other. In perspective representation, the flat surface of the painted picture is known as the *picture plane*; the horizon line is the horizontal *eye-level line* that divides the scene in the distance; and the *vanishing point* is located on the horizon line where parallel lines in the scene appear to converge:

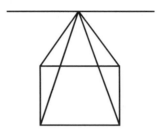

Elemental visual signifiers can be found in virtually all domains of representation and communication. Consider, for instance, the use of so-called *emoticons* (literally *icons* that convey *emotions*) in computer communication. These are strings of text characters that, when viewed sideways, form a face expressing a particular emotion. An emoticon is often used in an e-mail message or newsgroup post as a comment on the text that precedes it. Common emoticons include the smiley :-) or :) (meaning "I'm smiling at the joke here"), the winkey ;-) (meaning "I'm winking and grinning at the joke here"), :-(("I'm sad about this"), :-7 ("I'm speaking with tongue in cheek"), :D or :-D (big smile; "I'm overjoyed"), and :-O (either a yawn of boredom or a mouth open in amazement). In an e-mail message or newsgroup article, a letter, word, or phrase that is encased in angle brackets, and that, like an emoticon, indicates the attitude the writer takes toward what he or she has written is called an *emotag*. Often emotags have opening and closing tags, similar to HTML tags, that enclose a phrase or one or more sentences. For example: <joke> *You didn't think there would really be a joke here, did you?*<joke>. Some emotags are used as single tags, such as <grin>.

Visual signifiers are also used commonly in the drawing of such useful devices as diagrams and charts. These are used, incidentally, in science to represent unseeable things. The diagram of the atom as a miniature solar system with a nucleus and orbiting particles is, *ipso facto*, a theory of the atom, allowing us to envision it in a particular way.

Such diagrams reveal that sight is a basic analogue for understanding intellectual processes. The connection between such processes and sight has also left its imprint in language, as can be observed in the following common expressions and words:

- *seeing* a way out of a situation
- *see* the point of something
- *see* reason
- *see* hope

- *see* a point of view
- *see* what one can do
- *look* something up
- to have an *outlook*
- *look* into something
- the mind's *eye*
- more than meets the *eye*
- fore*sight*
- in*sight*
- hind*sight*
- over*view*
- *view*point
- *vision*ary

The science of geometry too is a product of this linkage. Geometry is all about "ideal visual forms" such as triangles, circles, and squares. Amazingly, such forms have allowed us to draw inferences about reality and about ourselves. This is perhaps why the basic geometric figures are imbued with symbolism in cultures across the world. Here are a few examples:

- The square symbolized the earth's surface in antiquity, indicating the four points of the earth's compass or the outermost points of the earth.

- The triangle has acquired many symbolic meanings throughout the world, of which the idea of "trinity" comes instantly to mind.

- The circle has been a symbol of perfection and infinity since antiquity. This is probably due to the fact that it suggests eternal recurrence.

- The cross has been used to represent everything from Christianity to the plus sign. If tilted it becomes an X, which can stand for a signature, something wrong, the x-character, something forbidden (as in X-rated movies), and so on.

MAPS

Maps are remarkable examples of how the link between knowledge and visual signs is an intrinsic one—with one implying the other in tandem. And yet, making a map is such a straightforward task that anyone can easily make a rudimentary one on the spot. Let's say a stranger wants to get to a certain destination. The stranger asks us to draw her a map of how to get there. We start by showing the stranger's location as point **A** on a piece of paper, which is at the intersection of two streets, one running north and south, the other east and west. The stranger wants to go to **B**, which is west two blocks and north three blocks of location **A**. In this case, the configuration of streets in the area is that of a grid. We can thus show **B**'s location by drawing the street on which it is located as a line meeting our previous east-west line at right angles. Compass directions can also be added to the map (**N** = north, **S** = south, **E** = east, **W** = west). Finally, we can indicate the blocks by adding two equally-calibrated units to the east-west line to the left of **A**; and three equally calibrated units added to the north-south line that represents the street on which **B** is located. This will show the stranger how to reach the desired location, **B**:

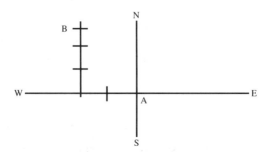

Remarkably, with this simple diagram we were able to represent real topographical structure *(Y)*, in its bare outline and in condensed form, on a surface *(X)*. This is a perfect example of how the $X = Y$ relation undergirds many of the practical things that we do.

A *map* can be defined, semiotically, as a text involving all three basic types of signification processes—indexicality, iconicity, and symbolism:

- A map is, overall, an *indexical* text, since it indicates where a territory is located on *terra firma*.
- Its layout is *iconic*, because it shows the features in a territory in topographical relation to each other.
- It involves *symbolism* because it is decipherable on the basis of conventionalized notational systems (key, scale, etc.).

As semiotic constructs, maps will thus tend to condition how social groups perceive and interpret represented territories. To illustrate how a map can do this, consider the technique of cylindrical projection in Western map-making. Developed by the Flemish geographer Gerardus Mercator (1512–1594), it consists in wrapping a cylinder around the globe, making it touch the equator, and then projecting (1) the lines of latitude outward from the globe onto the cylinder as lines parallel to the equator, and (2) the lines of longitude outward onto the cylinder as lines parallel to the prime meridian (the line that is designated 0° longitude, passing through the original site of the Royal Greenwich Observatory in England). The resulting two-dimensional map can be made to represent the world's surface as a two-dimensional plane figure such as a rectangle or an ellipse. Here's an example of the latter:

Because of the curvature of the globe, the latitude lines on the map nearest the poles appear closer together. This distortion makes the sizes of certain land masses appear smaller than they are. Indeed, the very concept of *worldview* derives from the fact that the ways in which we come to "view the world"

are, in part, a consequence of how that *world* is represented *for viewing* by the maps we make of it.

Although modern technology now makes it easy to construct three-dimensional maps, traditionally the term *map* has always designated a two-dimensional representation of an area; three-dimensional maps are more accurately known as *models*. All civilizations have developed map-making techniques to meet a host of social needs. In Western culture, these were elaborated and refined in tandem with the rise and growth of the mathematical sciences. Since Mercator invented the cylindrical projection method, most map-making techniques have, in fact, been devised in accordance with the principles of Cartesian coordinate geometry. By convention, longitude is marked 180° east and 180° west from 0° at Greenwich, England. Latitude is marked 90° north and 90° south from the 0° parallel of the equator. Points on a map can be accurately defined by giving degrees, minutes, and seconds for both latitude and longitude. Distances are represented with the technique of *scaling*, whereby two points on the earth are represented by two points on the map that relate to each other by means of a scale: for example, a scale of 1:100,000 means that one unit measured on the map (say 1 cm) represents 100,000 of the same units on the earth's surface. The varying heights of hills and mountains, and the depths of valleys, are portrayed instead with the technique known as *relief*. In earlier maps, this consisted in making small drawings of mountains and valleys on the maps. But this was extremely imprecise and thus came eventually to be supplanted by the use of contour lines. The shapes of these lines provide accurate representations of the shapes of hills and depressions, and the lines themselves show actual elevations, so that closely spaced contour lines indicate steep slopes. Other methods of indicating elevation include the use of colors, tints, hachures (short parallel lines), and shadings. When colors are used for this purpose, a graded series of tones is selected for coloring areas of similar elevations. Shadings or hachures, neither of which show actual elevations, are more easily interpreted than contour lines and are sometimes used in conjunction with them for achieving greater fidelity in representation.

How do we interpret a map? To say "I am here, but I want to get to there" on a map involves understanding (1) that *here* and *there* are indexes in map space standing for points in real space, and (2) that the movement from *here* to *there* on a map stands for the corresponding movement between two points in real space. In this way, maps involve several levels of the $X = Y$ relation.

The first known maps were made by the Babylonians around 2300 BC. Carved on clay tablets, they consisted largely of land surveys made for the purposes of taxation. More extensive regional maps, drawn on silk and dating from the second century BC, have been found in China. The precursor of the modern map, however, is believed to have been devised by the Greek philosopher Anaximander (c. 611–c. 547 BC). It was circular and showed the known lands of the world grouped around the Aegean Sea at the center and surrounded by the ocean. Anaximander's map constituted one of the first attempts to think beyond the immediate territorial boundaries of a particular society—Greece— even though Anaximander located the center of the universe in the Aegean Sea. Then, around 200 BC, the Greek geometer and geographer Eratosthenes (276?– 195? BC), introduced the technique of parallel lines to indicate latitude and longitude, although they were not evenly and accurately spaced. Eratosthenes' map represented the known world from present-day England in the northwest to the mouth of the Ganges River in the east and to Libya in the south. About AD 150, the Egyptian scholar Ptolemy (c. 100–c. 170 AD) published the first textbook in cartographic science, entitled *Geographia*. Even though they contained a number of errors, his were among the first maps of the world to be made with mathematical principles. At about the same time in China, map-makers were also beginning to use mathematically accurate grids for making maps.

The next step forward in cartography came in the medieval era when Arab seamen made highly accurate navigational charts, with lines indicating the bearings between ports. In the fifteenth century, influenced by the publication of Ptolemy's maps, European map-makers laid the foundations for the modern science of cartography. In 1507, for instance, the German cartographer Martin Waldseemüller (c. 1470–c. 1522) became the first to apply the name *America* to the newly identified trans-Atlantic lands, separating America into North and South—a cartographic tradition that continues to this day—and differentiating the Americas from Asia. In 1570 the first modern *atlas*—a collection of maps of the world—was put together by the Flemish cartographer Abraham Ortelius (1527–1598). The atlas, titled *Orbis Terrarum*, contained 70 maps.

Undoubtedly, the most important development in the sixteenth century came when Mercator developed the technique of cylindrical projection in 1569, as mentioned above. This allowed cartographers to portray compass directions as lines, at the expense, however, of the accurate representation of relative size. By the eighteenth century, the modern-day scientific principles of map-making were well established. With the rise of nationalism in the nineteenth century, a number of European countries conducted topographic surveys to determine political boundaries. In 1891, the International Geographical Congress proposed the political mapping of the entire world on a scale of 1:1,000,000, a task that occupied cartographers for over a century. Throughout the twentieth century, advances in aerial and satellite photography, and in computer modeling of topographic surfaces, have greatly enhanced the versatility, functionality, accuracy, and fidelity of map-making. Here are a few examples:

- The so-called Geographic Information System (GIS) consists of computers, computer programs, and extremely large amounts of information, which is stored as computer code and can include measurements or photographs taken from land, sea, or space. Cartographers can use such a system to produce many different maps from the stored data.
- Many types of maps are easily stored on CD-ROMs, which enable people to choose exactly the area they want to view, then print a map.
- In-vehicle navigation systems create maps to guide drivers of moving vehicles. These systems constantly track a vehicle's location by using signals from a group of space satellites called the Global Positioning System. A computer in the vehicle combines the position data with stored street map data and produces maps of the route to a destination. The maps change as the vehicle moves. Some in-vehicle systems show the map on a small screen. Other systems produce spoken directions.
- Aeronautical charts are used to navigate airplanes. Depending on their level of certification, pilots use Visual Flight Rules (VFR) or Instrument Flight Rules (IFR) charts. VFR charts show landmarks that pilots can see as they fly, such as roads, bridges, and towns. VFR maps also show airports and indicate the heights of mountains and other obstacles. IFR charts are designed for radio navigation. These charts show the location of transmitters of high-frequency radio signals. Pilots use these signals to determine their position and plot their course.
- Some airplanes are equipped with computer systems that produce heads-up display maps. These maps are projected near eye level where the pilot can see them without looking down.

Modern map-making is based on the principles of Cartesian geometry, which segments the map space into determinable points and calculable distances. The traditional maps of North American aboriginal peoples, on the other hand, were designed to show the interconnectedness among the parts within the map space through a distortion of distance, angulation, and shape. Western maps represent the world as an agglomeration of points, lines, and parts, related to each other in terms of the mathematics of the Cartesian plane; aboriginal maps represent the world instead as a holistic unsegmentable entity.

Arguably, maps have influenced the design of modern cities. Not only does the layout of the city of New York, for instance, mirror a Cartesian map, but the city also names its streets largely in terms of the grid system: for example, *52nd and 4th* refers to the intersection point of two perpendicular lines in the city grid. In a fundamental semiotic sense, modern cities are the "iconic byproducts" of the worldview that has been enshrined into our mindset by the widespread use of grid maps since the early sixteenth century.

As a final comment on map-making, it is relevant to note that maps have facilitated exploration of the world. In the same way that the sciences of geometry and trigonometry have allowed human beings to solve engineering problems since ancient times, the science of cartography has allowed explorers to solve travel problems with amazing accuracy. Exploration involves determining position and direction. Position is a point on the earth's surface that can be identified in terms of the grid or coordinate system. Direction is the position of one point relative to another within the coordinate system. The shortest distance between two points is a straight line, and since any line in the plane is a hypotenuse, then its length can be determined easily. In this way, maps have allowed explorers to fix points and determine distances to regions of the plane (= the earth's surface). Explorers setting out on a journey will not know what they will encounter along the way, nor will they know in advance if they will reach a land mass or a body of water. But they can still take that journey with a high degree of assurance that they will be able to find the intended destination, no matter what it is.

What is even more remarkable is that cartography has permitted us to describe the positions of heavenly bodies and to calculate their distances from Earth with accuracy. Suffice it to say here that mapping outer space involves the use of techniques that correspond to terrestrial point-fixing in terms of latitude and longitude lines. Simply put, the positions of stars relative to one another are regarded as points on a celestial map; the motion of the sun, the moon, and the planets is then indicated as a mean rate of progression across the celestial space. It is truly mind-boggling to think that with the aid of a simple representational device (the map), we have already been able to set foot on the moon and will no doubt be able to visit other places in the skies in the not-too-distant future.

THE VISUAL ARTS

The question of the function of the visual arts in human life has become part of a general social debate, as contemporary art galleries routinely put controversial "abstract" paintings and sculptures on display in many societies. One of the most famous versions of this debate was initiated by Andy Warhol (1928–1987), the American pop artist who produced paintings and silk-screen prints of commonplace objects, such as soup cans and photographs of celebrities. Take, for example, his painting of a Campbell's soup can (1964):

Campbell's Soup Can by Andy Warhol (1964)

When asked *what* it means, people will either (1) say that it means nothing, or (2) give responses such as "It is a symbol of our consumer society," "It represents the banality and triviality of contemporary life," and so on. The latter pattern of responses suggests that we tend to interpret certain texts as "works of art" because meanings and values are attributed to them by those who make them, by the society in which they live, and by those who look at them in later years. But, such "art" does not evoke the same response all over the world, nor does it capture the fancy of children (for instance). True art transcends the social, the present, and the purely conventional.

The modern idea of visual art as something to be appreciated individualistically by viewing it in a gallery or museum hides the fact that art in its origins had a public function. Art works were meant to decorate the public square or to commemorate some meaningful event. The idea of "authored" art is a modern one that took shape in the late Renaissance. And only after the Romantic nineteenth century did the idea of the "art gallery" as the appropriate locus for appreciating art emerge as an *idée fixe*.

The visual arts are divided into several main areas, of which painting and sculpture are the main ones. Since the early part of the twentieth century, however, photography and cinema have been added to the list. The earliest photographs on record were made by the French physicist Nicéphore Niépce (1765–1833). Then in 1831 the French painter Louis Daguerre (1789–1851) succeeded in developing a positive photographic image. The first camera for public use was produced by the American George Eastman (1854–1932) in 1889. During the 1950s, new manufacturing processes greatly increased the speed, or light sensitivity, of both black-and-white and color film. The decade was also marked by the introduction of electronic devices called light amplifiers, which intensify dim illumination, making possible the recording on photographic film of even the faint light of very distant stars. Such advances in mechanical devices systematically raised the technical level of both amateur and professional photography. Today, digital cameras, which were introduced in the early 1990s, can produce an image almost instantly. These filmless cameras have a light-sensitive mechanism called a charge-coupled device (CCD). The lens focuses light on the CCD, which changes the light into electronic signals. The images can be viewed immediately on cameras equipped with a liquid crystal display (LCD) screen.

Photography became an art form almost from the instant it was invented. Indeed, from the 1860s through the 1890s it was conceived of as an alternative to drawing and painting, allowing for greater fidelity. In other words, photography was viewed as a shortcut to traditional visual art. The Swedish photographer Oscar Gustave Rejlander (1813–1875) and the English photographer Henry Peach Robinson (1834–1901), for instance, emulated painting forms with their cameras. Like the painter, they claimed, the photographer inevitably makes a selection of what is to be recorded. This selection may be planned ahead of time or calculated on the spot. Lighting, focus, and camera angle may be manipulated to alter the appearance of the image; the developing and printing processes may be modified to produce desired results; or the photograph may be combined with other media to produce a composite art form.

Photography has become much more than an ersatz form of painting today. It now constitutes one of the mementos we utilize to remember people, events, and things. The photographs that adorn our tables and walls are, in effect, visual mementos and testimonials of who we are. Photographs capture a fleeting and irretrievable moment in time, extracting it from the flux of change that characterizes human life. Such captured moments have strong appeal because they provide eyewitness evidence, so to speak, that we do indeed exist in some enduring form, at least in the photographic space. This is why in Michelangelo Antonioni's 1966 movie masterpiece, *Blow-Up*, the search for clues to a crime in a blow-up of a photograph is a metaphor for the search for clues to our own existence in our photographic images.

CINEMA

The example of *Blow-Up* leads to the topic of *cinema*, which has become the art form to which most people today respond most strongly and to which they look for recreation, inspiration, and insight. Movies are aesthetically powerful because they juxtapose dialogue, music, scenery, and action in a visual-narrative way. Semiotically speaking, a film can be defined as a text which, at the level of the signifier, consists of a chain of images that represent real-life activities. At the level of the signified, films are metaphorical mirrors of life. The topic of cinema is, clearly, a central one for semiotics because movie genres constitute signification systems to which most people today respond and to which they look for recreation, inspiration, and insight at the level of the interpretant.

Most cinema historians trace the origin of cinema to the year 1896, when the French magician Georges Méliès made a series of films that explored the narrative potential of the new medium. In 1899, in a studio on the outskirts of Paris, Méliès reconstructed a ten-part version of the trial of French army officer Alfred Dreyfus and filmed *Cinderella* (1900) in 20 scenes. He is chiefly remembered, however, for his clever fantasies, such as *A Trip to the Moon* (1902), in which he exploited the new possibilities for offering perspective that the movie camera afforded. His short films were an instant hit with the public and were shown internationally. Although considered little more than curiosities today, they are significant precursors of an art form that was in its infancy at the time.

The theatrical fantasies of Méliès influenced the American inventor Edwin S. Porter, often called the father of the silent film, when he produced the first major American silent film, *The Great Train Robbery*, in 1903. Only eight minutes long, it greatly influenced the development of motion pictures because of its intercutting of scenes shot at different times and in different places to form a unified narrative, culminating in a suspenseful chase. With the production of D. W. Griffith's *The Birth of a Nation* (1915), small theaters sprang up throughout the United States, and cinema emerged as a *de facto* art form. Most films of the time were short comedies, adventure stories, or filmed records of performances by leading actors of the day.

Between 1915 and 1920, grandiose movie palaces proliferated throughout the United States. The film industry moved gradually to Hollywood. Hundreds of films a year poured from the Hollywood studios to satisfy the ever-increasing craving of a fanatic movie-going public. The vast majority of them were Westerns, slapstick comedies, and elegant romantic melodramas such as Cecil B. DeMille's *Male and Female* (1919). In the 1920s movies starring the comedian Charlie Chaplin ushered in the golden age of silent film.

After World War I, motion-picture production became a major American industry, generating millions of dollars for successful studios. American films became international in character and dominated the world market. Artists responsible for the most successful European films were imported by American studios, and their techniques were adapted and assimilated by Hollywood.

The transition from silent to sound films was so rapid that many films released in 1928 and 1929 had begun production as silent films but were hastily turned into sound films, or "talkies" as they were called, to meet the growing demand. Gangster films and musicals dominated the new "talking screen" of the early 1930s. The vogue of filming popular novels reached a peak in the late 1930s with expensively mounted productions of classic novels, including one of the most popular films in motion-picture history, *Gone with the Wind* (1939).

The trend toward escapism and fantasy in motion pictures was strong throughout the 1930s. A cycle of classic horror films, including *Dracula* (1931), *Frankenstein* (1931), and *The Mummy* (1932), spawned a series of sequels and spin-offs that lasted throughout the decade. One of the most enduring films of the era was the musical fantasy *The Wizard of Oz* (1939), based on a book by L. Frank Baum—a children's movie with a frightful theme that reflected the emerging cynicism of society at large, namely, that all human aspirations are ultimately make-believe, that the Wizard at the end of the road of life is really a fraud, a charlatan. The fun of living is getting to Oz, not finding out the truth about Oz.

One American filmmaker who came to Hollywood from radio in 1940 was the writer-director-actor Orson Welles, who experimented with new camera angles and sound effects that greatly extended the representational power of film. His *Citizen Kane* (1941) and *The Magnificent Ambersons* (1942) influenced the subsequent work of virtually every major filmmaker in the world. From the late 1940s to the mid-1970s, Italian cinema achieved an intimacy and depth of emotion that radically transformed cinematic art, starting with Roberto Rossellini's *Open City* (1945) and Vittorio De Sica's *The Bicycle Thief* (1949) to Lina Wertmuller's *Swept Away* (1975) and *Seven Beauties* (1976).

One of the most distinctive and original directors to emerge in post-World War II international cinema was Sweden's Ingmar Bergman (1918–), who brought an intense philosophical and intellectual depth to his films, treating the themes of personal isolation, sexual conflict, and religious obsession. In his film *The Seventh Seal* (1956) he probed the mystery of life and spirituality through the trials of a medieval knight playing a game of chess with Death. In *Wild Strawberries* (1957) he created a series of poetic flashbacks reviewing the life of an elderly professor. He dissected the human condition starkly in a series of films—*Persona* (1966), *Cries and Whispers* (1972), *Scenes from a Marriage* (1973), and *Autumn Sonata* (1978)—which excoriated the futile penchant in the human species to search for meaning in existence.

In the 1950s and 1960s color movies gradually replaced black-and-white film. But some filmmakers still prefer the latter, striving for "naked" realism. Such black-and-white films as *Psycho* (1960) by Alfred Hitchcock, *The Last Picture Show* (1971) by Peter Bogdanovich, *Raging Bull* (1980) by Martin Scorsese, *Zelig* (1983) and *Shadows and Fog* (1992) by Woody Allen, and *Schindler's List* (1994) by Steven Spielberg have become classics in the genre.

Of the many directors of the last part of the twentieth century, perhaps no one has been as successful at exploiting the film medium as a versatile art form as has Steven Spielberg (1947–). His *Jaws* (1975), about a killer shark that terrorizes a small beach community, became the model for a number of films in which fear-inspiring creatures threatened helpless victims. His *Close Encounters of the Third Kind* (1977) and *E.T.* (1982) capitalized on a widespread fascination with the possibility of extraterrestrial life. His other multimillion-dollar blockbusters include *Raiders of the Lost Ark* (1981), *Indiana Jones and the Temple of Doom* (1984), and *Indiana Jones and the Last Crusade* (1989), all imitative of the serial cliffhangers of the 1930s. Most of Spielberg's films rely heavily on high-tech special effects, especially his *Jurassic Park* (1993), which features frighteningly realistic computer-generated dinosaurs. Within the first four weeks of its release, *Jurassic Park* became one of the highest-grossing films up to that time, only to be surpassed by *Titanic* (1998) a few years later and some current-day ones.

The 1980s and 1990s saw a revolution in the home-video market, with major releases being made available for home viewing almost immediately after they left the movie theater. This development, combined with the advent of cable television, which features relatively current films on special channels, seemed to threaten the long-term survival of movie theaters and created a climate similar to that of the early 1950s, when television began to challenge the popularity of motion pictures. As a result, film companies increasingly favored large spectacles with fantastic special effects in order to lure the public away from home videos and back to the big screen. But despite the challenge from video, the traditional movie theater has remained as popular as ever—a testament to the power of cinema as a "social art form," much like the theater once was. Digital video discs (DVDs), invented in the 1990s, have stimulated even more interest in movies. Although they make it possible to enjoy movies in the home with all the technological splendor offered by movie theaters (given the right equipment), DVDs too are in fact entrenching movie-going even more so in social life, not replacing it.

As a "social art" involving people coming together to experience the performance of narrative as a group, cinema talks to the modern psyche in ways that perhaps theater cannot. Some kinds of narratives, moreover, can only be envisioned as cinema. As an example, consider Ridley Scott's 1982 classic movie *Blade Runner*, based on a science fiction story titled *Do Androids Dream of Electric Sheep?* by Philip K. Dick (1928–1982). This movie still attracts considerable interest from moviegoers of all kinds.

Against the depressing backdrop of a futuristic choking urban landscape, the protagonist of the movie, Rick Deckard, is one of a select few law-enforcement officers, nicknamed "blade runners," who have been trained to detect and track down "replicants," powerful humanoid robots who had been engineered to do the work of humans in space. But some of the replicants have gone amok. They have somehow developed the mental characteristics of humans and have started to ask fundamental philosophical questions about their own existence made urgent by the limited lifespan programmed into them. A desperate band of these killer replicants has made its way back to Earth, seeking to have their programmed deaths reversed. They are looking for the sinister corporate tycoon responsible for their creation, so that he can give them new life. Deckard's assignment is to track down these runaway replicants and terminate them, which is not an easy task given that the replicants look exactly like humans. But there is one feature that differentiates human anatomy from replicant anatomy—the eye. Deckard's main technique for identifying the replicants is, in fact, to record the ocular responses of his suspects. Replicants use their eyes exclusively to see; humans use them as well to show feeling and spirituality. Aware of the mysterious power of the human eye, the replicants kill their maker by poking out his eyes.

The movie, however, is not about bringing machines to life. It is about the nature of humanity. Interestingly, we are never sure if Deckard is himself a human or a replicant. This ambiguity is an intrinsic part of the movie's power. Deckard's search unfolds in an urban wasteland where punk mutants control the streets while the pathetic inhabitants of endless blocks of gloomy high-rises remain glued to their TV sets. Deckard relies on a VCR, complete with stop action and precision image-enhancers, to track the replicants through dark alleys abandoned to the forces of anarchy.

Somehow, the replicants have developed human emotions. Deckard falls in love with one of them, Rachel, whose name has Biblical reverberations and who, while helping Deckard track down replicants, falls in love with him. Significantly, Deckard is saved at the end by a replicant who shows him mercy, one of the quintessential human qualities. Wearing only a white cloth around his waist, in obvious allusion to the Crucifixion scene, he saves Deckard's life at the cost of his own. When Deckard and Rachel escape the gruesome city scene to the countryside, the dark, gloomy atmosphere suddenly clears up, the sun comes out, and a "new Biblical dawn" arises.

Blade Runner asks the fundamental questions of philosophy in a new way: What is a human being? What is real? Is there any meaning to existence? It does so by making the replicants mirror images of human beings, transforming their struggle to know who they are into a reflection of our own struggle to unravel who we are and why we are here. It is interesting to note that in the first decade of the twenty-first century, the themes that *Blade Runner* explored have become popular ones in cinema at large.

CONCLUDING REMARKS

Eyesight constitutes an important source of message- and meaning-making. There is no culture without some form of visual signification. All cultures have the equivalents of what we call diagrams, maps, drawings, paintings, sculptures, and so on. These bear witness to the fact that visual forms are perceived to be just as crucial to human understanding, if not more so, than words. This is perhaps why we have always felt a need to literally "extend" our ability to see, leading to the many scientific inventions that extend vision mechanically (the lens, the magnifying glass, the telescope, etc.). And this is perhaps why we have always equated sight with intelligence, as can be seen in expressions such as "He's so *bright*," "She has great *foresight*," and so on.

Language

Language is the mother of thought, not its handmaiden.

Karl Kraus (1874–1936)

PRELIMINARY REMARKS

What is a word? Consider as a case in point the word *green*. First, note that it is a legitimate signifier structurally—that is, it is made up with legitimate English sounds (known as *phonemes*) connected to each other in an appropriate structural fashion (according to the rules of English syllable structure). You would not recognize the signifier *çeñ*, on the other hand, as an acceptable English word because it contains two phonemes, represented by the alphabet characters *ç* and *ñ*, that do not exist in English. It violates paradigmatic structure. Nor would you perceive *gpeen* as a legitimate signifier, even though each of its sounds is in actual fact an acceptable English phoneme. The reason is that it violates syntagmatic structure (the sequence *gp* does not occur in English to start a word). Now, consider what *green* denotes. It refers, of course, to a specific gradation on the light spectrum. The story of *green* is not complete, however, until (as we have seen throughout this book so far) we consider its connotations. It can, in fact, stand for envy ("She's *green* with envy"), hope ("The grass is always *greener* on the other side"), youthfulness ("He's at the *green* age of eighteen"), and many other connotative meanings.

This semiotic sketch of the word *green* is intended to show how words are recognized, constructed, and used in all languages. But, then, language is not just a collection of words. When words are used for representational and/ or communicative purposes they allow people to make messages in truly powerful ways. But, to a semiotician, the texts that deliver verbal messages

– 93 –

are no different semiotically than are nonverbal texts. In semiotics, "verbality" is considered to be just one among other "semiosic modalities" used by humans to make their messages.

This chapter looks at language from a semiotic perspective. One of its objectives is to show that language has properties that hardly set it apart from nonverbal codes, but rather, as we saw already with respect to gesture in chapter 3, that it reveals the same forces of sign-creation at work—namely, iconicity, indexicality, and symbolism.

WHAT IS LANGUAGE?

Language is truly a remarkable phenomenon. Without it, human life as we know it would be inconceivable. The endless sea of written words contained in books, which have recorded human thoughts throughout the ages, and to which we can have access if we know the appropriate verbal codes, constitute a truly astounding achievement. If somehow all the books contained by the world's libraries were to be destroyed overnight, human civilization would have to start all over re-coding knowledge linguistically, by bringing together writers, scientists, educators, law-makers, etc. to literally "rewrite" knowledge.

Language has always been universally felt to constitute the capacity that, more than any other, sets humankind apart from all other species. There is a deeply felt conviction within us that if we were ever able to solve the enigma of how language originated in our species, then we would possess a vital clue to the mystery of life itself. One of the New Testament gospels starts off, as a matter of fact, with "In the beginning was the *Word*." Throughout the centuries, the debate on what language is has often focused on whether it was a gift from a divine source or a unique accomplishment of the human mind. In Ancient Greece, the term for "speech"—*logos*—designated not only articulate discourse but also the rational faculty of mind. For the Greeks, it was *logos* that transformed the human animal into a rational thinker.

The lengths to which some have gone to throw light on the enigma of language origins are quite extraordinary. It is reported by the Greek historian Herodotus (484?–425 BC) that in the seventh century BC the Egyptian king Psamtik (663–610 BC) devised an "experiment" to determine the original language of humanity. He gave two newborn babies of ordinary people to a shepherd to nurture among his flocks. The shepherd was commanded not to utter any speech before them. The children were to live by themselves in a solitary habitation. At the due hours the shepherd was instructed to bring to them, give them their fill of milk, and carry out the necessary tasks to ensure their survival. After two years the shepherd brought the babies raised in the prescribed manner before Psamtik. The first word uttered by the two sounded like *becos*–the ancient Phrygian word for bread. The ecstatic Psamtik immediately declared Phrygian to be the mother tongue of humanity. Whether or not Psamtik's "experiment" ever took place at all is an open historical question. But even if it had, it certainly would not have proved anything. The babbling sounds made by the children—in probable imitation of something they had heard—were interpreted, or more accurately misinterpreted, as constituting the word *becos* by Psamtik.

The question of language origins has spawned countless speculations throughout the millennia. This is why the Linguistic Society of Paris imposed a ban in 1866 on all discussions related to the question, as did the Philological Society of London a half century later in 1911. In the early 1970s, however, interest in this conundrum was rekindled, probably because of the intriguing and suggestive findings that were being accumulated in such interrelated fields of inquiry as archeology, paleography, animal ethology, psychology, neurology, anthropology, semiotics, and linguistics. Language scientists came to see these as tantalizing bits and pieces to the puzzle of language origins.

The ancient Greeks put forward one of the first theories of language origins, known as *echoic*, by which speech was said to have sprung from attempts to imitate sounds and/or react to emotions. To this day, the supporters of echoic theory point to the universal presence of onomatopoeic words and interjections in the world's basic vocabularies. The most serious shortcoming of this view, however, is its inability to account for the development of nonvocal languages, such as writing, gesture languages, and the like. Nevertheless, echoic theory cannot be dismissed entirely. After all, there really is no way to determine whether or not sound imitation played a much more pivotal creative role in prehistoric times than it does today. It is certainly not at all unreasonable to suggest that echoism was *one* of the factors leading to vocal language.

In actual fact, there are three basic versions of echoic theory. They are as follows:

- *Bow-wow theory*: This claims that language originated when our hominid ancestors started imitating the sounds of animals (bird calls, the barking of dogs, and so on).
- *Pooh-pooh theory*: This claims that language originated when our early ancestors starting uttering instinctive noises and interjections with their vocal apparatus in response to various emotional states.

- *Ding-dong theory*: This claims that language originated when our hominid ancestors started observing and then imitating correspondences between different objects and the various noises they made.

Competing with such theories is so-called gestural theory, also known as *La-la theory*: This claims that gesture preceded vocal speech, and that the latter emerged gradually from simulations between the organs of articulation and gesture forms: for example, wagging the tongue to say "bye-bye" to simulate the waving of the hand. The continual apposition of gestures with imitative movements of the vocal organs led eventually to the replacement of the former by the latter.

Neither echoic nor gestural theories address the possibility that speech arose from social cooperation. The theory that makes this very claim is known as *Yo-he-ho theory*. It posits, simply, that language originated in the chants and songs that early hominid groups used as they worked and played cooperatively together. But like echoic and gestural theories this scenario skirts around a fundamental question: What mental feature could have sparked the process by which work-related chants were transformed into full language? Moreover, as Sebeok (1986) suggests, speech or vocal communication is no specific function of language, since humans have many nonvocal modes of communication available to them.

At this point it is necessary to distinguish between *language* and *speech*. Speech is a physiological and anatomical phenomenon. It involves the intentional use of the organs of the vocal apparatus—the tongue, the teeth, the epiglottis, etc.—to articulate sounds and words. Language is a mental code. It is a system of signs commonly delivered as vocal speech; but it can also be expressed through other physical modes—through pictography, gesture, and so on. One can have language without speech (as do individuals with impaired vocal organs), because it exists in the mind. But one cannot have speech without language, because speech depends on the language code.

Language probably developed before speech. The evidence for this hypothesis is indirect. At birth, the position of the larynx in human infants is high in the neck, like it is in that of other primates. Infants breathe, swallow, and vocalize in ways that are physiologically similar to gorillas and chimps. But, during the first six months of life, the infant's larynx starts to descend gradually, dramatically altering the ways in which the child will carry out such physiological functions from then on. Nobody knows why this descent occurs. It is an anatomical phenomenon that is unique to humans. This new low position means that the respiratory and digestive tracts now cross above the larynx. This entails a few risks: food can easily lodge in the entrance of the larynx; and humans cannot drink and breathe simultaneously without choking. But in compensation, it produces a pharyngeal chamber above the vocal folds that can modify sound. That makes it possible to articulate sounds.

Interestingly, research on the casts of human skulls found at archeological sites has established that the lowered larynx did not occur earlier than 100,000 years ago. This was arrived at by reconstructing adult skulls, known as *endocasts*. Archeologists have established that the lowered larynx is typical of endocasts that are less than 100,000 years old; those that are older than 100,000 years show a high larynx. This critical paleoneurological finding suggests that there may have been language without speech in early hominid groups, since speech requires a lowered larynx. The most probable mode of delivery of language was gesture. This is probably why we still use gesture as a default mode of communication (when vocal speech is impossible), and why we gesticulate when we speak.

LEARNING TO SPEAK

Language literally comes *naturally* to us. We acquire it as vocal speech without effort or training during our infancy. Indeed, the only requirement for learning any language, or languages, is adequate exposure to samples of it from birth to about two. So natural is speech to us, in fact, that some, like the American linguist Noam Chomsky (1928–), have gone so far as to claim that language is a physical organ as congenital to the human being as, say, flight is to a bird. Is Chomsky right?

When one examines Chomsky's description of the organ more closely, one cannot help but become disappointed, for it ends up being no more than an organ consisting of grammar-making principles. Called a Universal Grammar (UG), it is purportedly present in the brain at birth and subjected to modification by the specific languages to which individuals are exposed in infancy. The attractive part of UG theory, of course, is its claim that all natural languages are built on the same basic plan and that differences among languages are explainable as choices of rule types from a fairly small inventory of principles. Hence the universality and rapidity of language acquisition—when the child learns one fact about a language, the child can easily infer other facts without having to learn them one by one. The part that is, however, disappointing is that the UG ends up being described as consisting of a small set of rules of syntax devised by linguists themselves. As such, UG theory ignores the critical link that seems to exist between language, gesture, and the other nonverbal modes of representation.

Moreover, UG theory disregards almost completely the use of imitation and the role that iconicity plays in early linguistic activities. The use of sound to model the world imitatively can already be seen when the child reaches six months of age and starts to emit monosyllabic utterances (*mu, ma, da, di*, etc.), which are imitations of what the child has heard in social context. These are called *holophrastic* (one-word) utterances, and have been shown to serve three basic functions: (1) naming an object; (2) expressing an action or a desire for some action; (3) conveying emotional states. Holophrases are typically reductions of adult words—*da* for *dog*, *ca* for *cat*, etc. Over 60% will develop into nouns; and 20% will become verbs. During the second year children typically double their holophrases—*wowo* "water," *bubu* "bottle," *mama* "mother," etc.

Another weakness of UG theory is its view of grammar rules as being independent of meaning factors, thus skirting the whole question of the relation between language and thought or, in semiotic terms, of the dynamic interplay between the X and Y components of signification $(X = Y)$. One of the first to look closely at this very interplay was the American anthropological linguist Benjamin Lee Whorf (1897–1941), even though philosophers and linguists before Whorf had debated it extensively. Whorf was not interested in debate. He looked for evidence of the interplay by gathering data on a language that was radically different from any of those spoken by North Americans and Europeans generally. The language he examined extensively was Hopi—an aboriginal language of North America spoken in the southwestern part of the US. After analyzing the grammar and lexicon of that language, he came to the conclusion that the structures acquired by native speakers of any language predispose them to attend to certain concepts as being necessary, others as not. But, as Whorf emphasized, this does not mean that languages cannot be used to innovate. Indeed, we use the resources of our native languages to create new ideas and new thoughts any time we want. For example, if for some reason we wish, or need, to refer to "adolescent boys between the ages of 13 and 16 who smoke," then by coining an appropriate word, such as *groon,* we would in effect etch this concept into our thoughts, because the presence of the word *groon* in memory, as Whorf argued, would predispose us to see its meaning as somehow necessary. When a boy with the stated characteristics came into view, we would immediately recognize him as a *groon.*

To grasp Whorf's notion that languages differed in how they encode reality, consider a practical example. In Italian, the word *orologio* is used to refer to any "time-keeping device," no matter what its shape, form, or function might be. In English, on the other hand, two words are used, *watch* and *clock*—the former refers to a time device that is carried, worn, or put on bodies (on wrists, around the neck, in pockets, etc.), while the latter refers to a time device that is placed in specific locations (on a table, on a wall, etc.) and not carried around. This does not mean Italians are incapable of making this very same distinction. They can do so by using the construction: *da* + *place*, with *da* meaning approximately "for": *orologio da polso* = wristwatch ("watch for wrist"), *orologio da tavolo* = table clock ("clock for table"), and so on. But, unlike speakers of English, they are not accustomed to differentiating conceptually between "time-keeping devices that can be conveniently carried and those that cannot." By the way, it is relevant to note that the word *watch* came into currency when people started strapping clocks around their wrists.

The Whorf Hypothesis, as it has come to be known, raises some interesting questions about social inequalities and the structure of the language that encodes them. In English, sexist terms like *chairman*, *spokesman*, etc., were often cited in the past as examples of how language predisposed its users to view certain social roles in gender terms. Feminist critics have maintained that English grammar was originally organized from the perspective of those at the center of the society—the men. This is why we once would say that a woman married into a man's family, and why at wedding ceremonies expressions such as "I pronounce you man and wife," are still used by some. In the not-too-distant past, and perhaps still today in many areas of Western society, women were defined in relation to men. Similarly damaging language is the kind that excludes women, such as "lady atheist" or "lesbian doctor," implying that atheists and doctors are not typically female or lesbian. The Whorfian Hypothesis suggests that by changing the language, we end up changing the attendant social behaviors. And, indeed, this seems to have transpired in the last few decades in the case of sexist language.

In some other societies the reverse situation has been true. Investigating grammatical gender in the Iroquois language, Alpher (1987) found that the feminine gender was the default one in that language, whereas masculine items were marked by a special subject prefix. Alpher related this to the fact that the Iroquois society is matrilineal—traditionally women hold the land, pass it on to their heirs in the female line, are responsible for agricultural production, control the wealth, arrange marriages, and so on. Iroquois grammar therefore is organized from the viewpoint of those at the center of that society too—in this case the women.

WORDS

Words are constructed with sounds known as *phonemes*. These are defined as the minimal sound units that allow native speakers of a language to differentiate and identify structures as legitimate words. For example, the difference between the two words *sip* and *zip* can be discerned in the initial sound—in pronouncing the /s/ of *sip* the vocal cords in the larynx do not vibrate, whereas in pronouncing the /z/ of *zip* they do. If the reader puts his or her index and middle fingers over the larynx and articulates these two sounds, this would become instantly obvious to him or her. The two sounds are otherwise articulated in the same way. That minimal difference, which is sufficient to signal a difference in meaning between the two words, is said to be *phonemic*.

To a semiotician, the phonemic construction of words reveals basic signification processes at work. Iconicity, for example, manifests itself across languages in such common ways as follows:

- in alliteration, or the repetition of sounds for various effects: *sing-song, no-no, tick tock, choo choo*, etc.
- in the lengthening of sounds for emphasis: *Yesssss!, Noooooo!*, etc.
- in the use of intonation to express emotional states: *Are you absolutely sure? Noooooo way!*
- in sound modeling, as in the language of cartoons and comic books: *Zap!, Boom!, Pow!*, etc.
- in onomatopoeic descriptions of people and things: e.g., a snake or person with snake-like characteristics is described as *slithery, slippery, sneaky*, etc.
- in the use of tone and volume—e.g., loudness conveys anger, an increased rate of speech, urgency, etc.

Many words, which are not directly perceivable as iconic, contain nonetheless in their very structure a kind of "latent" or "suggestive" iconicity—that is, they are constructed with sounds that suggest sonorous aspects of referents indirectly. As mentioned in chapter 2, this is known generally as sound symbolism. For example, many English words constructed with *sh* and *gl* represent concepts associated with light:

- *sh*ine
- *sh*een
- *gl*immer

- *gl*int
- *gl*eam
- *gl*itter
- *gl*isten
- *gl*ow

Words constructed with *sl*, on the other hand, suggest unpleasantries:

- *sl*ink
- *sl*udge
- *sl*urp
- *sl*um
- *sl*eaze
- *sl*ime

The American linguist Morris Swadesh (1971), who was a pioneer in the study of sound symbolism, drew attention, moreover, to such suggestive features as the presence in many of the world's languages of [i]-type vowels to express "nearness," in contrast to [a]- [o]- and [u]-type vowels to express the opposite notion of "distance." Such coincidences suggested to him that nearness concepts tended to be conveyed unconsciously by the relative nearness of the lips in the articulation of [i] and other front vowels, while the distance concepts tended to be conveyed by the relative openness of the lips in the pronunciation of [a], [æ], [u], and other mid and back vowels. Examples of this form of latent sound symbolism abound in many languages. Here are some from English:

Nearness Concepts	Distance Concepts
here = [hi:r]	there = [ðæ:r]
near = [ni:r]	far = [fa:r]
this = [ðÎ̂:s]	that = [ðae:t]

Iconicity manifests itself as well in other areas of language structure. The American linguist Ronald Langacker (e.g., 1987, 1990) has argued persuasively that certain aspects of grammar are explainable only in iconicity terms. Nouns, for instance, elicit images of referents that appear to trace a "region" in mind-space—for example a count noun is imagined as referring to something that encircles a bounded region, whereas a mass noun is visualized as designating a non-bounded region. The noun *water* elicits an image of a non-bounded region, whereas the noun *leaf* evokes an image of a bounded region. This conceptual dichotomy produces grammatical effects—*leaves* can be counted, *water* cannot; *leaf* has a plural form *(leaves)*, *water* does not (unless the referential domain is metaphorical); *leaf* can be preceded by an indefinite article *(a leaf)*, *water* cannot; and so on.

Indexicality and symbolism are also forces in word creation. For example, languages across the world have indexical words for: (1) *this, that, here, there, up, down,* etc., for referring to the relative location of things; (2) *before, after, now, then, yesterday, tomorrow,* etc., for referring to events that are in temporal relation to each other, and (3) pronouns like *I, you, he, she, the one, the other* for referring to the participants taking part in a situation. And many are the words constructed on the basis of social convention, agreement, or common practice. Symbolism practices can be seen, for instance, in the invention of recent words made with the prefix *cyber-* such as *cyberspace, cybercafé,* etc.

Words are, of course, signs. This means, concretely, that they reveal an intrinsic $X = Y$ structure. In fact, as Saussure correctly observed, the signifiers *(X)* of words instantly entail specific signifieds *(Y)*. The problem in semiotics and linguistics has always been how to flesh out not only the meaning of the $X = Y$ relation, but also how words, as basic structures, relate to each other. As mentioned in chapter 1, the technique called binary opposition was introduced into these two disciplines to solve the practical problem of doing exactly this in a systematic way. The technique posits that the meaning of $X = Y$ structures is something that cannot be determined in the absolute, but only in relation to other structures *(sip* vs. *zip)*. From such "oppositions" we can identify one or two features at a time that go into making a particular structure unique. This technique has made it possible to establish the following basic relations among the words in a language:

- *Synonymy.* This is the relation by which the meanings of different words overlap, as can be seen by oppositions such as *hide-conceal, big-large,* etc. The overlap is normally partial, and rarely completely coincidental.
- *Homonymy.* This is the relation by which two or more meanings are associated with the same word or phrase, as can be seen by oppositions such as *Shakespeare's play* vs. *He likes to play,* which reveal that *play* is a homonym.

- *Antonymy.* This is the relation by which different words stand in a discernible "oppositeness" of meaning to each other, as oppositions such as *love-hate, hot-cold,* etc., reveal. But antonymy is a matter of degree, rather than of categorical difference.
- *Hyponymy:* This is the relation by which the meaning of one word is included in that of another: e.g., the meaning of *scarlet* is included in the meaning of *red, tulip* in that of *flower,* and so on.
- *Proportionality:* This is the relation by which distinctions among certain subsets of words are maintained by the components that make up their meanings. These are isolatable through *proportions* that can be set up among signs that are similar to those used in logic and mathematics. For example, a *man* can be put into the same relation to *woman* as a *bull* to a *cow,* since they stand to each other in the same way—as "male" and "female" counterparts.

NAMES

A *name* is a special kind of word. It is particularly interesting semiotically, because of the fact that it links the possessor of the name to the culture in which he or she is born directly. The study of names falls more properly under the branch of both semiotics and linguistics called *onomastics* (from Greek *onoma* "name").

Across cultures, a neonate is not considered a full-fledged member of the culture until he or she is given a name. The act of naming a newborn infant is his or her first rite of passage in society, becoming identified as a separate individual with a unique personality. If a person is not given a name by his or her family, then society will step in to do so. A person taken into a family, by marriage, adoption, or for some other reason, is also typically assigned the family's name. Throughout the world the name is perceived as identical to the person. In Inuit culture, an individual is perceived to have a body, a soul, and a name; a person is not seen as complete without all three. A few years ago, a British television program called *The Prisoner* played on this very same latent perception in our own culture. It portrayed a totalitarian world in which people were assigned numbers instead of traditional names—*Number 1, Number 2,* etc. The idea was, obviously, that a person could be made to conform to the will of the state and could be more easily controlled by state officials if he or she did not have a name. The whole series was, in a sense, a portrayal of the struggle that humans feel to discover the meaning of Self. The use of numerical identification of prisoners and slaves is, in effect, a negation of their humanity and, ultimately, their existence.

All names have historical and culture-specific meanings, even though today we may no longer be aware of them. Documents reveal that early peoples gave someone a name with a definite knowledge of its meaning. In the Bible, for example, a widow exclaims, "Call me not Naomi (*pleasant*), call me Mara (*bitter*): for the Almighty hath dealt very bitterly with me" (Ruth 1:20). Most of the common given names in Western culture come from Hebrew, Greek, Latin, or Teutonic languages. Hebrew names taken from the Bible have traditionally provided the most important source of Western names—for example, *John* (gracious gift of God), *Mary* (wished for), *Michael* (who is like God), *David* (beloved), *Elizabeth* (oath of God), *James* (may God protect, or one who takes the place of another), *Joseph* (the Lord shall add), *Hannah* (God has favored me), and *Samuel* (God has heard). Greek and Latin names often refer to abstract qualities—for example, *Alexander* (helper of humanity), *Barbara* (stranger), *George* (farmer), *Helen* (light), *Margaret* (pearl), *Philip* (lover of horses), *Stephen* (crown or garland), *Clarence* (famous), *Emily* (flattering), *Patricia* (of noble birth), *Victor* (conqueror), and *Virginia* (maidenly). Teutonic names usually consist of two elements joined together without regard to their relationship. For example, *William* is composed of two name elements, *Wille* (will or resolution) and *helm* (helmet). Some of these name elements are found at the beginning, such as *ead* (rich) in *Edwin* and *Edmund*, or at the end, such as *weard* (guardian) in *Howard* and *Edward*.

In some countries, a child must be given an appropriate cultural name before he or she can be issued a birth certificate. Although this might seem like an extreme measure to us, in all cultures, name-giving is constrained by traditions and conventions, to lesser or greater extents. Modern naming practices are, however, much more eclectic than they have ever been. Modern names are now derived from contemporary personalities (*Elvis*, *Marilyn*), places (*Georgia*), and variant spellings (*JoEtta*, *Beverleigh*). They may even be completely fanciful. The late rock musician and composer Frank Zappa (1940–1993), for instance, named his daughter *Moon Unit* and his son *Dweezil*.

Until the late Middle Ages, one personal name was generally sufficient as an identifier. Duplications, however, began to occur so often that additional differentiations became a necessity. Hence, *surnames* were given to individuals (literally "names on top of a name"). These were at first indexical, in that they identified the individual in terms of place. For example, in England a person living near or at a place where apple trees grew would have been called "John where-the-apples-grow," hence, *John Appleby*. This is how surnames such as

Wood, Lake, Brook, Stone, Field, or *Ford* came into being. During the Middle Ages, few people could read. Signboards often exhibited the picture of an animal or object to designate a shop or inn. A person working or living at the place might thus be called *Bell, Star,* or *Swan.* A person might also be named after the town he or she came from, such as *Middleton* or *Kronenberg.* Many English place names may be also recognized by the endings *-ham, -thorp, -ton, -wic,* and *-worth,* meaning a homestead or dwelling. Another category was descendancy surnames, or names indicating parentage. Some were forged with prefixes such as *Mac-, Mc-* in Scotland or Ireland, or with *Ap-* in Wales. Suffixes such as *-son* in English names and *-sen* or *–dottir* in Scandinavian names were also used—for example, *Johnson* or *Jensen* "son of John," *Maryson* "son of Mary," *Jakobsdottir* "daughter of Jacob." Many other surnames were forged descriptively. For example, someone who could be described as "small" became *Robert, the Small,* or simply *Robert Small.* Names such as *Little, Gross, Reid* (red-haired), and *Tiny* were created in this way. Descriptive names were also coined to reflect medieval occupations, *Smith* being the foremost example with equivalents in Spanish (*Ferrer*), German (*Schmidt*), and Hungarian (*Kovacs*). Other common occupation surnames include *Baker, Farmer, Carpenter, Taylor, Weaver, Clerk* (or *Clarke*), *Cook,* and *Miller.*

The Chinese were the first known people to use more than one name. The Emperor Fuxi is said to have decreed the use of family names about 2852 BC. Today, the Chinese customarily have three names: (1) the family name, placed first, comes from one of the 438 words in the Chinese sacred poem *Baijia Xing* (also spelled *Po-Chia Hsing*); (2) a generation name, taken from a poem of 20 to 30 characters adopted by each family; and (3) a name corresponding to a Christian name. The Romans had initially only one name, but later also started using three names: (1) the *praenomen,* which stood first as the person's given name; (2) the *nomen,* which indicated the *gens,* or clan to which the person belonged; and (3) the last name, or *cognomen,* which designated the family. For example, Caesar's full name was *Gaius Julius Caesar.* A person sometimes added a fourth name, the *agnomen,* to commemorate an illustrious action or remarkable event. Family names became confused by the fall of the Roman Empire, and single names once again became customary.

Family names came into use again in northern Italy in the late tenth century, becoming common by the thirteenth. Nobles were the first to adopt family names, so as to set themselves apart from common people. The nobles made their family names hereditary, passing them on from father to children. A family name thus became the mark of a well-bred person, and so all classes of common people aspiring to ascend the social ladder began to adopt the practice too. The

Crusaders carried the custom of family names from Italy to the other countries of Western Europe. Throughout Europe, wealthy and noble families first adopted family names. These were thus not hereditary, initially, but merely described one person. For example, the son of Robert Johnson might be known as Henry Robertson, or Henry, son of Robert.

Name-giving is extended across cultures to inanimate referents. When this is done, the objects somehow take on, as if by magic, an animate quality of their own. Throughout the world, naming objects and artifacts is felt to bestow upon them a mysterious life force. When a child names a teddy bear, that toy comes to life in the child's imagination. Similarly, when we name storms or commercial products, they too seem to come to life. Things with names have a personality; those without names do not.

VERBAL COMMUNICATION

Among the various semiotic approaches to verbal communication, the one by the Moscow-born linguist and semiotician who carried out most of his work in the United States, Roman Jakobson (1896–1982), is perhaps the most insightful one. Jakobson posited six "constituents" that characterize all speech acts (Jakobson 1960):

- an *addresser* who initiates a communication;
- a *message* that he or she wishes to convey and which he or she recognizes must refer to something other than itself;
- an *addressee* who is the intended receiver of the message;
- a *context* that provides the framework for encoding and decoding the message—e.g., the phrase "Help me" would have a different meaning depending on whether it was uttered by someone lying motionless on the ground or by someone in a classroom who was working on a difficult math problem;
- a mode of *contact* by which the message is delivered between an addresser and an addressee;
- a *code* providing the signs for encoding and decoding messages.

Jakobson then pointed out that each of these constituents determines a different communicative function:

- *Emotive function.* The intent of the addresser in constructing a message is emotive in the sense that, no matter how literal the message might be, its mode of delivery invariably involves the latent presence of the addresser's emotions, attitudes, social status, etc.

- *Conative function.* The message invariably has an effect on its receiver, known as "conative," no matter what the message contents might be, because the way it is delivered by the addresser involves such subjective features as tone of voice, individual selection of words, and so on.
- *Referential function.* This refers to any message that is constructed to convey information ("Bloor Street is two blocks north of here").
- *Poetic function.* This refers to any message that is constructed to deliver meanings similarly to poetry ("Roses are red, violets are blue, and how's it going with you?").
- *Phatic function.* This refers to any message that is designed to establish, acknowledge, or reinforce social relations ("Hi, how's it going?").
- *Metalingual function.* This refers to any message that is designed to indicate the code used ("The word noun is a *noun*.").

Jakobson's analysis suggests that verbal discourse goes well beyond the function of simple information transfer. It involves determining *who* says *what* to *whom*; *where* and *when* it is said; and *how* and *why* it is said; that is, it is motivated and shaped by the setting, the message contents, the participants, and the goals of each interlocutor. Discourse makes an emotional claim on everyone in the social situation.

To Jakobson's set of functions, however, I would add two more. One can be named the *mystical function*, or the latent perception of the words used in communication as having primordial mystical power. This function is latent in all kinds of rituals and religious practices—the Catholic Mass is spoken; sermons, prep rallies, and other ceremonial gatherings are anchored in speeches, either traditionally worded or specifically composed for the occasion; and so on. The use of language in ritual is not to create new meanings, but to reinforce traditional ones and, thus, to ensure cultural cohesion. Societies are held together as a result of such verbal rituals. People typically love to hear the same speeches, songs, stories at specific times during the year (at Christmas, at Passover, etc.) in order to feel united with the other members of the culture. They are passed on from generation to generation with little or no modification.

Words in their origin were probably perceived as magical or mystical forms. Those who possessed knowledge of them were also thought to possess supernatural or magical powers. In many early cultures, even knowing the name of a deity was purported to give the knower great power—for example, in Egyptian mythology, the sorceress Isis tricked the sun god, Ra, into revealing his name and, thus, gained power over him and all other gods. In some cultures, the name given to the individual is perceived as having a "life force" independent of the individual, bringing with it the spirit of the previous individuals who shared that name. Throughout the world, the names of ancestors are perceived to weave a sort of magical protective aura around the individual named after them. In some traditional Inuit tribes, for instance, an individual will not pronounce his or her name, fearing that this senseless act could break the magical spell of protection that it brings with it. As Espes Brown (1992: 13) puts it: "the fact that when we create words we use our breath, and for these people and these traditions breath is associated with the principle of life; breath is life itself. And so if a word is born from this sacred principle of breath, this lends an added sacred dimension to the spoken word."

Belief in the mystical powers of language is not limited to tribal cultures. It abounds even in modern technological cultures. "Speak of the devil," we say in common parlance, and "he will appear." When someone sneezes, uttering "bless you" is meant to ward off sickness. As Ann Gill (1994: 106) puts it:

> By portraying experience in a particular way, words work their unconscious magic on humans, making them see, for example, products as necessary for success or creating distinctions between better or worse—be it body shape, hair style, or brand of blue jeans. Words create belief in religions, governments, and art forms; they create allegiances to football teams, politicians, movie stars, and certain brands of beer. Words are the windows of our own souls and to the world beyond our fingertips. Their essential persuasive efficacy works its magic on every person in every society.

The other side of sacredness is *taboo*. This word comes from the tribal language Tongan where it means "holy, untouchable." Taboos exist in all cultures, because there are certain forms of language that a society prefers to avoid. These are generally related to sexuality, the supernatural, excretion, death, and various aspects of social life. For example, among the Zuñi of New Mexico, the word *takka* "frogs" is prohibited during ceremonies. In our own culture, so-called four-letter words are generally considered obscene, but they can be perceived as taboo if uttered in sacred places like churches, sanctuaries, etc.

The other function I would add to Jakobson's typology can be called the *economizing function*. This claims that messages will be constructed and delivered in the most "economical" way possible, that is, with the least possible effort. Actually, "economization" is characteristic of all kinds of communication systems, not just language. It appears in various ways across cultures. For example, the more frequently a word or expression is used the more likely it will be replaced by a shorter equivalent. Known as "Zipf's Law" in the communication sciences, here are a few well-known examples of how it manifests itself in English:

- ad = *ad*vertisement
- photo = *photo*graph
- NATO = *N*orth *A*tlantic *T*reaty *O*rganization
- laser = *l*ight *a*mplification by *s*timulated *e*mission of *r*adiation

The economizing function can be seen today in the use of so-called "instant message" (IM) acronyms. Unlike e-mails, IMs are sent in real time, like a phone call, but with text rather than spoken words. To increase the speed at which messages can be inputted and received, IM has developed a series of common acronyms that are now part of computer language. Here are a few of them:

- b4 = before
- bf/gf = boyfriend/girlfriend
- f2f = face-to-face
- gr8 = great
- h2cus = hope to see you soon
- idk = I don't know
- j4f = just for fun
- lol = laughing out loud
- cm = call me
- 2dA = today
- wan2 = want to
- ruok = Are you OK?
- 2moro = tomorrow
- g2g = gotta go

WRITING

Writing too has always been perceived as having a mystical function. The ancient Egyptians called their writing system *hieroglyphic* because it was used to record hymns and prayers, to register the names and titles of individuals and deities, and to record various community activities—*hieroglyphic* derives from Greek *hieros* "holy" and *glyphein* "to carve." Indeed, in their origins most scripts were deemed to have sacred or mystical origins—for example, the Cretans attributed the origin of writing to Zeus, the Sumerians to Nabu, the Egyptians to Toth, the Greeks to Hermes, and the list could go on and on.

The earliest form of writing was *pictographic*; this consisted of drawing pictures to represent objects. So intuitive and functional is pictography that it comes as little surprise to find that it has not disappeared from even our alphabet-based world. The figures designating *male* and *female* on washrooms and the *no-smoking* signs found in public buildings, to mention but two common examples, are modern-day pictographs.

One of the first civilizations to institutionalize pictographic writing as a means of recording ideas, keeping track of business transactions, and transmitting knowledge was the ancient Chinese one. According to some archeological estimates, Chinese pictography may date as far as back the fifteenth century BC. Another fully developed ancient pictographic system was the Sumerian-Babylonian one that was developed nearly five thousand years ago. The Sumerians recorded their representations on clay tablets with wedge-shaped forms, hence the name *cuneiform*. Cuneiform writing was a very expensive and impracticable means of writing. For this reason it was developed, learned, and used primarily by rulers and clerics. In Egypt, hieroglyphic writing emerged around 2700 to 2500 BC. The Egyptians used papyrus (a type of early paper made from reeds) to record their writings, making it more practicable for many more classes of people. On the following page are some examples of Sumerian and Egyptian pictographs.

More abstract forms of pictographic signs are called *ideographs*. These may bear some resemblance to their referents, but assume much more of a conventional knowledge of the relation between picture and referent on the part of the user. International symbols for such things as public telephones, washrooms, etc., are all ideographic. More abstract ideographs are known as *logographs*. A logographic system combines various pictographs and/or ideographs for the purpose of indicating ideas that cannot be graphically represented. For example, the Chinese pictographs for *sun* and *tree* are combined to represent the Chinese spoken word for *east*. The first *syllabaries*—systems

SUMERIAN

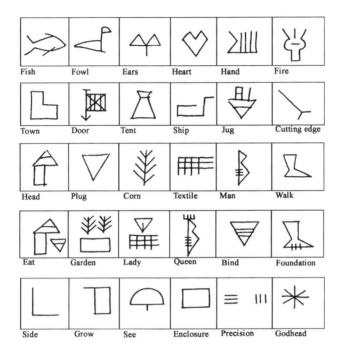

Fish	Fowl	Ears	Heart	Hand	Fire
Town	Door	Tent	Ship	Jug	Cutting edge
Head	Plug	Corn	Textile	Man	Walk
Eat	Garden	Lady	Queen	Bind	Foundation
Side	Grow	See	Enclosure	Precision	Godhead

EGYPTIAN

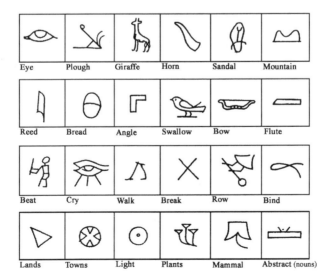

Eye	Plough	Giraffe	Horn	Sandal	Mountain
Reed	Bread	Angle	Swallow	Bow	Flute
Beat	Cry	Walk	Break	Row	Bind
Lands	Towns	Light	Plants	Mammal	Abstract (nouns)

of signs standing for syllables—developed from such amalgamated systems. Syllabaries are still used in some cultures. Japanese, for example, is still written with two complete syllabaries—the *hiragana* and the *katakana*—devised to supplement the characters originally taken over from Chinese.

To facilitate the speed of writing, the Sumerians and the Egyptians eventually streamlined their pictographs and transformed them into symbols for the actual sounds of speech. Called *phonographic* writing, it consisted of signs standing for parts of words, such as syllables or individual sounds. A complete phonographic system for representing single sounds is called *alphabetic*. The first alphabetic system emerged in the Middle East around 1000 BC, and was then transported by the Phoenicians (a people from a territory on the eastern coast of the Mediterranean, located largely in modern-day Lebanon) to Greece. It contained signs for consonant sounds only. When it reached Greece, signs for vowel sounds were added to it, making the Greek system the first full-fledged alphabetic one.

The transition from pictorial to sound representation came about to make writing rapid and efficient in its use of space. So, for example, instead of drawing the full head of an ox, only its bare outline was at first drawn. This then came to stand for the ox, which, eventually, came to stand for the word for ox (*aleph* in Hebrew). Finally, it came to stand just for the first sound in the word (*a* in *aleph*), which was represented by simply turning the pictograph 180° (and removing any minor details from it). In actual fact, archeological findings suggest that the Phoenician scribes, who wrote from right to left, drew the ox figure sideways (probably because it was quicker for them to do so). The Greeks, who adapted Phoenician letters, generally wrote from left to right, and so turned the **A** around the other way. Around 500 BC writing became more standardized and letters stopped changing directions. By that time the **A** assumed the upright position it has today—the ox had finally settled on its horns! The various stages in the development of the character **A** are summarized below:

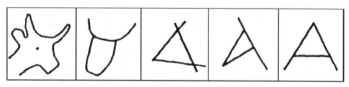

From the hieroglyph to the modern phonetic character A

The Greeks started the practice of naming each alphabet sign by such words as *alpha, beta, gamma*, etc., which were imitations of Phoenician words: *aleph* "ox," *beth* "house," *gimel* "camel," etc. Incidentally, the idea of an "alphabetic order" of letters from **A** to **Z** emerged because the letters were used to count the numbers in order—**A** stood for 1, **B** for 2, **C** for 3, and so on. The earliest record of alphabetic order is Psalm 37 where verses follow the Hebraic sequence.

Alphabetic writing has become the norm in many cultures. But in every alphabetic sign, there is a pictographic history and prehistory similar to the one described above for the letter **A.** The pictographic content of our letters goes unnoticed because our eyes are no longer trained to extract pictorial meaning from them.

VERBAL ART

The poems, stories, and plays that individuals throughout the world have created, and continue to create, with language are testaments to the need for verbal art in human life. Of all the verbal art forms, poetry seems to be the most fundamental and most universal. It can be defined as the use of words to reproduce natural sounds, to evoke feelings, and to provide insight into the intrinsic nature of things. The philosopher Vico, who was introduced in the second chapter, saw poetry as the primordial form of language. Vico called the first speakers "poets," which etymologically means "makers." At first, they formed a concept poetically as the image of a god or a hero—e.g., the ancient Greeks formed the concept of "valor" poetically through the character of the hero Achilles in the *Iliad*. This same pattern of concept-formation is noticeable in children, who seem to acquire concepts in poetic ways—through god-like and heroic characters who embody them.

Poetry is essentially "vocal music," since it is marked by rhythm and tone. Although poetry eventually gained an independent existence in our culture, in many others poetry and music are, in fact, still conceived of as identical. Some of the earliest written examples of poetic texts found by archeologists in ancient Sumer, Babylon, and other areas of the Middle East appear to confirm that poetry originated alongside music and drama as a communal expression to seek favor from, or give praise to, the gods. The musical aspect of poetry is still visible in many cultures. For example, in the Navajo culture, poetic forms are used as incantations for rain. But even in our modern technological culture, ritualistic uses of poetry abound—e.g., we use poetic language on greeting cards, on special kinds of invitations, to impart knowledge to children, in advertising jingles, and so on.

Interest in the nature and function of poetry goes back to ancient times. Plato asserted that poets were divinely inspired, but he regarded poetry as a pallid imitation of the actual world. Aristotle, on the other hand, argued that poetry was the greatest of all the creative arts, representing what is universal in human experience. The Roman poet Horace (65–68 BC) maintained that the function of poetry was to please and instruct. The rhetorician Longinus (AD 213–273) stressed that poetry was a means through which spiritual, moral, or intellectual knowledge could be achieved. In the Middle Ages, the great Italian poet Dante (1265–1321) showed the world how only poetry could express the various spiritual facets of human nature. In his masterpiece, the *Divine Comedy*, which he began around 1307 and completed shortly before his death, Dante took his readers on an imaginary journey through hell, purgatory, and heaven. In each of these three realms Dante encounters mythological, historical, and contemporary personages. Each character is symbolic of a particular fault or virtue, either religious or political, and the punishment or rewards meted out to the characters reflect Dante's portrayal of human actions as purposeful and teleological.

CONCLUDING REMARKS

Language is a truly distinctive achievement of the human species. With it, we can easily classify the world with words and entertain ourselves with jokes and stories. Without it, we probably would not have developed many of our institutions: How could we ever have devised religious practices without sacred texts? How could we ever have developed laws without words? How would we have organized and classified knowledge without such devices as dictionaries and encyclopedias? And the list of such questions could go on and on. No wonder, then, that so many philosophers across history have depicted language as our greatest faculty. To a semiotician, however, it has equal status to all the other faculties, such as music and art. In closing, I should mention that, as a branch of semiotics, the study of language is sometimes called *semiolinguistics* or *semiology*, to distinguish the approach from that used in *linguistics* proper.

Metaphor

Midway between the unintelligible and the commonplace, it is
metaphor which most produces knowledge.

Aristotle (384–322 BC)

PRELIMINARY REMARKS

If a young child were to ask you "What is love?" how would you answer him
or her? One answer you would not contemplate giving the child for sure is a
"dictionary" definition of love, such as "an affective response to some erotic,
emotional, affectionate signal emitted by another human being"! What you are
more likely to do is to relate the "experience" of love to something that is
familiar to children: "Well, you know, love is the feeling you get when your
mommy or daddy kisses you." Or else you might tell or read the child a story
that illustrates what love is all about for, as you know instinctively, children
learn about morals, ideas, and concepts through stories.

The illustrations we show children and stories we tell them are created
from *metaphorical reasoning*, which is, clearly, a kind of semiotic strategy
that allows us to make abstractions knowable to them in concrete ways. No
wonder, then, that interest in metaphor has become widespread in many
disciplines. But even so, by and large people still think of it as a stylistic device
of language, used by poets and writers to make their messages more effective
or ornate. Nothing could be further from the truth. If the recent research on
metaphor within semiotics and linguistics is even partially correct, then it can
no longer be viewed as a purely rhetorical device. On the contrary, it appears
to be the sum and substance of how abstract thinking unfolds. This is precisely

what we discover when we attempt to explain abstract concepts to children. Only through metaphor does the child grasp a concept such as *love* easily and permanently. George Lakoff and Mark Johnson (1980: 3) put it aptly as follows:

> Metaphor is for most people a device of the poetic imagination and the rhetorical flourish—a matter of extraordinary rather than ordinary language. Moreover, metaphor is typically viewed as characteristic of language alone, a matter of words rather than thought and action.... We have found, on the contrary, that metaphor is pervasive in everyday life, not just in language but in thought and action.

The focus of this chapter is on metaphorical signs. Semioticians have always known about the unique qualities of such signs. But, as mentioned, it is only in the last few decades that the semiotic view of metaphor has been spreading to other scholarly domains. The study of metaphor, sometimes called *metaphorology,* has always been a major target of sign theorists.

WHAT IS METAPHOR?

From ancient times, the use of figures of speech, or *tropes*, has been seen primarily as a rhetorical strategy employed by orators and writers to strengthen and embellish their speeches and compositions. In addition to metaphor—which is defined traditionally as the use of a word or phrase denoting one kind of idea in place of another word or phrase for the purpose of suggesting a likeness between the two (e.g., "Love is a rose")—the following primary tropes constitute the domain of rhetorical speech:

- *Climax* is an arrangement of words, clauses, or sentences in the order of their importance, the least forcible coming first and the others rising in potency until the last: "It is an outrage to scoff at her; it is a crime to ridicule her; but to deny her freedom of speech, what shall I say of this?"
- *Anticlimax* is the opposite trope, namely the sequencing of ideas that abruptly diminish in importance at the end of a sentence or passage, generally for satirical effect: "I will shoot him down first, and then I will talk to him."

- *Antithesis* refers to the juxtaposition of two words, phrases, clauses, or sentences contrasted or opposed in meaning in such a way as to give emphasis to contrasting ideas: "To err is human, to forgive divine."
- *Apostrophe* is the technique by which an actor turns from the audience, or a writer from his or her readers, to address a person who usually is either absent or deceased, or to address an inanimate object or an abstract idea: "Hail, Freedom, whose visage is never far from sight."
- *Euphemism* is the substitution of a delicate or inoffensive term or phrase for one that has coarse, sordid, or other unpleasant associations, as in the use of *lavatory* or *restroom* for *toilet.*
- *Exclamation* is a sudden outcry expressing strong emotion, such as fright, grief, or hatred: "Oh vile, vile, person!"
- *Hyperbole* is the use of exaggeration for effect: "My friend drinks oceans of water."
- *Litotes*, on the other hand, is the technique of understatement so as to enhance the effect of the ideas expressed: "Franz Boas showed no inconsiderable analytical powers as an anthropologist."
- *Simile* is the technique of specific comparison by means of the words *like* or *as* between two kinds of ideas or objects: "You're as light as a feather."
- *Metonymy* is the use of a word or phrase for another to which it bears an important relation, as the effect for the cause, the abstract for the concrete, etc.: "She's the head of our family."
- *Conceit* is an elaborate, often extravagant metaphor or simile, for making an analogy between totally dissimilar things: "Love is a worm."
- *Irony* refers to a dryly humorous or lightly sarcastic mode of speech, in which words are used to convey a meaning contrary to their literal sense: "I really love the pain you give me."
- *Onomatopoeia* is the imitation of natural sounds by words: *the humming bee, the cackling hen,* etc.
- *Oxymoron* is the combination of two seemingly contradictory or incongruous words: "My life is a living death."
- *Paradox* is a statement that appears contradictory or inconsistent: "She's a well-known secret agent."
- *Personification* is the representation of inanimate objects or abstract ideas as living beings: "Necessity is the mother of invention."
- *Rhetorical Question* is a questioning strategy that is intended not to gain information but to assert more emphatically the obvious answer to what is asked: "You do understand what I mean, don't you?"

- *Synecdoche* is the technique whereby the part is made to stand for the whole, the whole for a part, the species for the genus, etc.: "The President's administration contained the best brains in the country."

Since the 1970s, the trend in linguistics and psychology has been to consider metaphor, metonymy, synecdoche, and irony as manifestations of separate cognitive processes, rather than as types of tropes. As will become evident in this chapter, the reason for this is that they are much more than rhetorical devices.

Aristotle was the one who coined the term *metaphor*—itself a metaphor (*meta* "beyond" + *pherein* "to carry"). The great Greek philosopher saw the power of metaphorical reasoning in its ability to shed light on abstract concepts. However, he affirmed that, as conceptually powerful as it was, its primary function was stylistic, a device for sprucing up more prosaic and literal ways of communicating. Remarkably, this latter position became the rule by which metaphor came to be judged in Western philosophy ever since. But as a seminal 1977 study by Pollio, Barlow, Fine, and Pollio showed, Aristotle's original view was in effect the correct one. Those researchers found that speakers of English uttered, on average, 3,000 novel verbal metaphors and 7,000 idioms per week. Shortly thereafter, it became clear to language scientists that metaphor was hardly an optional flourish on literal language. On the contrary, they started discovering that it dominated everyday communication and was the source of many symbolic practices.

Defining metaphor semiotically poses an interesting dilemma. In the metaphor "The professor is a snake," there are two referents, not one, which are related to each other as follows:

- There is the primary referent, *professor*, which is known as the *topic* (or *tenor*) of the metaphor.
- Then there is a second referent, *snake*, which is known as the *vehicle* of the metaphor, which is chosen to say something about the topic.
- The linkage between the two creates a new meaning, called the *ground*, which is much more than the simple sum of the meanings of topic and vehicle.

Thus, metaphor can be seen to constitute a complex sign. First, the whole metaphor is itself a sign, showing $X = Y$ structure:

Structure of Metaphor

$$X \quad\quad = \quad\quad Y$$
$$\downarrow \quad\quad\quad\quad\quad\quad \downarrow$$

The professor   =   The professor is a sneaky,
is a snake   dangerous ... person

However, since the *snake* vehicle is itself a sign, the actual structure of the metaphor should show the *Y* part itself as an embedded "snake sign." The latter can be indicated with lower case letters *(x = y)*. Note, moreover, that it is not the denotative meaning of the vehicle that is embedded into the metaphor, but rather its connotative meaning:

Structure of Metaphor

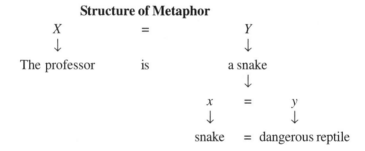

Metaphor reveals a basic tendency of the human mind to think of certain referents in this way. The question now becomes: Is there any psychological motivation for this? In the case of "The professor is a snake," the probable reason for correlating two apparently unrelated referents seems to be the *de facto* perception that humans and animals are interconnected in the natural scheme of things. Indeed, as we shall see below, metaphor is the strongest evidence in existence to support what can be called an *interconnectedness principle*. It reveals a knack for seeking out and establishing similarities among things, interconnecting them semiotically. Among the first to point this out was Vico (introduced in chapter 2). Before Vico, metaphor was viewed as a manifestation of analogy—an inductive form of reasoning whereby it is assumed that if two or more entities are similar in one or more respects, then a probability exists that they will be similar in other respects. For Vico, on the other hand, metaphor was hardly a manifestation of analogical reasoning; rather, it revealed how humans go about creating analogies. Paradoxically, and significantly, metaphor is so fundamental to how we form abstractions, such as analogies, that it is impossible to talk about it without resorting to metaphor.

METAPHORS WE LIVE BY

The first modern-day language scientists to argue that metaphors are traces to abstract concept-formation were George Lakoff and Mark Johnson in their groundbreaking 1980 book, *Metaphors We Live By* (introduced in chapter 4). Lakoff and Johnson meticulously illustrated in that book the presence of metaphor in everyday language, thus disavowing the mainstream view within linguistics that metaphorical utterances are figurative alternatives to literal ways of speaking. According to the traditional account of discourse, an individual would purportedly try out a literal interpretation first when he or she hears a sentence, choosing a metaphorical one only when a literal interpretation is not possible from the context (Grice 1975). But as Lakoff and Johnson convincingly argued, this is the case because people no longer realize that most of their sentences are based (unconsciously) on metaphorical structure. Moreover, many sentences are interpreted typically in a metaphorical way, no matter what their true meaning. When a sentence such as *The murderer was an animal* is uttered, almost everyone will interpret it as a metaphorical statement. Only if told that the *animal* was a real "animal" (a tiger, a bear, etc.) is the sentence given a literal interpretation.

First, Lakoff and Johnson assert what Aristotle claimed two millennia before, namely that there are two types of concepts—concrete and abstract. But the two scholars add a remarkable twist to the Aristotelian dichotomy— namely that many socially relevant abstract concepts are built up systematically from concrete ones through metaphorical reasoning. They then proceed to rename abstract concepts so formed as *conceptual metaphors*, defining them as generalized metaphorical thought formulas that underlie specific kinds of metaphorical utterances. For example, the expression "The professor is a snake" is really a token of something more general, namely the conceptual metaphor *people are animals*. This is why we also say that *John* or *Mary* or whoever is a *snake, gorilla, pig, puppy,* and so on. Each specific metaphor ("John is a gorilla," "Mary is a snake," etc.) is not an isolated example of poetic fancy. It is really a manifestation of a more general metaphorical idea— *people are animals*. Such formulas are what Lakoff and Johnson call, as mentioned, conceptual metaphors:

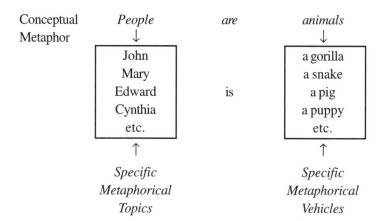

In our graph above, the level of the conceptual metaphor can be symbolized with $X' = Y'$ in order to distinguish it from a specific metaphor $(X = Y)$ and its embedded vehicle $(x = y)$. The structure of the metaphorical statement "The professor is a snake," can now be shown in its entirety as follows:

Structure of Metaphor

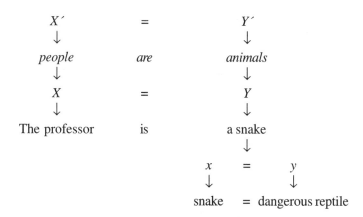

Each of the two parts of the conceptual metaphor is called a *domain*— *people* is the *target domain* because it is the general topic itself (the "target" of the conceptual metaphor), and *animals* is the *source domain* because it represents the class of vehicles, called the *lexical field*, that delivers the metaphor (the "source" of the metaphorical concept). Using the Lakoff-Johnson model, it is now easy to identify the conceptual metaphor in such expressions as those that follow:

- Those ideas are *circular*, getting us nowhere.
- I don't see the *point* of your ideas.
- Her ideas are *central* to the entire discussion.
- Their ideas are *diametrically opposite.*

In this case the target is *ideas* and the source domain *geometrical figures/ relations*. The conceptual metaphor is, thus, *ideas are geometrical figures/ relations*. Conceptual metaphors are unconscious thought formulas that permeate everyday language. This is why Lakoff and Johnson aptly call them "metaphors we live by." To get a firmer sense of how they shape discourse, consider the topic of *argument*. When this topic comes up in discourse, the most likely source domain enlisted for talking about it is *war*. The unconscious *argument is war* formula shows up in such common utterances as the following:

- Your claims are *indefensible.*
- You *attacked* all my *weak points.*
- Your criticisms were right *on target.*
- I *demolished* his argument.
- I've never *won* an argument.
- She *shot down* all my points.
- If you use that *strategy*, I'll *wipe you out.*

What does talking about argument in this way imply? It means, as Lakoff and Johnson suggest, that we feel within us that we actually "win" or "lose" arguments, and that our reactions to the argument situation will thus be similar to what they would be if we were involved in an actual physical battle: *we attack a position, lose ground, plan strategy, defend or abandon a line of attack*, etc. In a phrase, the *argument is war* conceptual metaphor structures the actions we perform when we argue and influences the feelings we experience during an argument.

Lakoff and Johnson trace the psychological source of conceptual metaphors to *image schemas*, a notion discussed already in chapter 4. These are mental impressions of our sensory experiences of locations, movements, shapes, etc. They link experiences with conceptual abstractions, permitting us not only to recognize patterns within certain bodily sensations, but also to anticipate their consequences and to make inferences and deductions. Thus, image schema theory suggests that the source domains enlisted in delivering an abstract topic were not chosen originally in an arbitrary fashion, but derived from the experience of events.

Lakoff and Johnson identify three basic types of image schemas (although a number of others have since been discovered). The first one involves the experience of orientation—*up vs. down, back vs. front, near vs. far*, etc. A second type involves *ontological* thinking. This produces conceptual metaphors in which activities, emotions, ideas, etc., are associated with entities and substances—for example, *the mind is a container* undergirds an expression such as "I'm *full* of memories." A third type, called structural, involves several image schemas at once: e.g., *time is a resource* is built from *time is a resource* and *time is a quantity*, as in "My time is *money*." Here is just a sampling of how image schemas underlie various concepts:

happiness is up/sadness is down
- I'm feeling *up* today.
- She's feeling *down*.
- That *boosted* my spirits.
- My mood *sank*.
- That gave me a *lift*.

health and life are up/sickness and death are down
- I'm at the *peak* of my health.
- She *fell* ill.
- Life is an *uphill* struggle.
- Her life is *sinking* fast.

knowledge is light/ignorance is darkness
- I was *illuminated* by that professor.
- I was left in the *dark* about what happened.
- That idea is very *clear*.
- That theory is *obscure*.
- His example *shed light* on several matters.

ideas are buildings
- That is a *well-constructed* theory.
- His views are on *solid ground*.
- That theory needs *support*.
- Their theory *collapsed* under criticism.
- She put together the *framework* of an exciting new theory.

ideas are plants
- Her ideas have finally come to *fruition*.
- That's a *budding* new theory, isn't it?
- The views of that ancient philosopher have contemporary *offshoots*.
- Number theory is a *branch* of mathematics.

ideas are commodities
- He certainly knows how to *package* his ideas, doesn't he?
- That idea just won't *sell*.
- There's no *market* for that idea.
- That's a *worthless* idea.

We do not detect the presence of metaphorical reasoning in such common expressions because of repeated usage. For example, we no longer interpret the word *see* in sentences such as "I don't *see* what you mean," "Do you *see* what I'm saying?" in metaphorical terms, because such uses of *see* have become so familiar to us. But the association between the biological act of seeing outside the body and the imaginary act of seeing within the mind was the original source of the conceptual metaphor *seeing is understanding or believing*, which permeates common discourse:

- There is more to this than *meets the eye*.
- I have a different *point of view*.
- It all depends on how you *look* at it.
- I take a *dim view* of the whole matter.
- I never *see eye to eye* on things with you.
- You have a different *worldview* than I do.
- Your ideas have given me great *insight* into life.

This conceptual metaphor has been documented across societies as a fundamental source for understanding abstractions such as *thinking, belief, understanding, knowledge*, and the like. Interestingly, this basic or "root" metaphor leads to further (or derived) metaphorizing. Consider the *thinking is visual scanning* thought formula in English as evidence of this:

thinking is visual scanning
- You must *look over* what you've written.
- I must *look into* what you've told me a bit further.

- She *saw right through* what you told her.
- I'm going to *see* this thing completely *out*.

These also suggest that thoughts, like objects, can be moved, arranged, located, etc., or else seen, looked into, scanned, etc., a concept encoded more explicitly by the *thoughts are objects* formula:

- *Work* that idea *over* in your mind.
- *Turn* that thought *over* in your mind.
- You should *rearrange* your thoughts carefully.
- *Put* your thoughts *in order* before going forward with your plans.

As Walter Ong (1977: 134) has also pointed out, the presence of such formulas in human language suggests that "we would be incapacitated for dealing with knowledge and intellection without massive visualist conceptualization, that is, without conceiving of intelligence through models applying initially to vision."

The last relevant point made by Lakoff and Johnson in their truly fascinating book is that cultural groupthink is built up from layers or clusters of conceptual metaphors. They call these clusters *idealized cultural* or *cognitive models* (ICMs). To see what an ICM implies, consider the target domain of *ideas* again. The following three conceptual metaphors, among many others, are used in English-speaking cultures to deliver the meaning of this concept in separate ways:

ideas are food
- Those ideas left a *sour taste* in my mouth.
- It's hard to *digest* all those ideas at once.
- Even though he is a *voracious* reader, he can't *chew over* all those ideas at once.
- That teacher is always *spoonfeeding* her students.

ideas are persons
- Darwin is the *father* of modern biology.
- Those medieval ideas continue to *live on* even today.
- Cognitive linguistics is still in its *infancy.*
- Maybe we should *resurrect* that ancient idea.
- She *breathed* new life into that idea.

ideas are fashion

- That idea went out of *style* several years ago.
- Those scientists are at the *avantgarde* of their field.
- Those revolutionary ideas are no longer in *vogue*.
- Semiotics has become truly *chic*.
- That idea is old *hat*.

Recall from examples cited above that there were other ways of conceptualizing ideas—for example, in terms of *buildings, plants, commodities, geometry,* and *seeing*. The constant juxtaposition of such conceptual formulas in common discourse produces, cumulatively, an ICM of ideas:

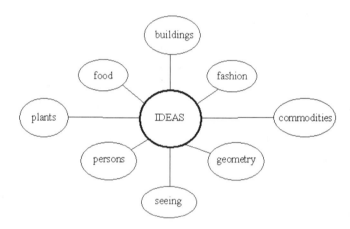

An ICM is, thus, definable as a clustering of source domains around an abstract concept. When the topic of ideas comes up in discourse, therefore, speakers of English can interpret it by navigating conceptually through the various source domains that cluster around it according to need, whim, or situation. For example, the sentence *Your ideas are enlightening because they have deep roots and are on solid ground* has been put together with three of the above source domains *(seeing, plants,* and *buildings)*.

ICM theory has many implications for the study of concepts. For example, several of the source domains for the above ICM—*food, people,* and *seeing*— are relatively understandable across cultures: that is, people from non-English-speaking cultures could easily figure out what statements based on these domains mean if they were translated or relayed to them. However, there are some source domains that are more likely to be culture-specific, such as, for instance, the *geometrical figures* domain, and thus beyond easy cross-cultural comprehension. This suggests that there are different categories of abstract concepts, some of which are more common in languages across the world than others. The *ideas are food* concept, for example, is a basic or root concept because it connects a universal physical process (*eating*) to an abstraction (*thinking*) directly. But the *ideas are geometrical figures* concept reveals a more culture-specific abstraction.

The notion of ICM also suggests a framework for comparing the productivity of concepts. By determining the number of source domains used to construct an ICM of a concept, we can get an idea of the productivity of that concept with relation to others, since the ICM is, in effect, the sum of all the source domains enlisted to form a specific concept. For example, as we saw above, in English *ideas* is rendered by such source domains as *food*, *people*, and *fashion*. I was able to uncover at least 89 source domains used commonly in English to deliver the concept of *ideas* (or more generally *thinking*). On the other hand, I unraveled only 36 source domains for the ICM of *love*. This would seem to suggest that *love* is a less productive concept than *thinking* in English.

What does this imply? It suggests, arguably, that in English culture, *thinking* is a concept that is given much more representational salience, so to speak, than is *love*. This does not mean that the latter is not important, but simply that there are fewer ways to conceptualize it in everyday discourse. When I compared the two English ICMs to Italian ones, I found that most of the source domains used to deliver the concept of *ideas* were identical or similar (87 in all). On the other hand, I determined that there were at least 99 source domains for the Italian ICM of *love*, indicating that it is probably a more productive concept in Italian (i.e., there are more ways to speak about it).

CONCEPTUAL METAPHOR THEORY

The theory laid out in *Metaphors We Live By* has led to extensive research on metaphor in both linguistics and psychology. However, for the sake of historical accuracy it should be mentioned that conceptual metaphor theory (CMT), as it is now called, traces its roots to the ideas of the literary critic I. A. Richards (1893–1979), who in 1936 suggested that metaphor resulted from an association of concepts, rather than of single words. Richards's crucial work opened the way for the serious investigation of metaphor within the social sciences. A 1955 study by the Gestalt psychologist Solomon Asch, for instance, showed that metaphors of sensation in several phylogenetically unrelated languages used the same sensory source domains (*warm, cold, heavy*, etc.), although the choice of specific items from a domain varied as to their application to a target domain. For example, he found that *hot* stood for *rage* in Hebrew, *enthusiasm* in Chinese, *sexual arousal* in Thai, and *energy* in Hausa. As Brown (1958: 146) aptly commented shortly after the publication of Asch's study, "there is an undoubted kinship of meanings" in different languages that "seem to involve activity and emotional arousal." Empirical work on metaphor proliferated in the 1970s and 1980s. By the early 1990s there was little doubt in the minds of many linguists and psychologists that metaphor was a guide to the workings of human abstract thinking.

Asch's work showing that the body is a primary source domain in conceptualization has been confirmed by the work on CMT. It would seem that in human cognition the body is the "measure of all things," metaphorically speaking of course. Here are some examples in English:

- a *body* of water
- the *body* of a work
- a *body* of people
- the *head* of the household
- the *head* of a table
- the *head* of an organization
- the *face* of a clock
- the *foot* of a mountain
- a *leg* of a race
- the *eye* of the needle
- the *eye* of a storm

Expressions such as these are found across cultures, suggesting that people the world over probably experience the cosmos as one huge body made up of bodily parts. This suggests, in essence, that anthropomorphism is a basic force in metaphor. It is the reason why we say that cups have *lips*, combs *teeth*, fixings *knuckles* and *joints*, texts *footnotes* and *appendixes*, and so on and so forth. And it is the reason why we describe various human social activities in bodily terms. Here are a few examples:

- *holding* a meeting
- taking things at *face* value
- *nosing* around
- *mouthing* lyrics

- *shouldering* a burden
- *knuckling* under
- going *belly up*
- *toeing* the line

Naming the world anthropomorphically is, as mentioned, a universal tendency. In the language spoken by the Batammaliba people who live in the border region between the West African states of Togo and the Benin Republic (Tilley 1999: 41–49) houses are named with body and organ metaphors. The diagram below shows how they are named with English glosses:

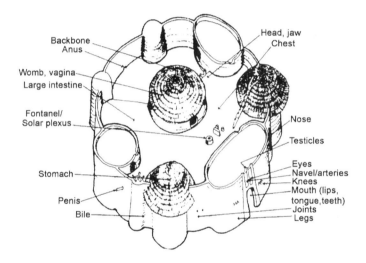

The research in CMT has also shown that, unlike many aspects of language, metaphor emerges spontaneously. Children do not even have to be exposed to it to be able to use it to understand things in their environment. When children refer to the sun or the moon as a "ball" they do so without having ever heard it named as such. I would like to give the example of my grandson, who was barely 15 months old when he used metaphorical reasoning in the following way. He knew how to refer to orange juice as "juice." One day, as our household cat, which had orange fur, came into view, he pointed to her and uttered the word "juice." He had, clearly, used metaphorical reasoning, extracting the property of "orangeness," which he had learned to perceive in another context, and applying it to a new referent that he perceived to possess the same property.

An identical form of metaphorical reasoning underlies the formation of color conceptual metaphors throughout the world, suggesting that many concepts (if not most) were originally forged as metaphors. Consider the concept of *red* once again. This color suggests "blood" and thus "vitality." In many tribal and cult-based rituals, it is thus common to slit the wrists of fellow members and rub them together so that they may become *blood brothers*. Red is also commonly associated with "love" and "passion." This is why a *red heart* is commonly used as a symbol of love and passion. The source for this is probably the physiological fact that such emotions involve an increase in the heartbeat and thus in the blood pumped by the heart. *Red* lipstick continues to be extremely popular today perhaps for the metaphorical reason that *redness* implies female fertility metaphorically. The list could on and on.

METONYMY AND IRONY

Before Lakoff and Johnson's trend-setting work, the study of metaphor fell within the field of rhetoric, where it was viewed as one of various tropes (listed above). But since the early 1980s the practice has been to use the term *metaphor* to refer to the study of all figurative language and to consider most of the other tropes as particular kinds of metaphor. Within this framework, *personification*, for instance, "My cat speaks English," would be seen as a particular kind of metaphor, one in which the target domain is an *animal* or *inanimate object* and the source domain *humans*. This kind of reasoning really reverses domains in the *people are animals* conceptual metaphor (*animals are people*), suggesting that rather than a mapping between domains, there really is an interaction, as Richards also argued—one domain influences the other in tandem, so that we see people as animals and animals as people simultaneously.

But there are two types that are regularly considered separately from metaphor in CMT—metonymy and irony. Metonymy is the process by which the name of one thing is used in place of that of another associated with or suggested by it (e.g., *the White House* for *the President*). In conceptual terms, it can be defined as the process of using a part of a domain to represent the whole domain.

Here are some examples of this interesting phenomenon (Lakoff and Johnson 1980: 35–40):

- She likes to read *Dostoyevsky* (= the writings of Dostoyevsky).
- He's in *dance* (= the dancing profession).
- My mom frowns on *blue jeans* (= the wearing of blue jeans).

- New *windshield wipers* will satisfy him (= the state of having new wipers).
- The *automobile* is destroying our health (=automobiles collectively).
- We need a couple of *strong bodies* for our teams (= strong people).
- I've got a new *set of wheels* (= car).
- We need *new blood* in this organization (= new people).

In parallelism with the notion of *conceptual metaphor*, the term *conceptual metonym* can be used to refer to generalized metonymical formulas. For example, the use of the face as a metonym for personality produces the conceptual metonym *the face is the person* that manifests itself commonly in expressions such as the following:

- He's just another pretty *face*.
- There are an awful lot of *faces* in the audience.
- We need some new *faces* around here.
- You can read his thoughts on his *face*.

Conceptual metonyms are abstractions, and like conceptual metaphors they are interconnected to other domains of meaning-making in a culture. The distribution of the concept *the face is the person* throughout the meaning pathways of a culture is the reason why portraits, in painting and photography, focus on the face. Here are some other examples of conceptual metonyms:

a body part for the person
- Get your *butt* over here!
- The Yankees need a *stronger arm* in right field.
- We don't hire *crew cuts*.

the producer for the product
- I'll have a *Heineken*.
- We bought a *Ford*.
- He's got a *Rembrandt* in his house.

the object used for the user
- My *piano* is sick today.
- The *meat and potatoes* is a lousy tipper.
- The *buses* are on strike.

the institution for the people in the institution
- *Shell* has raised its prices again.
- The *Church* thinks that promiscuity is immoral.
- I don't approve of *Washington's* actions.

the place for the institution
- The *White House* isn't saying anything.
- *Milan* is introducing new jackets this year.
- *Wall Street* is in a panic.

Irony constitutes the use of words to convey a meaning contrary to their literal sense ("I love being tortured"). It is, more formally, a cognitive strategy by which a concept is highlighted through its opposite, its antithesis, its antonym, or some other such "opposing" structure. In sign terms, it can perhaps be represented as a sign whereby the X (the actual statement) implies a meaning *(Y)* through its opposite *(-Y): X = -Y = Y.* This process creates a discrepancy between appearance and reality, thus creating a kind of "meaning tension by contrast." Irony is particularly productive in producing satirical, parodic, and other kinds of captious language. It is important to note that irony emerges late in verbal development (e.g., Winner 1988), and tends to be culture-specific. Such ironic works as Woody Allen's (1935–) movies, would hardly be understood by children before the age of puberty. Allen's films are ironic depictions of neurotic urban characters preoccupied with love and death. Movies such as *Bananas* (1971), *Everything You Always Wanted to Know About Sex* (1972), *Annie Hall* (1977), *Bullets over Broadway* (1994), and *Mighty Aphrodite* (1995) are ironic texts criticizing human habits, ideas, and vacuous rituals.

Irony is a culture-specific form of signification. Cultures throughout the world develop their own ironic forms and literary traditions derived from them. This is why ironic texts are not easily translated from one language to another.

METAPHOR AND GRAMMAR

The research in CMT has also been showing that conceptual metaphors may even shape grammar. The traditional view is, of course, that grammatical rules are impervious to semantic or conceptual factors. The work in CMT, however, provides evidence why this view is no longer tenable. As a concrete example of how grammar and metaphor might be interrelated, consider the use of the prepositions *since* and *for* in sentences such as the following in English:

- I have been living here *since* 1999.
- I have known Lucy *since* September.
- I have not been able to sleep *since* Monday.
- I have been living here *for* 15 years.
- I have known Lucy *for* 9 months.
- I have not been able to sleep *for* 21 days.

An analysis of the expressions that follow *since* reveals that they belong to a source domain based on an image schema of *time* as *a point on a line*. The specific *points* in the first three sentences above are "1999," "September," "Monday." The expressions that follow *for*, on the other hand, belong to a source domain based on an image schema of *time* as a *quantity*. The specific *quantities* in the last three sentences above are: "15 years," "9 months," "21 days." It would appear therefore that the different conceptual metaphors have specific effects at the level of grammar—expressions introduced by *since* are reflexes of the conceptual metaphor *time is a point*; those introduced by *for* are reflexes of the conceptual metaphor *time is a quantity*. This is, in fact, the kind of rule of grammar that explicitly interconnects conceptual metaphors and parts of speech. Research has documented similar reflexes in all domains of grammar and vocabulary in languages across the world.

Take, as one other example, the selection of certain verbs in particular types of sentences in Italian. The verb *fare* "to make" is used to relay the concepts of "heat" and "cold" in reference to their presence in the environment: *Fa caldo oggi* "It is hot today" (= literally "it makes heat"), *Fa freddo oggi* "It is cold today" (= literally "it makes cold"). The verb *avere* ("to have") is used instead when the "heat" and the "cold" are located in a human being: *Lui ha caldo* "He is hot" (= literally "He has heat"), *Lei ha freddo* "She is cold (= literally "She has cold"). Finally, when the "heat" and "cold" are in an object, the verb *essere* ("to be") is used: *Il caffè è caldo* "The coffee is hot," *Il tè è freddo* "The tea is cold." The use of one verb or the other—*fare, essere,* or *avere*—is motivated, clearly, by an underlying image schema of Nature, bodies, and objects as containers of heat and cold. So, it is the specific container in which the heat or cold are located that determines the verb to be employed. If the heat or cold is in the environment, it is "made" by Nature *(fa freddo)*; if it is in a human being, then the body "has" it *(ha freddo)* within itself; and if it is in an object, then the object "is" its container *(è freddo).*

Examples such as this abound in languages across the world. It would seem that the parts of speech, the rules of syntax, the rules of lexical selection, and so on are shaped and even derived from metaphorical thinking. If this turns out to be true in any significant way, then all of our models and theories of language structure will have to be radically revised.

METAPHOR AND CULTURE

Conceptual metaphors and metonyms are not only the most likely sources of grammatical categories in a language, but they appear as "conceptual factors" in rituals, symbolism, and other components of the semiosphere. Our own courtship rituals, for example, reflect the *love is a sweetness* metaphor ("She's my *sweetheart*," "I love my *honey*," etc.) in nonverbal ways: for example, sweets are given to a loved one on Valentine's day; matrimonial love is symbolized at a wedding ceremony by the eating of a cake; we sweeten our breath with candy before kissing our romantic partners, etc. Incidentally, Emantian (1995) has documented cross-cultural similarities in the ways in which romance is metaphorized. In Chagga, a Bantu language of Tanzania, the same concept found in our culture—*love is a sweetness*—manifests itself constantly in discourse about sex and romance. In Chagga the man is perceived to be the eater and the woman his *sweet food*, as can be detected in expressions that mean, in translated form, "Does she taste sweet?" "She tastes sweet as sugar honey" (Emantian 1995: 168).

Animal metaphors are also common across cultures as sources of symbolism. In our own culture, we use the names of animals for sports teams (*Chicago Bears, Detroit Tigers, Toronto Blue Jays, Denver Broncos*, etc.), so as to impart character to the team in terms of animal qualities; we name cartoon characters *(Bugs Bunny, Daffy Duck,* etc.) to represent human personality types; we tell our children animal stories in order to impart morals to them; and so on and so forth. The gods of many early cultures were conceived as animal figures—Egyptian gods had animal heads, the principal god of the Hindus is Ganesha the elephant, the godhead of the Aztecs was the green-plumed serpent Quetzalcoatl, and the list could go on and on. Animal symbolism was also applied to name the Christian evangelists as shown below:

John = Eagle   Matthew = Angel   Luke = Bull   Mark = Lion

And, of course, animals are used in astrology to symbolize human character and to predict destiny in tandem with the movement of celestial objects. Even though we may not believe outright in the power of astrological signs to predict our future, we nevertheless keep an open mind about them, as evidenced by the ubiquity of horoscopes in modern media.

Animal metaphors constitute the central idea behind *totemism*, an Ojibway word (Great Lakes region of North America). Totems are spiritual entities represented by animal species. A particular totem symbolizes a specific clan. People who share the same totems cannot marry. An individual may have a totem—a personal guardian spirit—but then can never eat the animal that represents his or her totem.

As examples such as these bring out, the relation between metaphor and culture cannot be underestimated. More often than not, metaphors are guides to a culture's past. A common expression such as "He has fallen from grace" would have been recognized instantly in a previous era as referring to the Adam and Eve story in the Bible. Today we continue to use it with only a dim awareness (if any) of its Biblical origins. Expressions that portray life as a metaphorical journey—"I'm still a long way from my goal," "There is no end in sight," etc.—are similarly rooted in Biblical narrative. As the literary critic Northrop Frye (1981) aptly pointed out, one cannot penetrate such expressions, or indeed most of Western literature or art, without having been exposed, directly or indirectly, to the original Biblical stories. These provide the source domains for many of the concepts we use today for judging human actions and offering advice, bestowing upon everyday life a kind of implicit metaphysical meaning and value.

Proverbs too are extended metaphors that people employ to provide sound practical advice when it is required in certain situations:

- You've got too many fires burning (= advice to not do so many things at once).
- Rome wasn't built in a day (= advice to have patience).
- Don't count your chickens before they're hatched (= advice to be cautious).
- An eye for an eye and a tooth for a tooth (= equal treatment is required in love and war).

Every culture has its proverbs, aphorisms, and sayings. They constitute a remarkable code of ethics and of practical knowledge that anthropologists call "folk wisdom." Indeed, the very concept of *wisdom* implies the ability to apply proverbial language insightfully to a situation. Preaching, too, would hardly be persuasive if it were not embedded in the metaphorical practices of a culture. An effective preacher is one who knows how to structure his or her oration around a few highly understandable conceptual metaphors such as *sex is dirty*, *sex is punishable by fire,* etc. These guide the preacher's selection of words, illustrations, turns of phrase, practical examples, etc.—"You must cleanse your soul of the filth of sex"; "You will burn in Hell, if you do not clean up your act"; and so on.

Proverbs often find their way into literature. Many of the characters in *The Canterbury Tales* (late 1300s) by Geoffrey Chaucer (1340?–1400) use proverbs to make sense of things. Miguel de Cervantes's (1547–1616) novel *Don Quixote* (1605, 1615) contains many proverbs that the author had heard from the Spanish peasants, who supposedly could carry on a sensible conversation for a whole evening in nothing but proverbs. The Hebrew Bible contains a whole book—titled appropriately the *Book of Proverbs*—containing the teachings of parents trying to raise their children to become successful and responsible adults. The *Book of Proverbs* has earned universal appeal because it contains material valuable to all people who hope to live a life of wisdom, honesty, responsibility, self-control, and respect for God. Many of the book's sayings have become part of everyday speech.

Scientific reasoning too is intertwined with metaphorical reasoning. Science often involves things that cannot be seen—atoms, sound waves, gravitational forces, magnetic fields, etc. So, scientists use their metaphorical imaginations to envision this hidden matter. That is why scientists describe waves as *undulating* through empty space, atoms as *leaping* from one quantum state to another, electrons as *traveling in circles* around an atomic nucleus, and so on. Metaphors are evidence of the human ability to see the universe as a holistic structure. As physicist Robert Jones (1982: 4) aptly puts it, for the scientist metaphor serves as "an evocation of the inner connection among things." When a metaphor is accepted as scientific fact, it takes on an independent conceptual existence in the real world, suggesting ways to bring about changes in and to the world. Even the nature of experimentation can be seen in this light. Experimentation is a search for connections, linkages, associations of some sort or other. As Rom Harré (1981: 23) has pointed out, most experiments involve "the attempt to relate the structure of things, discovered in an exploratory study, to the organization this imposes on the processes going on in that structure."

All this really could not be otherwise. Whereas individual signs create referential domains for humans to reflect upon, utilize, and store as knowledge, metaphor is the strategy the human species uses to interconnect such domains into increasingly layered orders of meaning—layers upon layers of metaphors. One metaphor suggests another, which suggests another, and so on. The central feature of human thinking is the fluid application of existing concepts to new situations.

CONCLUDING REMARKS

Lakoff and Johnson claim that virtually all our abstract thoughts are built from metaphorical reasoning. There is no doubt that much of it is. However, abstractions are formed by humans in other ways. If I were to add the suffix -*ness* to a simple concrete noun such as *cat* (*catness*), I would have in effect introduced a level of abstraction that was not there before. This has, clearly, nothing to do with metaphor. Similarly, in mathematics many theorems are built from observing facts and figures and extrapolating a pattern from them. Nevertheless, having said this, I tend to agree with Lakoff and Johnson that most abstractions are derived from metaphorical or associative thinking.

The topic of metaphor completes the first part of this book. Detailed and complementary discussions of the various topics treated in this part can be found in the bibliography at the end. The next part will focus on how messages and meanings are made with signs, that is on how the $X = Y$ relation is used to create texts, concepts, and all the other kinds of "messaging phenomena" that distinguish humanity from all other species.

Messages and Meanings

Myth and Narrative

There are only two or three human stories, and they go on repeating themselves as fiercely as if they had never happened before.

Willa Cather (1873–1947)

PRELIMINARY REMARKS

The penchant for stories is an integral part of the human condition. People all over the world cannot help but think even of their own lives as stories and proceed to describe them as such. An autobiographical story has an inherent "narrative logic" all its own that imparts sense and purpose to the teller's life, not simply mirroring what happened, but exploring and interpreting it for his or her audience. In a phrase, storytelling is as fundamental to human psychic life as breathing is to physical life. Indeed, the "narrative instinct" is as much a part of the constitution of human life as are any of the physical instincts.

The founding narratives of a culture are known as *myths*. Myths are so fundamental to human understanding that they continue to inform activities ranging from psychoanalysis to sports events such as wrestling. And since mythological thinking is universal, it may explain why although details of stories change from culture to culture, they all reflect the same kinds of mythic themes (good vs. evil, heroism, etc.).

The study of ancient myths comes under the semiotic rubric of *mythology*, and the general study of storytelling under that of *narratology*. Studying the ways in which narratives give sense and purpose to human existence is, needless to say, a fundamental focus of the semiotic approach to the study of culture.

NARRATIVE

A *narrative* is a text that has been constructed in such a way as to represent a sequence of events or actions that are felt to be logically connected to each other or intertwined in some way. The narrative sequence may be purely fact-based, as in a newspaper report or a psychoanalytic session, or fictional, as in a novel, a fairy-tale, etc. Needless to say, it is often difficult, if not impossible, to determine the boundary line between fact and fiction. Indeed, even in the recounting of life-stories, fiction is often intermingled with fact in order to give the stories more coherence and thus credibility. Psychologists call this the "Othello effect." It is defined as lying in order to emphasize the truth.

The meaning of the narrative text is not a straightforward process of determining the meanings of the individual words with which it is constructed; rather, it involves interpreting it holistically, as a sign, in which X is the actual narrative text and Y the meaning that can be extracted from it. The Y in this case is often called the *subtext*. The subtext is extracted by readers from cues within the main text. Some of the cues may come in the form of *intertexts,* which are allusions within the narrative to other texts. For example, the main text of the movie *Blade Runner* (chapter 4) unfolds as a science fiction detective story, but its subtext is, arguably, a religious one—the search for a Creator and thus a meaning to life beyond mere physical existence. This interpretation is bolstered by the many intertextual allusions to Biblical themes and symbols in the movie (as we saw).

Narrative texts can be verbal, nonverbal, or a combination of both. An example of a verbal narrative is a short story; an example of a nonverbal narrative is a silent movie that tells a story through image sequences. An example of a combined verbal-nonverbal narrative is a comic book story.

The essence of narrative is plot, character, and setting. The plot is basically what the narrative is all about; it is a kind of "macro-referent," to which the narrative, as a text, draws attention. Character refers to the people or beings about whom the narrative tells a story. Each character is a sign standing for a personality type—the hero, the coward, the lover, the friend, and so on. The setting is the location where, and the time when, the plot takes place. The teller of the story is called the narrator. The narrator can be a character in the narrative, the author of the text, or some other person or entity. Each type of narrator provides a different perspective on the story for the reader. The reader can thus feel a part of the narrative, looking at the action as if he or she were in it; or aloof from it, looking at the action as if from the outside.

By and large, people think of narrative as *fiction* (from Latin *fingere* "to form, make, put together"). But fictional narration did not become prevalent until the Middle Ages, although there is some evidence that fiction may have ancient roots nonetheless. Papyri from the fourth Egyptian Dynasty report on how King Cheops (2590–2567 BC) delighted in hearing the fictional stories that his sons told him. The Greek statesman and general Aristides (530?–468? BC), moreover, wrote a collection of what we would now call short stories about his hometown, Miletus, to celebrate the Greek victory over the Persians at Salamis. The Latin *Golden Ass* of Apuleius (AD 125?–200?) was also a fictional narration aimed at providing social and moral commentary. But by and large the ancient world told tales of the gods or of human foibles. They were hardly perceived as fictional. Fiction became a standard narrative craft only after the Middle Ages, especially after the Italian Giovanni Boccaccio (1313–1375) wrote the *Decameron* (1351–1353), a collection of 100 fictional tales set against the gloomy background of the Black Death, as the bubonic plague that swept through Europe in the fourteenth century was called. The *Decameron* is the first real example of fiction in the modern sense. To escape an outbreak of the plague, ten friends decide to take refuge in a country villa outside Florence. There, they entertain one another over a period of ten days with a series of stories made up for the occasion and told by each member of the party in turn.

Ever since, fictional narration has been a yardstick for probing human actions and human character. This is probably because narrative structure is felt to reflect the structure of real-life events. The "reality-inducing effect" of narrative structure was used a few decades ago by a popular program on American television called the *Wild Kingdom*. The show purported to explain animal behavior in scientific terms. Each week, a film would be shown of animals eating, hunting, mating, etc. Unedited, the actions of the animals caught on film would hardly make up a meaningful storyline. But with the help of film editors and scriptwriters the program produced an intriguing narrative account of the actions dispersed randomly on the unedited film. Although the program's creators extracted their ideas for the narratives from scientific sources, the particular ways in which they explained the animals' actions constituted human stories. They were not unlike the kinds of animal tales we tell children. Each story had a human theme to it—growing up, forming a family unit, and so on.

The study of narrative structure in semiotics proper can be traced to the work of Vladimir Propp (1928). Propp argued that a relatively small number of "narrative units," or plot themes went into the make-up of a universal "plot grammar." Propp's theory would, in effect, explain why stories seem to be similar the world over and why we tell stories to children instinctively. Stories allow children to make sense of the real world, providing the intelligible formats that give pattern and continuity to their observations of daily life. In effect, they impart the sense that there is a *plot* to life, that the *characters* in it serve some meaningful purpose, and that the *setting* of life is part of a meaningful cosmos. By age four or five, children are able to manage and negotiate narratives by themselves, especially during play, when they create imaginary narratives designed to allow others watching them a framework for interpreting their actions.

After Propp, the semiotician who most influenced the study of narrative was Algirdas Julien Greimas (1917–1992). Greimas expanded upon Propp's ideas, claiming that the stories of different cultures were devised with virtually the same types of characters, motifs, themes, settings, etc., which he called *actants*. The basic structure of narrative consists of:

- a *subject* (the hero of the plot)
- who desires an *object* (a sought-after-person, a magic sword, etc.)
- and who encounters an *opponent* (a villain, a false hero, a trial situation, etc.)
- and then finds a *helper* (a donor)
- who then gets an *object* from a *sender* (a dispatcher)
- and gives it to a *receiver*
- and the *action* unfolds accordingly
- until a *resolution* manifests or does not manifest itself, leading to different kinds of endings

One actant can be represented by several characters, and several actants by one and the same character. In a mystery novel, for instance, the subject, or hero, may have several enemies, all of whom function actantially as an opponent. In a love story, a male lover may function as both object and sender.

A serious work of fiction stimulates reflection and leads to a better understanding of some aspect of human reality. By creating characters, placing them in specific situations, and establishing a point of view, writers of fiction set forth judgments about moral, philosophical, psychological, or social problems. But by their very nature, narratives also bring out the relationship between signs and reality. To probe this relationship, some authors have abandoned traditional storytelling devices, such as plots, characters, and settings, so as to instill in readers a "sense of fiction as fiction." The Argentine writer Jorge Luis Borges (1899–1986), for instance, examined the relationship between fiction and truth in this way with his collection of stories called *Ficciones* (1944, 1962).

MYTH

The word *myth* derives from the Greek *mythos* "word," "speech," "tale of the gods." A myth is a narrative in which the main characters are gods, heroes, and mystical beings, the plot revolves around the origin of things or around the meaning of things, and the setting is a metaphysical world juxtaposed against the real world. In the beginning stages of human cultures, myths functioned as genuine theories of the world. All cultures have created them to explain their origins. The Zuñi people of North America, for instance, claim to have emerged from a mystical hole in the earth, thus establishing their kinship with the land; Rome was said to have been founded by Romulus, who as an infant had to be suckled by a wolf, thus alluding to a certain fierceness of the Roman people, and the list could go on and on. Myths create a metaphysical knowledge system for explaining human origins, actions, and character, as well as phenomena in the world. And this system is the one to which we instinctively resort even today for imparting knowledge of values and morals initially to children. It also manifests itself latently in other ways. Climatologists, for example, refer to the warming of the ocean surface off the western coast of South America that occurs every 4 to 12 years as a person, *El Niño* ("the little one" in Spanish). Although modern people do not believe El Niño to be a person, they nonetheless find it somehow more intuitively correct to blame an imaginary being for bringing about a climate change in the world. El Niño is, *ipso facto*, a mythic character.

By studying myths, we can learn how different societies have answered basic questions about the world and the human being's place in it. We can study myths to learn how a people developed a particular social system with its many customs and ways of life, and thus better understand the values that bind members of society into one group. Myths can be compared in order to discover how cultures differ and how they resemble one another, and why people behave as they do. We can also study myths as the referential frames underlying not only masterpieces of architecture, literature, music, painting, and sculpture, but also such contemporary things as advertising and television programs (as we shall see in due course).

The most important myth in a culture, known as a *cosmogonic* myth, explains how the world came into being. In some cosmogonic accounts, the world is created from nothing; in others it emerges from lower worlds. *Eschatological* myths, on the other hand, describe the end of the world. These usually predict the destruction of the world by a divine being who will send human beings either to a paradisiacal existence or to one of eternal torment, depending on the ways in which people have lived their lives. An apocalypse, such as a universal fire and a final battle of the gods, is a central element of eschatological mythology. To counteract the apocalypse, many cultures tell myths of birth and rebirth, which inform people how life can be renewed or about the coming of an ideal society or a savior. Myths of the *culture hero* are also common. These describe beings who discover a cultural artifact or technological process that radically changes the course of history.

Explanatory myths are those that attempt to explain natural processes or events. The Norse, who lived in medieval Scandinavia, believed that the god Thor made thunder and lightning by throwing a hammer at his enemies. The ancient Greeks believed that the lightning bolt was a weapon used by the god Zeus. To explain climatological phenomena, the ancient Romans invented Neptune, the god of the sea and brother of Jupiter, the supreme god of the skies. Originally a god of springs and streams, Neptune became identified with the Greek god of the sea, Poseidon. The myth of Neptune is a story created to explain the interconnectedness of natural phenomena, thus giving a metaphysical coherence to the world. In a fundamental cognitive sense, El Niño is a contemporary "descendant" of this mythological figure.

Many ancient societies explained death mythologically as well. The people of the Trobriand Islands in the Pacific Ocean believed that people were immortal when the world originated. When people began to age, they swam in a certain lagoon and shed their skin. They quickly grew new skin, renewing their youth. One day, a mother returned from the lagoon with her new skin. But her unexpected youthful appearance frightened her little daughter. To calm the child, the mother returned to the lagoon, found her old skin, and put it back on. From then on, according to this myth, death could not be avoided. Some myths even explained proper behavior through the actions of particular gods and heroes. The ancient Greeks strongly believed in moderation—that is, in the notion that nothing should be done in excess. They found this ideal in the behavior of Apollo, the god of purity, music, and poetry.

Mythical characters fall into several groups. Many gods and goddesses resemble human beings, even though they possess supernatural powers— they are born, fall in love, fight with one another, and generally behave like their human worshipers. These divinities are called anthropomorphic, from two Greek words meaning "in the shape of man." Greek mythology has many anthropomorphic divinities, including Zeus, who was the most important Greek god. Another group of mythical beings includes gods and goddesses who resemble animals. These characters are called theriomorphic, from two Greek words meaning "in the shape of an animal." Many theriomorphic beings appear in Egyptian mythology. For example, the ancient Egyptians sometimes represented their god Anubis as a jackal or a dog. A third group of mythical beings are those that have both human and animal features. An example is the famous sphinx of Egypt, which had a human head and a lion's body. Human characters can also play an important role in myth. Some mythical mortals have a divine father and a mortal mother. These characters are called heroes, although they do not always act heroically. Most stories about heroes are called *epics* or *legends* rather than myths, but the difference between them is not always clear.

Many myths describe settings where demons, gods and goddesses, or the souls of the dead live. Most of these places are in the sky, on top of mountains, or below the earth. For instance, the most sacred place in Japanese mythology is Mount Fuji, the tallest mountain in Japan. During part of their history, the Greeks believed their divinities lived on a mythical mountain called Olympus that was separate from the visible Mount Olympus in northern Greece. The Greeks also believed in mythical places beneath the ground, such as Hades, where the souls of the dead lived. The Norse believed in Hel, an underground home for the souls of all dead persons, except those killed in battle. The souls of slain warriors went to Valhalla, which was a great hall in the sky.

Myths are the sources of early symbolism. The Greeks symbolized the sun as the god Helios driving a flaming chariot across the sky. The Egyptians represented the sun as a boat. Animals, human beings, and plants have all stood as symbols for ideas and events in myths of all kinds, many of which are around to this day. The Greeks portrayed Asclepius, the god of healing, holding a staff with a serpent coiled around it. The staff is often confused with the caduceus of the god Mercury, which has two snakes coiled around it. Today, both symbols are used as emblems of the medical profession. In Babylonian mythology, the hero Gilgamesh searched for a special herb that made anyone who ate it immortal. To this day, herbs are considered to have healing powers. Rarely, in fact, do we realize how much of the symbolism used by modern cultures is cut from the fabric of early myths. From the Germanic and Roman myths we have inherited, for instance, the names of most of the days of the week and months of the year: for example, Tuesday is the day dedicated to the Germanic war god Tiu; Wednesday to the chief god Wotan, Thursday to Thor, Friday to the goddess of beauty Frigga; and Saturday is dedicated to the Roman god Saturn, January to Janus, and so on. Our planets bear a similar pattern of nomenclature: Mars is named after the Roman god of war, Venus after the Roman god of love, etc. The residues of mythic thinking can also be seen in the fact that we read horoscopes, implore the gods to help us, and cry out against Fortune.

The French anthropologist Claude Lévi-Strauss (1978) even saw myth as the original source for the development of conceptual thinking, which continues to reverberate with the binary oppositions constituting all myths—life vs. death, maternal vs. paternal, good vs. evil, raw vs. cooked, etc. The nature of myth and conceptualization, Lévi-Strauss suggested, lies in the endless combination and recombination of such oppositions:

Concept	Its Opposite
Good	Evil
Right	Wrong
Mother	Father
God	Devil
Female	Male
Day	Night
Life	Death
Oneness/unity	Nothingness
Heaven	Hell

Lévi-Strauss's notion seems to work at a practical level. If one were to ask you what evil is, you would tend to explain it in terms of its opposite (good), and vice versa. Similarly, if you wanted to explain the concept of right to someone, you are bound to bring up the opposite concept of wrong at some point.

The Italian philosopher Giambattista Vico (chapter 2) claimed that the original mythic stories led to the foundation of the first institutions. The gradual increase of control humans had over their environment and the increasing complexity of human institutions were then reflected in the functions that new gods assumed. For Vico, myth was not constructed on the basis of a rational logic but of what he called a *poetic logic*, a form of thinking based upon, and guided by, conscious bodily experiences that are transformed into generalized ideas by the human imagination. The course that humanity runs, according to

Vico, goes from an early mythical age, through a heroic one, ending at a rational one (before it starts over). Each age has its own kind of culture, language, social institutions, and narratives—the poetic mentality, for instance, generated myths; the heroic one, legends; and the rational one, narrative history.

In myth, psychoanalysts find traces to the motivations and complexes of individuals. Sigmund Freud (1913), for instance, saw the conflicts recounted in myths as attempts to come to grips with unconscious psychic life. In the myth of Oedipus—the king who was abandoned at birth and unwittingly killed his father and then married his mother—he found a narrative paradigm for explaining a subconscious sexual desire in a child for the parent of the opposite sex, usually accompanied by hostility to the parent of the same sex. Carl Jung (1965) saw in such stories evidence for a collective unconscious in the human species constituted by primordial images, which he termed *archetypes*, that continue to seek expression through symbolism and various forms of expression.

An interesting view of myth was set forth by the French sociologist Émile Durkheim (1858–1917). Durkheim rejected the notion that myth arises in response to extraordinary manifestations of Nature. To Durkheim, Nature was a model of regularity and thus predictable and ordinary. He concluded that myths arose as emotional responses to social existence, thus constituting a narrative moral code and a system of historical reasoning. Myths and the rituals stemming from them sustain and renew moral systems, keeping them from being forgotten, and binding people socially. He explained the remarkable similarities among the world's myths with the "collective conscious," by which the basic ingredients of myth are actually part of the human brain and thus common to every human being:

> The collective conscious is the highest form of the psychic life, since it is the consciousness of the consciousness. Being placed outside and above all individual and local contingencies, it sees things in this permanent and essential aspect, which it crystallizes into communicable ideas…it alone can furnish the mind with the molds which are applicable to the totality of things and which make it possible to think of them (Durkheim 1912: 12).

The anthropologist Bronislaw Malinowski (1884–1942) claimed that myth provided a rationale for such things as the domestication of plant life. He argued that, in its primitive form, myth was not merely a story, but a lived emotional reality. It was not fictional, and it lives on in our rituals, governing our modes of perception and controlling our conduct in an unconscious fashion. The German philosopher Ernst Cassirer (1946), too, saw myth as arising from a communal emotional response to Nature—awe of thunder, fear of lightening, etc. In myth, the identity and basic values of the group were thus given an absolute meaning.

The most popularized studies of myths in the twentieth century were those of the American scholar Joseph Campbell (1904–1987). In his bestselling books, Campbell combined insights from Jungian psychology and linguistics to formulate a general theory of the origin, development, and unity of all human cultures. If there is thunder in the sky, and one lacks the notion of "thunder," then it can be explained as the angry voice of a god; if there is rain, then it can be explained as the weeping of the gods, and so on. A myth is a telling of such events.

MYTHOLOGIES

As the foregoing discussion brings out, most scholars of myth emphasize that the original mythic themes are so fundamental to human cognition that they continue to reverberate in modern day symbolism and traditions. To distinguish between the original myths and their modern-day versions, the semiotician Roland Barthes (1915–1980) designated the latter *mythologies* (Barthes 1957). Mythologies are modern-day reflexes of mythic themes, plots, and characters. They come about through a blend of *mythos* (true mythical thinking) and *logos* (rational-scientific thinking). In early Hollywood westerns, for instance, the mythic conceptual opposition of good vs. evil manifested itself in various symbolic and expressive ways: e.g., heroes wore white hats and villains black ones; heroes were honest and truthful, villains dishonest and cowardly, and so on. Sports events, too, are felt to be mythological dramas juxtaposing good (the home team) vs. evil (the visiting team). The whole fanfare associated with preparing for the "big event," like the Superbowl of American football, has a ritualistic quality to it similar to the pomp and circumstance that ancient armies engaged in before going out to battle and war. Indeed, the whole event is perceived to be a battle of mythic proportions. The symbolism of the team's (army's) uniform, the valor and strength of the players (the heroic warriors), and the skill and tactics of the coach (the army general) has a powerful effect on the fans (the warring nations). The game is, as television and radio announcers constantly blurt out, "real life, real drama!"

Let us look more closely at the Hollywood western as a modern mythology, which revolves around cowboy hero who wins a "high noon" gun duel and then rides off into the sunset. The cowboy hero has all the traits of the classic mythic heroes—strength, physical beauty, honesty, and vulnerability. The cowboy villain has all the opposite traits—cowardice, physical ugliness, dishonesty, and cunning. The hero is beaten up at some critical stage, but against long odds he becomes a champion of ethics and justice. Because of the power of myth, it is little wonder to find that cowboy heroes such as Roy Rogers, John Wayne, Hopalong Cassidy, and the Lone Ranger, have become cultural icons, symbolizing virtue, heroism, and righteousness. Although Hollywood has also showcased female characters, most of the women portrayed in westerns play a subsidiary supporting role to the "Marlboro Man" hero. Hollywood broke away somewhat from this mythology in recent times, with films such as Clint Eastwood's *Unforgiven* (1992), but the tradition of the maverick loner fighting for justice remains the central mythic image even in contemporary cowboy narratives.

As Barthes noted, a mythology can also lead to the establishment of lifestyle and social trends. Childhood, for instance, emerged as a mythology during the Industrial Revolution of the nineteenth century, when for the first time in history children were considered to be human beings at a stage of life as yet uncorrupted and untainted by civilization. The concept of a period of life characterized by innocence, purity, simplicity did not exist in previous eras, nor is it a universal one today. Children are younger human beings undergoing growth in body, mind, and personality. They are different from adults, not any better or worse. The images of children as pure and innocent is part of a mythology, not a psychology or sociology of childhood. A child has no awareness whatsoever of being pure or innocent—adults do. In medieval and Renaissance paintings and portraits there are no children as such. The "babes" that do appear occasionally in portraits look more like adult midgets than they do children. Before the Industrial Revolution, most people lived in agricultural communities or settings. Children barely out of infancy were expected to share the workload associated with tending to the farm. There was, consequently, little distinction between childhood and adult roles—children were perceived to be adults with smaller and weaker bodies. During the Industrial Revolution, the center of economic activity shifted from the farm to the city with many moving into the city (urbanization). This led to the construction of a new social order with different social role categories. The result was that children were left with few of their previous responsibilities, and a new mythology emerged, proclaiming children as vastly different from adults, needing the time to learn at school, to play, etc. Child labor laws were passed and public education became compulsory. Protected from the harsh reality of industrial work, children came to assume a new pristine identity as innocent, faultless, impressionable, malleable creatures.

Once the mythology of childhood entered cultural groupthink, it started to shape attitudes and lifestyle patterns profoundly. As a case in point of how powerful the mythology of childhood has become, let's turn the cultural clock back to the 1983 Christmas shopping season to revisit semiotically the "Cabbage Patch doll craze." Hordes of parents were prepared to pay almost anything to get one of the dolls for their daughters. Scalpers offered the suddenly and unexplainably out-of-stock dolls (a marketing ploy?) for hundreds of dollars through the classified ads. Grown adults fought each other in line-ups to get one of the few remaining dolls left in stock at some mall toy outlet.

How could a simple doll have caused such mass hysteria? To a semiotician, only something imbued with mythological signification could have possibly triggered such intense commotion. It is instructive to note, incidentally, that the Cabbage Patch dolls came with "adoption papers." This is a concrete clue as to what the dolls really meant semiotically. Each doll was given a name—taken at random from 1938 state of Georgia birth records—which, like any act of naming, conferred upon it a personality and human existence. And, thanks to computerized factories, no two dolls were manufactured alike. The doll was a "person substitute," a being who was adopted into the family as a sibling. No wonder, then, that the Cabbage Patch episode was fraught with so much hysteria. Parents did not buy a simple doll; they bought their child another member of the family. Toys, as the name of a major toy chain overtly puts it, are indeed us *(Toys "R" Us).*

BIOGRAPHY

One of the most interesting uses of narrative is in the telling of life stories. Through such stories we not only recreate personal histories; we interpret them. And only in narrative form do memories of people survive. This is why rulers of the ancient world had their deeds recorded by biographers, so as to perpetuate their memory beyond the grave. Perhaps the best-known biographical work of the ancient world is the *Parallel Lives* by the Greek biographer Plutarch (46?–120)—a collection of biographical sketches of legendary personages. Incidentally, Shakespeare drew from the *Lives* for his plays based on Roman history (*Coriolanus, Julius Caesar, Antony and Cleopatra*).

Until about the middle of the seventeenth century, written biography was generally commemorative in Western society—it was meant to condemn malefactors and tyrants, and to exalt heroes and heroines. This started to change in the Renaissance. In 1560 the Italian artist Giorgio Vasari (1511–1574) published his *Lives of the Artists*, an event that reflected the new spirit of humanism and the idea that each individual life, not just the lives of heroes, had intrinsic worth. In 1640, Izaak Walton (1593–1683) published *Life of Donne*, a biography of English poet John Donne. Over the next 25 years, it was revised and developed by its author becoming a prototype for modern biographical writing. The first modern narrative biography is considered to be *The Life of Samuel Johnson, LL.D* (1791) by James Boswell (1740–1795). Since then, many significant biographies have appeared, becoming staples of literary traditions. During the nineteenth century such significant works as the *Life of Sir Walter Scott* (7 volumes, 1837–1838) by John Gibson Lockhart became bestsellers. In the twentieth century biography retained its broad appeal as various literary fashions came and went. People's fascination with the lives of media personalities and popular figures alike was satisfied late in the century by the television medium, as programs such as *Biography* on the Arts and Entertainment channel became a staple of television programming in the 1990s. In recent years a *Biography Channel* has also appeared, offering up biographies to viewers on a 24-hour basis.

Among the most famous modern-day biographical writers, the Frenchman André Maurois (1885–1967) and the Austrian Stefan Zweig (1881–1942) require some mention. Maurois's *Life of Shelley* (1923) made popular the romanticized biography, a form of biography written in an engaging popular style and relying more on imaginative interpretation than on scholarly originality. Zweig's *Three Masters* (1920), a collection of biographical sketches of Honoré de Balzac, Charles Dickens, and Fyodor Dostoyevsky, started the trend in literary criticism of evaluating the artist's work against the background of his or her life experiences.

THE NOVEL

There are many types of narrative. But perhaps the most widely influential one in human history, before the advent of cinema, has been the *novel*. The plots, characters, and settings of popular novels have become sources for many semiotic practices over the centuries—children are named after characters in novels, real places after places described in novels, and so on and so forth. Novels such as Dostoyevsky's *Crime and Punishment* (1866) have also been used as templates for evaluating some real-life event or action in a society. It is amazing indeed to contemplate that a text that is essentially a lie (fiction) is used nevertheless to get at the truth, about people, life, and the universe.

As mentioned above, fictional narratives were composed in the ancient world, and to these the term *novel* is sometimes applied. But the novel did not emerge as an autonomous narrative fictional form until the Middle Ages. Many scholars regard the eleventh century *Tale of Genji*, by the Japanese baroness Murasaki Shikibu (978?–1026?), as the first true novel, since it depicts the amorous adventures of a fictional Prince Genji and the staid lives of his descendants. The novel paints a charming and apparently accurate picture of Japanese court life in the Heian period. Among its chief delights are the portraits of the women in Prince Genji's life. These women are individually characterized, with their aristocratic refinements, talents in the arts of music, drawing, and poetry, and love for the beauties of nature. As the work nears its conclusion, the tone becomes more mature and somber, colored by Buddhist insight into the fleeting joys of earthly existence.

Fiction became popular with the rise of the long verse tale, the prose romance, and the Old French *fabliau* in the medieval period, culminating, as mentioned above, with Boccaccio's *Decameron*. In Spain during the sixteenth century, the novel form gained great social importance with the advent of the so-called picaresque novel, in which the hero is typically a vagabond who goes through a series of exciting adventures. The classic example is the novel by Miguel de Cervantes Saavedra (1547–1616), *Don Quixote de la Mancha* (Part I, 1605, Part II, 1615), which is considered the first truly great novel of the Western world.

The novel became the dominant and most popular form of narrative art in the eighteenth and nineteenth centuries, as more and more writers started devoting their lives to this art form. Novels became more psychologically real, depicting and often satirizing contemporary life and morals. During this same era, the novel spawned its own genres, including the didactic novel, in which theories of education and politics were explored, and the Gothic novel, which aimed to horrify readers by depictions of bizarre supernatural happenings. The first Gothic novel was *The Castle of Otranto* (1764) by Horace Walpole (1717–1797). But perhaps the most well-known example of the genre is *Frankenstein* (1818) by Mary Wollstonecraft Shelley (1797–1851). Another genre of the period was the comedy of manners, which explored the imposed artificial structure of social relations. The novels of Jane Austen (1775–1817) are probably the most important of the genre.

Throughout the nineteenth century, and for most of the twentieth, the novel became a powerful medium for probing human nature. Novelists were as popular and well known as media personalities are today. Their critiques led to social change; their characters gave the early psychologists insights into human nature. The French writer Marcel Proust (1871–1922), for instance, explored the nature of memory; the German author Thomas Mann (1875–1955) searched for the roots of psychic angst in social systems; and English authors Virginia Woolf (1882–1941) and James Joyce (1882–1941) plumbed the emotional source of human thoughts and motivations. After World War II the novels of an increasing number of writers in developing countries came to the forefront. Many of these portray with vivid realism the clash between classes and races, the search for meaning in a world where materialism reigns supreme, and the desire to reform the world.

Narrative techniques in novels vary from simple first-person storytelling to complex stream-of-consciousness narration, designed to reveal a character's feelings, thoughts, and actions, often following an associative rather than a logical sequence, without commentary by the author. The latter technique is considered by many to be the maximal achievement of the novel form. Not to be confused with interior monologue, it attempts to portray the remote, preconscious state that exists before the mind organizes its thoughts logically. The term "stream of consciousness" was first used by William James (1842–1910), the American philosopher and psychologist. Major exponents of the genre were American novelist William Faulkner (1897–1962), British writer Virginia Woolf, and Irish writer James Joyce, who perhaps brought the technique to its highest point of development in *Ulysses* (1922) and *Finnegans Wake* (1939). In those two masterpieces the inaccessible corners of human memory and the recurrent repertory of feeling and form within the psyche are laid bare before us.

But evaluations of the novel's worth to human history have varied. Twentieth-century Marxist critics, for instance, saw literary works as great only when they were "progressive," that is, when they supported the causes of the society in which they were created. Freudian critics, instead, believed that the value of narrative art lay in its therapeutic nature. The conflicts, fantasies, and daydreams of fictional characters, they claimed, are those of ordinary people, and thus can be read by someone as a means for coming to grips with his or her own real-life conflicts, fantasies, and daydreams. The French philosopher and writer Jean-Paul Sartre (1905–1980), on the other hand, saw narrative art as providing an "escape hatch," so to speak, from inner psychic turmoil, because he saw it as eradicating the guilt from which people ordinarily suffer, thus opening the way for genuine emotional freedom.

Perhaps the most radical view of narrative ever to have been formulated comes from the pen of the French philosopher Jacques Derrida (1930–), who contends that the traditional, or metaphysical, way of interpreting literary works makes a number of false assumptions about the nature of such texts. A traditional reader believes that the author of a text is the source of its meaning. Derrida has challenged both this belief and the idea that a text has an unchanging, unified meaning. The author's intentions in writing, Derrida has claimed, cannot be unconditionally accepted. There are an infinite number of legitimate interpretations of a text.

THE COMICS

In closing this chapter, a comment on a modern-day form of narrative, the *comics*, is in order, not only because it has become a target of great interest among semioticians, but also because of its importance to the development of contemporary pop culture. The predecessors of the modern-day comic book are the caricatures or satirical portraits of famous people that became popular in seventeenth-century Italy. The form spread quickly throughout Europe. In the early nineteenth century, caricatures were expanded to include speech balloons, giving birth to the modern comic book form.

Comics are narratives told by means of a series of drawings arranged in horizontal lines, strips, or rectangles, called *panels*, and read like a verbal text from left to right. Comics usually depict the adventures of one or more characters in a limited time sequence. Dialogue is represented by words encircled by a balloon, which issues from the mouth or head of the character speaking. Movement is illustrated largely through the use of lines of different sizes. For example, long thin lines trailing a running horse show speed. Short broken lines indicate a jumping frog.

The senses are illustrated by lines, symbols, and words. The lines and stars around the thumb suggest pain. The lines leading from a dog's nose represent smell.

One of the first American works with the essential characteristics of a comic strip was created by Richard Felton Outcault and appeared in the series *Hogan's Alley,* first published on May 5, 1895, in the New York *Sunday World.* The setting depicted squalid city tenements and backyards filled with dogs and cats, tough-looking characters, and ragamuffins. One of the urchins was a flap-eared, bald-headed, Oriental-looking child with a quizzical, yet shrewd, smile. He was dressed in a long, dirty nightshirt, which Outcault often used as a placard to comment on the cartoon itself. Other early comics were the *Little Bears* by James Guilford Swinnerton, which first appeared in the San Francisco *Examiner* in 1892, *The Katzenjammer Kids* by Rudolph Dirks, which first appeared in *The American Humorist* in 1897, and *Mutt and Jeff,* which first appeared as *Mr. A. Mutt* in a November 1907 issue of the *San Francisco Chronicle.* Newly formed newspaper syndicates subsequently introduced the latter comic strip to a wide audience, and it became the first successful daily comic strip in the US. To satisfy demand, newspapers published collections of the cartoons, and a 1911 *Mutt and Jeff* collection was the first comic book to be published (to the best of my knowledge). Its success led to the first comic book published independently of any newspaper, containing material specially prepared for it. Called *The Funnies,* it ran for 13 issues in 1929. Starting in 1933, a number of comic books, reprinted from well-known newspaper comic strips such as *Joe Palooka* and *Connie,* were published and distributed as premiums with certain merchandise. The first comic book to be sold on newsstands was *Famous Funnies,* which appeared in 1934.

A great impetus was given to the comic book industry by the phenomenal success in 1938 of *Action Comics,* of which the principal attraction was the *Superman* comic strip, later published in separate *Superman* comic books. Indeed, only a year after, *Superman* spawned a series of comic-book hero clones in the early 1940s—the decade that saw the debuts of *Batman, The Flash, Green Lantern, Wonder Woman,* and *Captain America.*

Like the pop culture they reflect, it is impossible to dismiss comics as just "entertainment texts." A number of strips have, in fact, found a devoted following among intellectuals. *Krazy Kat,* for instance, has been regarded by many as one of the most amusing and imaginative works of narrative art ever produced in America. The art of Charles Schultz (1922–2000), too, falls into this category. His comic strip *Peanuts,* which was originally titled *Li'l Folks,* debuted in 1950, becoming one of the most popular comic strips in history, appearing in more than 2000 newspapers and translated into more than 24 languages. His characters—Charlie Brown; his sister Sally; his dog Snoopy; his friends Lucy, Linus, Schroeder, Peppermint Patty, and Marcie; and the bird Woodstock—have become icons of pop culture. At the same time, religious and philosophical meanings have been attributed to the characters and to the simple existence they lead.

Starting in the 1970s, many individuals and small companies began competing with the larger publishers. Independent or "alternative" artists experimented with new styles, more sophisticated formats, and stories suited to adults. For example, the graphic novel is a book-length comic book that tells a single complex story for adults. The most celebrated examples are *Maus: A Survivor's Tale* (1986) and *Maus II* (1991) by Art Spiegelman. They tell of the artist's relationship with his father and the experiences of his father and mother in the Holocaust.

Comics are narratives for the modern world, both reflecting modern life and helping to mold it. Even before the advent of television, they set the style for clothing, coiffure, food, manners, and mores. They have inspired plays, musicals, ballets, motion pictures, radio and television series, popular songs, books, and toys. Language is replete with idioms and words created for the comics. For example, the code word for the Allied Forces on D-Day was "Mickey Mouse," and the password for the Norwegian Underground was "The Phantom." Numerous contemporary painters and sculptors have incorporated comic-book characters into their art works; motion picture directors have adapted techniques of the comics into their films; and of course, Bugs Bunny (with his "What's up, Doc?"), Homer Simpson (with his "D'oh"), Rocky and Bullwinkle (with their wry humor), the Grinch, the Flintstones, Fat

Albert, Popeye, Scooby-Doo, Arthur, Winnie the Pooh, Mr. Magoo, Felix the Cat, Yogi Bear, Mighty Mouse, Batman, Woody Woodpecker, Tom and Jerry, to mention just a few, have become household names.

Today, there are many online *e-toons*. For example, *Gary the Rat* (mediatrip.com) is about a ruthless New York lawyer who gets turned into a huge rat, in obvious parodic imitation of Franz Kafka's (1883–1924) horrifying masterpiece *Metamorphosis*. The rat is hated by his landlord, who wants to evict him, and chased by an exterminator who is out to eliminate him. Yet, Gary the rat is adored by his boss because clients are eager to work with him. *Queer Duck* (icebox.com) satirizes the gullibility of people who listen to "radio shrinks." It is about a gay duck and his animal pals who are frequent crank callers to a well-known "radio psychologist." *The God and Devil Show* (entertaindom.com) is a cartoon talk show hosted by a bearded ruler of heaven and a sexy leader of hell. Other popular online e-toons are: *The producer* (thethreshold.com), which parodies media producers and production; *Kung Fu 3D* (entertaindom.com), which is a web animation update of the American TV series starring David Carradine (1972–1975); *The Critic* (shockwave.com), which features an animated film critic who comments satirically on current movies and actors; and *Star Wars Network* (atomfilms.com), which spoofs the whole subculture spawned by the *Star Wars* series.

CONCLUDING REMARKS

Whether it be a founding myth, a fictional novel, or a comic strip, narrative is a form of text-making that provides humans with a powerful means of making messages and meanings. It is an "instinctual" capacity, as can be seen from the fact that from the beginning of life we respond to stories "instinctively," with no tutoring as to what they are. Indeed, they come so naturally to us that they constitute both how we come to know the world culturally (through founding myths) and personally (through the childhood stories to which we are exposed in cultural context).

Art

Art for art's sake? I should think so, and more so than ever at the
present time. It is the one orderly product which our middling
race has produced. It is the cry of a thousand sentinels, the echo
from a thousand labyrinths, it is the lighthouse which cannot be
hidden. It is the best evidence we can have of our dignity.

E. M. Forster (1879–1970)

PRELIMINARY REMARKS

The capacity to draw and extract meaning from pictures, to make and enjoy
music, to dance, to put on stage performances, to write poetry, is a truly
extraordinary and enigmatic endowment of the human species. The "art instinct"
allows everyone, regardless of age class, or abilities, to indulge in the entire
range of feelings and spiritual emotions that truly differentiate humans from
other life forms. It is indisputable evidence of the workings of what Vico
called *fantasia*. Artistic traditions are passed on from generation to generation
throughout the world as precious tokens because they are perceived universally
as transcending time, as saying something true and profound about the human
condition.

The subfield of semiotics that deals with art is called *aesthetics*; the related
subfield of art interpretation is called *hermeneutics*. The two are concerned
with such phenomena as human responses to sounds, forms, and words and
with the ways in which the emotions condition such responses. In this chapter,
therefore, the focus is on the messages and meanings of art. Actually, some of
the arts have already been discussed in this book: dancing in chapter 3, visual

art and cinema in chapter 4, and poetry in chapter 5. Thus, the focus here will be on theater, music, and so-called "postmodern art."

WHAT IS ART?

Defining *art* is as impossible a task as defining *culture*. Indeed the two are often used as synonyms. Art is something that everyone recognizes, but which no one can quite define. It involves a disciplined, skilled form of representation that entails a distinctive way of looking at the world. The word *art*, in fact, derives from the Latin *ars,* meaning "skill." This is why this word is used frequently as a synonym for *skill*—e.g. the "art of gardening," the "art of chess." In its broader meaning, however, it involves not only specialized skill, but also a creative imagination and a point of view about the world that is etched into the artistic text.

In classical and medieval times, poets were praised and recognized for their endeavors, whereas musicians, painters, sculptors, and other artists who used physical skills were considered less important and, therefore, remained anonymous. However, starting in the Renaissance, those skilled in the visual and performing arts gradually gained greater recognition and social prestige, and thus the right to authorship. By the eighteenth century, a more sophisticated public felt the need to distinguish between art that was purely aesthetic and art that was practical or ornamental. Thus, a distinction was made between the fine arts—including literature, music, dance, painting, sculpture, and architecture—and the decorative or applied arts—such as pottery, metalwork, furniture and carpet making, etc.—which for a time were demoted to the rank of crafts. Because the prestigious École des Beaux-Arts in Paris taught only the major visual arts, the term *art* has since been reserved in the West to refer only to drawing, painting, architecture, and sculpture. However, since the mid-twentieth century, greater appreciation of all types of art, of non-Western art, and of folk artistic traditions has expanded the view of what constitutes art considerably and given back to the word its broader meaning.

Many scholars believe that art originally had a ritualistic and mythic function. The notion of artists as individualists and eccentric creators is a relatively modern one. In ancient cultures, art was created to be used as part of communal ceremonies. It was made by all members of the community, rather than by professionals alone. In traditional aboriginal cultures of North America art continues, in fact, to be perceived as one aspect of community rituals that are designed to ensure a good harvest or to celebrate a significant life event such as a birth or a marriage. But even in modern Western culture, art entails ritual. At a performance of a classical piece of music in a concert hall, for instance, there is ritualistic silence. At a rock concert, on the other hand, there is communal shouting and physical involvement. Hanging a painting in an art gallery invites an individualistic appreciation, but drawing something on a city wall invites social participation (graffiti, commentary, modifications, etc.).

THEORIES OF ART

The first aesthetic theory of any scope was that of Plato, who believed that art was an imitation of ideal forms. However, he also felt that art encouraged immorality, and that certain musical compositions caused laziness and immoderacy. He thus suggested banishing some types of artists from society. Aristotle also saw art as imitation, but not in the same way that his teacher Plato did. The role of art, thought Aristotle, was to complete what Nature did not finish, separating the form from its content, such as the human bodily form from its manifestation in people, and then transferring that form onto some physical medium, such as canvas or marble. Thus, art was not pure imitation, but rather a particular representation of an aspect of things that had the capacity to profoundly affect the human observer and thus eventually transform him or her. In his *Poetics,* Aristotle argued that tragedy, for instance, so stimulates the emotions of pity and fear that by the end of the play the spectator is purged of them. This *catharsis,* as he called it, makes the audience psychologically healthier and thus more capable of happiness.

The third-century philosopher Plotinus (AD 205–270), born in Egypt and trained in philosophy at Alexandria, also gave art great importance. In his view, art revealed the true nature of an object more accurately than ordinary experience did, thus raising the human spirit from the experience of the mundane to a contemplation of universal truths. According to Plotinus, the most precious moments of life were those mystical instants when the soul is united, through art, with the divine.

Art in the Middle Ages was considered to be primarily a servant of religious traditions. It was during the Renaissance that art reacquired its more secular functions. The Renaissance, moreover, saw little difference between the artist and the scientist. Indeed, many were both—Leonardo da Vinci was a painter, writer, and scientist, Michelangelo a visual artist and writer, to mention but two. It was only after the Enlightenment and the Romantic movement that an unfortunate, artificial split came about, pitting artists against scientists. The view of the artist as a unique kind of genius impelled by his or her own creative energies to free himself or herself from the shackles of culture is very much a product of Romanticism. In ancient times artists were merely laborers, paid by rulers for their services. Ancient Egyptian architects, for instance, were hired to build structures designed to glorify the pharaoh and life after death. In pious medieval Europe, visual artists and playwrights were hired by the Church to create art texts designed to extol Christian themes. The choice to be an artist was a matter of social custom, not of some esoteric inclination at birth. Artists, like other people, customarily followed their fathers' profession. It was only after the eighteenth century that the choice to become an artist became an individual one. But the romantic view of the artist as an individualist, who is the opposite of the scientist, continues on to this day. Specialization in the arts and specialization in the sciences is a fact of life in the modern world.

Why is art so effective emotionally, no matter who produces it or at which period of time it was produced? Perhaps the best known, and most widely accepted, contemporary theory for explaining the potency of art is the one put forward by the American philosopher Susanne Langer (1895–1985) during the middle part of the twentieth century. We do not experience art, she emphasized, as individual bits and pieces (notes, shapes, words, etc.), but as a total emotional experience. It is only when an individual tries to understand rationally why the art work had such an effect on him or her that the holistic experience is transformed by reasoning and language into one in which its parts can be taken apart, discussed, critiqued, etc. like the individual words in a sentence. But, no matter how many times people try to understand the aesthetic experience logically, it somehow escapes understanding, remains larger than the sum of its parts. One can analyze the opening movement of Beethoven's *Moonlight Sonata* as a series of harmonic progressions and melodic figures based on the key of C# minor. But the elements of melody and harmony come into focus as components of the work only during an analysis of the sonata's structure. When one hears it played as an artistic performance, on the other hand, one hardly focuses on these bits and pieces. One cannot help but experience the music holistically. And this is what makes it emotionally "moving," as the expression goes. In effect, no theory of art is really possible.

Langer remarked, further, that because of its emotional qualities, great art transforms human beings and cultures permanently. It is truly a "mirror of the soul." Humanity has never been the same since, for example, Michelangelo sculpted his *David,* Shakespeare wrote his *King Lear*, Mozart composed his *Requiem,* Beethoven composed his Ninth Symphony, and so on and so forth. The spiritual meanings and the aesthetic effects in such great art works are constantly being experienced across time, across cultures. Such works seem to have been constructed with the universal spiritual blueprint of humankind.

A HISTORY OF THEATER

The word *performance* refers to the physical means employed for executing an art text before an audience. Performances are generally given spatial prominence through a raised stage, and they typically involve props and paraphernalia such as costumes, masks, musical instruments, and materials of various kinds. They are put on according to a socially defined tradition. They are prepared, scheduled, and set up in advance; they have a beginning and an end; they unfold in terms of a structured sequence of parts (e.g., acts in a play); and they are coordinated for public participation. Performances are both reflective and constitutive of cultural meanings: they both shed light upon the values of the culture and critique them. If they are aesthetically powerful, they end up becoming part of common traditions and may even transcend the cultures for which they were originally designed. This is why citations from Shakespeare or Molière, allusions to actions in famous plays, references to dramatic characters for explaining certain aspects of human nature (Oedipus, Antigone, Hamlet, Ophelia, Lear) are commonplace.

The performing arts include theater, dancing, singing, instrumental music, mime, vaudeville, circus acts, pageantry, and puppetry. In this section we will focus on the theater, which can be defined as a performance representing some event in Nature, in life, or in society, put on by actors on a stage, around which an audience can view the performance. In general, theater puts on display actions and events that we somehow consider vital to our existence. It does so typically through the narrative medium. The dramatic text is usually verbal, but it can also be based purely on bodily movement. The latter genre is referred to more precisely as *pantomime,* or the art of theater based on facial expressions and bodily movements rather than on a verbal text. In the great open-air theaters of ancient Greece and Rome, where the audience could see more easily than it could hear, pantomime became an important aspect of verbal theater as well, leading to the use of stylized pantomimic gestures to portray character in Western theatrical art generally.

The term *theater* is used to describe both the performance itself and the place where it takes place. Stages and auditoriums have had distinctive forms in every era. New theaters today tend to be eclectic in design, incorporating elements of several styles. A theatrical performance, however, need not occur in an architectural structure designed as a theater, or even in a building. Many earlier forms of theater were performed in the streets, in open spaces, in market squares, in churches, or in rooms and buildings not intended for use as theaters. Much of contemporary experimental theater, too, rejects the formal constraints of the traditional stage performance, attempting to create the sense of auditorium through the actions of the performers and the natural features of the acting space.

Most scholars trace the origin of the theater to ancient ceremonial practices. These were intended as fertility or harvest rites, put on in order to appease the gods. Even in ancient Greece the first dramas revolved around tales of the gods. The plays of Aeschylus (c. 525–456 BC), Sophocles (c. 497–405 BC), and Euripides (c. 485–406 BC) were drawn from myth and legend, though their focus was not a simple performance of the mythic storyline, but rather a consideration of the tragedy of human actions. The actors of those dramas wore masks, a practice that also had a ritualistic source. Masks are expressive devices, shifting the focus from the individual actor to the character he or she is portraying, thus clarifying aspects of theme and plot as well as imparting a sense of greater universality to the character. In modern theater, make-up and facial expression has taken over from masks.

Comedy was developed in ancient Greece alongside tragedy for criticizing and satirizing both individuals and society in general. The first great comedic playwright was, no doubt, Aristophanes (c. 445–385 BC), who became famous for satirizing both public figures and the gods, to the delight of large audiences. The comedic approach became even more popular in the Roman plays of Plautus (c. 250–184 BC) and Terence (c. 85–159 BC). But, with the fall of the Roman Empire in AD 476, the emerging Christian Church saw comedy as too bawdy and scatological, discouraging it for more than 500 years, and promoting instead a liturgical form of theater based on Bible stories. By the fifteenth century, the latter had evolved into the *morality play*, which was a self-contained drama performed by professional actors, and which dealt, typically, with the theme of the individual's spiritual journey through life.

Interest in comedic theater was revived by the movement known as the *commedia dell'arte*, an improvised comedy genre that arose in sixteenth-century Italy and spread throughout Europe over the subsequent 200 years. The six to twelve players in the *commedia* wore half-masks to portray the exaggerated features of a character. They did not use a script; rather, they improvised skits both on outdoor, impromptu stages and in conventional staging areas. Each actor played the role of a stereotypical character as, for instance, Harlequin, the clownish valet; the Doctor, who used meaningless Latin phrases and often suggested dangerous remedies for other characters' imagined illnesses; and

Pulcinella, who concocted outrageous schemes to satisfy his animal-like cruelty and lust. Unlike traditional theater, *commedia* troupes featured skilled actresses rather than males playing the female characters. From the cast of stock characters, each troupe was able to put on hundreds of plays. *Commedia* actors also developed individual comic routines, called *iazzi*, which they could execute on demand, especially when it was felt that a sudden laugh was needed. For instance, a *commedia* performer might pretend to trip and tumble into a pail of bath water during the exit sequence. Many of the routines and ideas of the *commedia* live on in contemporary forms such as vaudeville, burlesque, and even television sitcoms.

By the mid-sixteenth century a new, dynamic secular theater had developed. The most important concept in its design was *verisimilitude*—the appearance of truth. Characters were common individuals. The plays had a single plot, which took place within a 24-hour period, and occurred only in one locale. In the Romantic nineteenth century, theater took another turn, concentrating on a search for the spiritual nature of humankind. One of the best examples of Romantic drama is *Faust* (Part I, 1808; Part II, 1832), by the German playwright Johann Wolfgang von Goethe (1749–1832). Based on the classic legend of a man who sells his soul to the devil, the play depicts humankind's attempt to master all knowledge and power in its constant struggle with the universe.

As plays attracted larger and larger audiences, playwrights became more and more involved in writing about everyday life, focusing on the psychological realism of the characters and on social problems. They sought to present a "slice of life" on the stage. This new realistic trend in theater led to the notion of the *director* as the one who interprets the text, determines acting style, suggests scenery and costumes, and gives the production its overall quality—a tradition that continues to this day.

MODERN THEATER

By the first decades of the twentieth century, a reaction against realism erupted in the world of theater. Paralleling contemporaneous radical visual art and musical movements, a movement known as *absurdist* theater emerged. The emphasis of this new form of theater was on the absurdity of theater and of the human condition it glorified. The subtext in all absurdist drama was that of humanity as lost in an unknown and unknowable world, where all human actions are senseless and absurd. Absurdism reached its peak in the 1950s, but continues to influence drama to this day.

Take, as a well-known case in point, the play *Waiting for Godot,* published in 1952 by the Irish-born playwright and novelist, Samuel Beckett (1906–1989). *Godot* is a powerful indictment of the wretchedness of the human condition. It continues to have great appeal because, like the two tramps in the play, many people today seem to have become cynical about the meaning of human existence. The play perseveres in challenging the ingrained belief system that there is a meaning to life, insinuating that language, religion, and philosophy are no more than illusory screens we have set up to avoid the truth—that life is an absurd moment of consciousness on its way to extinction.

The play revolves around the actions of two tramps, Vladimir and Estragon, stranded in an empty landscape, who are attempting to pass the time away with a series of banal activities reminiscent of those of slapstick comedians or circus clowns. The two tramps seem doomed to repeating their senseless actions and words forever. They call each other names; they ponder whether or not to commit suicide; they reminisce about their insignificant past lives; they threaten to leave each other but cannot quite do it; they perform silly exercises; and they are constantly waiting for a mysterious character named Godot, who never comes. A strange pair, named Lucky and Pozzo, appear, disappear, reappear, and finally vanish in the second act, which is virtually a duplicate of the first. Pozzo whips Lucky, as if he were a cart horse. Lucky kicks Estragon. The two tramps tackle Lucky to the ground to stop him from shrieking out a deranged parody of a philosophical lecture. Vladimir and Estragon go back to talking about nothing in particular, and wait with mindless exasperation for Godot, engaging in mindless discourse replete with tired clichés. Allusions to the Bible narrative and scenery are sardonic—there is a bare tree on stage suggesting the Biblical tree of life, and the tramps constantly engage in senseless theological discourse. The play ends with the two tramps still waiting. There is no meaning to life, nor will there ever be. Life is meaningless, a veritable circus farce!

But despite the play's nihilism, people seem paradoxically to discover meaning in it. The tramps are perpetually waiting for Godot—a name coined as an obvious allusion to God. Godot never comes in the play. But deep inside us, as audience members, we yearningly hope that Beckett is wrong, and that on some other stage, in some other play, the design of things will become known to us—that God will indeed come.

Waiting for Godot questions traditional assumptions about certainty and truth. It satirizes language, portraying it as a collection of senseless words that can refer only to other words. It also deconstructs classic theater, which drew its stories and characters from myth or ancient history. The objective of the ancient dramas was to consider humanity's place in the world and the consequences of individual actions. The classical actors wore costumes of everyday dress and large masks. Movement and gesture were stately and formal. The plots emphasized supernatural elements, portraying how humans and the gods struggled, interacted, and ultimately derived meaning from each other. Similarly, medieval morality plays put on display principles of human conduct that informed the populace about what was meaningful to existence. Shakespeare's great tragedies continued in this vein. *Waiting for Godot* is a critique of this kind of theater. The ancient dramas portrayed a world full of metaphysical meanings; Godot portrays a world in which there is only a void. In the ancient dramas, human life was portrayed as having great meaning. In *Godot,* human beings fulfill no particular purpose in being alive—life is a meaningless collage of actions on a relentless course leading to death and to a return to nothingness. But Beckett's bleak portrait of the human condition somehow forces us to think about that very condition, paradoxically stimulating in us a profound reevaluation of the meaning of life.

Absurdist theater was deconstuctionist, taking apart common beliefs and forcing people to reevaluate them. It continues to inform contemporary theatrical trends. In a play such as *American Buffalo* (1976) by David Mamet (1947–), for instance, little action occurs and the focus is on mundane characters and events. The language is fragmentary, as it is in everyday conversation. And the settings are indistinguishable from reality. The intense focus on seemingly meaningless fragments of reality creates a nightmarish effect on the audience.

Today, the functions of the theater have been largely replaced by cinema, although theater continues to attract a fairly large following. Musical theater has also emerged as a popular entertainment art form. Already in the 1920s musicals were transformed from a loosely connected series of songs, dances, and comic sketches to a story, sometimes serious, told through dialogue, song, and dance. The form was extended in the 1940s by the team of Richard Rodgers (1902–1979) and Oscar Hammerstein II (1895–1960) and in the 1980s by Andrew Lloyd Webber (1948–) with such extravagantly popular works as *Cats* (1982) and *Phantom of the Opera* (1988).

It should be mentioned, as a final word on theater, that theatrical practices in Asia—in India, China, Japan, and Southeast Asia—have started to attract great interest from the West. The central idea in Asian performance art is a blend of literature, dance, music, and spectacle. The theater is largely participatory—the audience does not actually take part in the performance, but participation unfolds like a shared experience. The performances are often long, and the spectators come and go, eating, talking, and watching only their favorite moments. The West discovered Asian theater in the late nineteenth century, a discovery that has gradually influenced many contemporary forms of acting, writing, and staging.

MUSIC

Music is an art form involving the organized use of sounds through a continuum of time. Music plays a role in all societies, and it exists in a large number of styles, each characteristic of a geographical region or a historical era. Indefinite border areas exist, however, between music and other sound-based arts such as poetry (chapter 5). For this reason, societies differ in their opinion as to the musicality of various sounds. Thus, chanting, half-spoken styles of singing, or sound texts created by a computer program may or may not be accepted as music by members of a given society or group. Often, it is the social context in which the sounds occur that determines whether or not they are to be regarded as music. Industrial noises, for instance, are not perceived as musical unless they are presented as part of a concert of experimental music in an auditorium, with a composer.

Various strata of musical art may exist. In our own, the following three apply: (1) *classical music*, composed and performed by trained professionals originally under the patronage of aristocratic courts and religious establishments; (2) *folk music*, shared by the population at large; and (3) *popular music*, performed by professionals, disseminated through electronic media (radio, television, records, film) and consumed by a mass public. But the boundaries among these strata are not clear—e.g., melodies from the realm of classical music are sometimes adopted by the folk and pop communities, and vice versa.

Although an isolated cuneiform example of Hurrian (Hittite) music of 2000 BC has been tentatively deciphered, the earliest precursor of Western music known is that of the ancient Greeks and Romans, dating from about 500 BC to AD 300. Fewer than a dozen examples of Greek music survive, written in a notation that has still not been deciphered entirely. The rhythm of Greek music was closely associated with language. In a song, the music was composed to duplicate the rhythms of the verbal text. In an instrumental piece it was made to follow the rhythmic patterns of the various poetic meters. The internal structure of Greek music was based on a system of sound modes that combined a scale with special melodic contours and rhythmic patterns. A similar organization exists today in Indian music. Because each Greek mode incorporated rhythmic and melodic characteristics, listeners could easily distinguish between them. Greek theories on the nature and function of music are discussed by Pythagoras, Aristotle, and Plato. They believed that music originated with the god Apollo, the musician Orpheus, and other mythical figures, and that it reflected in microcosm the laws of harmony that rule the universe. They also believed that music influenced human thoughts and actions.

Opinions differ as to the original motivation for, and the spiritual value of, music. In some African societies music is seen as the faculty that sets humans apart from other species; among some Native Americans it is thought to have originated as a way for spirits to communicate with human beings. In Western society music is regarded generally as an art form. But in some others it is considered to be of low value, associated with sin and evil, and thus something to be restricted or even prohibited. This view is not unknown to America, where attempts in the 1950s to ban rock 'n' roll were based on the argument that it was an obscene and sinful form of musical expression. Some even called it "the devil's music."

The minimal unit, or signifier, of musical organization is the *tone*—a sound with specific pitch and duration. Musical texts are put together by combining individual tones to make melodies and harmonies, on the structural plan of regularly recurring beats. The makers of musical texts are known, appropriately enough, as composers, since the principal creative act in music is based on arranging sounds into sonorous texts known as compositions. Musical performances are based on compositions, but can also include improvisation, or the creation of new music in the course of performance. Improvisation usually takes place on the basis of some previously determined structure, such as a tone or a group of chords; or it occurs within a set of traditional rules, as in the *ragas* of India or the *maqams* of the Middle East.

Music is used frequently to accompany other activities. It is universally associated, for example, with dance. It is a major component in many types of religious services, secular rituals, and theater. In some societies it is also an activity carried out for its own sake. In Western society, for example, music is often listened to at concerts, on the radio, etc.

The power of music to transform people was brought out brilliantly by the 1984 movie *Amadeus* directed by Milos Forman (1932–). The movie is based on the 1979 play by British playwright Peter Shaffer (1926–) about the eighteenth-century rivalry between Austrian composer Wolfgang Amadeus Mozart and Italian composer Antonio Salieri. The play plumbs the meaning of art, genius, and the central role of music in the spiritual life of human beings.

The film captures these themes by juxtaposing the emotionally powerful music of Mozart against the backdrop of dramatized events in his life and the truly splendid commentaries of Salieri, who guides the audience through the musical repertoire with remarkable insight and perspicacity. Forman's camera shots, close-ups, angle shots, tracking shots, and zooming actions allow us to literally probe Mozart's moods (his passions, his tragedies, etc.) on his face as he conducts or plays his music, as well as those of his commentator Salieri (his envy, his deep understanding of Mozart's art, etc.) as he speaks through his confessor to us. Forman thus blends music, plot, and commentary through camera artistry to create a truly effective *mise-en-scène* that is narrative, drama, musical performance, and historical documentary at once. The movie conveys the power of music to transform human evolution. A world without the music of Mozart can be envisioned, but it would be a greatly impoverished one.

POSTMODERN ART

A movement in the arts known as *postmodernism* took a foothold in Western society in the 1980s and 1990s. The term was coined originally by architects to designate a style that was meant to break away from an earlier modernist style (skyscrapers, tall apartment buildings, etc.) that had degenerated into sterile and monotonous formulas. Postmodern architects called for greater individuality, complexity, and eccentricity in design, along with allusions to historical symbols and patterns. Shortly after its adoption in architecture, the notion of postmodernism started to catch on more broadly, becoming a more general idea in philosophy and the arts.

To understand the roots of this movement it is instructive to step back in time to the origins of *modernism*—the belief that science was the means for answering life's great questions. Modernism can be traced to the Renaissance. It received its greatest impetus after the Enlightenment, known also as the "age of reason." In the nineteenth century, the dizzying growth of technology and the constantly increasing certainty that science could eventually solve all human problems further entrenched modernism into cultural groupthink. At mid-century, Charles Darwin (1809–1882) introduced the controversial notion of natural selection, which posed a serious challenge to traditional religious worldviews. By the end of the century, the now famous assertion that "God is dead," by the German philosopher Friedrich Nietzsche (1844–1900), expressed in a nutshell the radical change in worldview that modernism had brought about in Western society. Postmodernism in philosophy and the arts is a reaction to the modernist perspective. In postmodernism, nothing is for certain, and even science and mathematics are constructs of the human imagination, as subject to its vagaries as are the arts. The essence of postmodern technique in all the arts was, and continues to be, irony and parody of the modernist belief in scientific certainty. The technique has been expanded to encompass destructive critiques of modernist society itself. As the sociologist Zygmunt Bauman (1992: vii–viii) has perceptively remarked, postmodernism constitutes "a state of mind marked above all by its all-deriding, all-eroding, all-dissolving *destructiveness.*"

A well-known example of postmodern technique in the area of cinema is Godfrey Reggio's brilliant 1983 film *Koyaanisqatsi*—a film without words that unfolds through a series of discontinuous, narrativeless images. On the one hand, the movie shows us how narrativeless, disjunctive, and distracted the twentieth-century world had become; on the other hand, it is an example of what postmodern art is all about, being at one level a parody of documentary-style films and TV programs. The film has no characters, plot, dialogue, commentary: in a word, nothing recognizable as a narrative. The camera juxtaposes contrasting images of cars on freeways, atomic blasts, litter on urban streets, people shopping in malls, housing complexes, buildings being demolished, etc. We see the world as the TV camera sees it. And it is a turgid, gloomy world indeed with no identifiable purpose or meaning. People move around like mindless robots. To bring out the insanity of a world characterized by countless cars, decaying buildings, and crowds bustling aimlessly about, Reggio incorporates the mesmerizing music of Philip Glass (1937–) into the movie's visual structure. The music acts as a guide to understanding the images, interpreting them tonally. We can feel the senselessness of human actions in such a world in the contrasting melodies and rhythms of Glass's music. His slow rhythms tire us with their heaviness, and his fast tempi—which accompany a demented chorus of singers chanting in the background—assault our senses. When the filmic-musical frenzy finally ends, we feel an enormous sense of relief.

In a certain sense, the whole film can be conceived of as a musical sonata with an opening part or exposition, a middle developmental section, and a final recapitulation with coda. The film starts off with a glimpse into a vastly different world—the world of the Hopi peoples of the southwestern US. This is a world firmly implanted in a holistic view of existence, a view that does not separate humans from Nature. Glass's choral music in this exposition is spiritual, sacred, and profound. It inspires reverence for the bond that links the human spirit to the physical world. This stands in dark contrast to the development of the filmic sonata—a cornucopia of dissonant images of a decaying, senseless, industrialized world. Then we are taken back, at the end, to the Hopi world. As in any recapitulation, the opening profound strains of the choir come back, hauntingly, awesomely, and with a warning this time (the coda), which is projected onto the screen:

> *koyaanisqatsi* (from the Hopi language)
> 1. crazy life
> 2. life in turmoil
> 3. life out of balance
> 4. life disintegrating
> 5. a state of life that calls for another way of living

As Jean-François Lyotard (1984: xxiv) states, in postmodern art "narrative function is losing its functors, its great heroes, its great dangers, its great voyages, its great goal." However, in making Western culture more aware of its narrative presuppositions and its preoccupation with words, postmodernism has ended up engendering a profound reevaluation of belief systems. Postmodern art is powerful to the modern imagination because it is so critical and reflective. But ultimately, the human spirit cries out for something more emotionally satisfying, something more *poetic*. Indeed, today movies such as *Koyaanisqatsi* are no longer being produced, except maybe by small experimental production companies. Nevertheless, postmodernism has left its mark in cinema. A recent example of its legacy is *The Matrix* (1999) and its sequel *The Matrix Reloaded* (2003), both of which struck a resounding chord with young audiences brought up in a world dominated by computers. The movie exposes the artificial world of the computer screen, with intertextual allusions to the Bible. It critiques those "technophiles" who are totally engrossed in their "e-lives." The "computer nerds" rule, but what kind of world have they brought into existence? The search for a higher state of consciousness, free of objects, is ultimately what satisfies humanity.

Another commendable example of postmodern technique is the 2001 film *Memento*, written and directed by Christopher Nolan and based on a short story written by his brother Jonathan Nolan (*Memento Mori*). The main character, Leonard, is forced to live entirely in the present, unable to create new memories after a head injury. The movie revolves around his attempts to get revenge for the killing and raping of his wife. Leonard writes notes on his body, he takes Polaroid photos, and keeps pieces of paper so that he can remember what he has discovered—hence the name *Memento* to indicate that his memory is a series of external mementos, which he is unable to connect to any life story and therefore to any sense of reality. The time sequence of the narrative is presented in reverse manner, so that the audience is denied the key clues of which the protagonist is also deprived, due to his amnesia. The viewer is thus projected directly into the horror of having lost one's memory. Fragmentation and dislocation in the narrative and in memory lead to doubt about the reality of consciousness and existence.

We get the idea that Leonard's wife was killed at the very start. Leonard was hit on the head in the act, and is left without short-term memory. He carries a picture of a man he suspects of the murder. The death of this man, and the inference that he (i.e., Leonard) killed him, ends the tale. Leonard goes on to write a letter, in the style of previous mementos, perhaps to himself, knowing that he would otherwise forget that he was the one who wrote them.

The movie is replete with symbols of time—alarm clocks ringing, a wristwatch, notepads, etc. The movie however destroys the sense of time created by such artifacts by showing the plot in both forward and reverse time, distinguishing the two sequences by black-and-white and color cinematography. Color sequences show what actually happened; black-and-white ones what Leonard believes happened. The first color scene, in which Leonard shoots and kills the suspected man Teddy, is in actual fact the last scene of the narrative. In that scene we see a Polaroid undevelop, a bullet fly back into the barrel of a gun and Teddy come back to life after the sound of a shot is heard. This is followed immediately by a black-and-white scene of Leonard in a motel room talking to an anonymous person on the phone explaining his circumstances.

To make the movie even more horrifying, Nolan intersplices the parallel story of a man named Sam Jenkins. As an insurance investigator, Leonard came across a medical claim from Sam Jenkins, who eerily had the same memory problem that he has now. Leonard investigated the case and had the insurance company deny giving Sam the money he sought, believing that Sam was faking his condition. Sam's wife also wasn't sure if her husband was faking. So, she came up with a memory test. She had diabetes and it was Sam's job to administer the shots of insulin. If she repeatedly had to ask for the shots, she would be able to prove that his condition was real. To her dismay, Sam administered the shots automatonically, forgetting he had just given her one. Eventually, she slipped into a coma from the overdoses and died, leaving Sam a patient in a mental institution. The Sam Jenkins subplot clearly creates a sense that Leonard may, himself, be a patient in the same mental institution, and that he also killed his wife.

Ultimately, the movie raises an ancient philosophical question in a kind of "neo-postmodern" style: What is truth? It is, it seems, what we make of it in our minds. The horror comes when we "lose the mind" that creates the truth.

Postmodern art came forward to destabilize the rational and logocentric worldview that has taken hold of Western society since the Renaissance. However, in making Western culture more deconstructive of its belief systems, it has concomitantly engendered a kind of spiritual renewal within us.

CONCLUDING REMARKS

Perhaps nothing else differentiates human beings from all other species like art does. It is an innate faculty that allows us, from infancy on, to extract meaning from drawings, music, performances, and the like. It is a testament that we are, after all, spiritual beings searching for an explanation to the universe. Whereas science asks questions and seeks answers to the meaning of life with a blend of imaginative and logical thinking, art probes the meaning of life through the emotions. This is why the experience of art is called an aesthetic experience, and the experience of science an intellectual one. But it would be a mistake to see the two types of probes as categorically different. Both are used by human beings to probe the same questions.

Clothes

Nudity is the uniform of the other side; nudity is a shroud.
Milan Kundera (1929–)

PRELIMINARY REMARKS

Like any other common object or artifact, we interpret *clothes* as signs, standing for such things as the personality, the social status, and overall character of the wearer. Once again, the semiotician's basic method of asking *what, how* and *why* something means what it means applies to clothes. To get a concrete grasp of how clothes signify, imagine the following situation. Suppose you had an appointment for a job interview at the head office of a bank. In addition to appropriate grooming, the question of how you would dress is hardly a trivial one. It will depend, first, on whether you are male or female. This is because the *dress code* involved is *gendered*. So, let's assume you are a male. What is the appropriate dress code for a "male head office bank employee"?

Here are the kinds of options (clothing signifiers) that constitute this code:

Dress Code	Selections and Options
Shirt	white or some other conservative color, long sleeves, no designs, preferably buttoned at the collar
Tie	conservative color that should match the suit, tied neatly around the neck with a standard knot; its use is becoming increasingly optional
Jacket	gray or blue, or some other color that does not stand out

| Pants | matching color |
| Shoes | black (preferably with shoelaces) |

There is, needless to say, some latitude to the options and selections you can make. But you know for certain that you cannot put on sneakers or wear a red shirt or yellow jacket, because if you did the chances are that you would not even get past the door of the job interviewer with whom you have an appointment. Although conformity with the dress code will not guarantee you a job in a bank, it will at least get you past that door. Dressing for the occasion is indeed a social requirement. Along with appropriate grooming practices, it is a primary means of presenting persona.

Now, let's switch the situation from the standpoint of gender. Suppose you are a female. What is the appropriate dress code for a "female head office bank employee"? Here are some of the kinds of options (clothing signifiers) that constitute the female code:

Dress Code	Selections and Options
Blouse	soft colors, preferably white
Jacket	gray, blue, or some other conservative color
Skirt or pants	color should match the jacket
Shoes	preferably with high or semi-high heels and a dark color

Although there are some differences in the female dress code, there are also many similarities—many more than there once were. This suggests that the job type now cuts across gender categories. Indeed, dressing "unisexually" originated in social trends that date back to the counterculture 1960s, designed to symbolize equality in the job workplace, in the family, and in society generally.

In effect, this vignette was designed to impress upon you that clothes *make* the person. Clothing is more than mere bodily covering for protection. It is a sign system that is interconnected with the other sign systems of society through which we can send out messages—about our attitudes, our social status, our political beliefs, etc. This is why uniforms are required by special groups like sports teams, military organizations, religious institutions, and the like. And this is why we dress for occasions such as job interviews.

The purpose of this chapter is to examine what clothes mean. The branch of semiotics that focuses on the meaning of material objects and artifacts is sometimes called *artifactual semiotics* or, in the present case, simply *clothing semiotics*.

CLOTHING VS. DRESS

Because clothes are put on bodies, and because (as we have seen) bodies are signs of Selfhood, clothes can be defined as signs extending the basic meaning of bodies in cultural context. Clothes and the bodies they enfold are thus imbued with moral, social, and aesthetic significance. In ancient Greece the body was glorified as a source of pleasure; in ancient Rome it was perceived as a source of moral corruption. As a consequence, the two cultures represented the body in different ways. The Christian Church has always played on the duality of the body as a temple and as an enemy of the spirit. The perception of the body as something morally significant is typical of tribal cultures too. As the anthropologist Helen Fisher (1992: 253–254) observes, even in the jungle of Amazonia Yanomamo men and women wear clothes for sexual modesty. A Yanomamo woman would feel as much discomfort and agony at removing her vaginal string belt as would a North American woman if one were to ask her to remove her underwear. Similarly, a Yanomamo man would feel just as much embarrassment at his penis accidentally falling out of its encasement as would a North American male caught literally "with his pants down." As these considerations bring out, clothing and decorating the body for social presentation is a basic form of Self-representation. It is also intrinsically intertwined with sexual, romantic, and courtship meanings. When a young Zulu woman falls in love, she is expected to make a beaded necklace resembling a close-fitting collar with a flat panel attached, which she then gives to her boyfriend. Depending on the combination of colors and bead pattern, the necklace is a courtship device designed to convey a specific type of romantic message: e.g., a combination of pink and white beads in a certain pattern would convey the message *You are poor, but I love you just the same* (Dubin 1987: 134).

At a biological level, clothes have a very important function indeed—they enhance our survivability considerably. They are, at this denotative level, human-made extensions of the body's protective resources; they are additions to our protective bodily hair and skin thickness. As Werner Enninger (1992: 215) aptly points out, this is why clothing styles vary according to geography and topography: "The distribution of types of clothing in relation to different climatic zones and the variation in clothes worn with changes in weather conditions show their practical, protective function." But as is the case in all human systems, clothes invariably take on a whole range of connotations in social settings. These are established on the basis of the various *dress codes* (from Old French *dresser* "to arrange, set up") that inform people how to clothe themselves in social situations.

Predictably, dress codes vary across cultures. To someone who knows nothing about Amish culture, the blue or charcoal *Mutze* of the Amish male is just a jacket. But to the Amish the blue *Mutze* signals that the wearer is between 16 and 35 years of age, the charcoal one that he is over 35. Similarly, to an outsider the Russian *kalbak* appears to be a brimless red hat. To a rural Russian, however, it means that the wearer is a medical doctor. It is interesting to note, too, that clothing, like other types of signs, can be used to lie about oneself: con artists and criminals can dress in three-piece suits to look trustworthy; a crook can dress like a police officer to gain a victim's confidence, and so on. To discourage people from deceiving others through clothing, some societies have even enacted laws that prohibit misleading dressing, defining who can dress in certain ways. In ancient Rome, for instance, only aristocrats were allowed to wear purple-colored clothes; and in many religiously oriented cultures differentiated dress codes for males and females are regularly enforced.

For some semioticians and cultural historians, the history of clothing fashions is the history of a culture. Let us take, therefore, a rapid and highly selective trip through the maze of Western clothing history as a case in point. After the fall of the Western Roman Empire in AD 476, invaders from the north introduced fitted tunics and hoods into clothing styles. Shortly thereafter, the élite of the Byzantine Empire adopted Oriental traditions of dress, with no apparent concession to sexual attraction or to utility. After Charlemagne (AD 742?–814) became Holy Roman Emperor in AD 800, a relatively uniform style of dress appeared in Europe. Charlemagne's own everyday attire consisted of an undertunic and an overtunic, with breeches cross-gartered to the knee. This introduced the "tunic style" to other European monarchs. Court ladies also started wearing long tunics, under supertunics hitched up to show the tunics beneath. A cloth veil concealed the hair. These garments made up the basic wardrobe of the European aristocracy throughout the Middle Ages.

In the 1100s the Crusades had a startling effect on fashion, as crusaders brought back luxurious Oriental fabrics and new styles. The Oriental long, trailing tunic became the main form of aristocratic dress in the 1300s and evolved into the doublet, which survived into the 1600s as the basic male outer garment. Its modern version is the waistcoat or vest. The period also produced an early form of the corset for women. Throughout the Middle Ages, long skirts reached to the floor to hide women's ankles.

In the Renaissance, the development of new fabrics and materials brought about a desire for elaborate clothing styles. By the early 1600s, fashion had literally become the craze with lace edges, frills at the neck and sleeves, collars that eventually became the cravat and the necktie, and breeches for men. This period also saw the introduction of the wig for men. Light colors and fabrics characterized the 1700s, typified by the loose gown. Soft lace replaced the starched, formal ruffs of the previous century. With the French Revolution (1789–1799) came radical changes, as men began wearing trousers for the first time in 600 years. No basic change in men's clothing has taken place since. Women's fashion reverted to what was deemed the "classical style," a look featuring thin fabrics and bare arms—emphasizing a new sexual freedom for females.

Up until the nineteenth century fashion was, clearly, mainly the privilege of the aristocracy. The Industrial Revolution, however, projected fashion for the masses into the realm of economic possibility. Since then fashion crazes for everyone have become an intrinsic feature of modern living. Outside the Western world, however, clothing styles continue to be anchored in religious and/or ritualistic traditions. Where non-Western cultures have come into conflict with Western ideas, traditional garments have tended to be displaced. Nevertheless, in Africa, the Middle East, and the Far East many aspects of traditional dress have survived.

During the 1950s, a new paradigm of dress codes cropped up in Western society that mirrored the power of youth culture. That was, in fact, the period when the clothes worn by rock 'n' roll musicians and adolescent media personages became the dress models for teenagers to emulate. In the 1960s, adolescent clothing styles started to make their way into the mainstream, as the clothes worn by hippies became items of general fashion almost overnight. Since then, those who dictate fashion are hardly aristocrats; they are adolescents in tandem with the media. In the mid-1970s teens wishing to be members of so-called "punk groups" would have had to dye their hair with bizarre colors and cut it in unconventional ways; they would have had to wear unusual clothes and various kinds of bizarre props (e.g., safety pins stuck through their nostrils) to send out counter-culture messages. Although the punk movement started as a political statement from working-class youths in England, by the time its symbolism was acquired by a larger segment of the teen subculture, the punk dress code had become all things to all classes. Elements of that code are now part and parcel of many other kinds of dress codes. The same story repeats itself in relation to all other teen dress codes, from hip-hop to girl power codes.

DRESS CODES

The broad range of connotations associated with dress codes is inextricably interconnected with social trends and political movements. Until the early 1950s, females in our culture rarely wore pants. The one who "wore the pants" in a family meant, denotatively and connotatively, that the wearer was a male. With the change in social role structures during the decades of the 1950s and 1960s, women too began to wear pants regularly, sending out the new social messages that this entailed. The reverse situation has never transpired. Except in special ritualistic circumstances—e.g., the wearing of a Scottish kilt—men have never adopted wearing women's skirts in modern-day Western society. If they do, then we label it as an act of "transvestitism." A double standard still lurks below the surface.

Dressing for social reasons is a universal feature of human cultures. Even in cold climates, some people seem more interested in decorating their bodies than in protecting them. In the 1830s, for example, the famous British biologist Charles R. Darwin (1809–1882) traveled to the islands of Tierra del Fuego, off the southern tip of South America. There he saw people who wore only a little paint and a small cloak made of animal skin, in spite of the cold rain and the sleet. Darwin gave the people scarlet cloth, which they took and wrapped around their necks. Even in the cold weather, these people wore clothing more for decoration than for protection.

No one knows exactly why or when people first wore clothes. But they probably began to wear clothing more than 100,000 years ago—and probably for much the same reasons we wear clothes today. Early people may have worn clothing to protect themselves, to improve their appearance, and to tell other people something about themselves. For example, a prehistoric hunter may have worn the skin of a bear or a reindeer in order to keep warm or as a sign of personal skill, bravery, and strength as a hunter. By the end of the Old Stone Age—about 25,000 years ago—people had invented the needle, which enabled them to sew skins together. They had also learned to make yarn from the threadlike parts of some plants or from the fur or hair of some animals. In addition, they had learned to weave yarn into cloth. At the same time, people had begun to raise plants that gave them a steady supply of materials for making yarn. They had also started to herd sheep and other animals that gave them wool.

So, almost from the beginning of history, people have worn clothes not only for protection, but also for identification and identity. Today, bus drivers, mail carriers, nurses, police officers, and priests wear special clothing to help other people recognize who they are. Dress also conveys people's beliefs, feelings, and general approach to life. Confident people often show more independence in choosing their style of dress than do those who are shy or unsure of themselves. The confident individual is likely to try new clothing styles. A shy person may seek security by following current styles. Others may be unconcerned about their dress and care little whether they dress in what others consider attractive clothing. Some people wear plain clothes because of strong beliefs about personal behavior. Such people believe it is wrong to care about wearing clothes as decoration. They believe that, instead, people should be concerned with other matters. Members of the Amish religious group have this kind of belief system. Amish men wear plain, dark clothes, and Amish women wear long, plain dresses.

In all societies, certain items of clothing and the colors used have special meanings. For example, people in mourning may wear black clothes. Most brides in the US wear white gowns; but the people in India would interpret the use of this color in clothing as a sign of mourning. In this regard, the hat is a clothing item that requires special mention. Hats vary widely in material and style, depending largely on climate and people's customs. For example, a Russian farmer wears a fur hat to protect himself from the cold. A South American cowboy wears a felt gaucho hat as part of his traditional costume, and the American cowboy wears a wide-brimmed hat for protection from the sun. The members of a nation's armed services wear a hat as part of their uniform. The hats of coal miners, fire fighters, and matadors indicate the wearer's occupation. Many clowns wear colorful, ridiculous hats to express fun and happiness. To the Amish, the width of the hat brim and the height of the crown can communicate whether the wearer is married or not.

Throughout the centuries, the desire of people to be fashionable has resulted in many kinds of unusual hats. During the 1400s, many European women wore a tall, cone-shaped hat called a *hennin*. This hat measured from 3 to 4 feet (0.9 to 1.2 meters) high and had a long, floating veil. The Gainsborough hat became popular with both men and women in the late 1700s. It had a wide brim and was decorated with feathers and ribbons. Hats are, and have always been, props in dress codes, communicating various things about the people who wear them. Most people wear a hat that they believe makes them look attractive. This is why much protective headgear today, such as fur hoods and rain hats, is both attractive and stylish. Even the caps of police officers and military personnel are designed to improve the wearer's appearance.

No one knows when people first wore hats. People in various cold climates may have worn fur hoods as far back as 100,000 years ago. Through the centuries, people have worn headgear to indicate their social status. In ancient Egypt, the nobility wore crowns as early as 3100 BC. They have also worn them to be fashionable. Some ancient Greeks wore hats known as *pelos* for fashion. These were usually made from wool fibers. Pelos can still be found in parts of southern Siberia today. They are similar to the brimless, tasseled hat known as a *fez*. By the fourteenth century, people wore hats increasingly for fashion, resulting in the development of a large variety of hats and frequent changes in hat styles. People in one area often adopted the hat styles worn in another. During that century, for example, women in western Europe wore a type of hat that resembled a turban. They adopted this style from the headgear worn by people who lived in the Middle East and the Orient. During the twentieth century, hat styles varied more widely than ever before. In the 1920s, women wore a drooping, bell-shaped hat called the *cloche*. In the 1930s, they wore the harlequin hat, which had a wide, upturned brim. A variety of hats were worn in the 1940s and 1950s. The cap became a central accouterment of male teen style, during the heyday of the rap movement in the mid to late 1990s, when it symbolized clique solidarity.

NUDITY

The human being is the only animal that does not "go nude," so to speak, without triggering off some form of social repercussion (unless, of course, the social ambiance is that of a nudist camp). Indeed, nudity can only be interpreted culturally. We are all born nude, but we soon learn that nudity has negative connotations. Moreover, what is considered "exposable" of the body will vary significantly from culture to culture, even though the covering of genitalia seems, for the most part, to cross cultural boundaries.

To see how we assign meanings to nudity, consider the "art" of stripteasing (male and female). A semiotician would ask of course: What does it represent? Why do people attend (or desire to attend) performances whose sole purpose is the removal of clothing to reveal the body or parts of the body? The semiotician would, as usual, seek answers to these questions in the domain of signification.

Stripteasing is an act of erotic "clothing removal." In an audience setting it has, first and foremost, something of a pagan ritualistic quality to it. The dark atmosphere, the routines leading up to the act, and the predictability of the performance itself, with its bodily gyrations and mimetic portrayals of sexual activities and sexual emotions, constitute a hedonistic performance. There is no motive for being at such performances other than to indulge in a fascination with the sexuality that clothing conceals. As the psychoanalyst Sigmund Freud (1856–1939) suggested, clothing the body has, paradoxically, stimulated curiosity and desire in the body itself. Covering the body is an act of modesty. But this has in effect imbued it with secret desirability. So, at a striptease performance, the shedding of clothes does several symbolic things at once: it removes imposed moral restrictions on sexuality; it reveals those covered bodily parts that have become desirable; it engages viewers in a communal ritual similar to the many carnivals put on throughout the world.

The nude body is, in a word, a powerful sign. This is why visual artists have always had a fascination with the nude figure. The ancient Greek and Roman nude statues of male warriors, Michelangelo's (1475–1564) powerful *David* sculpture, Rodin's (1840–1917) nude sculpture *The Thinker* are all suggestive of the potency of the male body. It is this kind of body image that enhances the attractiveness of the male in our society. A male with a "weakling" body is hardly ever perceived as sexually attractive. On the other side of this semiotic paradigm, paintings and sculptures of female nude figures have tended to portray the female body ambiguously as either: (1) soft and submissive, as can be seen in the famous ancient Greek statue known as the Venus de Milo, which represents Aphrodite, the Greek goddess of love and beauty (Venus in Roman mythology), or (2) feral and powerful (as can be seen in the sculptures of Diana of Greek mythology). It is (2) that came to the forefront again in the 1990s. Known as the "girl power" movement, representations of women in pop culture now emphasize the second type of the two representations.

Human anatomy clearly evokes a coded system of meanings. This system undergirds representations in virtually all areas of human social life. The body is a truly powerful sign system in itself! Artists know this better than anyone else. Even in his scientific drawings, Leonardo da Vinci (1452–1519) always emphasized the inherent beauty of idealized human proportions, as can be seen, for example, in his classic drawing called *Vitruvian man*:

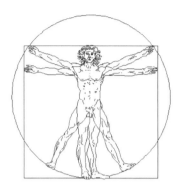

Encircled by two ideally perfect geometric figures, the circle and the square, da Vinci's painting brings out the idealized form of human anatomy perfectly. The modern-day fascination with erotic materials is a contemporary testament to our age-old fascination with nudity as a sign system of such perfection. In my view, those who see danger in such materials, and seem to be prepared to become everyone else's moral guardians by censoring them, are probably more overwhelmed by the connotative power of nudity than most others. Censorship is an attempt to control the form and contents of representational activities, by claiming to have the best interests of society at heart. Gazing at the human body depicted in sexual poses or activities reveals, to this semiotician at least, the signifying power of the clothing vs. nudity opposition. Indeed, in sexual representations, clothing plays a central role in emphasizing sexuality, not hiding it. This is why shoes, stockings, and other gear are used in erotic representations. Only when such depictions are restrained does a perilous fascination with gazing surface.

Aware of this, some, called "nudists," have even gone so far as to advocate the practice of not wearing clothes on principle. The proponents of nudism maintain that clothing should be abandoned when not absolutely necessitated by the rigors of the weather, as clothing serves to focus erotic attention on the body, thereby exciting an unhealthy interest in sex. The shame customarily associated with nakedness in much of modern society results, according to nudists, from centuries of cultural conditioning against complete exposure of the body in public. By correcting in its practitioners this false sense of shame, nudism aims to enhance their self-assurance and furnish them with a new appreciation of the essential beauty and dignity of the human body. Whatever the case, the interplay between clothing and nudity as sign systems cannot be ignored. They are intertwined and interconnected with the entire signifying order of a culture.

FASHION

As discussed above, fashion was, until at least the Renaissance, the privilege of the rich. Since the early decades of the twentieth century, however, it has become an intrinsic component of daily life. Fashion statement has become personal statement.

Fashion can be defined as the prevailing style or custom of dress. It is a kind of "macro" dress code that sets style standards according to age, gender, class, etc. To understand how fashion codes emerge, let us return briefly to the code with which we started off this chapter—the business suit, and specifically the male business suit. The subtextual message underlying the apparel text is, of course, *dress for success*. How did this subtext crystallize in our culture? A look at the history of the business suit provides an interesting answer to this question.

In seventeenth-century England there existed a bitter conflict in social ideology between two forces—the Royalist "Cavaliers," who were faithful to King Charles I, and the Puritans, who were followers of Oliver Cromwell (1599–1658), the military, political, and religious figure who led the Parliamentarian victory in the English Civil War (1642–1649). This conflict was a battle of lifestyles, as the two warring camps sought to gain political, religious, and cultural control of English society. The Cavaliers were aristocrats who only superficially followed the teachings of the Anglican Church. Their main penchant was for a life of indulgence (at least as the Puritans perceived it). They wore colorful clothes, flamboyant feathered hats, beards, and long flowing hair. This image of the Cavalier as a "swashbuckler" has been immortalized by literary works such as *The Three Musketeers* (Alexandre Dumas, 1844) and *Cyrano de Bergerac* (Edmond Rostand, 1897). The Puritans, on the other hand, frowned precisely upon this type of fashion, because of the "degenerate lifestyle" that they perceived it represented. Known as the "Roundheads," Cromwell's followers cropped their hair very short, forbade all carnal pleasures, and prohibited the wearing of frivolous clothing. They wore dark suits and dresses with white shirts and collars. Their clothes conveyed sobriety, plainness, and rigid moralism.

The Cavaliers were in power throughout the 1620s and the 1630s. During this period the Puritans escaped from England and emigrated to America, bringing with them their lifestyle, rigid codes of conduct, and clothing styles. In 1645 the Puritans, led by Cromwell, defeated the Royalist forces and executed the king in 1649. Subsequently, many Cavaliers also emigrated to America. Since the Puritans had set up colonies in the northeast, the Cavaliers decided to set up colonies in the south. The king's son, Charles II, escaped to France to set up a court in exile. For a decade, England was ruled by the Puritans. Frowning upon all sorts of pleasure-seeking recreations, they closed down theaters, censored books, enforced Sunday laws, and forbade the wearing of flashy clothing.

With Cromwell's death in 1658, the Puritans were eventually thrown out of power and England welcomed the exiled king, Charles II, back in 1660. Known as the Restoration, the subsequent twenty-five year period saw a return to the lifestyle and fashions of the Cavaliers. For two centuries the Puritans had to bide their time. They were excluded from holding political office, from attending a university, from engaging in any socially vital enterprise. Nevertheless, throughout the years they maintained their severe lifestyle and dress codes.

By the time of the Industrial Revolution, the Puritans had their revenge. Their lifestyle—based on thrift, diligence, temperance, and industriousness, which some have called the "Protestant work ethic"—allowed them to take advantage of the economic conditions in the new industrialized world. In America and in England, Cromwell's descendants became rich and eventually took over the reigns of economic power. Ever since, Puritan ethics and fashion in the workforce have influenced British and North American culture. The origins of modern corporate capitalism are to be found in those ethics. The belief that hard work and "clean living" were necessarily interrelated, and that this combination led to wealth and prosperity, had become a widespread one by the turn of the present century. To this day, there is a deeply felt conviction in our culture that hard work and strict living codes will lead to success in both this life and the afterlife.

The business suit is a contemporary version of Puritan dress. The toned down colors (blues, browns, grays) that the business world demands are the contemporary reflexes of the Puritan's fear and dislike of color and ornament. During the "hippie" 1960s and early 1970s, the office scene came briefly under the influence of a new form of fashion. "Cavalierism," with its emphasis in the wearing of colorful suits, of turtleneck sweaters rather than of white shirts, of longer hair, of sideburns, of Nehru jackets, of medallions, and of beards made its pitch to take over the world of corporate capitalism. But this fashion experiment was bound to fail, as the Cavalier 1960s were overtaken by conservative neo-puritanical forces in the late 1970s and 1980s. The "business suit" model became once again the dress code for all of corporate North America, with only minor variations in detail.

The business suit somehow endures—perhaps because it is so tied to the history of capitalism. But, nowadays, even this fashion code has become rather eclectic. Take, for example, the length of skirts in the female business suit code. The mini, maxi, and normal length skirts are alternatively in and out of fashion. Evidently, a detail such as length of skirt is, in itself, meaningless. What appears to count is what it implies as a signifier about the ever-fluctuating perceptions of femininity in the workplace. When the mini is "in," it might imply an increased emphasis on sexual freedom in the culture at large. When it is "out," then it might imply the opposite—a decreased emphasis on sexuality in the culture at large. Whatever the case may be, the point to be made here is that the specific elements and features of a fashion code will invariably have connotative value that is a derivative of larger connotative frames and codes within the culture.

Fashion codes, as we have seen, can also constitute ideological statement. The hippies dressed to emphasize "love" and "freedom" in the 1960s. Motorcycle gang members have always worn leather jackets, boots, and various items such as brass knuckles to convey toughness. Clearly, clothing communicates. Like language, it can be endearing, offensive, controversial, delightful, disgusting, foolish, charming.

As mentioned, fashion was the privilege of the aristocracy until the late Middle Ages. Before then, common people wore clothes that reflected the long-standing customs of their communities, and clothing styles changed extremely slowly. Fashion, however, causes styles to change rapidly for a variety of historical, psychological, and sociological reasons. A clothing style may be introduced as a fashion, but the style becomes a custom if it is handed down from generation to generation. A fashion that quickly comes and goes is called a fad.

True fashions began to appear in northern Europe and Italy when a system of social classes developed in the late Middle Ages with the rise of the so-called bourgeois class. At this time, the people of Europe began to classify one another into groups based on such factors as wealth, ancestry, and occupation. The clothes people wore helped identify them as members of a particular social class. Before the late Middle Ages, only wealthy and powerful individuals concerned themselves with the style of their clothes. But when the class system developed, the general population began to compete for positions within society. Fashion was one means by which people did this. One of the first true fashions appeared among young bourgeois Italian men during the Renaissance. While their elders dressed in long traditional robes, the young Italian males began wearing tights and short, close-fitting jackets called doublets. German soldiers set another early fashion when they slashed their luxurious silk clothes with knives to reveal another colorful garment underneath.

Before the 1800s, many countries controlled fashion with regulations called sumptuary laws. Sumptuary laws controlled the amount of money people could spend on private luxuries. Many such laws were designed to preserve divisions among the classes and regulated fashion according to a person's rank in society. In some countries, only the ruling class could legally wear silk, fur, and the colors red and purple. In Paris in the 1300s, middle-class women were forbidden by law to wear high headdresses, wide sleeves, and fur trimmings. Other sumptuary laws forced people to buy products manufactured in their own country to help the country's economy. For example, an English law in the 1700s prohibited people of all classes from wearing cotton cloth produced outside of England. But the lure of fashion caused many people to break this law. The cloth was so popular that people risked arrest to wear it.

Essentially, then, most fashions originated in the past in the upper classes and trickled down to the lower ones. Ordinary people have always hoped to raise their social position by following the fashions of privileged people. In a way, this still happens. But today, such celebrities as singers and athletes, rather than aristocrats, set trends. Fashions considered appropriate for men and women have changed as standards of masculinity and femininity have changed. Until the late 1700s, upper-class European men dressed as elaborately as women did. It was acceptable for men to wear bright-colored or pastel suits trimmed with gold and lace, hats decorated with feathers, high-heeled shoes, and fancy jewelry. But by the mid-1800s, men had abandoned such flamboyance in favor of plain, dark-colored wool suits. Society came to view this new fashion style as democratic, businesslike, and masculine. Until the early 1900s, European and American women rarely wore trousers, and their skirts almost always covered their ankles. By the 1920s, however, standards of feminine modesty had changed to the point that women began to wear both trousers and shorter skirts.

Contrary to popular belief, political events seldom cause fashions to change. However, political events do sometimes speed up changes that have already begun, as we saw in the case of the business suit. For example, during the French Revolution (1789–1799), simple clothing replaced the extravagant costumes made fashionable by French aristocrats. But simple styles had become popular years earlier when men in England started wearing practical, dark suits instead of elegant, colorful clothes. English people identified these plain suits with political and personal liberty. Because many French people admired

English liberty, this style was already becoming fashionable in France before the revolution.

In the nineteenth century, the invention of mechanical looms, chemical dyes, artificial fabrics, and methods of mass production made fashions affordable to many more people. In addition, new means of mass communication spread European and American fashions throughout the rest of the world. The Industrial Revolution created a "fashion global village." Since then, fashion shows and fashion magazines have proliferated. And, as semiotician Roland Barthes (1915–1980) pointed out frequently in his clever writings, they change constantly because rapid turnover guarantees economic success. It is the only constant in fashion.

CONCLUDING REMARKS

Like all sign systems, clothing is interconnected with the other sign systems of the semiosphere. For instance, it is intertwined with religious ceremonies and rituals—the clothing worn at a religious service, during certain religious feasts and festivals, for example, is designed to send out religious messages. It is also intertwined with daily life routines. Just think of what you do every day after you get up in the morning. Typically, after grooming yourself (showering, brushing your teeth, putting on make-up or shaving, etc.), the next thing you do is to dress yourself appropriately, selecting your clothes on the basis of what you are going to do that day (work, go out for recreation, go on a vacation, etc.). In other words, you synchronize your dress code to your lifestyle and social options on a routine daily basis.

Clothing and fashion offer humans an opportunity to make messages and meanings of all kinds. The semiotic study of clothing shows, thus, that clothing is hardly just a study of physical survival. Rather, it is about the penchant for turning anything we put onto the body into a sign.

Food

Roast Beef, Medium, is not only a food. It is a philosophy. Seated at Life's Dining Table, with the menu of Morals before you, your eye wanders a bit over the entrées, the hors d'oeuvres, and the things à la though you know that Roast Beef, Medium, is safe and sane, and sure.

Edna Ferber (1887–1968)

PRELIMINARY REMARKS

Like clothing, food is much more than survival substance. As a concrete example, imagine having adopted a furry little bunny a few years back as a household companion, whom you have named Peter. You have come to depend on Peter for companionship and affection. He has become another family member. You would hardly perceive Peter to be a potential meal.

Now, imagine having been recently invited over to dinner one evening by a family of a different cultural background for whom you have great admiration. For your first dish, you are served a delicious plate of pasta. After eating the savory noodles, you commend your gracious hosts on the exquisiteness of the cuisine. Next, a plate is brought out and you are served a portion of the cooked meat on the plate. It looks appetizing. You are ready to taste it. But before you put the fork in your mouth, you ask one of your hosts what kind of meat it is. "Rabbit," is the answer you receive.

How will you react? Undoubtedly, the image of Peter will come to your mind, and instinctively, you will probably take the fork away from your mouth and place it gently on your plate. Your frame of mind will probably not allow you to swallow the meat, feeling disgusted. What are you going to do? Will you refuse the meat openly and thus risk offending your hosts? Chances are that you will contrive some excuse for not eating it, designed strategically not to insult your hosts, such as: "I'm really too full to eat anything else after that marvelous dish of pasta!" "I really must make room for dessert!" or something similar.

The foregoing vignette was meant to emphasize that food is much more than substance for nourishment and sustenance. It is a sign imbued with meaning. We eat, first and foremost, to survive. But in a social ambiance, food takes on significance that transcends this function and that affect perceptions of edibility. This chapter is about the semiotics of food, an area of substantive interest to contemporary semioticians.

FOOD VS. CUISINE

Survival without food is impossible. So, denotatively food is, as mentioned, survival substance. But, in the semiosphere, food and eating invariably take on a whole range of connotations. The term that is often used to designate the system of connotations that food evokes is *cuisine*. Cuisine informs us as to what certain people eat, how they make it, and what it reveals about them.

The earliest people probably ate whatever plant food they could find, including wild fruits, mushrooms, nuts, roots, and seeds. They caught fish and small land animals, and ate the meat of dead animals they found. In time, people developed weapons to hunt large animals, and probably spent much time searching for them. If the food supply in an area ran out, they apparently moved on. They roasted some of their food over burning wood from fires that started naturally. After they discovered how to make fire, they could roast food more often. After they learned how to make pots, they could also boil and stew food.

By about 8000 BC, people had begun to raise plants and animals for food—hence the rise of farming as a communal activity, assuring people of a steadier food supply. It also meant settling in one area instead of traveling about in search of food. Grains were especially important crops for the early farming communities. So was the raising of cattle, goats, sheep, and other animals for meat and milk. Some groups of prehistoric people were nomadic. They traveled across the countryside in patterns, raising such animals as camels, goats, and sheep. Between 3500 and 1500 BC, the first great civilizations developed in river valleys, such as the Nile Valley in Egypt, the Tigris-Euphrates Valley in what is now Iraq, the Indus Valley in what are now Pakistan and northwestern

India, and the Huang He Valley in China. All these valleys had fertile soil and a favorable climate, which enabled farmers to produce abundant yields. In ancient Egypt, for example, farmers along the Nile could raise two or three crops a year on the same fields. They grew barley and wheat and such vegetables as beans, lettuce, and peas. The Egyptians also cultivated such fruits as grapes and melons. Their livestock included cattle, goats, and sheep.

At first, the ancient Greek and Roman societies could not produce enough food for their growing populations. They thus had to import large quantities of food from other countries. This may be the reason why both civilizations took the decision to conquer and colonize lands that had plentiful food supplies. By the third century AD, the Roman Empire covered much of Europe, most of the Middle East, and the Mediterranean coast of Africa. Most of the empire's large farms specialized in raising wheat, which formed the basis of the Roman diet.

The foregoing sketch only gives a schematic outline of the origin of hunting and farming. The point that it is intended to make is that the origin of true culture is a consequence of efforts to secure a source of food and to invent a technology to make the provision of food abundant and stable. As the anthropologist Claude Lévi-Strauss (1964) pointed out, the origin of culture can, in fact, be traced to the advent of "cooking technology." Lévi-Strauss claims that this transformation was accomplished by two processes—roasting and boiling—both of which were among the first significant technological advances made by humanity. Roasting is more primitive than boiling because it implies a direct contact between the food and a fire. But boiling reveals an advanced form of technology, since the process in this case is mediated by a pot. Boiling was the event that led to the institution of true culture—which implies the sharing of food in the community of others. At that point food takes on symbolic meanings.

To grasp how this may have come about, imagine being in a "Robinson Crusoe" situation—Robinson Crusoe being protagonist in the Daniel Defoe's (1660?–1731) famous novel, *The Life and Adventures of Robinson Crusoe*, which appeared in 1719. Although the novel is the fictional tale of a shipwrecked sailor, it is however based on the real adventures of a seaman, Alexander Selkirk, who had been marooned on an island off the coast of Chile. The novel chronicles Crusoe's ingenious attempts to overcome the hardships he faces on the island. Like Robinson Crusoe, imagine being abandoned on an isolated island in the middle of nowhere. Without the support and security of a social ambiance, your first instincts are to survive in any way that you can. In such a situation, your need for food and water takes precedence over all else. You will hardly be fussy about what to eat. In effect, you will eat whatever you find.

Now, suppose that after living alone on the island for a few years you discover other similarly abandoned individuals, each one on some remote part of the island, all of whom speak the same language as you do. Since there is strength in numbers, you all decide to join forces as a group. The group decides that it is wise to assign specific roles to separate individuals for the procurement, storage, and preparation of food. This division of labor assigns different roles to the individuals. As time passes, other "social contracts" and arrangements are made, all designed to ensure survival. The food eaten and its method of preparation will start at that point to take on meanings that transcend survival. The group may want to reserve a day of the week to eat a special type of food, cooked in a special way, to symbolize the gratitude each one feels (for having survived).

This vignette was meant to exemplify how food cooked for a community of eaters is bound to take on a meaning beyond that of "survival substance." When especially favorable food sources became available, early humans settled in permanent, year-round communities, learning to domesticate plants and animals for food, transportation, clothing, and other uses. With greater population concentrations and permanent living sites, cultural institutions developed, united by religious ceremonies and ritualistic food exchanges. These early hunting-gathering societies soon developed complex belief systems with regard to the supernatural world, and the behaviors of spirits and gods. Food thus became a part of ritual and a source of symbolism. To this day, food invariably is a primary constituent of all kinds of ceremonies and rituals, from feasts (weddings, Bar Mitzvahs, etc.) to simple social gatherings. We schedule "breakfast," "lunch," and "dinner" events on a daily basis. Indeed, we plan our days around meals. Even going out on a common date would be virtually unthinkable without some eating component associated with this courtship ritual (ranging from the popcorn eaten at movie theaters to the elaborate meals consumed at trendy restaurants).

FOOD AS SYMBOLISM

Let's now look at some specific examples of food symbolism. Take, for example, bread. We talk of the *bread of life*, of *earning one's bread*, and so on because, as in many other cultures, bread is a symbol for life. The word *companion*, incidentally, comes from Latin and means literally the person "with whom we share bread." As Margaret Visser (1992: 2–3) aptly points out:

> This is true even in our own day, when people eat far less bread than they used to, and when bread comes to us from a factory, bleached, squishy, ready-cut (so much for "breaking bread"), wrapped in plastic or cellophane. Yet we still expect to have bread on hand at every meal, as background, as completion, as dependable comforter and recompense for any stress or disappointment the rest of the meal might occasion. Bread is for us a kind of successor to the motherly breast, and it has been over the centuries responsible for billions of sighs of satisfaction.

The probable reason for the association of bread with life may be the fact that it is one of the oldest foods eaten and cooked by humans. Prehistoric people made flat bread by mixing grain meal with water and baking the resulting dough on rocks that they had heated. Historians believe the Egyptians learned to make yeast bread around 2600 BC. The ancient Greeks learned bread-making from the Egyptians and later taught the method to the Romans. By the first century AD, the Romans passed it on to people in many parts of Europe.

Many of the symbolic meanings of food derive from accounts of human origins. The story of Adam and Eve in the Western Bible, for instance, revolves around the eating of a forbidden fruit. The representation of this fruit as an apple came in medieval pictorial representations of the Eden scene. Since then, the Biblical symbolism of the apple as "forbidden knowledge" continues to resonate in our culture. This is why the apple tree symbolizes the "tree of knowledge"; why the "Apple" computer company has probably chosen this fruit for its company name and logo, and so on.

The discovery and cultivation of the apple dates back to 6500 BC in Asia Minor. Ramses II of Egypt cultivated apples in orchards along the Nile in the thirteenth century BC. The Ancient Greeks also cultivated apple trees from the seventh century BC onwards. They designated the apple "the golden fruit," since in Greek mythology the apple was given to Hera from the Garden of the Hesperides as a wedding present when she married Zeus.

As another example of food symbolism, consider lamb meat, which is a particularly important Easter food in central and eastern European countries. It is eaten at this time period of the liturgical year because it represents Jesus and relates His death to that of the lamb sacrificed on the first Passover. This is why Christians traditionally refer to Jesus as "the Lamb of God." In many homes, a lamb-shaped cake also decorates the table at Easter. Many Eastern Orthodox Christians even hang pictures of the Easter lamb in their homes.

Similar historical accounts can be sketched for virtually any of the traditional foods we continue to eat today. Symbolism is also the reason why the meat of certain animals is not eaten by the people of certain cultures. And it is also the reason for fasting. Fasting is one of a number of rites in which physical activities are reduced or suspended, resulting in a state of quiescence symbolically comparable to death, or to the state preceding birth. Fasts have been part of fertility rites since prehistoric times.

Closely associated with fasts to induce fertility are fasts intended to avert catastrophe or to serve as penance for sin. Among the peoples of the Old World, the Assyrians and the Babylonians observed fasts as a form of penance. Among Jews, too, fasting as a form of penitence and purification is observed annually on the Day of Atonement, Yom Kippur. The fast observed by Muslims during the month of Ramadan is an expression of atonement. The early Christians associated fasting with penitence and purification. Although most Protestant churches retained fasting after the Reformation in the sixteenth century, stricter Protestants such as the Puritans condemned traditional fasts. The Orthodox Church observes fasts rigorously. Native North Americans hold tribal fasts to avert impending disasters. Political fasting, known as "hunger striking," has also been employed as a political weapon ever since Mohandas Gandhi, leader of the struggle for India's freedom, used it effectively in the early and mid-1900s.

The counterpart to fasting is indulging in food. One tradition based on indulging is *carnival*, which in Christian traditions consists of feasting and merrymaking just before Lent. The Mardi Gras in New Orleans is a famous American carnival. From this tradition the modern concept of a carnival as a form of outdoor amusement that consists of exhibits, games, rides, and shows gradually developed.

THE EDIBLE AND THE NON-EDIBLE

Recall the unpleasant and difficult situation into which you were projected above. The fact that in our culture rabbits are defined as "household companions" forces us to perceive cooked rabbit meat as "inedible." On the other hand, in our culture bovine meat (beef steaks, hamburgers, etc.), lamb meat, and poultry meat are eaten routinely, with few negative perceptions and gustatory reactions. In India, however, a cow is considered by religious tradition to be sacred and, therefore, to be inedible. Anglo-American culture does not classify foxes or dogs as edible food items, but the former is reckoned a delicacy in Russia, and the latter a delicacy in China. And the list could go on and on.

Historically, the ancient Romans were the ones who had domesticated the rabbit, which flourished throughout their empire as a source of food. In sixteenth-century England, rabbits were prized instead for their fur. So, they were bred selectively in order to enhance their rich coats. In the nineteenth century, England passed strict game laws prohibiting rabbit hunting. By the turn of the twentieth century, rabbits were redefined in Anglo-American culture as household animals. The reinforcement of the anthropomorphic connotations that the rabbit has since taken on can be seen in the popularity of fictional rabbit characters (*Bugs Bunny*, the *Easter Bunny*, *Benjamin Bunny*) that have become a part of the mythology of childhood.

Edibility is more a product of Culture than of Nature. Outside of those that have a demonstrably harmful effect on the human organism, the species of flora and fauna that are considered to be edible or inedible are very much the result of history and tradition. We cannot get nourishment from eating tree bark, grass, or straw. But we certainly could get it from eating frogs, ants, earthworms, silkworms, lizards, and snails. Most people in our culture would, however, respond with disgust at the thought of eating such potential food items. However, there are cultures where they are not only eaten for nourishment, but also as part of symbolic traditions. Our expression *to develop a taste* for some "foreign" food reveals how closely tied edibility is to cultural perception. Left alone on that hypothetical Robinson Crusoe island described above, the question would certainly not be one of "taste," but of "survival" at any taste.

So close is the association between food and culture, that it is used commonly and stereotypically as a template for evaluating other people and other cultures. People perceive gustatory differences in cuisine as fundamental differences in worldview and lifestyle—as differences between "us" and "them." It is interesting to note that when people come to accept the cuisine of others as not only tasty but as a delicacy, the culture of the food-makers concomitantly takes on greater importance.

FOOD CODES

Food codes, like all other kinds of social codes, are regulatory systems—they regulate what kinds of food are eaten, when they are eaten, who is allowed to eat them, and so on and so forth. Predictably, these vary considerably from culture to culture (Goode 1992: 236–245). Here are a few examples:

- The adult !Kung Bushmen of the Kalahari Desert in southern Africa never eat the scavenged contents of a bird's nest, but will use it to make soup for their children.
- In traditional Chinese households, the eldest eat first, followed by the next generation, on down to the youngest.
- At certain intervals, the richest members of the Kwakiutl society of the Pacific Northwest put on a lavish feast during which they give away material gifts as a sign of bonding with all the members of the society.
- At matrimonial ceremonies throughout the world, specific kinds of codes may dictate the organization of parts of the ceremony (e.g., the wedding party normally sits apart from the invited guests).

Above all else, food codes dictate how eating events are organized, including:

- the order in which dishes are presented
- what combinations can be served in tandem
- how the foods are to be placed on the table
- who has preference in being served
- who must show deference
- who does the speaking and who the listening
- who sits where
- what topics of conversation are appropriate

These can be seen to be relevant to all kinds of eating events, but particularly so the dinner invitation. As Visser (1991: 107) remarks, "dinner invitations can be fraught with hope and danger, and dinner parties are dramatic events at which decisions can be made and important relationships initiated, tested, or broken."

Eating events are so crucial to the establishment and maintenance of social relations and harmony that there exists virtually no culture that does not assign an area of the domestic abode to eating functions and ceremonies. All cultures, moreover, have a discrete set of table rituals and manners that are inculcated into the members of the culture from birth. If you do not know the *table-manner code* of a certain culture, then you will have to learn it in order to continue living in that culture without censure and disapprobation. Let's take a concrete example. If you have never eaten spaghetti before, then you will have to learn that the "correct" way is to eat it with a fork if you find yourself in Italy. Incidentally, in nineteenth-century Naples, where the modern-day version of this dish comes from, people ate spaghetti with their hands by raising each string of pasta in the hand, throwing back the head, and lowering the string into the mouth without slurping. Today, the correct manner of eating spaghetti is to wind it around a fork in small amounts and place in the mouth. Eating it in any other way would be a breach of the relevant table-manner code.

Table-manner codes clearly involve the use of flatware. Knives, spoons, forks, and other specialized implements for eating and serving food have until recent times been the privilege of the aristocracy. In Egypt, Greece, and Rome knives and spoons of the aristocracy were made of precious materials, including silver and gold, and were sometimes decorated. The Romans also possessed skewers that were forerunners of the fork. From the Middle Ages until the Renaissance, the knife remained the principal table utensil. Forks came into common table use in Italy in the 1500s. At the same time spoons made the transition from kitchen utensils to table items. From that time onward, flatware came to be used by all peoples of all classes. During the nineteenth century numerous other items of flatware were created, such as teaspoons, butter knives, and salad forks.

FAST FOOD

Expressions such as *fast living*, *the fast lane*, and the like tell us an awful lot about the way we live today in our consumerist culture. Everything seems to be "moving too fast," as the expression goes. Even the way we eat has become "fast." Since the 1960s, the "fast food" business has become a multi-billion dollar industry. Why has this happened? The sociologist or the psychologist would look for an answer in some social or behavioral pattern. The semiotician would look for it in the meanings associated with fast food eateries.

The semiotic probe into the nature of fast food would, thus, start by seeking to determine why people go to fast-food restaurants. Evidently, people do so to be with family or friends, because the food is affordable and the atmosphere is generally congenial. Indeed, some people today probably feel more "at home" at such restaurants than in their own households. This is, in fact, the semiotic key to unlocking what contemporary fast food restaurants are all about.

Consider the case of McDonald's. The first hamburger stand was opened up in 1940, in a drive-in near Pasadena, California, by movie theater co-owners Richard and Maurice McDonald. The modern-day restaurant chain was founded in 1955 by Raymond A. Kroc, a distributor of machines for making milk shakes. Kroc learned of a hamburger stand that had eight of the machines. He visited the stand, which was called McDonald's, and was impressed with how quickly customers were served. Kroc persuaded the stand's owners to let him start a chain of fast-service restaurants of the same name. Kroc opened the first McDonald's restaurant in Des Plaines, Illinois, in 1955. It is significant to note that this event coincided with the rise of youth culture in the 1950s. As a consequence, the number of McDonald's eateries began to proliferate, as young people flocked to it to be together. By 1961 Kroc had established more than 200 stands, building McDonald's into a powerful business.

But the astute Kroc knew that in order to survive in the long run, he needed to attract adults as well. Aware that fewer and fewer families had the time to prepare meals within the household, Kroc wisely decided to change the image of McDonald's into a place where the family could eat together. His plan worked beyond expectations. Families started en masse to eat at McDonald's more and more often for lunch and/or dinner. The golden arches logo reflected the new image perfectly. Arches reverberate with mythic symbolism—they beckon good people to march through them where they can expect a world of cleanliness, friendliness, hospitality, and family values. Kroc made sure that McDonald's was, in fact, run like a religion. From the menu to the uniforms, he exacted and imposed standardization, in the same way that religions do.

Kroc's advertising campaigns reinforced this new image effectively, entrenching it throughout society. McDonald's was a place that would "do it all for you," as one of their slogans phrased it, keeping family members united at meal times. Many outlets even installed miniature amusement parks in them for children. Kids meals were introduced throughout the restaurant chain. As a family-oriented company, McDonald's started sponsoring Ronald McDonald House Charities, which operates hundreds of Ronald McDonald Houses worldwide in which the families of critically ill children may stay when the young patients undergo medical treatment away from their homes. Over a few decades McDonald's had, in effect, turned fast food into family food.

Incidentally, the origin of the Ronald McDonald clown is informative. The McDonald's Corporation's first mascot was a winking little chef named Speedee, who had a head in the shape of a hamburger. The character was later renamed Archie McDonald. In 1960 a Washington D.C. franchisee, named Oscar Goldstein, decided to sponsor "Bozo's Circus," a local children's television show. Bozo's appearance at the Washington restaurant drew a large crowd. When the local NBC station canceled the show, the franchisee hired its star to invent a new clown who would make restaurant appearances. An ad agency designed the clown's outfit and the rhyming name of Ronald McDonald was given to the clown.

CONCLUDING REMARKS

The semiotic investigation of food brings out how Nature (the biosphere) and Culture (the semiosphere) intersect constantly in human life. At a denotative level, food means exactly what Nature has decreed it to be—survival substance. However, in cultural settings, food items become signs that assume specific kinds of meanings. Cultures vary widely as to the types and the degree of meaning they assign to food and eating. But throughout the world, food is as much symbolic substance as it is survival substance.

Objects

Electronic aids, particularly domestic computers, will help the inner migration, the opting out of reality. Reality is no longer going to be the stuff out there, but the stuff inside your head. It's going to be commercial and nasty at the same time.

J. G. Ballard (1930–)

PRELIMINARY REMARKS

In human life, there is virtually no object or artifact that is not imbued with meaning. Indeed, objects are signs that evoke a broad range of meanings across the world's cultures. Although the terms *object* and *artifact* are often used interchangeably, they are distinguished in both semiotics and archaeology as follows: objects are things found in the environment, artifacts are things made by humans. This distinction, however, is not necessary here, since the purpose is to focus on the meanings that material things in general embody.

In this chapter, therefore, our trek through the landscape of the semiosphere takes us through the domain of objects. Like all the other dimensions and components of culture, the meanings of objects are coded with the same kinds of properties that characterize, say, clothing, bodily presentation, language, food, etc. Studying why people make things, how they design their objects, what role these play in the life of a culture, is another important aspect of contemporary semiotics.

OBJECTS

The objects that are found in a culture are hardly perceived to be meaningless "things" by members of the culture. They cohere into a system of signification that mirrors, in microcosm, the meaning structures of the entire culture. This is why archaeologists reconstruct ancient societies on the basis of the artifacts they discover at a site. The jewelry, clothes, furniture, ornaments, tools, toys that they find there are signs that allow them to reconstruct the society's traditions, values, rituals to varying degrees of completeness. Artifacts provide truly valuable clues as to what an extinct culture was probably like. Especially significant are those that were thought to possess mysterious powers. The symbolism of objects, in fact, was the basis of the ancient craft of alchemy, defined as the art of transmuting materials that lasted well into the medieval ages and continues to have some adherents to this day. The principal activity of the alchemists was the search for the "philosopher's stone"—popularized as a unique object by the highly popular Harry Potter movies of the early 2000s—and the production of gold by artificial means. Gold meant (and continues to mean in many ways) power, deification, and immortality.

For the reasons just mentioned, archaeology can be defined as a semiotic study of objects and artifacts. It traces its roots to the Renaissance when antiquaries collected ancient artifacts and speculated about their significance. Near the end of the eighteenth century, Danish geological research led to the conception of the Stone, Bronze, and Iron ages. At the same time, Egyptian and Persian writing was deciphered. By the mid-nineteenth century, archaeology became a firmly-established science. Between World War I and World War II, many American archaeologists focused on local and regional areas. Significant work also occurred in Greece, Latin America, and Israel. At the same time, the development of the radiocarbon (carbon-14) dating method (1947) made archaeological conclusions more accurate.

The essence of archaeological method is semiotic. Archaeologists review ancient texts before they begin collecting data. They look for sites with undisturbed, layered deposits of artifacts that will allow them to establish a clear chronology, which will allow them, in turn, to reconstruct the cultural system of each layer. They then reconstruct cultural and ecological systems, because each artifact invariably indicates something about the culture and its ecosystem, reflecting activities during the period when humans occupied a site. Pots, for instance, reveal an awful lot of how early cultures cooked their food and, thus, organized their social systems. In the early Bronze Age (5000–2500 BC), several agricultural groups emerged, each with its own pottery style. Asian sites from the subsequent Iron Age show the emergence of state-level organization, iron tools, and new pottery types. In China, 500,000 year-old hearths probably represent the earliest evidence for the use of fire by humans.

There is a common belief throughout the world that objects are not only signs standing for conventional social meanings, but that they also possess some inner force above and beyond the physical. An extreme manifestation of this belief is referred to as *fetishism*—the conviction that some inanimate objects, known as *fetishes* (from Portuguese *feitiço* "artificial, charm," from Latin *facticius* "artificial"), are imbued with supernatural attributes. The fetish is typically a figure modeled or carved from clay, stone, wood, or some other material, resembling a deified animal or some sacred thing. Sometimes it is the animal itself, or a tree, river, rock, or place associated with it. In some societies belief in the powers of the fetish is so strong that fetishism develops into idolatry. In such cases, the belief system is referred to as an extreme form of *animism*—the view that spirits either inhabit or communicate with humans through material objects. The term *fetishism* has been applied in our culture to describe sexual urges and fantasies that persistently involve the use of objects by themselves or, at times, with a sexual partner. Common fetishes in our society are feet, shoes, and articles of intimate female apparel.

Animism is not limited to tribal or pre-modern cultures. On the contrary, it is alive and well even in modern cultures, whether or not people realize it. In addition to the fetishes that incite sexual urges or fantasies in some people, there are many behaviors and trends that surface in the world today that can only be explained as the manifest effects of a latent form of animism. In the 1970s, for example, American society went mad for "pet rocks." Many considered the fad a ploy foisted upon a gullible public spoiled by consumerism by a craft manufacturer, and thus simply a quick way to make money. But to a semiotician, that craze could not have been perpetrated in the first place, unless some signification force was at work—and that force was animism. The same animistic tendencies can be seen in the common view held by people that some objects are unexplainably magical. This is why, if they are lost, then impending danger is feared. If, however, they are found serendipitously—as for instance when one finds a "lucky penny"—then it is believed that the gods or Fortune will look auspiciously upon the finder.

Animism is evidence that people perceive certain objects as special kinds of signs. This is why objects of all kinds are preserved and why they have historical value—the making of one leading to the making of another and then to the making of yet another, and so on. Like works of art, objects are felt to be reflections of innate forms of thought that seek expression in real-world physical forms. Some objects are even perceived to be extensions of the Self. Consider, for instance, the automobile, which is experienced by many as an extension of the body and thus as a protective shell of the Self. In the public world of traffic, it creates a space around the physical body that is as inviolable as the body itself. Interestingly, but not unexpectedly, this perception is not confined to our culture. The anthropologist Basso (1990: 15–24) found that the Western Apache of east-central Arizona also perceive the car as a body, even going so far as to use the names of body parts to refer to analogous automobile parts: e.g., the hood is called a "nose," the headlights "eyes," the windshield "forehead," the area from the top of the windshield to the front bumper a "face," the front wheels "hands and arms," the rear wheels "feet," the items under the hood "innards," the battery a "liver," the electrical wiring "veins," the gas tank a "stomach," the distributor a "heart," the radiator a "lung," and the radiator hoses "intestines."

Animism is also latent in the perception of toys as childhood objects— recall, from chapter 7, the mass hysteria caused by Cabbage Patch dolls in 1983. Children have always played with objects—broom handles can be imagined to be swords, rocks can be imagined to be baseballs, and so on. But a toy is different. It is an adult-made object that is given to children according to social traditions. Dolls are particularly interesting in this regard because they are icons of the human figure. As early as 600 BC dolls were made with movable limbs and removable garments so as to reinforce their resemblance to human anatomy. Dolls have been found in the tombs of ancient Egyptian, Greek, and Roman children. Evidently the objective was to provide the children with a lifelike human form, so that they could play with someone in the afterlife.

Interestingly, in many societies dolls have similar metaphysical meanings. In the aboriginal Hopi culture of the United States, for instance, *kachina* dolls are given as sacred objects to children as part of fertility rites. In many Christian traditions, dolls have been used since the Middle Ages to represent the Holy Family in the Nativity scene, as part of Christmas observations. In Mexico, dolls representing Our Lady of Guadeloupe are ceremonially paraded every year. And in some cultures of the Caribbean, it is believed that one can cause physical or psychological damage to another person by doing something injurious to a doll constructed to resemble that person.

The commercialization of dolls as both fashion "models" and playthings for children can be traced to Germany in the early fifteenth century. Fashion dolls were made on purpose to model clothing of German women. Shortly thereafter, manufacturers in England, France, Holland, and Italy also began to manufacture dolls dressed in fashions typical of their respective locales. The more ornate ones were often used by rulers and courtiers as gifts. By the seventeenth century, however, simpler dolls, made of cloth or leather, were being used primarily as playthings by children.

During the eighteenth century, doll manufacturing became more sophisticated. The fashion dolls looked so lifelike that they were often used to illustrate clothing style trends and were sent from one country to another to display the latest fashions in miniature form. After the Industrial Revolution, fashion dolls became commonplace toys of little girls. By the early part of the twentieth century, it was assumed that all female children would want to play with dolls. Noteworthy design innovations in dolls manufactured between 1925 and World War II included sleeping eyes with lashes, dimples, open mouths with tiny teeth, fingers with nails, and latex-rubber dolls that could drink water and wet themselves. Since the 1950s, the association of lifelike dolls with female childhood has been entrenched further by both the quantity of doll types produced and their promotion in the media. Since their launch in 1959, the "Barbie" dolls, for instance, have become part of the experience of growing up for many little girls in North America. Incidentally, the Barbie dolls also started the trend of making fashionable clothing and accessories for dolls, thus enhancing their human iconicity even more.

TECHNOLOGY

The making of objects and artifacts with tools is known as technology. Technology has become a major force in human evolution. The great Canadian communications theorist Marshall McLuhan (1911–1980) claimed throughout his illustrious career that objects and tools are extensions of human anatomy and mentation. For instance, the telescope has extended the capacities of humans to see farther than their eyesight would otherwise permit; the wheel has extended the range and power of human locomotion; the computer has extended the speed and accuracy of logical thinking, and so on. The study of technology is thus a study in human evolution through the semiosphere, rather than the biosphere.

Technology is, more specifically, the general term used for describing the systematic processes by which human beings fashion objects and machines to increase their understanding of, and control over, the material environment. The term is derived from the Greek words *tekhne,* which refers to an "art" or "craft," and *logia,* meaning an "area of study," hence the meaning of technology as the "craft of object-making." Many historians of culture argue that technology has not only become an essential condition of advanced civilizations, but also a "force" that now has its own dynamism, and that does not respect geographical limits or social systems. Technology, in a phrase, is transforming our perception of the human condition permanently.

Early human sites have been found to contain axes, scrapers, knives, and other stone instruments indicating that the ax was used as a tool for making tools. This capacity for creating tools to make other tools distinguishes human beings from other animals, although there is some evidence of advanced tool-use among elephants (Chevalier-Skolnikoff and Liska 1993), which may serve as a form of adaptation enabling elephants to cope with parasites and weather changes.

The next major step in the history of technology was the control of fire. Besides the benefits of light and heat, fire was also used to bake clay pots that were used for cooking. Early peoples also learned to create objects out of copper and bronze. Eventually human societies shifted from nomadic hunting to the practice of agriculture. The early agricultural societies constructed stone buildings, used sickles to harvest grain, developed a primitive plowstick, and advanced their skills in metalworking. They also built two-wheeled carts for transportation. After 4000 BC, the first cities were built within walls for defense reasons and thus designed structurally for battle and conquest. Greece came to power through its skill in shipbuilding, allowing it to effectively carry out the colonization of the places strewn along the Mediterranean Sea. The Romans' skill at technology also allowed them to conquer and transform other civilizations. Using cement and the principle of the arch, Roman engineers built roads across their vast empire. They also built numerous arenas, aqueducts, sewers, and bridges. In the Middle Ages, a heavier plow with wheels, a horizontal plowshare, and a moldboard were developed, enhancing the ability of societies to provide a semi-permanent source of alimentation to larger and larger agglomerations of people. One of the most important inventions of medieval times was the windmill. This made it possible to increase grain and timber production. Two other medieval inventions, the clock and the printing press, also influenced all aspects of human life. The printing press set off a social revolution, as the written word became available to a wider audience. Intellectual life was no longer the exclusive domain of church and court, as literacy became a "commodity" for virtually everyone.

The Industrial Revolution introduced the first factories in 1740, concentrating on textile production. Factory workers were not required to be artisans and did not necessarily have to possess craft skills. Thus the work of men, women, and children became just another commodity in the production process. Engineering achievements of the era included the development of telegraphic communications and railroads, which connected cities with one another. In the late nineteenth century the light bulb was invented by Thomas Edison (1847–1931). Shortly thereafter, every industrial nation started generating electric power for lighting and many of the other devices and activities based on electricity that now define modern life—such as radio, motion pictures, television, and so on. The development of computers and transistors and the accompanying trend towards miniaturization over the last few decades continues to have a profound effect on society. The opportunities it offers are enormous, but so are the possibilities for invasion of privacy and for unemployment caused by automated systems. The growth of technology since the Renaissance has, in a word, had profound consequences on the evolution of the semiosphere, creating the conditions for the coalescence of cultures into a worldwide global culture.

The event that made globalization a possibility in the first place was, no doubt, the invention of print technology in the fifteenth century and the subsequent widespread use of the book to codify knowledge. The forerunners of books were the clay tablets, impressed with a stylus, used by the Sumerians, Babylonians, and other peoples of ancient Mesopotamia. These were followed by the scrolls of the ancient Egyptians, Greeks, and Romans, which consisted of sheets of papyrus, a paper-like material made from a pith of reeds, formed into a continuous strip and rolled around a stick. The strip, with the text written with a reed pen in narrow, closely spaced columns on one side, was unrolled as it was read. Later, during the fourth to first centuries BC, a long roll was subdivided into a number of shorter rolls, stored together in one container. In the first century AD, this was replaced by the rectangular codex, the direct ancestor of the modern book. The codex, used at first by the Greeks and Romans for business accounts and schooling, was a small, ringed notebook consisting of two or more wooden tablets covered with wax, which could be marked with a stylus, smoothed over, and reused many times. It was easier for readers to find their place in a codex, or to refer ahead or back. In the Middle Ages, codices were used primarily in the observance of the Christian liturgy. Indeed, the word *codex* is part of the title of many ancient handwritten books on topics related to the Bible.

The spread of books made literacy a possibility for one and all, thus changing the evolutionary course of human cognition radically. Literacy introduces a level of abstraction in human thought that forces people to separate the maker of knowledge from the knowledge made. And this in turn leads to the perception that knowledge can exist on its own, spanning time and distance. This is precisely what is meant by the term *objectivity*: knowledge unconnected to a knower. Before literacy became widespread, humans lived primarily in oral cultures, based on the spoken word. The human voice cannot help but convey emotion, overtly or implicitly. In such cultures, the knower and what he or she knows are seen typically as inseparable. On the other hand, in literate cultures, the written page, with its edges, margins, and sharply defined characters organized in neatly layered rows or columns, induces a linear-rational way of thinking in people. In such cultures, the knowledge contained in writing is perceived as separable from the maker of that knowledge primarily because the maker of the written text is not present during the reading of the text. The spread of print literacy since the Renaissance has, *ipso facto*, been the determining factor in the "objectification" of knowledge.

Marshall McLuhan characterized the world of knowledge shaped by print literacy as the "Gutenberg Galaxy" after the European inventor of the printing press, the German printer Johannes Gutenberg (1395?–1468?). Through books, newspapers, pamphlets, and posters, McLuhan argued, the printed word became, after the fifteenth century, the primary means for the propagation of knowledge and ideas. More importantly, given the fact that books could cross political boundaries, the printing press set in motion the globalization of culture. Paradoxically, however, as McLuhan (1962) also observed, this process did not simultaneously lead to the elimination of tribalism. On the contrary, he claimed that it was impossible to take the tribe out of the human being, so to speak, no matter how advantageous a global culture would seem to be. McLuhan insisted that tribal tendencies resonate continually within modern-day people. The impersonal global culture, on the other hand, is really an abstraction. Tribalism is also a means by which people cope with impersonal social systems. It is manifest in the formation of subcultures and parallel cultures within cultural mainstreams.

COMPUTERS

Objects are extensions of ourselves. Bicycles and cars extend the human foot, weapons our hands, nails, and teeth, clocks our internal rhythms, houses our body's heat-control system, clothing our skin, the computer our central nervous system, and so on. These extensions are real and tangible. This extensive process can be called, simply, *objectification*. Today, this process is particularly evident in the role that computers have come to assume.

The first general-purpose all-electronic computer was built in 1946 at the University of Pennsylvania by the American engineer John Presper Eckert, Jr., and the American physicist John William Mauchly. Called ENIAC, for *Electronic Numerical Integrator and Computer*, the device contained 18,000 vacuum tubes and could perform several hundred multiplications per minute. ENIAC's program was wired into its processor, so that reprogramming required manual rewiring. The development of transistor technology and its use in computers in the late 1950s marked the advent of smaller, faster, and more versatile machines than those that were built with vacuum tubes. Because transistors use much less power and have a much longer life, they introduced "second-generation computers." Late in the 1960s the integrated circuit was invented, making it possible for many transistors to be fabricated on one silicon board with interconnecting wires plated in place. In the mid-1970s with the introduction of large-scale integrated circuits with many thousands of interconnected transistors etched into a single silicon board, the modern-day personal computer was just around the corner.

The computer is one of humanity's greatest technological achievements. It has had a definite impact on the human semiosphere, parallel to the one that the printing press had five centuries ago. It all started with the advent of the personal computer (PC), which can be traced to the *Apple II* in 1977 created by American computer designers Steven Jobs and Stephen Wozniak. It had a color video display and a keyboard that made the computer easy to use. Jobs and Wozniak later founded Apple Computer Corporation. Their initial plan was to manufacture PCs to run games software for people to pit their logical skills against those of software programmers. In 1984 the first Apple Macintosh was manufactured. That machine featured a graphical user interface (GUI), as mentioned in chapter 2. The Macintosh GUI combined icons with windows (boxes that contain an open file or program). The Macintosh user interface made computers easy and fun to use, eliminating the need to type in complex commands. They were characterized, appropriately, as "user-friendly."

PCs have since become as intrinsic to the system of everyday life as automobiles and TV sets. PCs now enable artists to create images. Musicians use them for composing and recording music. Businesses keep track of their finances and forecast performance using PCs. Journalists, students, instructors, and many more professionals can now compose their verbal texts on portable PCs and electronically communicate them to others from remote locations. Many people work at home and communicate with fellow workers with their PCs. PCs can also be used to interface with worldwide communication networks in order to find information on any subject.

The computer has also introduced a new form of text-making and text-usage known as *hypertextuality*. Reading a printed page is, at the level of the signifier (i.e., of deciphering the actual signs on the page), a linear process, since it consists in decoding the individual words and their combinations in sentences in the framework of a specific signification system (a novel, a dictionary, etc.). Information on any specific sign in the text must be sought out physically: for example, if one wants to follow up on a reference in the text, one has to do it by consulting other printed texts or by asking certain people. This is also what must be done when one wants to determine the meaning of a word found in a text. Dictionaries serve this very purpose.

The computer screen has greatly facilitated such tasks, by introducing a hypertextual dimension. The term *hypertext* was coined in 1965 to describe an interlinked system of texts in which a user can jump from one to another. This was made possible with the invention of *hyperlinks*—portions of a document that can be linked to other related documents. By clicking on the hyperlink, the user is immediately connected to the document specified by the link. Web pages are designed in this way, being written in a simple computer language called HTML (Hypertext Markup Language). A series of instruction "tags" are inserted into pieces of ordinary text to control the way the page looks and these can be manipulated when viewed with a Web browser. Tags determine the typeface or act as instructions to display images, and they can be used to link up with other Web pages.

As opposed to the linear structure of paper-produced texts such as books, hypertextuality permits the user to browse through related topics, regardless of the presented order of the topics. The links are often established both by the author of a hypertext document and by the user, depending on the intent of the document. For example, "navigating" among the links to the word *language* in an article contained on a website or a CD-ROM might lead the user to the *International Phonetic Alphabet*, the science of *linguistics*, samples of languages, etc. Hypertextuality was introduced as a regular feature of PCs in 1987 when Apple began distributing a new program called *Hypercard* with its new PCs. This was the first program to provide a linking function permitting navigation among files of computer print text and graphics by clicking keywords or icons. By 1988 compact disc players were built into computers, introducing CD-ROMs into the computer market.

Interpreting a text involves three types of cognitive processes. First, it entails the ability to access the actual contents of the text at the level of the signifier, that is, the ability to decode its words, images, etc. Only someone possessing knowledge of the codes (verbal and nonverbal) with which the text has been assembled can accomplish this. If it is in Finnish, then in order to derive an interpretant (a specific kind of meaning) from it, the decoder must know the Finnish language, the conceptual metaphors that characterize Finnish modes of speaking, and so on and so forth. The second process entails knowledge of how the $X = Y$ relation unfolds in the specific text, that is, of how the text (X) generates its meanings (Y) through a series of internal and external signification processes. This requires some knowledge on the part of the interpreter of cultural codes other than the strictly verbal and nonverbal ones used to physically create the text. This is, in fact, the level of the signified that is alluded to in the question: *What does it mean?* Finally, various contextual factors enter into the entire process to constrain the interpretant. This will determine what the individual interpreter will get from the text. When viewed globally, these processes suggest that text interpretation is, de facto, hypertextual, because it involves being able to navigate among the three processes simultaneously. In effect, the physical structure of hypertextuality on the computer screen may constitute a kind of "mirror model" of how people process all kinds of texts.

THE DIGITAL GALAXY

In the 1960s, at the same time that computers were becoming faster, more-powerful, and smaller, networks were being developed for interconnecting them. The Advanced Research Projects Agency (ARPA) of the US Department of Defense, along with researchers working on military projects at research centers and universities across the country, developed a network called the ARPANET for sharing data and mainframe computer processing time over specially equipped telephone lines and satellite links. Used at first for military purposes, the ARPANET became the first functional major electronic-mail network right after the National Science Foundation connected universities and nonmilitary research sites to it. ARPANET was subsequently renamed the Internet—a term conveying that it was designed as an "interconnected" network serving many different functions, not just military ones.

Today, the Internet is the largest and most prevalent computer network in the world. Commercial online service providers—such as America Online, CompuServe, and the Microsoft Network—sell Internet access to individual computer users and companies. Smaller networks for specific utilization are also available. People can now use computers to design graphics and full-motion video, send electronic mail, make airline or hotel reservations, search for all kinds of information, play games, listen to radio, watch some television programs, and even visit "electronic rooms" to chat with other people over the World Wide Web. In the history of human communications, no other device has made it possible for so many people to interact with each other virtually instantaneously, irrespective of the distances between them. We no longer live in the Gutenberg Galaxy (as McLuhan called the world dependent upon print technology for encoding and storing information and knowledge). Rather, we now live in a "Digital Galaxy." Documents and programs can now be downloaded so easily that with some manipulation any text can easily be appropriated and used as if it were one's own. The Gutenberg Galaxy made the notion of authorship a critical one; the Digital Galaxy is leading to a fundamental reevaluation of this very notion.

Until the early 1990s, most information on the Internet consisted only of printed text. The introduction of the World Wide Web (WWW) made it possible to include graphics, animation, video, and sound. The WWW contains tens of millions of documents, databases, bulletin boards, and electronic publications, such as newspapers, books, and magazines in all media forms (print, visual, etc.). The miasma of information it contains made it immediately obvious to Internet users, shortly after its introduction, that appropriate technology was needed for them to be able to locate specific types of information. This led to the development of *uniform resource locator* (URL) technology. Using software that connects to the Internet—called *navigation* or *browser* software—a computer operator can select a URL that contains information he or she wishes to access. The computer then contacts that address, making the information available to the operator. With millions of separate URLs, classification and indexing have clearly become critical Internet functions. Indexing services— located on the Internet itself—enable users to search for specific information by entering the topic that interests them. The URL of the main Web page for the American White House, for instance, is http://www.whitehouse.gov/. The http indicates that the document is on the WWW. The next part, www.whitehouse.gov, is the hostname and identifies the computer, www. The .gov extension identifies the computer as belonging to the United States government. Next comes the path, or chain of directories, and finally the document name.

There is no question that the Internet has already changed the way we live. A new breed of worker, called the "teleworker," has already emerged. He or she works at his screen anywhere he or she desires to—not in any specific location, such as in an office room in a building. The computer has also become *the* primary reference tool in most areas of study, research, information, and entertainment. Unlike published print materials, the information on the Internet can be updated constantly. All the major newspapers now have an online version of their text. All kinds of music companies now also have their sites to which access will guarantee music content. Cyberspace is fast becoming the only kind of space to which some people will resort to interact socially and intellectually.

But perhaps the most radical influence the Digital Galaxy has had on human intellectual and social life is the perpetuation of the process that has been called objectification in this chapter. In movies, TV programs, comic books, and other media, it is now a common thing to find robots, cyborgs, and other "intelligent" machines featured as heroes or villains, and possessing qualities that the heroes and villains of myth and legend were once portrayed as embodying. The representation of machines as having human qualities has been a popular one in all media for some time. But the interest in intelligent machines is not limited to the media. In certain sciences of the mind, such as artificial intelligence (AI), the question is now raised with all sincerity if truly intelligent computers can be built to live alongside humans. This is why specific kinds of computers are being constructed with the sole purpose of duplicating the complex functions of human thought. But, amid all this "cyber excitement," it is misguided, in my view, to assume a similarity between human and machine intelligence. The former grew out of lived experience and developed through historical forces; the latter has been literally invented by humans themselves.

The belief of AI researchers that computers can become truly intelligent is not something that has crystallized in the Digital Galaxy. It is, as a matter of fact, an ancient one. In some Sumerian and Babylonian myths, for instance, there are descriptions of inanimate matter being brought to life. The AI version derives its impetus, however, not from myth but from the mathematical concept of machine, which traces its roots to the work of the great mathematician Alan Turing (1912–1954). Turing showed that four simple operations on a tape—*move to the right, move to the left, erase the slash, print the slash*—allowed a computer to execute any kind of program that could be expressed in a binary code (as, for example, a code of blanks and slashes). As long as one could specify the steps involved in carrying out a task and translating them into the binary code, the *Turing machine*—now called a *computer program*—would be able to scan the tape containing the code and carry out the instructions.

Although Turing himself was well aware of the limitations of his notion, openly admitting that it could never come close to emulating the more spiritual aspects of human consciousness, to many AI theorists his insights suggested that humans too were, in effect, special kinds of protoplasmic machines, whose cognitive states, emotions, and social behaviors were not only representable in the form of computer programs, but that mechanical machines themselves could eventually be built to think, feel, and socialize like human beings. For such scientists, therefore, consciousness is really no more than a consequence of the workings of a biological program that allows individual human machines to express and modify the emotions of their brains and the impulses of their bodies.

The AI movement is really a contemporary outgrowth of the "Cartesian project" that ushered in the modern era of science. According to Descartes, all human problems, whether of science, law, morality, or politics could eventually be solved by developing a universal method of philosophy based on the laws of mathematics. This project seemed realizable when the engineer Claude Shannon demonstrated that information of any kind, in both animal and mechanical systems of communication, could be described in terms of binary choices between equally probable alternatives (see chapter 15). By the 1950s, enthusiasm was growing over the possibility that computers could eventually carry out human thinking processes, since the brain was thought to be really no more than a Turing machine operating on the basis of its own kind of biological binary code. By the 1960s, phenomenal advances in computer technology seemed to make the Cartesian project a reality.

But true intelligence by machines has never been realized, nor will it be realized in the future, because it is beyond the capacities of machines to feel, imagine, invent, dream, construct rituals, art works, and the like. These are derivatives of bodily and psychic experiences. AI theories and models of consciousness can perhaps give us precise information about the nature of the formal properties of mental states, but they tell us nothing about how these states were brought about in the first place.

In a fundamental sense, the AI movement is a product of metaphorical thinking: *the mind = a machine* (chapter 6). This is not to imply that technological discoveries are purely imaginary. On the contrary, technology is a product of human ingenuity; metaphor is a cognitive strategy for understanding the products of that ingenuity. Indeed, such metaphorical thinking extends across the various "media" we have invented to communicate ideas. Here are some examples:

From Print Media:

- He has a great *character*.
- I cannot *read* your mind.
- Make a mental *note* of what I just said.
- It is time to turn over a new *leaf*.
- His life is an open *book*.
- You must start over *tabula rasa*.
- Her story is *written* in my heart.

From Electronic, Photographic, and Cinematic Media:

- I just had a *flashback*.
- What mental *picture* do these words evoke?
- My mind is out of *focus*.
- He has a *photographic* memory.
- I am going over what you said in *slow motion*.

From the Computer Medium:

- He is *hard-wired* for action.
- My mental *software* no longer works.
- I can't quite *retrieve* that memory.
- I haven't yet *processed* what he said.
- Did your *store* away what I told you?

Such expressions suggest that we perceive our media as extensions of our mental selves. More importantly, they reveal that we know virtually nothing about the mind and, therefore, we are forced to resort to metaphor in order to fill in the signification gap. That is something, obviously, that some AI scientists have yet to realize.

POP ART

There is one other manifestation of objectification that merits some discussion here by way of conclusion. In a society where objects of all kinds are being produced for mass consumption, there arises an incessant craving for new objects. The semiotician Roland Barthes (1915–1980) referred to this excessive form of objectification as "neomania" (Barthes 1957). To encourage the acquisition of objects, obsolescence is, in fact, regularly built into the marketing strategies of a company, so that the same product can be sold again and again under new guises. This is also why advertisers rely on a handful of Epicurean themes—happiness, youthfulness, success, status, luxury, fashion, beauty—to peddle their products.

Neomania has even spawned its own art forms and movements. One of these, called *pop art* (short for *populist art*), emerged shortly after World War II. It was inspired directly by the mass production and consumption of objects. For pop artists, the factory, supermarket, and garbage can become their art school. But despite its apparent absurdity, many people loved pop art, no matter how controversial or crass it appeared to be. In a certain sense, the pop art movement bestowed on common people the assurance that art was for mass consumption, not just for an élite class of cognoscenti. Some artists duplicated beer bottles, soup cans, comic strips, road signs, and similar objects in paintings, collages, and sculptures; others simply incorporated the objects themselves into their works. Using images and sounds that reflected the materialism and vulgarity of modern consumerist culture, the first pop artists sought to provide a view of reality that was more immediate and relevant than that of past art. They wanted the observer to respond directly to the object, rather than to the skill and viewpoint of the artist.

The pop art movement surfaced in the 1940s and 1950s, when painters like Robert Rauschenberg (1925–) and Jasper Johns (1930–) strove to close the gap between traditional art and mass culture. Rauschenberg constructed collages from household objects such as quilts and pillows, Johns from American flags and bull's-eye targets. The first full-fledged pop art work was *Just What Is It That Makes Today's Home So Different, So Appealing?* (1956, private collection) by the British artist Richard Hamilton. In this satiric collage of two ludicrous figures in a living room, the pop art hallmarks of crudeness and irony are emphasized.

Pop art developed rapidly during the 1960s, as painters started to focus their attention on brand-name commercial products, producing garish sculptures of hamburgers and other fast-food items, blown-up frames of comic strips, or theatrical events staged as art objects. Pop artists also appropriated the techniques of mass production. Rauschenberg and Johns had already abandoned individual, titled paintings in favor of large series of works, all depicting the same objects. In the early 1960s the American Andy Warhol (1928–1987) carried the idea a step further by adopting the mass-production technique of silk-screening, turning out hundreds of identical prints of Coca-Cola bottles, Campbell's soup cans, and other familiar subjects, including identical three-dimensional Brillo boxes (see chapter 4).

But the rage over pop art has, finally, subsided at the start of the twenty-first century. Along with pop music, blockbuster movies, bestseller novels, television programs, fashion shows, and most commercial products, it was destined to become quickly obsolete. It was both a product and a victim of neomania.

CONCLUDING REMARKS

Objects are hardly just that—objects. In the human semiosphere they become signs and sign systems. In a psychological sense they are extensions of human physical, sensory, and intellectual qualities. But in an almost completely objectified world today, something strange is happening. As digital technologies continue to advance the possibility of global communication "on the spot," and as electronic devices and satellite systems allow people to break down barriers of nationhood, there is a strong desire in people to live in the "real" world. Indeed, the more the computer is used to conduct everyday affairs, the more people seem to resort to traditional forms of meaning-making and interaction. The paradox of everyday life in the Digital Galaxy is that it engenders both "globalism" and "tribalism" at once.

Space and Buildings

We shape our buildings: thereafter they shape us.

Sir Winston Churchill (1874–1965)

PRELIMINARY REMARKS

Imagine being introduced to a stranger of the opposite sex. As part of the social contact ritual, you know enough to extend your hand to initiate a typical handshake. Now, how close will you stand to the stranger? Will you hold on to the person's hand delicately or with force for a relatively short or for a protracted period of time? Will you touch any other parts of his or her body to execute the greeting? Without going into a detailed analysis of this situation, there's no doubt that you will know exactly the answer to all these questions. You certainly would not stand very close to your interlocutor, for that would constitute a breach of "personal space." You would also not touch any other part of his or her body—arms, face, etc. The reason for the predictability of these answers is the fact that contact rituals are regulated by *spatial* codes.

Like clothing, food, and objects, the spaces people maintain when interacting, and the spaces they enclose with buildings, are invariably interpreted as signs or sign systems. The objective of this chapter is to look at some of these. The fact that all social groups build and design the abodes and public edifices of their villages, towns, and cities in characteristic ways is a clear indication that these too are sign systems. Indeed, a building is hardly ever perceived by the members of a society as simply a pile of bricks, wood, straw, etc., put together to provide shelter. Rather, its shape, size, features, and location are perceived to be signifiers that refer to a range of culture-specific meanings.

INTERPERSONAL SPACE

Animals reside in territories that they have appropriated as their own, or in some negotiated arrangement with other animals, so that they can procure shelter, alimentation, and habitation. This applies to humans as well. But, unlike other species, humans also manifest a unique compulsion to ascribe meanings to the territories in which they are located as social groups.

Biologists define *territoriality* as: (1) an innate survival mechanism that allows an animal to gain access to, and defend control of, critical resources such as food and nesting sites that are found in certain habitats, and (2) as the instinctive need of an animal to procure a "safe boundary" around itself. The Austrian zoologist Konrad Lorenz (1903–1989) was among the first scientists to identify and document the patterns animals display in marking territoriality. Such patterns, he proposed, were an important part of an animal's repertory of survival strategies, as critical in evolutionary terms as its physiological characteristics. Lorenz also suggested that human aggression and warfare were explainable as residual territoriality impulses. Lorenz's controversial theory gained widespread popularity through a best-selling book written in 1966 by Robert Ardrey, *The Territorial Imperative*—a book that subsequently generated a heated debate in academia and society at large on the nature and origin of human aggression. The notion of territoriality in human life continues to receive much support because of its intuitive appeal—intrusions into appropriated territories (e.g., into one's home, car, etc.) are indeed perceived typically as signals of aggression, in the same way that a cat, for example, would likely react aggressively to another cat intruding upon the boundaries it has proclaimed by urination.

The territoriality mechanism became the target of behavioral psychologists in the mid part of the twentieth century, whose experiments received much media attention because of the implications they seemed to have at the time for life in modern crowded urban centers. The gist of the experiments can be condensed as follows. When two laboratory rats were enclosed in the same cage, the researchers found that each one would instinctively seize an area of approximately equal dimensions. When a third rat would be introduced into the same cage, then a tripartite arrangement of subdivided areas would seem to be negotiated among the three rats. However, there always seemed to be some initial reluctance to do so, as signaled by minor altercations among the three rats at the beginning of the negotiations. As each extra rat would be introduced progressively into the cage, more reluctance and aggression would ensue until a "critical mass" would apparently be reached whereby the rats in the cage would either fight relentlessly or demonstrate some form of capitulation behavior. The implications for "urban overcrowding" that those experiments apparently had were not missed by journalists and reporters. They also seemed to provide an explanation as to why some people "snap," as the expression goes, when this critical mass is surpassed, and why others seek rational solutions such as escaping into the suburbs, moving into the country, etc.

Another implication that was derived from the above experiments was the fact that we all need to maintain a boundary around ourselves for our protection and sanity. Edward T. Hall (1966) was among the first to see the relevant social implications of this, and thus to investigate the zone patterns people establish and maintain between each other when interacting. He noted that these could be measured very accurately, allowing for predictable statistical variation, and that the dimensions varied from culture to culture. In North American culture, Hall found that a distance of under 6 in. between two people was perceived as an "intimate" distance, while a distance at from 1.5 to 4 feet was the minimum one perceived to be a safe distance. Intruding upon the limits set by this boundary causes considerable discomfort. For example, if a stranger were to talk at a distance of only several inches away from someone, he or she would be considered rude or even aggressive. If the "safe" distance is breached by some acquaintance, on the other hand, it would be interpreted as a sexual advance.

Hall identified four types of culturally elaborated zones: *intimate, personal, social,* and *public*. He further subdivided these into "far" and "close" phases:

- *Intimate distance* (0 in.–18 in.)
  At intimate distance, all the senses are activated and the presence of the other person or persons is unmistakable. The close phase (0 in.– 6 in.) is an emotionally charged zone reserved for love-making, comforting, and protecting; the far phase (6 in.–18 in.) is the distance where family members and close friends interact. Touch is frequent at both phases of intimate distance.

- *Personal distance* (1.5 ft.–4 ft.)
  This is the minimum comfortable distance between non-touching individuals. In the close phase (1.5 ft.–2.5 ft.), one can grasp the other by extending the arms. The far phase (2.5 ft.–4 ft.) is defined as anywhere from one arm's length to the distance required for both individuals to touch hands. Beyond this distance the two must move to make contact (e.g., to shake hands). In essence, this zone constitutes a small protective space.

- *Social distance* (4 ft.–12 ft.)
  This distance is considered non-involving and non-threatening by most individuals. The close phase (4 ft.–7 ft.) is typical of impersonal transactions and casual social gatherings. Formal social discourse and transactions are characteristic of the far phase (7 ft.–12 ft.). This is the minimum distance at which one could go about one's business without seeming rude to others.

- *Public distance* (12 ft. and beyond)
  At this distance, one can take either evasive or defensive action if physically threatened. Hall noted that people tend to keep at this distance from important public figures or from anyone participating at a public function. Discourse at this distance will be highly structured and formalized (lectures, speeches, etc.).

The study of such zones, and of interpersonal behaviors generally, falls under the rubric of *proxemics*, the term coined by Hall himself. Semiotically, the maintenance of proxemically meaningful zones is explained in terms of spatial codes. The zones themselves are, of course, signs. And the signifieds of these signs are distributed in other codes, such as language, as can be detected as well in the use of space metaphors in common discourse—"Keep your *distance*," "They're very *close*," "We've *drifted* far apart," "You're *trespassing* into my personal space," "I can't quite *get* to him," "Please keep in *touch*," and so on.

In addition to zones, interpersonal spatial codes also regulate bodily orientation. If someone is standing up at the front of an audience, he or she is perceived as more important than those sitting down. Speeches, lectures, classes, musical performances, etc., are oriented in this way. Officials, managers, directors, etc., sit behind a desk to convey importance and superiority. Only their superiors can walk behind the desk to talk to them. To show "friendliness," the person behind the desk will have to come out and sit with his or her interlocutor in a different part of the room.

SPATIAL CODES

Spatial codes fall into three main categories—*public*, *private*, and *sacred*. Public spatial codes are those that regulate how people interact at public sites; private spatial codes are those that regulate how they interact in private spaces; and sacred spatial codes are those that regulate interaction at those locales that are purported to have metaphysical, mythical, or spiritual qualities. Spatial codes are the reason why, for example, one must knock on the door of a friend's house to announce one's presence, but why one does not knock on the door of a retail store; they are also the reason why one may sit and wait for someone in a foyer, atrium, or lobby, but why one does not normally wait for someone in a public washroom; they are also the reason why one can walk on a public sidewalk, but why one cannot walk on someone's porch without permission; and they are the reason why when one enters a sacred place like a church or chapel, one feels and behaves differently than when one enters a bank or a stadium.

Public spaces are felt to be extensions of the "communal body." This is why societies are often described by people as being "healthy," "sick," "vibrant," "beautiful," "ugly," etc. Outsiders habitually judge a society at first sight on how the public places appear to the eye—as "neat," "dirty," "organized," "disorganized," etc. And this is why when someone defaces public places, he or she is felt to have violated the entire community. Conflicts between tribes or nations are, in actual fact, often triggered by such acts against the communal body.

Within the communal body, public places are set aside so that members of a society can gather for reasons of entertainment, recreation, celebration, etc. They provide appropriate locales where ritualistic behaviors can unfold. The spatial codes that relate to such places involve everything from dress to zone maintenance. They give coherence and thus overall purpose to social activities and routines, producing recognizable effects on how people experience places— the space in one's home feels more personal than the space in a bank. At a party, a feast, or a traditional ceremony people assume the social personae that they are either assigned or expected to play, that is, they know what clothes to wear, what behaviors are appropriate, etc. The end result is that the public event is experienced as a collective bodily experience.

Public places set aside for the display and exchange of goods are characteristic of all cultures. In many large contemporary urban societies, this function is served by shopping malls. But the mall has become much more than just a locus for the acquisition of goods. The modern mall satisfies several psychic and social needs at once. It is perceived as a safe and purified space for human socialization; it is felt to be a haven for combating loneliness and boredom; it provides a theatrical atmosphere proclaiming the virtues of a consumerist utopia; it imparts a feeling of security and protection against the world of cars, mechanical noises, and air pollution outside; it shields against rain, snow, heat, cold; it conveys a feeling of control and organization—in a phrase, the mall is placeless and timeless.

Officially, the first mall was Country Club Plaza in Kansas City, Missouri (although department stores already existed in the nineteenth century in Europe). A small collection of Spanish Colonial buildings surrounded by a parking lot, it opened in 1922. Since then, malls have gradually evolved into self-contained consumerist fantasylands, where one can leave the problems and hassles of daily life literally "outside." In the controlled "inside" environment of the mall everything is clean, shiny, cheery, and optimistic. The mall is commonly experienced as a nirvana of endless shopping, cosmeticized and simplified to keep grisly reality out of sight and out of mind. In the same way that one can "switch" from TV scene to TV scene with a remote-control, one can switch from clothing store to coffee stand, to pinball parlor, to lottery outlet with great ease at a mall. The mall subtext is essentially *shopping = paradise on earth*. But this is ultimately an empty, vacuous subtext. Very few people will claim that their experiences at shopping malls are memorable, rewarding, or meaningful. Indeed, they do not remember them for very long once they have left.

In the same way that public spaces are perceived to be parts of a semiotic communal body, so too private spaces are felt typically to be extensions of semiotic Self-space. A home, whether a crude hut or an elaborate mansion, is a shelter providing protection from weather and intruders. It is felt, therefore, to be an extension of the body's protective armor. Indeed, when one steps inside, one feels as if one has entered into one's own body. Thus, when people build and decorate their homes, they are primarily engaged in making images of themselves to suit their own eyes. The identification of Self with the home is characteristic of all cultures.

In tribal societies the house tends to be a single volume, a room for all activities, reflecting an uncomplicated experience of Self. It is usually built directly against neighboring structures and often close to the tribal meeting-house or religious site as well. In city cultures, the experience of home is much more diversified. In China, for instance, the walled-in form of the courtyard house, which has persisted for centuries, reflects the need for privacy that is inherent in Chinese social traditions. But rows of single-volume dwellings, each with a small court or garden, are also found in China, reflecting a different type of perception. At the other end of the scale are the imperial palace compounds, of which the Forbidden City in Beijing is the outstanding example. The various buildings of these compounds, laid out to form a vast, symmetrical complex, constitute an architectural text symbolizing the divine claims of the emperors and the society they governed.

Within the home, the rooms are themselves meaningful "sign spaces" eliciting a specific constellation of emotive connotations. Concealing bedrooms seems to have a biological basis. Humans are extremely vulnerable when sleeping, and so it is certainly judicious, if not essential, to keep sleeping areas hidden from view. This is perhaps why people are especially protective of their bedrooms. In a bedroom, an individual unwinds, relaxes, and expresses his or her inner Self through decoration and personal objects. The bedroom is a refuge and asylum from the outside world. Only intimates are allowed to share that space physically and symbolically. This is why when someone steals something from a bedroom, or defiles it in some way, it is felt to be a personal violation. When people cannot procure a personalized space, living, for example, in public institutions such as prisons, it should come as no surprise to find that they tend to lose respect for the institution and even for themselves, thus often engaging in defacement and vandalism. "Cleanliness" and "dirtiness," moreover, are signs that appertain to spatial contexts. In a home "dirt" is really no more than displaced matter. If earth is found in a garden it is hardly considered to be dirt; however, if found on a kitchen floor it takes on that very meaning. We define a kitchen as a space that should be kept "dirt-free." We find "dirty" kitchens repellent. We can tolerate "dirty" bedrooms much more because they do not involve food and because they are out of sight (Douglas 1966).

It is instructive to note that the Industrial Revolution was a turning point in the way private homes were built and thus perceived. The city poor lived in reasonable, well-built rows of small houses. But it was the emerging middle class that attained the economic ability to buy land and to build fairly comfortable large houses. In the twentieth century, new transportation systems, and the desire of the middle class to own a plot of land, produced suburbs, where a majority of independently situated family houses are found today. As population increased, technology responded. By the late nineteenth century the construction of houses had become a major focus of architecture. Small one-story dwellings, each on its own tract of land, proliferated especially in America. Large ornate houses became fairly common, closely adjacent to neighbors in the older cities, standing alone in the newer towns and the suburbs. Distinctive styles of domestic architecture rose in popularity and waned shortly thereafter.

Houses that broke with historical architectural styles were slow to be accepted. As early as 1889 the American architect Frank Lloyd Wright (1869–1959) built a house embodying new concepts of spatial flow from one room to another. He and others, both in Europe and in the US, soon moved towards a domestic architectural style of metric forms and simplified surfaces largely free of decoration. Contemporaneous changes in painting and sculpture were allied to this movement, and by the 1920s *modernist* architecture, though by no means universally accepted, had arrived. By the 1950s the modern house—a more or less standard, one-floor, two- or three-bedroom house—was commonplace in North America.

Wright created the philosophy of "organic architecture," which maintains that a building should develop out of its natural surroundings. His designs for both private and public structures contrasted with ornate Victorian styles. Wright believed that architectural form must be determined by the particular function of a building, its environment, and the type of materials used. His interiors emphasized spaciousness. To achieve this, Wright initiated many new techniques, such as the use of precast concrete blocks reinforced by steel rods. He also introduced air conditioning, indirect lighting, and panel heating. By 1908 he had originated most of the principles that serve as fundamental concepts of modern architecture today.

Sacred places are sites where humans believe they can secure some form of contact with or proximity to the divinities. The spatial codes that relate to these places are emotionally powerful. In a Catholic church, for example, a confessional is felt to be a very intimate enclosure. Therefore, it cannot be lit or be made amenable to social interaction. It signifies a space in which one is expected to look into the dark depths of the soul. The altar area is perceived as more sacred and therefore less traversable than the area containing the pews. As a table for eating spiritually along with Christ, it was once put against the wall of the church with the priest facing it and with his back to the people. This removed the priest and the Mass from the people, making the whole celebration more detached and ethereal. The language spoken was Latin, which further imbued the celebration with a far-removed, spiritual quality. Nowadays the altar and the priest face the faithful. More interaction is encouraged by this new configuration. There is a greater feeling of "communion" among the people. The change in the orientation of the altar reflected, clearly, a change in emphasis on the part of the Church and its faithful.

Every culture has its designated sacred spaces, usually with some building on them. The place and building are designed for worship. In tribal societies, one building was enough to host the congregation, but in large urban societies, many such buildings are needed. These all have the same goal of making the individuals of a culture feel that they have entered a special place. Indeed, the word *church* comes from New Testament Greek *ekklesia*, meaning "those called out," that is, those called by God away from their daily life to form a new and spiritually deeper relation with the divine.

The salient characteristic of all sacred spaces is that they are designed to impart a spiritual sense. Some are considered to be supernatural, because of miracles that took place on them. For example, the Madonna appeared to St. Bernadette at Lourdes in 1858, and the grotto where she was said to have talked with the peasant girl has ever since been considered sacred, capable of curing disease and bringing spiritual healing. Similar places exist throughout the world.

ARCHITECTURE

Many animals have the ability to construct appropriate shelters within their habitats to protect themselves from the elements and to procure a safeguard against intruding enemies: for example, beavers build dams of stick, mud, brushwood, or stone to widen the area and increase the depth of water around their habitats; marmots (groundhogs) make burrows in the ground where they can hibernate safely during the winter; birds build nests for their young to survive, and the list could go on and on. Humans too build shelters. Thus, while building styles and practices may vary according to available technologies in a culture, the primary functions of buildings remain the same the world over—protection against intrusions and avoidance of discomforts caused by an excess of heat, cold, rain, or wind. But the semiotic story of buildings does not stop there. It reveals that buildings are signs of identity, status, power, and so on. Temples, churches, mosques, as we have seen, are designed to allow people to celebrate the mysteries of religion and to provide assembly places where divinities can be propitiated and where people can be instructed in matters of belief and ritual. Fortresses and castles are designed with defense in mind. Palaces, villas, and skyscrapers are created to display power and wealth. In a phrase, architectural practices mirror social organization and lifestyle. A proliferation of building types, for instance, reflects the complexity of modern life. In large urban centers, more people live in mass housing and go to work in large office buildings; they spend their incomes in large shopping centers, send their children to different kinds of schools, go to specialized hospitals and clinics when sick, linger in airports on the way to distant hotels and resorts.

Some buildings are perceived to be artistic signs. This is why the aesthetic response to them is varied. They differ from, say, sculpture only in the fact that the observer can be inside the art text (the building). The aesthetic response to buildings is affected by construction materials used, by the way they have been assembled, by the lighting conditions, by the form and style of windows, doors, floor design, and ceiling height. Movement through the spaces within a building also has narrative force, since the parts of a building are interpreted as being as structured as are the parts of a sentence or a story. Buildings are thus "read" as narrative texts with specific meanings. This is why one listens with great interest to a tour guide's story as he or she takes us through an historically significant building.

The various elements of the building text are, of course, signifiers. Consider, for instance, how the height of a building can convey a specific kind of meaning. The cities built during the medieval period had one outstanding architectural feature—the tallest building noticeable along their skyline was the bell tower of the church or the church itself. The spires on medieval churches rose majestically upwards to the sky, reflecting semiotically the fact that there is something overpowering about looking up at tall buildings, making one feel small and insignificant by comparison bringing out a desire for heavenly aspiration in a concrete way. The height of churches thus came to symbolize the power and wealth of the Church. But, with the rise of secularism after the Renaissance, cities were gradually redesigned architecturally to reflect a new political order. The tallest buildings were the palaces of aristocrats and rich bourgeoisie—such as the buildings constructed in Urbino, Italy. Today, the tallest buildings in sprawling urban centers are certainly not churches or palaces. The tallest structures in cities like Dallas, Toronto, Montreal, New York, Chicago, Los Angeles are owned by large corporations and banks. Wealth and power now reside literally and symbolically in these institutions. Inside these mammoth buildings there is an architectural structure that mirrors the social hierarchical structure within it—the jobs and positions with the lowest value are at the bottom of the building; the more important ones are at the top. The company's executives reside, like the gods on Mount Olympus, on the top floor. The atmosphere on this level is perceived to be rarefied and other-worldly. This architectural symbolism is the reason why we use such expressions as "to work one's way *up*," "to make it to the *top*," "to climb the *ladder* of success," "to set one's goals *high*," etc.

The foregoing discussion emphasizes that buildings and cities are much more than agglomerations of buildings. They allow us to understand social structure. The Assyrian city of Khorsabad, built during the reign of Sargon II (722–705 BC) and excavated in 1842, is one of the oldest city sites to have been found, and has become the basis for studying the architecture and social order of the Mesopotamian world. Many of the architectural trends in the West trace their origins to the building styles and practices of ancient Greece and Rome. Both were noteworthy for grandiose urban design, as exemplified by the Parthenon (448–432 BC) which crowns the Athenian Acropolis and Hadrian's Villa (125–132) near Tivoli.

From the fourth century until the early Renaissance, Christianity influenced and even dictated social structure, including architectural trends, prompting the building of many new churches. Byzantine churches, domed and decorated with mosaics, proliferated throughout the Byzantine Empire. The secularizing trends of the Renaissance brought about a revival of the principles and styles of ancient Greek and Roman architecture. The Italian architect Filippo Brunelleschi (1377–1446) was among the first to revive the classical forms, championing a new architecture based on mathematics, proportion, and perspective. In 1418 he was commissioned to build the dome of the unfinished Florence Cathedral. His design for the dome was a great innovation, both artistically and technically:

Duomo, Florence
Italian Cultural Institute

Brunelleschi also developed the technique of perspective in art and architecture, perfected a little later by the German painter and printmaker Albrecht Dürer (1471–1528). In the sixteenth century, Rome became the leading center for architectural innovation. Saint Peter's Basilica in the Vatican was the most important of many sixteenth-century architectural projects. Towards the middle part of the century such leading Italian architects as Michelangelo, Baldassare Peruzzi, Giulio Romano, and Giacomo da Vignola started the trend of using the classical Roman elements in ways that became known as the *mannerist* style, characterized by arches, columns, and entablatures that enshrined the techniques of perspective and depth in Western architecture.

The best known architect of the period was the sculptor Gianlorenzo Bernini (1598–1680), designer of the great oval piazza in front of St. Peter's Basilica.

In the eighteenth century a new style arose, called *rococo*, reflecting a new affluence and elegance in society at large. But little less than a century later, with the advent of the Industrial Revolution, a new world order came into existence, accompanied by architectural trends that set the stage for the growth of industrialized building trends and the widespread use of cast iron and steel. At the beginning of the twentieth century, the American architect Louis Sullivan (1856–1924) and his apprentice Frank Lloyd Wright (mentioned previously) designed the first true skyscrapers. The "art of the modern skyscraper" was, actually, an idea put forward by the so-called *Bauhaus school* (based in Weimar, Germany, around 1919–1925), which brought together architects, painters, and designers from several countries to formulate the goals of the visual arts in the modern age, under its first director Walter Gropius (1883–1969). The Bauhaus style prevailed throughout the 1940s, 1950s, and most of the 1960s. Often referred to with the term *modernism*, its approach can be seen in the chaste elegance and subtle proportions of the Seagram Building (1958) in New York. Gropius wanted to rebuild the landscape by stripping it of its past symbolism, substituting a geometrically pure style that intentionally excluded references to the past. The Bauhaus School envisioned a working-class architectural landscape. Buildings were to be fashioned as box-like forms so as to eliminate all the symbols of traditional power. Out of this movement, modern office towers, housing projects, hotels, and other public buildings were built with the same basic cubic blueprint.

Between about 1965 and 1970, architects started to reject modernism, which they found to be too monolithic and formulaic, promoting a new style that came to be known as *postmodern*. The postmodern architects wanted to inject individuality, intimacy, complexity, humor, and irony into building design. The American architect Robert Venturi (1925–), for instance, defended the new vernacular architecture—gas stations, fast-food restaurants, etc.—and attacked the modernist establishment with incisive criticism. By the early 1980s, postmodernism had become the dominant trend in American architecture and an important phenomenon in Europe as well. Its success in the US owed much to the influence of Philip C. Johnson (1906–). His AT&T Building (1984) in New York City (see next page) instantly became a paragon of postmodern design, perhaps because it was so simple yet captivating:

Vivid color and other decorative elements have since been effectively used to build everything from office towers to private houses. But another paradigm shift in architecture has been fomenting. New office buildings in the twenty-first century emphasize high-tech and glamorous professions. Once again the city landscape, and thus the mindscape that it mirrors, are changing.

In a sense, architecture is all about imposing order on space. Architecture is based on the general principle that when things look right, they feel right. In China this principle has even been given expression in the form of the "art of placement," which interprets the forces of Nature and of the cosmos to enhance well-being through design. Born out of the 3,000-year-old *I Ching*, the art of *Feng-Shui*, as it is called, is a mixture of geometry, geography, architecture, and psychology. Practitioners use an octagonal template called the *ba-gua* to assess an area as large as the floor of a building or as small as a desktop. The orientation, layout, and placement of objects within an area are considered to be significant. While some may dismiss such arts as the products of superstition, I see in them a profound sense of spatial pattern that, in one form or other, we assume to be interconnected with destiny and the human condition.

CITIES

The origin of cities is to be found in mixed tribal settlements that came onto the scene around 5,000–6,000 years ago. To protect themselves and their food supplies against predatory nomads, animals, and changes in climate, the people in these settlements built their dwellings within a walled area or a naturally fortified place, such as the acropolis of ancient Greek cities. Because the availability of water was also a key consideration, these early settlements were usually located around, near, or along a river. Gradually, the expanding configuration of buildings and spaces of the settlement created the need for a specialization of labor. Markets developed in which artisans could exchange their specialties for other kinds of goods. They became centers of commerce, learning, and technology.

The spread of the city concept in Europe was a result of the breakup of feudalism. At the beginning of the sixteenth century Europe had six or seven cities of 100,000 or more inhabitants; at the end of the century it had twice as many. During the seventeenth century, although the population of Europe remained stationary, that of the cities increased. But it was not until the late nineteenth century that the process of urbanization—more and more people moving into cities at the expense of rural districts—became a general trend. Its principal causes were the development of the factory system, improvements in transportation, and the mechanization of agriculture, which reduced the need for farm labor. Many modern cities were, in fact, planned as industrial centers near sources of raw materials. In 1890, barely 16 percent of the population of the US lived in cities of 100,000 or more. In 1990 just over one-fourth of the population did so, and three-fourths of the total population lived in cities and towns of 2500 or more.

City design reflects cultural values, beliefs, and emphases. In ancient Greece, religious and civic citadels were oriented in such a way as to give a sense of aesthetic balance to the inhabitants—streets were arranged in a grid pattern and housing was integrated with commercial and defense structures. In the Renaissance, the design of cities around piazzas was in sharp contrast to the narrow, irregular streets of medieval cities. Renaissance city planners stressed wide, regular radial streets forming concentric circles around a central point, with other streets radiating out from that point like spokes of a wheel. To this day, the downtown core is known as *centro* in Italy, reflecting this Renaissance view of cities as circles.

After the Industrial Revolution the concept of the grid started to gain a foothold on city designs. The grid conveys rationalization, efficiency of movement, and precision. This is evident in New York City's plan of 1811, which divided Manhattan into identical rectangular blocks that were even named in terms of the grid system—1st and 7th, 2nd and 31st, and so on. Since the middle part of the twentieth century, many new grid-type designs have emerged. And hotels and other recreational buildings (e.g., casinos) are taking on some of the symbols of power that were once associated exclusively with the banks and the corporations. The city of Las Vegas is a classic example of a city designed to cater to our modern-day craving for recreation and consumption. The tall hotel towers that mark its landscape are symbols of a world of fast money, quick recreational fixes, and consumerist delights.

Sociologists have made various predictions about urban communities of the future. They believe that metropolitan areas will continue to grow in both population and area. In 1990, about 2.3 billion people in different parts of the world lived in urban places. By the year 2010, the number is expected to rise to about 4 billion people. The development of new towns and cities is a slow, costly process. Private developers are reluctant to take on such projects because of the uncertainty of, and the long wait for, profits. Many governments have been unable or unwilling to finance such projects. For these reasons, sociologists predict that almost all the additional millions of people who will live in urban places in the future will crowd into existing communities. More and more of the land around central cities will be filled by people. The suburbs will spread out so far that some metropolitan areas will run together with no rural areas between them. Such a continuous stretch of metropolitan areas is called a *megalopolis*. A megalopolis has already formed between Boston, New York City, Philadelphia, Baltimore, and Washington, DC.

CONCLUDING REMARKS

In perceiving territories, spaces, and shelters as signs and sign systems, humans the world over have fashioned for themselves environments that are increasingly breaking away from Nature. This has, of course, had many positive consequences. But it has also brought about some extremely dangerous ones as well. One of these is the level of pollution that invariably seems to plague modern cities.

The effort to free cities of pollution is something that is now of great concern throughout the world. Entire urban communities may be enclosed in plastic domes in the future. Temperature and humidity inside the domes would be controlled, and electronic filters would keep the air clean and fresh. The world, however, would be a vastly different place, physically and semiotically.

Television

In Beverly Hills they don't throw their garbage away. They make
it into television shows.

Woody Allen (1935–)

PRELIMINARY REMARKS

Television is so common that we hardly ever take notice of what it is and does
to us. TV has created a form of literacy that informs and engages more people
than any other form has been capable of doing at any time in human history. It
has also become the medium that many people blame for helping to entrench
our materialistic and shallow culture. Since the 1970s scientific research papers
on the effects television has purportedly had on society have also proliferated.
Today, it is common to accuse television for causing virtually everything that
is bad, from obesity to street violence. Are the critics right? Has television
spawned a "psychologically toxic" world? Are the victims of TV programs, as
Key (1989: 13) suggests, people who "scream and shout hysterically at rock
concerts and later in life at religious revival meetings?" In my view, the critics
are only partially correct. There is no doubt that TV has had an impact on
culture and on individuals living in it, but so has every other form of
representation—from religious texts to paperback novels. In actual fact, TV is
hardly ever innovative or inspiring, as are some other kinds of texts. TV puts
on programs that reinforce already-forged lifestyle trends. TV moguls are
more intent on adopting and recycling such trends than in spreading
commercially risky innovations of their own.

Critics of TV also conveniently overlook the fact that it has been
instrumental in bringing about significant and important changes in society.

For instance, the TV images of the Vietnam War broadcast daily on news programs in the late 1960s and early 1970s brought about protest and ultimately an end to the war. The constant exposure to, and treatment of, sexual themes on TV have also, through the years, greatly reduced the hypocrisy that previously existed with regard to sexual matters in society at large. The changes were successful because TV guaranteed that they did not involve just "intellectuals," but large segments of the populace.

The semiotic study of TV is, clearly, of great social importance. It comes, logically, under the rubric of *media semiotics*—a branch of semiotics started primarily by the French semiotician Roland Barthes with the publication of his highly popular 1957 analysis of pop culture called *Mythologies.*

THE ADVENT OF TV

In 1884 the German engineer Paul Nipkow designed a scanning disk that created crude television images. Nipkow's scanner was used from 1923 to 1925 in experimental television systems. Then in 1926 the Scottish scientist, John Logie Baird (1888–1946), perfected the scanning method. And in 1931 the Russian-born engineer, Vladimir Zworykin (1889–1982), built the electronic scanning system that became the prototype of the modern TV camera. The first home television receiver was exhibited in Schenectady, New York, in 1928, by American inventor Ernst F. W. Alexanderson. The images were small, poor, and unsteady, but the set was thought by many entrepreneurs at the time to have commercial potential.

By the late 1930s, television service was in place in several Western countries. The British BBC, for example, started a regular service in 1936. By the early 1940s there were 23 television stations operating in the US. But it was not until the early 1950s that technology had advanced to the point that made it affordable for virtually every North American household to own a television set. Immediately thereafter, TV began to take an emotional hold on society. Television personages became household names, looming larger than life. Actors and announcers became lifestyle trend-setters. People began more and more to plan their daily lives around television programs.

Throughout the 1950s and 1960s television programming developed rapidly into more than an assortment of fact and fiction narratives; it became itself a *social text* for an increasingly larger segment of society, functioning as a kind of code through which people gleaned a large portion of their information, intellectual stimulation, and distraction. Today, 98% of North American households own a television set, and a large portion of these have more than one. People continue to this day to glean a large portion of their information, intellectual stimulation, and recreation from television. TV's total integration into modern society can be seen by the fact that TV sets are now ubiquitous—in hotel rooms, airports, schools, elevators, office waiting rooms, cafeterias, washrooms, and even outer space. The successful US manned landing on the moon in July 1969 was documented with live broadcasts made from the surface of the moon. The world, it would seem, has become one big television monitor.

Technology has constantly improved TV viewing. Digital television receivers, which convert the analog or continuous electronic television signals received by an antenna into an electronic digital code (a series of ones and zeros), are doing to television what the compact disc did to sound recording in the 1980s. Known as high-definition television (HDTV), the technology was developed originally in the mid-1980s. HDTV offers sharper pictures on wider screens, with cinema-quality images. A fully digital system was put on display in the US in the early 1990s. Recently, engineers have devised ways of making HDTV compatible with computers and telecommunications equipment so that HDTV technology can be applied to other systems besides home television, such as medical devices, security systems, and computer-aided manufacturing. HDTV is making sure that TV sets will continue to be bought and used throughout society.

TV GENRES

Network programming began in large scale in the late 1940s and early 1950s. At first, TV simply adapted previous radio genres to the screen. For instance, the highly popular *I Love Lucy* (1951–1957) sitcom, which starred Lucille Ball, was adapted from her radio show *My Favorite Husband* (1948–1951). It established dramatic elements that have been adopted by subsequent sitcoms—the battle between the sexes, arguments among neighbors or work colleagues, and other mundane conflicts. TV developed its own particular brand of sitcoms shortly thereafter. Some of these, such as *Father Knows Best* (1954–1960) and *The Cosby Show* (1984–1992), focused on child rearing issues; others raised the "critical coefficient" of their contents considerably by providing controversial social commentary. Prime examples of the latter were *All in the Family* (1971–1979) and *M*A*S*H* (1972–1983). Some sitcoms have also occasionally used fantasy characters as vehicles for comedy—e.g., *Bewitched* (1964–1972) and *I Dream of Jeannie* (1965–1969). Currently, sitcoms have become eclectic in content. The majority, however, are designed to appeal primarily to young adults, dealing openly with problems of sexuality, romance, and marriage.

The TV comedy-variety genre was, at first, a hybrid of vaudeville and nightclub entertainment. In the early years of television, many of the medium's first great stars were, as a matter of fact, comedy-variety performers, including Milton Berle, Sid Caesar, Jackie Gleason, Martha Raye, and Red Skelton. A comedy-variety hour typically consisted of short monologues and skits featuring the host, which alternated with various show-business acts, including singers, bands, stand-up comedians, trained animal acts, and other novelties. The variety show—a related genre in which the host served only as master of ceremonies— also emerged in the early period of TV. The *Ed Sullivan Show* (1948–1971), for example, hosted by newspaper columnist Ed Sullivan on CBS, featured entertainers as diverse as Elvis Presley, the Beatles, and the Bolshoi Ballet.

The early years of television also brought serious drama to large segments of society, which had never before been exposed to it. Hour-long works by Paddy Chayefsky (1923–1981), Rod Serling (1924–1975), and other television playwrights were presented live on such programs as *Goodyear-Philco Playhouse* (1951–1960) and *Studio One* (1948–1958). As with radio, however, serial dramas proved to be much more popular and, therefore, the more serious programs gradually disappeared. The format and style of the series had mass appeal. They included police dramas, such as *Dragnet* (1952–1959, 1967– 1970), *The Mod Squad* (1968–1973), and *Hawaii Five-O* (1968–1980); private-eye series, such as *77 Sunset Strip* (1958–1964), *The Rockford Files* (1974–1980), and *Magnum, P.I.* (1980–1988), in which the personality of the detective was as important as the criminal investigation; and westerns, such as *Gunsmoke* (1955–1975), *Wagon Train* (1957–1965), and *Bonanza* (1959– 1973), which focused on the settling of the West. Other types of TV series have included war programs, such as *Rat Patrol* (1966–1967), spy series, such *as The Man from U.N.C.L.E.* (1964–1968), and science-fiction series, such as *Star Trek* (1966–1969). Dramatic series based on the exploits of lawyers, doctors, or rich business entrepreneurs also became part of the early TV menu. These have included *Perry Mason* (1957–1966), *L.A. Law* (1986–1994), *Ben Casey* (1961–1966), *Marcus Welby, M.D.* (1969–1976), and *Dallas* (1978– 1991).

TV soap operas, like their radio counterparts, have always explored romance, friendship, and familial relations in narrative form. Among the most popular of the early TV era were *The Guiding Light* (1952–) and *The Edge of Night* (1956–1984). At first, the soaps were no more than afternoon "romance interludes" for stay-at-home wives; now they appeal to male and female audiences alike, dealing with many aspects of relationships.

From the outset, TV news broadcasting has held wide appeal for all kinds of audiences. The speed with which TV broadcasting could reach entire populations redefined the role of news reporting in society. Print journalism has, as a consequence, become a supplemental medium to TV journalism, focusing on in-depth coverage and editorial opinion. Actually, the earliest years of television offered little more than newspaper-style reporting, but this changed in the mid-1950s. In 1956, NBC introduced *The Huntley-Brinkley Report*, a half-hour national telecast presented in the early evening and featuring filmed reports of the day's events. The other networks followed suit shortly thereafter. With the advent of videotape, the cost of such coverage dropped significantly, allowing individual stations to initiate and expand local news coverage. Network and local news programming has now become an integral part of TV.

In addition to daily news coverage, the networks capitalized on the popularity of news reporting by developing weekly prime-time newsmagazine series, such as *60 Minutes* (1968–) and *20/20* (1978–). Such shows consist of a mixture of cultural reporting, investigative reporting, and human-interest stories. They have proliferated in prime-time broadcasting. And, of course, all-news cable channels have become popular since the mid-1980s. The first of these, CNN (Cable News Network), was founded in 1980 by American businessman Ted Turner. CNN was the first 24-hour television network devoted entirely to news broadcasts. In 1991, the network received wide publicity when its reporter Peter Arnett remained in Iraq during the Persian Gulf War to broadcast his reports. In effect, Arnett gave a "play-by-play" account of the conflict, not unlike what a TV sportscaster does in describing a football or baseball match. During the Iraq campaign of 2003, reporters were even "embedded" in army units and tanks, so that viewers could see the "play-by-play'" as it unfolded in real time. Clearly, TV news reporting has become as much entertainment and "reality drama" as it is information transfer. War is real; the broadcasts, however, transform the events of war into adventure serials imbued with all the elements of a fictional narrative.

In the US, TV has even had a noticeable effect on electoral politics and on the evolution of the modern form of political campaigning. This can perhaps be traced to 1960, when presidential candidates Richard M. Nixon and John F. Kennedy agreed to a series of debates, which were broadcast simultaneously on television and radio. According to surveys, most radio listeners felt that Nixon had won the debates, while television viewers picked Kennedy. Kennedy won the general election that fall. This showed the power of the TV image, radically transforming the conduct and form of political campaigns ever since.

Other TV genres that have proven to be durable include: talk shows (providing a daily dose of gossip, scandal, and information, all mixed into one), sports coverage, children's programming, game shows, music programs, animation programs, and religious programs. One recent genre that requires special comment is the so-called reality program. The various *Survivor, Temptation Island*, and *Bachelor/Bachelorette* programs that cluttered the prime time airwaves in the early 2000s pitted real-life people, not actors, into situations imbued with all the dramatic elements of the soaps—intrigue, betrayal, romance, sex. Andy Warhol's prediction that everyone would have his or her "15 minutes of fame" in the media age was superseded by such unscripted programs. Common people now have a whole program's time of fame available to them, not just 15 minutes.

Unscripted TV is not new. It has been a staple of cable networks and some public broadcasting outlets for years. Britain's Channel 4's fine series *1900 House*, for instance, was much more intriguing than any *Survivor* or *Temptation Island* format, since it followed the misadventures of a family that agreed to live as the Victorians did for three months. The series combined elements of narrative with those of documentary and drama producing a TV sociology of family life that was truly powerful. Similarly, the American 1971 documentary of the Loud family—involving seven months of uninterrupted shooting and 300 hours of nonstop broadcasting—created a portrait of the banality of modern life that remains memorable to this day. The hyperreal Loud family, incidentally, fell apart, begging the question: Did the TV cameras cause this?

Reality TV is just one symptom of voyeurism in the Digital Galaxy. With the use of webcams (cameras made for Internet transmission), millions of people throughout the world are now letting strangers peer into their daily lives. A growing number of people simply seem to find "living in public" more exciting than living privately. The world is quickly becoming one huge "peep show." Maybe at some deep unconscious level we are trying to understand what human life is all about through such gratuitous people-watching. Who knows? But it certainly seems to be a bizarre way of doing so.

Today, TV genres have diversified significantly, as TV networks are forced to compete with smaller private channels that offer specialty programming. Still, the traditional genres seem to have much life left in them, despite their apparent inanity. *Seinfeld* (1990–1998), for instance, was notable for being about "nothing," unlike other sitcoms of the same era that focused on family issues (*Roseanne,* 1988–1997), gender issues (*Home Improvement,* 1991–1999), or various kinds of social issues (*Third Rock from the Sun,* 1996–).

THE EFFECTS OF TV

Marshall McLuhan was among the first to descry that TV had an impact far greater than that of the material it communicated. And indeed, just as he predicted, with advances in satellite communications, TV now allows viewers to see themselves as "participants" in a global village, as McLuhan called it. TV has, in fact, been a primary source since the 1950s for determining celebrity status, for documenting contemporary history, and for shaping how we process information.

I will refer to the "celebrity-making" effect as the *mythologizing effect,* because the celebrities that television creates are perceived as mythic figures, larger than life. Like any type of privileged space—a platform, a pulpit, etc., that is designed to impart focus and significance to someone—television creates mythic personages by simply "containing" them in a box-like space, where they are seen as suspended in real time and space, in a mythic world of their own. The "box" is psychologically similar to any kind of magic speaking box of many fantasies. TV personages are infused with a deified quality by virtue of the fact that they are seen inside the mythical box. This is why meeting TV actors, sitcom stars, etc., causes great enthusiasm and excitement in many people. They are otherworldly figures who have "stepped out" of the box to take on human proportions, in the same way that a mythic hero such as Prometheus did by coming into our human world to live among us.

I will use the term *history fabrication effect* to refer to the fact that TV has become not only the main way in which we document history, but also a source for fabricating it. The events that are showcased on TV are felt as being more significant and historically meaningful to society than those that are not. A riot that gets airtime becomes a historical event; one that does not is ignored. This is why terrorists are seemingly more interested in simply getting on the air, than in having their demands satisfied. TV imbues their cause with significance. Political and social protesters frequently inform the news media of their intentions, and then dramatically stage their demonstrations for the cameras. Sports events such as the World Series, the Super Bowl, the Stanley Cup Playoffs or the World Cup of soccer are transformed by television coverage into battles of Herculean proportion. Events such as the John Kennedy and Lee Harvey Oswald assassinations, the Vietnam War, the Watergate hearings, the Rodney King beating, the O. J. Simpson trial, the death of Princess Diana, the Bill Clinton sex scandal, the 9/11 attack, and so on are perceived as portentous and prophetic historical events through the filter of TV coverage. People also make up their minds about the guilt or innocence of others by watching news and interview programs; they see certain behaviors as laudable or damnable by tuning into talk shows or docudramas, and the list could go on and on.

In a phrase, TV has become the maker of history and its documenter at the same time. People now experience history through TV, not just read about it in a book or study it at school. Edward R. Murrow (1908–1965) of *CBS News* became a cultural hero when he stood up to the fanatical senator Joseph McCarthy (1908–1957), who led a campaign against a purported Communist subversion of the media in the early 1950s on his *See It Now* documentary program. In 1954, Murrow used footage of McCarthy's own press conferences to expose the excesses of his anticommunist campaign. This led to the Senate reprimanding McCarthy and paralyzing him politically. The horrific images of the Vietnam War that were transmitted into people's homes daily in the late 1960s and early 1970s brought about an end to the war, mobilizing social protest. Significantly, an MTV flag was hoisted by East German youths over the Berlin Wall as they tore it down in 1989. More people watched the wedding of England's Prince Charles and Princess Diana, and later Diana's funeral, than had ever before in human history observed such events at the same time. The Bill Clinton-Monica Lewinsky sex scandal allowed common people to become privy to the sexual flaws of a powerful political figure. The images of the two planes smashing into the World Trade Center buildings on September 11, 2001, brought about an international reaction, whose consequences are still being felt.

The history-making power of TV has led many to stage events for the cameras. The social critic W. T. Anderson (1992: 125–130) calls these appropriately "pseudoevents," because they are never spontaneous, but planned for the sole purpose of playing to TV's huge audiences. Most pseudoevents are intended to be self-fulfilling prophecies. As Anderson (1990: 126–127) aptly puts it, this is because the "media take the raw material of experience and fashion it into stories; they retell the stories to us, and we call them reality."

Finally, I will use the term *cognitive compression effect* to refer to the fact that the TV medium presents its stories, information, and features in compacted form for time-constrained transmission. Consequently, viewers have little time to reflect on the topics, implications, and meanings contained in TV information. This leads, generally speaking, to a cognitively compressed mode of "reading" the TV text.

Take TV news programs as a case in point. The amount of information presented in a short period of time on a news program is torrential. We are able to take it all in because the various stories have been edited and stylized beforehand for effortless mass consumption. The camera moves in to selected aspects of a situation, to show a face that cares, that is suffering, that is happy, that is angry, or whatever, and then shifts to the cool handsome face of an anchorman or to the attractive one of an anchorwoman to tell us what it's all about. The news items, the film footage, and the commentaries are all fast-paced and brief. They are designed to present dramatic snippets of easily digestible information in visual form. "Within such a stylistic environment," remarks Stuart Ewen (1988: 265), "the news is beyond comprehension." Thus it is that as "nations and people are daily sorted out into boxes marked 'good guys,' 'villains,' 'victims,' and 'lucky ones,' style becomes the essence, reality becomes the appearance" (Ewen 1988: 265–266).

I should mention that, although I have applied the notion of cognitive compression effect to the television medium, it applies to various (if not most) other media to greater or lesser extents. It is applicable to decipherment of a movie or printed narrative. Novels have chapters that can only be understood by "compressing" them into a whole—the underlying narrative. It is only after reading the whole novel that it makes sense. However, the visual image is much more difficult to "dissect reflectively" than is a sentence or paragraph in a printed book. The visual image, by its very nature, forces us to compress its content more than does any other medium, especially when it comes to us through a miasma of other images.

TV AS A SOCIAL TEXT

TV is itself a type of sign that can be called a *social text*. This can be defined as an overarching text from which an entire culture extracts meaning for its daily life routines. To see what this means, it is useful to step back in time with one's imagination to a village in medieval Europe. What would daily life have been like in that era? How would one have organized it? What *social text*, in effect, would one have been likely to live by?

As history records, daily life schemes in the era were informed and guided by a religious social text. Residual elements of this text are still around today. Religious dates such as Christmas and Easter, for instance, are still regularly planned yearly events around which many people in our society organize social activities. In medieval Europe, the religious social text regulated life on a daily basis. In that era, people went to church regularly, lived by strict moral codes derived from the religious text, and listened conscientiously to the admonitions and dictates of clergymen. The underlying subtext was that each day brought one closer and closer to one's true destiny—salvation and an afterlife with God. Living according to the text no doubt imparted a feeling of security, emotional shelter, and spiritual meaning to people's lives.

After the Renaissance, the Enlightenment, and the Industrial Revolution the religious social text came gradually to be replaced by a more secular form of textuality. Today, unless someone has joined a religious community or has chosen to live by the dictates of a religious text, the social text by which people in general live is hardly a religious one. We organize our day around work commitments, social appointments, etc., that have hardly anything to do with salvation, and only at those traditional "points" in the calendar (Christmas, Easter, etc.) do we synchronize our secular text with the more traditional religious one. The secular social text necessitates partitioning the day into "time slots." This is why we depend so heavily upon such devices as clocks, watches, agendas, appointment books, calendars, etc. We would be desperately lost without such things. In this regard, it is relevant to note that in his great 1726 novel, *Gulliver's Travels*, Jonathan Swift (1667–1745) satirized the tendency of people to rely on the watch to organize their daily routines—the Lilliputians were baffled to note that Gulliver did virtually nothing without consulting his watch! Like Gulliver, we need to know continually "what time it is" in order to carry on with the normal conduct of our daily life.

Outside of special cases—such as in cloisters and monasteries—the textual organization of the day is hardly ever conscious. If we started to reflect upon the value of our daily routines, it is likely that we would soon start to question them and eventually to abandon them. This does indeed happen in the case of those individuals who have decided to "drop out" of society, that is, to live their lives outside of the dictates of social textuality.

Now, since the 1950s, when it first entered the social scene, TV became almost instantly the medium through which our secular social text was delivered, and through which people gleaned information about life. If one looks through the daily TV listings and starts classifying the programs into morning, noon, and evening slots, one will get an idea of what this means. With cable television and satellite dishes, the range of programming offered would, at first, appear to be a broad and random one. But a closer critical look at the listings will reveal a different story.

Consider morning programming. Virtually all the networks start off their daily fare of offerings with several stock types of shows. These are, invariably, information programs (news, weather, sports), children's shows, exercise programs, and talk and quiz shows. There is very little digression from this menu. One may, of course, subscribe to a cable movie channel or to some special interest channel to suit one's fancy. But, as ratings research has shown, most people are inclined to watch the regular fare of network-based morning programs. The morning part of the TV text changes somewhat on weekends, reflecting the different kinds of social requirements associated with Saturdays and Sundays. But on weekday mornings "Wake up people" is the underlying subtext. "Here's what you need to know," blurt out the newscasters. "You're too fat and sluggish, so get into shape," exclaim the fitness instructors. "You're bored and need to gossip, so tune in to meet people with bizarre or heart-wrenching stories," bellow the talk show hosts. In the same way that the morning prayers reassured medieval people that their life was meaningful, so too does morning TV assure us that our busy lives have sense and purpose.

In the afternoon the primary viewing audience is made up of stay-at-home people. The soap opera continues to be the main staple of this time frame. It started on radio as a drama, typically performed as a serial characterized by stock characters and sentimental situations. It was given its name because it was originally sponsored by soap detergent companies. Rather than go out and chitchat or gossip, as did medieval people, we do virtually the same thing by peering daily into the complicated lives of soap opera personages. As the soaps change, so do social mores. One reflects the other.

The afternoon is also the time for TV's version of medieval morality plays and public confessions. Talk shows and interview programs allow modern-day people to reveal and confess their "sins" or their tragedies in public. A large viewing audience can thus participate cathartically in other people's acts of self-revelation, repentance, or emotional healing. As Stern and Stern (1992: 123) write, talk shows "are a relief in the sense that it is always nice to see people whose problems are worse than yours." The afternoon is thus a time slot for moral issues, acted out upon a media stage that has replaced the pulpit as the platform from which they are discussed publicly. TV hosts, like medieval priests, comment morally upon virtually every medical and psychological condition known to humanity.

The third part of the TV text has traditionally been called "prime time," the period in the evenings, from about 7 PM to 10 PM, when most people are home to watch TV. It is significant that the prelude to evening programming is, as it is for the morning time-slot, the "news hour." After this, quiz shows and gossip journalism maintain curiosity and interest, until family programming commences for a couple of hours, with sitcoms, adventure programs, documentaries, movies, and the like. The 1980s also introduced soap operas into this time frame, but with only limited success. Prime-time programming meshes fictional narrative with moral and social messages for the entire family. Documentary programs in particular showcase real-life events, often bolstered by dramatic portrayals of these events, so that appropriate moral and social lessons can be learned.

Prime time is followed by "late night" programming—a kind of *coda* to the daily text. There was nothing for medieval people to do past the early evening hours. If they did not go to bed early, then they would congregate and converse in village squares. But in contemporary consumerist societies, when the kids are safely in bed, TV programs allow viewers to indulge their more prurient interests. Under the cloak of darkness and with "innocent eyes and ears" fast asleep, one can fantasize and talk about virtually anything under the sun on TV with social impunity.

Needless to say, there are now many more alternatives to this fare of programs, given the huge number of specialty channels that are available. But, as it turns out, these do not impugn the overall TV text in any way. Specialty channels provide the same kinds of options that specialized books in libraries do. One can immerse oneself in any hobby or subject area by taking out the appropriate books from a library. But this in no way impugns the general reading preferences in the culture. The same applies by analogy to TV.

TV MYTHOLOGIES

Given the increasing diversity of consumerist societies, it is little wonder that the TV social text has become similarly diverse. There are now specialty channels for sports, movies, and music enthusiasts, for instance. But one thing has remained constant; TV is the locus where modern mythologies are forged, developed, and eventually discarded. Consider, as a case-in-point, the mythology of fatherhood that TV constructed and continually changed from the 1950s to the late 1990s.

1950s sitcoms like *Father Knows Best* and *The Adventures of Ozzie and Harriet* sculpted the father figure to fit the template of the traditional patriarchal family structure. Therefore, most of the early sitcoms painted the family in a rose-colored fashion. The father was in charge, with his wife working behind the scenes to maintain emotional harmony among the family members. This mythology of fatherhood reflected the social mindset of the 1950s. TV reinforced it and gave it a narrative form for people to take in on a weekly basis, allowing them to evaluate their own family situations in tandem. There were two notable exceptions to this: *The Honeymooners* and *I Love Lucy*, both of which revolved around strong-willed wives who were, in effect, precursors of later TV feminist characters. But, in general, the subtext to the 1950s TV sitcom was: *father = know-all and be-all.*

In the 1960s and early 1970s the subtext was changed drastically as the mythology was changed to reflect new times. The TV father was being portrayed more and more as a ludicrous character. The sitcom that reflected this new subtext brilliantly was *All in the Family*. In the early 1970s, the North American continent was divided, ideologically and emotionally, into two camps—those who supported the views and attitudes of the TV father, Archie Bunker, a staunch defender of the Vietnam War, and those who despised the War and thus the persona of Archie Bunker. What was happening inside the TV Bunker family was apparently happening in families across the continent. North American society had entered into a period of emotional turmoil and bitter debate over such controversial issues as war, racism, the role of women in society, and the hegemony of the patriarchal family. The new subtext that was informing the sitcoms of that era was: *father = opinionated, bigoted character*. Its symbolic embodiments were TV characters such as Archie Bunker.

The total "deconstruction" of the 1950s mythology of fatherhood took place in sitcoms from the mid-1980s to the late 1990s. A typical example was *Married, with Children*, a morbid parody of fatherhood and of the nuclear family. The father on that program, Al Bundy, was little more than a physical brute, a reprehensible character who was hardly deserving of the title of *father*. Indeed, as the name of the sitcom suggested, he was merely "married" and who just happened to have "children," just as shallow and despicable as he was—Bud, his boorish, sex-crazed son, and Kelly, his empty-headed and over-sexed daughter. There was no sugar-coating in that sitcom. *Married, with Children* was implanted on a new parodic subtext: *the father = moron*.

The television programs of the 1950s and 1960s reflected a patriarchal mythology of fatherhood. That mythology was challenged not only by *All in the Family*, but also throughout the 1970s by programs such as *The Mary Tyler Moore Show*, *Wonder Woman*, *Rhoda*, *Maude*, *The Days and Nights of Molly Dodd*, *Cagney and Lacey*, and others that portrayed strong, independent women who were attempting to survive, socially and professionally, in a world that was disassembling patriarchal structures. By the late 1980s the deconstruction of patriarchy was complete. *Married, with Children*, and other sitcoms similar to it (e.g., the cartoon sitcom *The Simpsons*), constituted a scathing indictment of traditional family values. The fathers on those sitcoms were anti-heroes, who had all the wrong answers to family problems.

It is interesting to note that in the midst of the reconfiguration, the *Bill Cosby Show*—a throwback to the 1950s—achieved unexpected success throughout the 1980s. In hindsight, there were a number of reasons for its success. First and foremost was the fact the Bill Cosby himself was a great comedian who could easily endear himself to a large audience. But, more importantly, the *Bill Cosby Show* was appropriate for the 1980s. Throughout the 1970s, programs like *All in the Family* and *The Jeffersons* were reflexes of an iconoclastic movement to tear down authority models and figures. But during the 1980s, with the ascendancy of a new right-wing moralism, as evidenced by the election of Ronald Reagan in the US, the mythology of patriarchal authority was attempting to make a comeback. Once more, audiences were searching for TV father figures who were gentle and understanding at the same time. Bill Cosby fit this image perfectly. But there was a difference. Unlike the wife in *Father Knows Best*, Cosby's wife had a more assertive role to play in the family. The "new-look" patriarchal family provided a symbolism of reassurance in traditional values to those who perceived that the world was in moral flux.

DIGITAL TV

The history of TV genres up to the last few years has been shaped by the fact that the audience for TV programming was fairly homogeneous in its tastes and expectations. But this has been rapidly changing with the rise of cable and satellite TV, along with the use of digital technologies. The new kind of TV audience is demanding, and getting, programming that is much more tailored to individualized needs and much more based on a diversity of lifestyles. Like modern society, TV has become in recent years a diverse, eclectic source of news, entertainment, information, and delectation.

Before cable and satellites, it was syndicated programming that made inroads into the hegemony that the main networks enjoyed. Syndicated programs are programs rented or licensed by their producers to other companies for broadcast, distribution, or exhibition. Programs such as *The Wheel of Fortune* (1983–) came forward in the mid-1980s to challenge the dominion over audiences that the networks had. It continues to be a popular prime time quiz program.

Cable television was first developed in the late 1940s to serve shadow areas—that is, areas that are blocked from receiving signals from a station's transmitting antenna. Today, cable and satellite TV have become the norm. Digital data-compression techniques, which convert television signals to digital code in an efficient way, have increased cable's capacity to 500 or more channels.

Cable television has introduced *narrowcasting* into TV. This can be defined, simply, as the use of genre channels designed to cater to individual tastes. Currently, these include: cultural/educational channels (Knowledge TV, Discovery Channel, Arts & Entertainment Channel, the Learning Channel), movie channels (Home Box Office, Showtime, the Movie Network), news channels (CNN, the Weather Channel, Fox News), music channels (MTV, VH-1), religious channels (Vision TV, the Christian Network), government channels (C-Span, S-Span), sports channels (ESPN, TSN), shopping channels (Home Shopping Network, QVC), animation channels (the Cartoon network), etc. In addition to basic service channels, some of these are part of a pay-per-view system, which allows individuals access to many other kinds of specialized programs, from adult erotic movies to wrestling and boxing tournaments, video game channels, such as *The Nintendo Channel*, musical channels for highly specialized tastes, and print-based services specializing in news headlines, program listings, weather updates, and the like. Cable companies now also offer computer and Internet services.

Although there appears to be much more choice for viewers in the Digital Galaxy, narrowcasting has in fact produced "more of the same thing," as media conglomerates gain control of the channels. With every merger, "homogenizing formulas" are established. There may be a hundred channels, but, as many subscribers quip, "there's nothing on." Indeed, the explosion in the number of channels has simply resulted in a multiplicity of mediocrities that all have the same pre-packaged contents. Every new television station looks like every other one. And in most of the new programs the intent is to appeal to younger audiences.

One of the consequences of narrowcasting is the fact that TV no longer has the same kind of "unifying power" to influence society as a group. People once watched programs such as *All in the Family* and debated them in other media and in their social milieus. Now, it is unlikely that people will watch the same programs at the same time as a social group. This fragments interpretation and reaction to programs and, consequently, diminishes the control that TV has over social trends. As a consequence, TV is losing its dominance as a social text.

Another important trend is the advent of interactive TV. Currently, services such as *TiVo, Replay TV,* and *America Online TV* offer interactive formats permitting viewers to have more of a choice in what they can see at a certain time. Actually, a form of interactive TV can be traced as far back as 1953, in the infancy of television broadcasting, when a kid's show called *Winky Dink* featured a quasi-interactive component. To interact with the show, viewers bought a kit that included a piece of plastic to cover the TV screen and a Magic Crayon. Kids could then help the hapless Winky character out of jams. Prompted by the show's announcer, they could draw a bridge for him, for example, so that he could cross over a ravine and then erase the bridge, as instructed by the announcer, so that the bad guys would plunge into the ravine. The show ran for four years, and was revived in 1970.

Regardless of the form and contents of TV, it has always been a powerful medium because of its ability to unite vast national populations to view as a global community political and cultural events, such as the address of a leader, a singer's performance, a comedian's monologue, a tear-jerking drama, or a sports event. Although still possible, assembling a homogeneous audience for any single event is becoming increasingly rare as the number of viewing alternatives available to society continues to increase.

CONCLUDING REMARKS

As a final word, I should emphasize that, like all human inventions of the past, TV is unlikely to be permanent, at least in its current form. Its importance to modern history, however, is undeniable. As a mass medium, it has made entertainment, education, hobbies, and much more available to one and all. Since the 1950s, in fact, TV has been perceived as a source of entertainment and distraction for mass audiences. Inevitably, as TV choices, options, and devices proliferate, so too will audience fragmentation. Fragmentation is the salient characteristic of the digital culture in which we live.

Advertising

Advertisers are the interpreters of our dreams— Joseph interpreting for Pharaoh. Like the movies, they infect the routine futility of our days with purposeful adventure. Their weapons are our weaknesses: fear, ambition, illness, pride, selfishness, desire, ignorance. And these weapons must be kept as bright as a sword.

E. B. White (1899–1985)

PRELIMINARY REMARKS

The contemporary advertising industry was founded at the threshold of the twentieth century on the premise that sales of a product would increase if the product could be linked to lifestyle and socially-significant trends and values. Indirect proof that product advertising has, in fact, achieved its goal of blurring the line between the product and social consciousness of it can be seen in the fact that it is now used as a persuasion technique by anyone in society who wants to influence people to do something—to endorse a political candidate, to support a cause, and so on and so forth. Business firms, political parties and candidates, social organizations, special-interest groups, and governments alike use advertising routinely to create favorable "images" of themselves in the minds of people. Since the 1960s, advertising campaigns have also been mounted and directed towards issues of social concern (cancer, AIDS, human rights, poverty, etc.).

But it is the messages of product advertising that are everywhere. They are on billboards, on the radio, on television, on buses and subways, in magazines and newspapers, on posters, on clothes, shoes, hats, pens—and the list could go on and on. To say that advertising has become a ubiquitous form of message-making in today's "global market culture" is an understatement—it is estimated that the average American is exposed to over 3000 advertisements a day and watches three years' worth of television commercials over the course of a lifetime. Using both verbal and nonverbal techniques to make its messages as persuasive as possible, advertising has become an integral category of modern-day culture designed to influence attitudes and lifestyle behaviors by covertly suggesting how we can best satisfy our innermost urges and aspirations.

The semiotic study of advertising has become a hugely popular one. The basic focus of such study is, of course, the view of advertising as a sign-creating system. That will be the focus of this chapter as well.

WHAT IS ADVERTISING?

The term *advertising* derives from the medieval Latin verb *advertere* "to direct one's attention to." It designates any type or form of public announcement intended to promote the sale of specific commodities or services, or to spread some kind of social or political message. Advertising is to be distinguished from other materials and activities aimed at swaying and influencing opinions, attitudes, and behaviors, such as *propaganda,* the term used in reference to any systematic dissemination of doctrines, views, beliefs reflecting specific interests and ideologies (political, social, philosophical, etc.); *publicity*, the term used in reference to the craft of disseminating any information that concerns a person, group, event, or product through some public medium; and *public relations,* the term commonly used to refer to the activities and techniques deployed by organizations and individuals to establish favorable attitudes towards them among the general public or special groups.

In the twentieth century, advertising evolved into a form of persuasive social strategy intended to influence how people perceived the buying and consumption of goods. Over the century, it became a privileged discourse that replaced, by and large, the more traditional forms of discourse—sermons, political oratory, proverbs, wise sayings, etc.—which in previous centuries had rhetorical force and moral authority. To this day, the advertising subtext aims to exalt and inculcate Epicurean values. As pointed out in chapter 11, Roland Barthes (1957) used the term *neomania* to emphasize the overall social consequences of living in a consumerist society informed by advertising messages. He defined neomania as an insatiable appetite for new objects of consumption induced into groupthink by ads and commercials constantly blurting out one promise to all: "Buy this or that and you will not be bored, but you will be happy!" With a handful of hedonistic themes—happiness, youth, success, status, luxury, fashion, and beauty—the general message of the advertising subtext is that solutions to human problems can be found in buying and consuming.

Advertising falls into three main categories: (1) *consumer advertising*, which is directed towards the promotion of some product, (2) *trade advertising,* in which a sales pitch is made to dealers and professionals through appropriate trade publications and media, and (3) *political-social advertising*, which is used by special-interest groups (such as anti-smoking groups) and politicians to advertise their platforms. The focus of this chapter is on the first type, which can be defined semiotically as a form of representation designed to promote the sale of marketable goods and services through persuasion.

Consumer advertising, incidentally, gave birth to the first agency for recording and analyzing data on advertising effectiveness in 1914 with the establishment of the Audit Bureau of Circulations in the US, an independent organization founded and supported by newspaper and magazine publishers wishing to obtain circulation statistics and to standardize the ways of presenting them. Then, in 1936 the Advertising Research Foundation was established to conduct research on, and to develop, advertising techniques with the capacity to enhance the authenticity, reliability, efficiency, and usefulness of all advertising and marketing research. Today, the increasing sophistication with statistical information-gathering techniques makes it possible for advertisers to target audiences on the basis of where people live, what income they make, what educational background they have, and so on in order to determine their susceptibility to, or inclination towards, certain products.

Advertising is thus closely interconnected with marketing. Advertisers and marketing agencies conduct extensive and expensive surveys to determine the potential acceptance of products or services before they are advertised at costs that may add up to millions of dollars. If the survey convinces the manufacturer that one of the versions exhibited will attract enough purchasers, a research crew then pretests various sales appeals by showing provisional product designs to consumers and asking them to indicate their preference. After the one or two best-liked designs are identified, the manufacturer produces a limited quantity of the new product and introduces it in a test market. On the basis of this market test the manufacturer can make a decision as to whether a national campaign should be launched.

THE ADVENT OF ADVERTISING

The first advertising materials of human civilization were the many outdoor signs displayed above the shop doors of ancient cities of the Middle East. As early as 3000 BC, the Babylonians used such signs to advertise the stores themselves. The ancient Greeks and Romans also hung signs outside their shops. Since few people could read, the merchants of the era used recognizable visual symbols carved in stone, clay, or wood for their signs. Throughout history, poster and picture signs in marketplaces and temples have, in fact, constituted popular media for disseminating information and for promoting the barter and sale of goods and services. With the invention of the printing press in the fifteenth century, flyers and posters could be printed quickly and cheaply, and posted in public places or inserted in books, pamphlets, newspapers, etc. The printing press also spawned a new form of advertising, known as the *handbill*. This had an advantage over a poster or sign because it could be reproduced and distributed to many people living near and far apart.

The growing use and influence of advertising in the nineteenth century led to the establishment of the first advertising agency by Philadelphia entrepreneur Volney B. Palmer in 1842. By 1849, Palmer had offices in New York, Boston, and Baltimore in addition to his Philadelphia office. In 1865, George P. Rowell began contracting with local newspapers as a go-between with clients. Ten years later, in 1875, N. W. Ayer and Son, another Philadelphia advertising agency, became a rival of Rowell and Palmer. In time, the firm hired writers and artists to create print ads and carried out complete advertising campaigns for clients. It thus became the first *ad agency* in the modern sense of the word. By 1900, most agencies in the US were writing ads for clients, and were starting to assume responsibility for complete advertising campaigns. By the 1920s, such agencies had become themselves large business enterprises, constantly developing new techniques and methods that would be capable of influencing the so-called "typical consumer." It was at that point in time that advertising came to be perceived primarily as an instrument of persuasion by corporate executives. Business and psychology had joined forces by the first decades of the twentieth century, broadening the attempts of their predecessors to build a semiotic bridge between the product and the consumer's consciousness.

In the 1920s, the increased use of electricity led to the possibility of further entrenching advertising into the social landscape through the use of new electronic media. Electricity made possible the illuminated outdoor poster; and photoengraving and other printing inventions helped both the editorial and advertising departments of magazines create truly effective illustrative material that could be incorporated into ad texts. The advent of radio, also in the 1920s, led to the invention and widespread use of a new form of advertising, known as the *commercial*—a mini-narrative or musical jingle revolving around a product or service. The commercial became immediately a highly popular form of advertising, since it could reach masses of potential customers, print literate or not, instantaneously. The commercial became even more influential as a vehicle for disseminating advertising messages throughout society with the advent of television in the early 1950s. TV commercials of the day became instantly familiar across society, creating a perception of the product as being inextricably intertwined with the style and content of the commercials created to promote it. Recently, the Internet has come forward to complement and supplement both the print and commercial (radio and TV) forms of advertising. As in TV commercials, Internet advertisers use graphics, audio, and various visual techniques to enhance the effectiveness of their messages.

The language of advertising has become the language of virtually everyone—even of those who are critical of it. As Twitchell (2000: 1) aptly puts it, "language about products and services has pretty much replaced language about all other subjects." We assimilate and react to advertising texts unwittingly and in ways that parallel how individuals and groups have responded in the past to various kinds of artistic texts. They thus shape social trends in a synergistic fashion. Advertising has become one of the most ubiquitous, all-encompassing forms of social discourse ever devised by humans. There are now even websites, such as AdCritic.com, that feature ads for their own sake, so that audiences can view them for their aesthetic qualities alone.

The two main techniques that make advertising so powerful are called *positioning* and *image-creation. Positioning* is the placing or targeting of a product for the right people. For example, ads for Budweiser beer are normally positioned for a male audience, whereas ads for Chanel perfume are positioned, by and large, for a female audience. The advertising of the Mercedes Benz automobile is aimed at socially upscale car buyers; the advertising of Dodge vans is aimed, instead, at middle-class suburban dwellers. Creating an *image* for a product inheres in fashioning a "personality" for it so that a particular type of product can be positioned for specific market populations. The image is a sign that is made up of an amalgam of the product's name, packaging, logo, price, and overall presentation which create a recognizable character for it that is meant to appeal to specific consumer types. Take beer as an example. What kinds of people drink Budweiser? And what kinds drink Heineken instead? Answers to these questions would typically include data about the educational level, class, social attitudes, etc., of the consumer. The one who drinks Budweiser is perceived by people as socially different from the one who drinks Heineken. The former is imagined to be a down-to-earth (male) character who simply wants to "hang out with the guys," the latter a smooth sophisticated type (male or female). This personification of the product is reinforced further by the fact that Budweiser commercials are positioned next to sports events on television, whereas Heineken ads are found next to current affairs programs, and certain types of sitcoms. The idea behind creating an image for the product is, clearly, to speak directly to particular types of individuals, not to everyone, so that these individuals can see their own personalities represented in the lifestyle images created by advertisements for certain products.

Product image is further entrenched by the technique of *mythologization*. This is the strategy of imbuing brand names, logos, product design, ads, and commercials with some mythic meaning. For instance, the quest for beauty, the conquest of death, among other mythic themes, are constantly being worked into the specific images that advertisers create for beauty products—a strategy that can be literally seen in the people who appear in ads and commercials, who are, typically, attractive people, with an "unreal," almost deified, mythic quality about the way they look. In a phrase, the modern advertiser stresses not the product, but the social or mythic meanings that may be expected to materialize from its purchase. The advertiser is, clearly, quite adept at setting foot into the same subconscious regions of psychic experience that were once explored only by philosophers, artists, and religious thinkers.

Advertisers are also among the most creative users of new technologies. Since young people are highly expert Internet users, advertisers are using this new medium in ways that are pushing advertising techniques in new and interesting directions. On the site for Barbie dolls, for instance, visitors are invited to design their own doll and then buy it. At the Hot Wheels website, visitors are invited to play games, and then buy the toy cars.

No wonder then that advertising has become an issue of debate and a target of legislation across the world. For example, in some countries, the law prohibits or restricts the use of women simply to attract attention in advertisements unless the product is relevant for women as consumers. In other countries, advertising for sanitary products and toilet paper is forbidden. Clearly, in the global village some cultures are scrambling to protect themselves against the images that emanate from the advertising image factory—images that emphasize sex, attractiveness, youth, and pop culture trends that have become routine and part of the global village.

BRAND NAMES AND LOGOS

To create a personality for a product, one must construct a signification system for it. This is achieved, first and foremost, by giving it a *brand name* and, whenever possible, creating a visual symbol for it known as a *logo*. By assigning it a name, the product, like a person, can be recognized in terms of its name. No wonder, then, that *trademarks*—which is the legal term for *brand name*—are so fiercely protected by corporations and manufacturers. So important is the brand name as an identifier of the product that, on several occasions, it has become the general term to refer to the product type. Examples include *aspirin*, *cellophane*, and *escalator*.

In effect, the name on its own generates a signification system for the product. Here are some examples:

- Names referring to the actual manufacturer evoke connotations of "tradition," "reliability," "artistry," "sophistication," etc.: e.g., *Armani, Benetton, Folger's.*
- Names referring to a fictitious personality elicit specific kinds of images associated with the names: e.g., *Wendy's* evokes the image of a "friendly young girl," *Mr. Clean* of a "strong toiler."
- Names referring to some aspect of Nature bestow upon the product the qualities associated with Nature: e.g., *Tide, Surf, Cascade, Aqua Velva, Mountain Dew.*
- Names constructed as hyperboles emphasize product "superiority," "excellence," etc.: e.g., *MaxiLight, SuperFresh, UltraLite.*
- Names constructed as combinations of words elicit composite meanings: e.g., *Fruitopia* ("fruit + Utopia"), *Yogourt* ("yogurt + gourmet").
- Some names are designed to tell what the product can do: e.g., *Easy Off, Lestoil, One Wipe, Quick Flow, Easy Wipe.*
- Some names are designed to show what can be accomplished by using the product: e.g., *Close-Up Toothpaste, No Sweat Deodorant.*

To continue to be effective, however, brand-naming must keep in step with the times. In early 2000 some carmakers, for instance, started looking at newer naming trends that were designed to appeal to a new generation of customers accustomed to an Internet style of communication. Cadillac, for instance, announced a new model with the monogram name CTS in 2001.

Acura also transformed its line of models with names such as TL, RL, MDX, RSX. On the other side of the naming equation, such abbreviations are hard to remember, especially for older customers who have not yet tapped into Internetese.

Brand names, clearly, do much more than just identify a product. As the above examples show, they are constructed to create signification systems for the product. At a practical informational level, naming a product has, of course, a denotative function; that is, it allows consumers to identify what product they desire to purchase (or not). But at a connotative level, the product's name generates images that go well beyond this simple identifier function. Consider Armani shoes as a specific case in point. Denotatively, the name allows us to identify the shoes, should we desire to buy them rather than, say, Russell & Bromley shoes. However, this is not all it does. The use of the manufacturer's name, rather than some invented name, assigns an aura of craftsmanship and superior quality to the product. The shoes are thus perceived to be the "work" of an artist (Giorgio Armani). They constitute, in effect, a "work of shoe art," not just an assembly-line product for everyone to wear.

In the world of fashion, designer names such as Gucci, Armani, and Calvin Klein evoke images of *objets d'art*, rather than images of mere clothes, shoes, or jewelry; so too do names such as Ferrari, Lamborghini, and Maserati in the world of automobiles. The manufacturer's name, in such cases, extends the meaning of the product considerably. When people buy an Armani or a Gucci product, they feel that they are buying a work of art to be displayed on the body; when they buy Poison, by Christian Dior, they sense that they are buying a dangerous, but alluring, love potion; when they buy Moondrops, Natural Wonder, Rainflower, Sunsilk, or Skin Dew cosmetics they feel that they are acquiring some of Nature's beauty resources; and when they buy Eterna 27, Clinique, Endocil, or Equalia beauty products they sense that they are getting products made with scientific precision. No-name products do not engender such arrays of connotations.

Iconic brand names are also effective, because they are memorable. A name such as Ritz Crackers, for example, assigns a sonority to the product that is simulative of sounds that crackers make as they are being eaten, as well as associating the product with the extremely expensive Ritz Hotel in London.Another example is the name Drakkar Noir, chosen by the Guy Laroche for one of its cologne products. The dark bottle conveys an imagery of "fear," the "forbidden," and the "unknown." Forbidden things take place under the cloak of the night, hence *noir* (French for "black"). The sepulchral name of the cologne is clearly iconic with the bottle's design at a connotative level, reinforcing the idea that something desirous in the "dark" will happen by splashing on the cologne. The name Drakkar is also obviously suggestive of Dracula, the deadly vampire who mesmerized his sexual prey with a mere glance.

Incidentally, branding was, originally, the searing of flesh with a hot iron to produce a scar or mark with an easily recognizable pattern for identification or other purposes. Livestock were branded by the Egyptians as early as 2000 BC. In the late medieval period, trades people and guild members posted characteristic marks outside their shops, leading to the notion of the trademark. Medieval swords and ancient Chinese pottery, for instance, were also marked with identifiable symbols so buyers could trace their origin and determine their quality. Among the best-known trademarks surviving from early modern times are the striped pole of the barbershop and the three-ball sign of the pawnbroker shop. Many trademarks are, in fact, indistinguishable from logos.

Names were first used towards the end of the nineteenth century. Previously, everyday household products were sold in neighborhood stores from large bulk containers. Around 1880, soap manufacturers started naming their products so that they could be identified—e.g., Ivory, Pears', Sapolio, Colgate, etc. The first modern-day brand names were thus invented. As Naomi Klein (2000: 6) aptly observes, branding became the general practice among manufacturers of products because the market was starting to be flooded by uniform mass-produced and, thus, indistinguishable products: "Competitive branding became a necessity of the machine age." By the early 1950s, it became obvious that branding was not just a simple strategy for product differentiation, but the very semiotic fuel that propelled corporate identity and product recognizability. Even the advent of no-name products, designed to cut down the cost of buying them to the consumer, have had little effect on the semiotic power that branding has on the consciousness of people. Names such as Nike, Apple, Body Shop, Calvin Klein, Levi's, etc., have become "culture signs" recognized by virtually anyone living in a modern consumerist society. As Klein (2000: 16) goes on to remark, for such firms the brand name constitutes "the very fabric of their companies."

Logos (an abbreviation of *logogriphs*) are the pictorial counterparts of brand names. They are designed to reinforce the signification system for a product through the visual channel.

Consider the apple logo adopted by the Apple Computer Company:

It is, clearly, an iconic sign suffused with latent religious symbolism suggesting, above all else, the story of Adam and Eve in the Western Bible, which revolves around the eating of an apple that contained forbidden knowledge. The logo reinforces this symbolic association because it shows an apple that has had a bite taken from it. The creator of the logo, a man named Rob Janoff of Regis McKenna Advertising, denies any intent to connect the logo to the Genesis story, claiming instead that he put the bite there in order to ensure that the figure was not interpreted as a tomato. Whatever the truth, the bite in the apple evokes the Genesis story nonetheless because we cannot help but interpret signs in cultural terms.

Logos can sometimes harbor a complex signification system. Consider the Playboy logo of a bunny wearing a bow tie:

Its ambiguous design opens up at least two interpretive paths:
- rabbit = "female" = "highly fertile" = "sexually active" = "promiscuous" = etc.
- bow tie = "elegance" = "night club scene" = "finesse" = etc.

The appeal and staying power of this logo is due, arguably, to this inbuilt ambiguity. Ambiguity, as a matter of fact, is what makes signs psychologically powerful. By not being able to pin down what the Y is in the $X = Y$ relation, we start experiencing the sign more holistically and, thus, attributing great significance to it (at least unconsciously).

Logos have now become part of an everyday visual symbolism that interconnects products with daily life. Until the 1970s, logos on clothes, for instance, were concealed discreetly inside a collar or on a pocket. But since then, they have been displayed conspicuously, indicating, not surprisingly, that our society has become "logo conscious." Ralph Lauren's polo horseman, Lacoste's alligator, and Nike's "swoosh" symbol, to mention but three, are now shown prominently on clothing items, evoking images of heraldry and, thus, nobility. They constitute symbols of "cool" (Klein 2000: 69) that legions of people are seemingly eager to put on view in order to convey an aura of high-class "blue-blooded" fashionableness. To see why logos are so powerful semiotically, consider briefly the Nike symbol:

As a visual sign suggesting speed, it works on several levels, from the iconic to the mythical. At the iconic level, it implies the activity of running at top speed with the Nike shoe; at the mythic level, it taps into the idea of speed as symbolic of power and conquest (such as in the Olympic races). The combination of these two signifying levels creates a perception of the logo, and thus the product, as having a connection to both reality and narrative history.

Given their psychological power, it is little wonder to find that logos are used as well by non-commercial enterprises and organizations. One of the most widely known of this kind is the peace sign, often worn on chains and necklaces:

Derived from an ancient runic symbol of despair and grief, it became the logo for philosopher Bertrand Russell's (1872–1970) "Campaign for Nuclear Disarmament" in the 1950s. The logo's first widespread exposure came when it surfaced in the 1962 sci-fi film *The Day the Earth Caught Fire*, leading to its adoption by the counterculture youth of the era.

The concepts of brand and logo have been extended to include not just products, but entire corporations (IBM, Ford, etc.) and even specific characters that represent, in some way, a corporation. Take, for example, the Disney Corporation cartoon character Mickey Mouse. In 1929, Disney allowed Mickey Mouse to be reproduced on school slates, effectively transforming the character into a logo. A year later Mickey Mouse dolls went into production and throughout the 1930s the Mickey Mouse brand name and image were licensed with huge success. In 1955 *The Mickey Mouse Club* premiered on US network television, further entrenching the brand and image—and by association all Disney products—into the cultural mainstream. The case of Mickey Mouse has repeated itself throughout modern corporate society. The idea is to integrate the brand with cultural spectacles (movies, TV programs, etc.) and render it indistinguishable as a sign from other culturally-meaningful signs and sign systems. In the case of the Disney Corporation, for example, toys, TV programs, films, videos, DVDs, theme parks, and the like have become part of the mythology of childhood. This is why children now experience their childhood through such products.

ANALYZING THE AD

It was Roland Barthes (1957) who drew the attention of semioticians to the value of studying advertising. Today there is considerable interest in this area. If there is one theme that can be extracted from this line of inquiry that is of specific relevance to the present discussion, it is that many ads are interpretable at two levels—a surface and an underlying one. The surface level is the actual ad text. The way in which the text is put together, however, is both a reflex of, and a trace to, an underlying subtextual level: that is, the surface elements cohere into signifiers that conjure up an array of connotations in the underlying subtext. The main intent of a large portion of contemporary advertising, as this line of analysis shows, is to speak indirectly to the unconscious mind.

To elucidate how the subtext is constructed, it is instructive to analyze a lifestyle print ad. For this purpose, I have selected an ad for *Marilyn Peach*, a sparkling wine, that was found in many European magazines a few years ago:

The peach background (which is not discernible in the black-and-white reproduction here) matches both the color and the taste of the wine. Subtextually, however, the idea that comes to mind is that of the dawn, and thus the connotations that it evokes, as can be discerned in expressions such as *the dawn of creation*, *the dawn of life*, and so on. Are there any surface level signifiers to help us ascertain the subtext? The woman's hand is holding out a drinking glass in an obvious toasting gesture. Is this a social gesture or a temptation? The fact that the woman is wearing a bracelet in the form of a snake suggests the latter—in the Book of Genesis, the devil came to Eve in the body of a snake to prod her on to tempt Adam. A male partner is probably the one who is being seductively offered the glass. Will he take it? Since, "his glass" is on the table, it would appear that he cannot resist. If you still have doubts about this analysis, just read the accompanying French verbal text— *La pêche, le nouveau fruit de la tentation* ("Peach, the new fruit of temptation")—and you will be left with little doubt about the Garden of Eden subtext built into the ad. Note as well the name of the wine—*Marilyn*—which is suggestive of pop culture's version of Eve, the late actress Marilyn Munroe, who became an icon of tragic femininity in the 1950s and early 1960s.

Whether or not this ad will induce consumers to buy *Marilyn Peach* is open to question. It is certainly not the point of semiotic analysis to determine this. Nor is it the goal of semiotics to criticize makers of such ads. On the contrary, a semiotician should, in theory, approach an ad like he or she would any text. Advertising textuality provides an opportunity to examine how varied sign processes are realized in a contemporary textual form.

It should also be pointed out that the interpretation of any advertising text is just that—one possible interpretation. Indeed, disagreement about what something means is not only unavoidable, but part of the fun of semiotics. Differences of opinion fill the pages of the semiotic journals and lead, like in other sciences, to a furthering of knowledge in the field. The point of the above analysis was simply to illustrate the technique of semiotic analysis itself, not to provide a definitive interpretation of the *Marilyn Peach* ad. The key to unlocking the underlying subtext is to consider the surface signifiers in a chain, like a comic strip, in order to see where they lead. This technique can thus be called "connotative chaining." In the above ad the connotative chain is:

the peach background = dawn = dawn of creation = Garden of Eden scene = Eve tempting Adam = prodded on by a serpent (bracelet) = he who drinks the wine will yield to temptation (*La pêche, le nouveau fruit de la tentation*).

In most ads, the subtext can be wrested from the technique of connotative chaining, which also involves taking into account the shape of a product (e.g., a perfume bottle), shadows and colors in the ad text, the name of the product, and all the relevant surface level signifiers.

THE LANGUAGE OF ADS

The above caption, *La pêche, le nouveau fruit de la tentation*, is evidently designed to reinforce the subtext. In advertising, language is generally a means for reinforcing, alluding to, or simply stating the subtextual meaning. There are many verbal techniques that advertisers use to realize this objective and, more generally, to get the product into social consciousness. Some of these are:

- *Jingles and Slogans*: These enhance memory of the product: *Have a great day, at McDonald's; Join the Pepsi Generation.*
- *Use of the Imperative Form*: This creates the effect of advice coming from an unseen authoritative source: *Drink milk, love life; Trust your senses.*

- *Formulas*: These create the effect of making meaningless statements sound truthful: *Triumph has a bra for the way you are; A Volkswagen is a Volkswagen.*
- *Alliteration*: The repetition of sounds in a slogan or jingle increases the likelihood that a brand name will be remembered and be imbued with a poetic quality: *The Superfree sensation* (alliteration of *s*); *Guinness is good for you* (alliteration of *g*).
- *Absence of language*: Some ads strategically avoid the use of any language whatsoever, suggesting, by implication, that the product speaks for itself.
- *Intentional omission*: This capitalizes on the fact that secretive statements like *Don't tell your friends about...; Do you know what she's wearing?* grab people's attention.
- *Metaphor:* Metaphor creates powerful imagery for the product: e.g., *Come to where the flavor is ... Marlboro country.*
- *Metonymy:* Metonymy also creates powerful imagery for the product: *Bring a touch of Paris into your life.*

In addition to these, the brand name itself, as mentioned, is a signifier in creating a signification system for a product and, thus, for understanding the subtext of any ad created for the product. Consider, again, the Drakkar Noir product. The ad below filled the pages of Italian magazines a few years ago. Note, first, that the perfume bottle has a portentous, ominous black color but aesthetically pleasing elliptical shape:

Darkness connotes fear, evil, the unknown. Forbidden things take place under the cloak of night. The sepulchral name, Drakkar Noir—obviously suggestive of Dracula—instills both a surreptitious fear and cupidity in the viewer. It thus reinforces the subtextual message that something dark, scary but nevertheless desirable, will happen by dousing oneself with the cologne, as suggested by the visual text:

darkness = evil = something desirable = Dracula = sexuality = etc.

This is reinforced by the caption *L'altro Drakkar, intenso come la notte* ("The other Drakkar, intense like the night"). The "other" Drakkar is, by implication, the other Dracula (the one who buys the cologne?) who is intense like the night. Note, as well, that the statement is at the top of the page, descending upon the bottle and, thus, reinforcing the sense that something truly mythic and metaphysical is involved in the whole scene.

Whatever the ad means, the point to be made here is that it is completely synchronized with the signification system built into the product name. The ad can almost be compared to a work of surrealist or abstract art, whereby interpretation is a matter of sense and feel, rather than of straightforward understanding.

AD CULTURE

As the foregoing discussion implies, advertising is an art form. This has in fact been acknowledged concretely by the fact that it has its own prize category at the annual Cannes Film Festival. Advertising is adaptive, constantly seeking out new forms of representation reflecting fluctuations in social trends and values. Although we may be inclined to condemn its objectives, as an aesthetic-inducing experience we invariably enjoy advertising. Advertisements sway, please, and seduce.

Aware of this, some societies have enacted restrictive legislative measures to constrain advertisers. Sometimes, however, these backfire. In early 1998, the US Congress was mulling over banning the Joe Camel and Marlboro Man figures from cigarette advertising. In response, the ad creators came up with ingenious alternatives. In an ad for Salem cigarettes, for instance, there is a pair of peppers curled together to look like a pair of lips, with a cigarette dangling from them. Benson and Hedges ads in the same year portrayed cigarettes acting like people—floating in swimming pools, lounging in armchairs, etc.

Ironically, the new, "government-permissible" form of advertising was a huge success, as cigarette-smoking rates among young people rose dramatically. The ads were even more effective in communicating the glamour and "cool" of smoking than was the Joe Camel figure.

The signification systems that are built into brand names and logos are transferred creatively to ad texts. And these now tend to become part of general culture. This integration into the mainstream is perpetuated and reinforced by the ad campaign, which can be defined as the systematic creation of a series of slightly different ads and commercials based on the same theme, characters, jingles, etc. An ad campaign is comparable to the theme and variations form of music—where there is one theme with many variations.

One of the primary functions of ad campaigns is to guarantee that the product's image keep in step with the changing times. Thus, for example, the Budweiser ad campaigns of the 1980s and early 1990s emphasized rural, country-and-western ruggedness, and female sexuality seen from a male viewpoint. The actors in the commercials were "Marlboro men," and the women their prey. In the early 2000s, the same company changed its image with its "Whassup!" campaign to keep in step with the changing sociopolitical climate. Its new ad campaign showed young urban males who hung around together, loved sports, and generally behaved typically. So appealing was the "Whassup!" campaign that its signature catch phrase was joked about on talk shows, parodied on websites, mimicked in other media, and used by people commonly in their daily conversations. The makers of Budweiser had clearly adapted their advertising style to social changes and trends.

Indeed, the most effective advertising strategy is not only to keep up with the times but also to co-opt them, so to speak. In the 1960s, for example, self-proclaimed "rebels" and "revolutionaries" referred to generally as "hippies," who genuinely thought they were posing a radical challenge to the ideological values and lifestyle mores of the mainstream consumerist culture, ended up becoming the incognizant trend-setters of the very culture they deplored, providing it with features of lifestyle and discourse that advertisers, since then, have been able to adapt and recycle into society at large. Counterculture clothing fashion was quickly converted into mainstream fashion, counterculture music style into mainstream music style, counterculture symbolism and talk into society-wide symbolism and discourse—hence the crystallization of a social mindset whereby every individual, of every political and ideological persuasion, could feel that he or she was a symbolic participant in the "youth revolution."

The Pepsi Generation and the Coke universal brotherhood ("I'd like to teach the world to sing in perfect harmony…") campaigns directly incorporated the rhetoric and symbolism of the hippie counterculture, thus creating the illusion that the goals of the hippies and of the soft drink manufacturers were one and the same. Rebellion through purchasing became the subliminal thread woven into the ad campaigns. The Dodge Rebellion and Oldsmobile Youngmobile campaigns followed, etching into the nomenclature of the cars themselves the powerful connotations of rebellion and defiance. Even a sewing company, alas, came forward to urge people to join its own type of surrogate revolution, hence its slogan *You don't let the establishment make your world; don't let it make your clothes.* In effect, by claiming to "join the revolution," advertising created the real revolution. This is why, since the late 1960s, the worlds of advertising, marketing, youth trends, and entertainment have become synergistically intertwined.

Today, the integration of ad campaigns into social discourse has become so versatile and ubiquitous that we hardly realize how pervasive it is. Here are some of its current forms:

- using the something-for-nothing lure (*Buy one and get a second one free! Send for free sample! Trial offer at half price! No money down!*);
- using humor to generate a feeling of goodwill towards a product (as in the Budweiser campaigns);
- getting a product endorsed by celebrities;
- inducing parents to believe that giving their children certain products will secure them a better life and future;
- appealing to children to "ask mommy or daddy" to buy certain products, thus increasing the likelihood that parents will give in to their children's requests;
- promoting such goods and services as insurance, fire alarms, cosmetics, and vitamin capsules by evoking the fear of poverty, sickness, loss of social standing, and/or impending disaster;
- the use of erotic, sensual, mythic, and other kinds of psychologically powerful themes and symbols in campaigns.

These techniques have become so common that they are no longer recognized consciously as stratagems. Advertising has become the fuel for an entertainment-driven society that seeks artifice on a daily basis as part of its routine of escapism from the deeper philosophical questions that would otherwise beset it.

CONCLUDING REMARKS

It is no exaggeration to say that the history of modern culture is intrinsically interwoven with the history of advertising. In looking back over the last century, it is obvious that the messages of advertisers, their ad campaigns, and their peculiar uses of language have become the norm in other creative domains, from cinematography to pop music. As McLuhan (1964: 24) aptly put it, advertising has become the "art of the modern world."

The answer to curtailing the power of advertising is not to be found in censorship or in any form of state control of media, as some proclaim. Even if it were possible in a consumerist culture to control the content of advertising, this would invariably prove to be counterproductive. The answer is, in my view, to become aware of how advertising produces meanings with semiotic analysis. In that way, we will be in a much better position to fend off the undesirable effects that it may cause.

Communication

I and my public understand each other very well: it does not hear
what I say, and I don't say what it wants to hear.
Karl Kraus (1874–1936)

PRELIMINARY REMARKS

Why do animals communicate with each other? Is it just for survival? Are
there any other reasons? How does communication unfold? These are questions
that fall under the rubric of *communication theory*, and as such have traditionally
fallen outside the purview of semiotics proper. However, since communication
involves the exchange of signs, messages, and meanings, it is nonetheless of
obvious interest to semioticians. This was certainly the opinion of the late
Thomas A. Sebeok (1920–2001), one of this century's leading semioticians
and linguists, who was instrumental in expanding the perimeter of semiotics
proper to include the study of communication among all species. Known as
the *biosemiotic* movement, Sebeok has shown that in studying cross-species
communication, we end up getting a better idea of what makes human
communication unique.

Research has, in fact, shown how remarkably rich and varied animal
communication systems are. Scientists have recorded and identified, for
instance, birdcalls for courting, mating, hunger, food bearing, territoriality,
warning, and distress, and elaborate vocal signals that whales and dolphins
deploy to communicate over long distances underwater. Biosemiotics aims to
investigate such patterns, seeking to understand how animals are endowed by
their nature with the capacity to use specific types of signals and signs for
survival (*zoosemiosis*), and thus how human semiosis (*anthroposemiosis*) is
both linked to, and different from, animal semiosis. The objective of this new

branch of semiotics is to distill common elements of semiosis from its manifestations across species, integrating them into a taxonomy of notions, principles, and procedures for understanding the phenomenon of communication in its globality.

The goal of this final chapter is to take a schematic overview of communication theory, touching briefly on what it entails in semiotic terms.

WHAT IS COMMUNICATION?

Communication is, simply, the exchange of information. It is to be distinguished from representation, which is the depiction of something (Y) in some specific way (X) to create a message $(X = Y)$. Communication is the delivery, broadcasting, or transmission of the message $(X = Y)$ in some way—through the air, by means of touch, visually, and so on and so forth. At a purely biological level, a message can be received successfully (i.e., recognized as a message) by another species only if it possesses the same kind of sensory modality used to transmit it (as will be discussed below). Of these, the tactile modality is the one that seems to cut across human and many animal sensory systems. There is no doubt in my mind that a household cat and a human enter into a rudimentary form of tactile communication on a daily basis. Sharing the same living space, and being codependent on each other for affective exchanges, they do indeed transmit their feeling-states to each other by sending out body signals and especially by touching each other. However, even within the confines of this versatile communicative mode, there is no way for humans to be sure that cats have the ability to understand a broader range of tactile feeling-states implied by words such as "embrace," "guide," "hold," "tickle," etc. Clearly, interspecies communication is realizable, but only in a restricted sense. It can occur in some modalities, partially or totally, according to species. If the sensory systems of the two species are vastly different, however, then virtually no message transmission is possible.

Messages can also be transmitted through technology, i.e., through some artifact or invention. Early societies developed simple tools for transmitting messages, such as drums, fire and smoke signals, and lantern beacons, so that they could be seen or heard over short distances. Messages were also attached to the legs of carrier pigeons trained to navigate their way to a destination and back home. In later societies, so-called "semaphore" systems of flags or flashing lights, for example, were employed to send messages over relatively short but difficult-to-cross distances, such as from hilltop to hilltop, or from one ship to another at sea.

Marshall McLuhan (1964) claimed that the type of technology developed to record and transmit messages determines how people process and remember them. Any major change in how information is represented and transmitted brings about a concomitant paradigm shift in cultural systems. Ancient cuneiform writing, impressed indelibly into clay tablets, allowed the Sumerians to develop a great civilization; papyrus and hieroglyphics transformed Egyptian society into an advanced culture; the alphabet spurred the ancient Greeks on to extraordinary advances in science, technology, and the arts; the alphabet also made it possible for the Romans to develop an effective system of government; the printing press facilitated the dissemination of knowledge broadly and widely, paving the way for the European Renaissance, the Protestant Reformation, and the Enlightenment; radio, movies, and television brought about the rise of a global pop culture in the twentieth century; and the Internet and the World Wide Web ushered in McLuhan's "global village" as the twentieth century came to a close.

The term *information* invariably comes up in any discussion of communication, and thus requires some commentary. Information can be defined simply as data that can be received by humans or machines. In the modern theory of information, it is considered as something mathematically probabilistic—a ringing alarm signal carries more information than one that is silent, because the latter is the "expected state" of the alarm system and the former its "alerting state." The man who developed the mathematical aspects of information theory was the American telecommunications engineer Claude Shannon (1916–2001). He showed, essentially, that the information contained in a signal is inversely proportional to its probability. The more probable a signal, the less information "load" it carries with it; the less likely, the more.

Shannon devised his mathematical model in order to improve the efficiency of telecommunication systems. It essentially depicts information transfer between two humans as a unidirectional process dependent on probability factors, i.e., on the degree to which a message is to be expected or not in a given situation. It is called the *bull's-eye model* because a sender is defined as someone or something aiming a message at a receiver as if he, she, or it were in a bull's-eye target range:

Sender → Message → Receiver

Shannon also introduced several key terms into the general study of communication: *channel, noise, redundancy,* and *feedback:*

- *Channel* is the physical system carrying the transmitted signal. Vocally produced sound waves, for instance, can be transmitted through air or through an electronic channel (e.g., radio).
- The term *noise* refers to some interfering element (physical or psychological) in the channel that distorts or partially effaces a message. In radio and telephone transmissions, *noise* is equivalent to electronic static; in vocal speech transmissions, it can vary from any interfering exterior sound (physical noise) to the speaker's lapses of memory (psychological noise).
- Noise is why communication systems have *redundancy* features built into them. These allow for a message to be decoded even if noise is present. For instance, in verbal communication the high predictability of certain words in many utterances ("Roses are red, violets are...") and the patterned repetition of elements ("Yes, yes, I'll do it; yes, I will") are redundant features of language that greatly increase the likelihood that a verbal message will get decoded successfully.
- Finally, Shannon used the term *feedback* to refer to the fact that senders have the capacity to monitor the messages they transmit and modify them to enhance their decodability. *Feedback* in human verbal communication includes, for instance, the physical reactions observable in receivers (facial expressions, bodily movements, etc.) that indicate the effect that a message is having as it is being communicated.

Shannon's model is useful in providing a terminology for describing aspects of communication systems, but it tells us nothing about how messages and meanings shape and ultimately determine the nature of human communication events (as we saw in the case of verbal discourse in chapter 5). The main objective of this book has, in fact, been to investigate precisely how such events unfold in semiotic terms.

ANIMAL COMMUNICATION

A truly remarkable thing happens around a beehive. Worker honey bees returning to the hive from foraging trips have the extraordinary capacity to inform the other bees in the hive about the direction, distance, and quality of a food cache with amazing accuracy through movement sequences which biologists call a "dance," in obvious analogy to human dancing as a sequence of preset, repeatable bodily movements. The noteworthy thing about bee dancing is that it appears to share with human communication the feature of displacement, i.e., of conveying information in the absence of a stimulus.

Several kinds of dance patterns have been documented by entomologists. In the "round" dance, the bee moves in circles alternately to the left and to the right. This dance is apparently deployed when the cache of food is nearby:

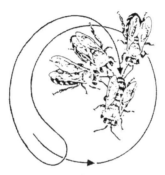

When the food source is further away, then the bee dances in a "wagging" fashion, moving in a straight line while wagging its abdomen from side to side and then returning to its starting point:

The straight line in this dance points in the direction of the food source, the energy level of the dance indicates how rich the food source is, and the tempo provides information about its distance. Now, as remarkable as this seems, it is ultimately an instinctual form of communication that cannot be learned by other bees (such as the queen bee). It is part of the beehive's survival system.

The study of animal communication systems comes under the rubric of *ethology*. Many are the fascinating findings coming out of this field, and many are the areas of study that the field now encompasses. One particular area of interest to semiotics is the teaching of human language to primates. Primates are very similar neurologically and physiologically to humans. But there is one critical anatomical difference—they lack the requisite vocal apparatus for producing speech. So, to investigate whether or not they are capable of language, the first primate communication experimenters chose American Sign Language (ASL) as the code for teaching them to speak. One of the first subjects was a female chimpanzee named Washoe, whose training by the Gardner husband and wife team (Gardner and Gardner 1969, 1975) began in 1966 when she was almost one year of age. Remarkably, Washoe learned to use 132 ASL signs in just over four years. What appeared to be even more extraordinary was that Washoe began to put signs together to express a small set of syntactically based ideas.

Inspired by such results, others embarked upon an intensive research program throughout the 1970s and the 1980s aimed at expanding upon the teaching procedures of the Gardners. The Premacks (e.g., Premack and Premack 1983), for example, whose work actually began as far back as 1954 with a five-year-old chimpanzee named Sarah, taught their subject a form of written language. They instructed Sarah to arrange and respond to vertical sequences of plastic tokens on a magnetic board that represented individual words: e.g., a small pink square = "banana"; a small blue triangle = "apple"; etc. Sarah developed the ability to respond to combinations of such symbols, which included references to abstract notions.

Although there was an initial wave of enthusiasm over such results, with the media reporting on them on a regular basis, there really has emerged no solid evidence to suggest that chimpanzees and gorillas are capable of verbal communication in the same way that humans are, nor of passing on to their offspring what they have learned from their human mentors. Nevertheless, the results obtained are truly unprecedented. It would seem that, with training, primates are capable of forming many of the abstract concepts (love, suffering, friendliness, altruism, etc.) that were once thought to be the exclusive domain of humans. This fascinating research is still ongoing.

The study of primate communication is a *biosemiotic* area of investigation. The question in biosemiotics is not whether primates can speak like humans, but rather, what semiotic capacities they possess. It is more likely that certain properties or features of semiosis cut cross species, while others are specific to one or several species. Determining the universality or specificity of particular properties is the primary target of the biosemiotic movement. The late Thomas A. Sebeok, for instance, documented the manifestations of iconicity in vastly different species. As a case in point, consider termite mound constructions. These mounds have extremely hard walls, constructed from bits of soil cemented with saliva and baked by the sun. Inside the walls are numerous chambers and galleries, interconnected by a complex network of passageways. Ventilation and drainage are provided, and heat required for hatching the eggs is obtained from the fermentation of organic matter, which is stored in the chambers serving as nurseries. Of more than 55 species common in the US, the majority build their nests underground. The subterranean termites are extremely destructive, because they tunnel their way to wooden structures, into which they burrow to obtain food. Upon closer scrutiny, such mound displays reveal the constituents of the termite's social evolution, even after the colony itself has become extinct. Indeed, the mounds are iconic signs or displays of the genetically coded social behavior of these insect architects: that is, they visually mirror this very behavior. This is an example of *unwitting iconicity* manifesting itself in Nature as a property of a specific life scheme.

Biosemiotics takes its impetus from the work of the biologist Jakob von Uexküll (1909), who provided empirical evidence to show that an organism does not perceive an object in itself, but according to its own particular kind of mental modeling system. This allows the organism to interpret the world of objects and events in a biologically unique way and, subsequently, to respond to them in semiosically specific ways. The modeling system of a species routinely converts its external world experiences into internal states of knowing and remembering that are unique to the species. Access to those states without possessing the same mental modeling system is never going to be complete. Thus, we will never be able to really understand what an animal feels, what it thinks about, and more importantly how it thinks about something.

HUMAN COMMUNICATION

In 1960 the linguist Charles Hockett put forward a typology of 13 design features that has remained a basic one for comparing animal communication systems and linguistic communication:

Design Feature	Properties and Manifestations in Language
1. Auditory-vocal transmission and directional reception	vocal language and communication involves mainly mouth and ear work, as opposed to visual, tactile, or other modes of communication.
2. Broadcast	a verbal signal can be heard by any auditory system within ear range, by which the source can be located using the ears' direction-finding capacity.
3. Rapid fading	auditory signals are transitory and do not await the hearer's convenience.
4. Interchangeability	speakers of a language can reproduce any linguistic message they can understand.
5. Total feedback	speakers of a language hear and can reflect upon everything that they say (unlike the visual displays often used in animal courtship signaling).
6. Specialization	speech sound waves have no function other than to signal meaning.
7. Semanticity	the elements of the linguistic signal convey meaning through their stable reference to real-world situations.
8. Arbitrariness	there is no necessary dependence of the element of a verbal signal on the nature of the referent.
9. Discreteness	speech uses a small set of sound elements (phonemes) that form meaningful oppositions with each other.
10. Displacement	language has the capacity to refer to situations remote in space and time from their occurrence.
11. Productivity	language users have the infinite capacity to express and understand meaning by using old elements to produce new ones.

12. Traditional transmission language is transmitted from
                              one generation to the next primarily
                              by a process of teaching and learning
                              (not only by genetic inheritance).
13. Duality of patterning   vocal sounds have no intrinsic meaning
                              in themselves but combine in different
                              ways to form elements (e.g., words)
                              that do convey meanings.

Hockett applied his typology to various animal systems of communication, including the bee dance, showing how only language possesses all of these features simultaneously (Hockett 1960: 10–11):

Feature	Bee Dancing	Language
Auditory-vocal channel	no	yes
Broadcast transmission and directional reception	yes	yes
Rapid fading	?	yes
Interchangeability	limited	yes
Total feedback	?	yes
Specialization	?	yes
Semanticity	yes	yes
Arbitrariness	no	yes
Discreteness	no	yes
Displacement	yes	yes
Productivity	yes	yes
Traditional transmission	probably not	yes
Duality of patterning	no	yes

What makes human communication unique among species is however not just language, but the fact that, whatever form it takes, it can enlist more than one mode and medium. Human communication is *multimodal* and *multimedial*, whereas most other communication systems are unimodal and unimedial. To grasp what this implies, consider the following basic typology of sensory modes of communication:

Sensory Mode	Features
Auditory-vocal	This mode characterizes speech, physiological vocal signals and symptoms (e.g., coughing and snoring), musical effects (e.g., whistling), and voice modulation (to communicate identity and feeling states).
Visual	This mode characterizes sign languages, writing, visual representation (drawing, sculpting, etc.).
Tactile	This mode characterizes communication by means of touch.
Olfactory	This mode characterizes communication by means of smell.
Gustatory	This mode characterizes communication by means of taste.

Now, it is clear that only humans have the ability to use all sensory modes to communicate, in part, in tandem, or in exclusivity: the auditory-vocal mode is used in speech, the visual one in writing, the tactile one in such interactions as handshaking, the olfactory one in perfumes, the gustatory one in artificial food tastes, and so on. In a word, human communication is multimodal. Communication between humans and animals will thus probably occur in some modes, but not in all. If the communicative mode or modes of the species are vastly different, however, then virtually no message exchange is possible. It is unlikely that humans and ants will ever enter into a communicative exchange such as the one that has evolved over the years between humans and cats or dogs.

The multimedial nature of human communication is also unique among species. The three main kinds of media that characterize human communication are:

- *natural media*, such as the voice (speech), the face (expressions), and the body (gesture, posture, etc.);
- *artifactual media*, such as books, paintings, sculptures, letters, etc.;
- *mechanical media*, such as telephones, radios, television sets, computers, videos, etc.

A verbal message, for instance, can be delivered through natural transmission, if it is articulated with the vocal organs; or else it can be transmitted by means of markings on a piece of paper through the artifactual medium of writing; and it can also be converted into radio or television signals for mechanical (electromagnetic) transmission. To sum up, human communication is a multimodal and multimedial system, involving virtually the entire body, objects, and other devices. For this reason it stands apart from all other communication systems.

Of all the mechanical media, the digital one has become a truly powerful one today, given the instantaneity and reach that such a medium allows. Most online services provide news, bulletin boards, databases, games, software libraries, and many other such things. Of these, electronic mail (e-mail) is one of the most-used digital communication systems in the world. Just as every website or Internet location has an electronic address, so too does every individual computer connected to a local access provider or online service. The user can write an e-mail message in a word-processing program, then transfer it to a communications program. The user can also write the message in an e-mail form—a box displayed on the monitor. Most communications software and online services provide such forms. After completing the message, the user can attach nonverbal material, such as graphics files, to it. He or she then addresses the message, and can send it to several addresses without rewriting it, by merely entering all the addresses as instructed by the computer. An electronic mailbox at each computer address stores the mail.

E-mail has made regular mail appear cumbersome and inefficient. And because of listservs—electronic mailing lists that make it possible to send e-mail to special-interest groups—it has truly created a worldwide system of time-efficient communications. With the advent of Instant Messaging (IM), this capacity is being enhanced further. IM is instantaneous, thus bypassing the lag time inherent in sending and receiving e-mail. With IM a line typed on one PC is seen almost instantly on the screen of the receiving PC.

In the Digital Galaxy, it is no longer valid to talk about "competing" media. Advances in digital technology and in telecommunications networks have led to a *convergence* of all media into one overall digital system of communications.

Convergence is manifest, first and foremost, in the digitization of all media technologies and in the integration of different media into computer networks:

- *Telephone*
  The first telecommunications medium to be digitized was the telephone in 1962, with the installation of high-speed lines in phone networks

capable of carrying dozens of conversations simultaneously. Phone equipment of all kinds is now fully digitized. Moreover, the phone is the technological device that permits people to gain access to the Internet. A new high-speed phone technology, called *Digital Subscriber Line* (DSL), is being currently installed across the globe. It has the capacity to transmit audio, video, and computer data over both conventional phone lines and satellite. Of course, the advent of cell phones has radically transformed how this technology is being used. Such phones have made communication with others literally a "portable thing." They allow people to connect to the Digital Galaxy without phone lines and terrestrial infrastructure.

* *Print*

The digitization of print media started in 1967. Today, most major newspapers and magazines are produced by means of digital technology and are available in online versions.

* *Film*

The special effects created for the movie *Star Wars* in 1977 introduced digital technology into filmmaking. The first computer-generated movie, *Toy Story*, debuted in 1995. Such movies are now common. In the domain of home video technology, the *Digital Video Disc* (DVD) is gradually supplanting the VHS tape.

* *Recordings*

The digitally produced *Compact Disc* (CD) started replacing vinyl records and audiocassette tapes in the mid-1980s, shortly after its introduction in 1982. The Internet has also become a source of music, not only for listening purposes, but also increasingly as a means for recording it—a process known as *downloading.*

* *Television*

Cable TV went digital in 1998, allowing broadcasters to increase their number of channel offerings. This technology was introduced primarily to meet competition from the *Direct Broadcast Satellite* (DBS) industry, which started producing digital multi-channel programming for reception by home satellite dishes in 1995. TV broadcasting in general has also become digitized. So-called *High-Definition Television* (HDTV), which consists of transmitters and receivers using digital formats, became commercially available in 1998.

* *Radio*

Digital Audio Broadcasting (DAB) is the corresponding technology in radio broadcasting to television's DBS system. Radio stations now use digital technology for creating their programs.

The convergence of the computer with all other media technologies is the defining characteristic of mass communications today. Computers can now be put on top of TV sets so that people can interface with the Internet as well as the new digital TV services. More and more computer boxes are being built into digital sets. Personal data assistants (PDAs), pocket-sized information devices that accept handwriting, keep people in contact with the Internet and other media as well. In the near future, computers will be in charge of most communication channels, turning the world into a true digital global village.

But all this has its setbacks. Over-reliance on computers and digital media has induced a mindset that sees digitation as an intrinsic, almost mythical, component of the human condition. This became apparent on the threshold of the year 2000 when the "millennium bug" was thought to be a harbinger of doom. So reliant had people become on the computer that a mere technological problem—making sure that computers could read the new "00" date as "2000, and not "1900" or some other "…00" date—was interpreted in moral and apocalyptic terms. That was striking evidence that computers had acquired connotative signification that far exceeded their original function as "computing machines." Constant exposure to cyberspace, moreover, is leading surreptitiously and gradually to an entrenchment of a bizarre modern form of Cartesian "dualism," the view that the body and the mind are separate entities. Incidentally, the term *cyberspace* was coined by American writer William Gibson in his 1984 science fiction novel *Neuromancer*, in which he described cyberspace as a place of "unthinkable complexity." The term has given rise to a vocabulary of "cyberterms," such as *cybercafes* (cafes that sell coffee and computer time), *cybermalls* (online shopping services), and *cyberjunkies* (people addicted to being online).

According to Baudrillard (1998), digital media have put people in the position of having to rebuild cultures from the ashes of the "dead signs" of the "real" world. But, as it turns out, these new signs are not that much different from the old ones. So, Baudrillard predicts, in a short time "virtual communication" will become "real communication" again, as people begin to realize that their bodies are as much a part of creating signs as are their minds. Paradoxically, Baudrillard goes on to quip, the computer will engender a desire to "re-embody" communication and interaction, that is, to get people to literally talk to each other with the voice.

CONCLUDING REMARKS

The topic of communication and media brings this introductory treatment of semiotics to a conclusion. Hopefully this trek through the science that aims to study how we make messages and meanings will have been a useful one. Many other kinds of paths could have been undertaken, given the interdisciplinary nature of the field. And, indeed, the reader is encouraged to seek these through the general bibliography provided at the end.

A large segment of contemporary semiotic work continues to analyze the nature of signs, codes, texts. But, more and more, semioticians have started searching for the *raison d'être* of representational activities. In effect, the study of representation is a study in the basic metaphysical questions that haunt humans everywhere: Why are we here? Who or what put us here? What, if anything, can be done about it? Who am I? and so on. As Johan Huizinga (1924: 202) has eloquently put it, these questions constitute the psychic foundations of cultural systems: "In God, nothing is empty of sense ... so, the conviction of a transcendental meaning in all things seeks to formulate itself." The languages, myths, narratives, rituals, art works, etc., that human beings learn to employ early in life guide their search to discover answers to the above questions.

Semiotics does not attempt to answer why these questions exist in the human species, because it knows that an answer is unlikely. Rather, it limits itself to a less-grandiose scheme—describing the representational activities they animate. Nevertheless, the semiotic agenda is starting to be shaped more and more by a search for the biological, psychic, and social roots of the human need for *meaning*, of the "metaphysical story" behind human signs.

As a concluding reflection, the question "What is Semiotics?" with which we started this introduction to the field can be answered simply: "It is the science of meaning." Semiotics is a dynamic, vibrant, ever-changing science. It is indeed remarkable to note that with barely a handful of notions and concepts, it can be used so powerfully to describe and explicate such phenomena as art, advertising, language, clothing, buildings, and, indeed, anything that is "interesting in itself." Hopefully, the reader will have come away from this book with the singular verity, expressed so well by Charles Peirce, that as a species we are programmed to "think only in signs."

Appendices

Exercises and Questions for Discussion

CHAPTER 1

1. List some connotations of the following English color terms:
   (a) green
   (b) blue
   (c) orange
   (d) yellow
   (e) orange
   (f) purple
   (g) brown
   (h) black
   (i) white

2. What are the three basic questions of semiotic analysis?

3. Describe the difference between a *concrete* and an *abstract* concept.

3. What is the difference between *semiotics* and *communication theory*?

4. What is the difference between *meaning* and *signification*?

5. Analyze each of the following signs as $X = Y$ structures, using the three basic questions of semiotics to guide you.

Words:

(a) dog
(b) table
(c) friend
(d) love
(e) democracy

Symbols:

(a)

(b)

(c)

(d)

6. Give the denotative meanings first and then several connotative meanings
    of the following words and pictorial symbols:

    Words:

    (a) blue
    (b) cat
    (c) car
    (d) life
    (e) person

    Symbols:

    (a) ?
    (b) ♣
    (c) ♥
    (d) Ω

7. Make up two or three simple texts using (1) words, (2) numbers, and (3)
    visual symbols. For example, with words you can make up a poem; with
    numbers you can make up an addition problem, with visual symbols you
    can make up a poster.

8. Explain the relation among *semiosis*, *representation*, and *interpretation* in
    your own words.

9. As an exercise in using the semantic differential, ask people to rate the following concepts using the scales provided. Then, quantify the results by taking the average ratings for each scale. Discuss the results afterwards in class.

father

kind	_	_	_	_	_	_	_ stern
	1	2	3	4	5	6	7

liberal-minded	_	_	_	_	_	_	_ conservative
	1	2	3	4	5	6	7

lenient	_	_	_	_	_	_	_ disciplinarian
	1	2	3	4	5	6	7

fashionable	_	_	_	_	_	_	_ individualistic
	1	2	3	4	5	6	7

talkative	_	_	_	_	_	_	_ laconic
	1	2	3	4	5	6	7

mother

kind	_	_	_	_	_	_	_ stern
	1	2	3	4	5	6	7

liberal-minded	_	_	_	_	_	_	_ conservative
	1	2	3	4	5	6	7

lenient	_	_	_	_	_	_	_ disciplinarian
	1	2	3	4	5	6	7

fashionable	_	_	_	_	_	_	_ individualistic
	1	2	3	4	5	6	7

talkative	_	_	_	_	_	_	_ laconic
	1	2	3	4	5	6	7

music piped in an elevator

pop	_	_	_	_	_	_	_	classical
	1	2	3	4	5	6	7	

fast-paced	_	_	_	_	_	_	_	slow
	1	2	3	4	5	6	7	

soft	_	_	_	_	_	_	_	loud
	1	2	3	4	5	6	7	

vocal	_	_	_	_	_	_	_	instrumental
	1	2	3	4	5	6	7	

joyful	_	_	_	_	_	_	_	sorrowful
	1	2	3	4	5	6	7	

10. Identify and discuss which paradigmatic feature(s) keeps the following pairs distinct:
    (a) a men's watch vs. a women's watch
    (b) a happy sound vs. a sad sound
    (c) the words *pink* vs. *punk*, *pink* vs. *rink*; *punk* vs. *punt*
    (d) a triangle vs. a rectangle
    (e) a pianoforte vs. an organ

11. Identify and discuss the syntagmatic structure of the following:
    (a) the word *thrill*
    (b) a happy face
    (c) a square
    (d) a football uniform
    (e) an automobile

12. Identify and discuss the analogical feature(s) that allow for the substitution of one item for the other:
    (a) the substitution of a button for a checker piece (to play chess)
    (b) the substitution of a Cyrillic alphabet character with a Roman alphabet character
    (c) the substitution of a linear equation for an actual line (in analytical geometry)
    (d) the substitution of coordinates for a position on a map

(e) the substitution of computer terms for the human mind (e.g., processing, filtering, storing, etc.).

13. Make up an appropriate text for each the following, and then explain the code(s) you used to make up the text:
(a) a poem for a child to teach him or her about cats (à la Dr. Seuss)
(b) a sign informing people politely that smoking is not allowed in a certain place
(c) a drawing of the classroom
(d) a map of the campus

14. Explain why the different meanings of the following vary according to context:
(a) a pipe in an ashtray vs. a pipe displayed as a sculpture in an art gallery
(b) The pig is ready to eat uttered by a farmer looking at his pig vs. *The pig is ready to eat* uttered by a cook
(c) a wig worn by an actor on stage vs. a wig worn by a bank robber
(d) a rose given to a lover vs. a rose given to a mother

QUESTIONS FOR DISCUSSION

1. Do you think that culture (the semiosphere) shapes human actions and ideas? If so, how is innovation or creativity possible?

2. After one chapter, would you be able to explain what semiotics is to an acquaintance? What illustrations would you use to make semiotics understandable to your acquaintance?

3. Do you think that representation and communication are interconnected? Do you think that signs exist for purposes other than communication? If so, what are those purposes?

CHAPTER 2

EXERCISES

1. Compare Saussure's to Peirce's model of the sign.

2. Give examples of:
    (a) visual iconicity
    (b) vocal iconicity
    (c) olfactory iconicity
    (d) gustatory iconicity
    (e) tactile iconicity

3. Is there any evidence to suggest that iconicity is a primordial form of representation?

4. Give examples of:
    (a) spatial indexicality
    (b) temporal indexicality
    (c) person indexicality

5. Give examples of verbal and nonverbal symbolism.

6. Give examples of your own of the power of symbolic representation in mathematics and science.

7. Classify the following signs as icons, indexes, or symbols (or a combination of these):
    (a) chat
    (b) erase
    (c) Ouch!
    (d) Wow!
    (e) 1001
    (f) ↑
    (g) $
    (h) ∞

8. Provide appropriate signifieds for the following signifiers:

Signifiers	Signifieds
chair	
justice	
up	

down	
bang	
swoosh	
$\Rightarrow$	
&	
Σ	
$\frac{1}{12}$	

9. Now provide appropriate signifiers for the following signifieds:

Signifiers	Signifieds
	leftward direction
	upward movement
	the sound of something breaking
	a structure for human habitation
	a shriek
	a long, smooth object
	a jagged, rough object
	infinity
	the afterlife
	nothingness

10. Provide appropriate signs for the following, explaining each one as you make it.

Icons to represent:
(a) a happy face
(b) a sad face
(c) the length of an object
(d) the quantity "three"

Indexes to represent:

(a) the presence of another person

(b) an event occurring before another in time

(c) the relative location of an object with respect to another

(d) direction to the right

Symbols to represent:

(a) peace

(b) friendship

(c) the relation of equality

(d) an unknown insect that looks like a grasshopper

QUESTIONS FOR DISCUSSION

1. Do you think that sign systems shape worldview? Defend your answer.

2. Do you agree with Peirce that iconicity is the "default" form of representation? Give reasons why you do or do not agree.

3. Is it possible to integrate Peircean with Saussurean views of the sign? In what ways?

4. Do you think that modern humans could live without culture? Explain your answer.

5. Do you agree with the idea that modern-day behaviors reverberate with tribal tendencies? Explain your answer.

CHAPTER 3

EXERCISES

1. Provide appropriate signs for the following, explaining each one as you make it.

   Signals made with the eyes and face:

   (a) to indicate agreement

   (b) to indicate disagreement

(c) to indicate disinterest

(d) to indicate acknowledgment

2. Give examples of:
    (a) iconic gestures
    (b) indexical gestures
    (c) symbolic gestures
    (d) iconic gesticulants
    (e) metaphoric gesticulants
    (f) beat gesticulants
    (g) cohesive gesticulants
    (h) deictic gesticulants

3. Discuss the differences between *sex* and *gender*.

4. Give examples of how grooming and appearance codes influence how we currently perceive gender and age. Be specific as to the use of the following signifiers (if applicable):
    (a) make up
    (b) hairstyle
    (c) facial decoration
    (d) jewelry
    (e) facial alterations

5. Find expressions in addition to those used in this chapter showing how we perceive the face (e.g., *He's just another pretty face*).

6. Compare contact patterns between any cultures you know.

7. Give examples of other kinesic codes like the one regulating the elevator scene (e.g., How would you orient your body in making your way down an aisle in a movie theater?).

8. Give examples of gestures for:
    (a) hello
    (b) good-bye
    (c) stop
    (d) uncertainty
    (e) sureness

(f) surprise

(g) anger

9. Give a summary of the reasons for, and functions of, *dance* in human societies.

10. Describe a dance form, ballet, or other dancing activity that you really like. Explain why.

11. Indicate who of the following you would touch while interacting, and where you would touch him or her:
(a) a professor while discussing a grade
(b) a parent while saying good-bye to him or her for a while
(c) a lover while making small talk
(d) a child while congratulating him or her on some achievement

QUESTIONS FOR DISCUSSION

1. If you have a pet, explain how you "get your message across." Do you understand the messages sent to you by your pet? How so?

2. Do you agree that the face is perceived as *persona*? Give reasons to support your answer.

3. Do you agree that what is perceived as obscene is a matter of cultural decisions? Give reasons for your answer.

4. Why do you think dancing originated in human life?

CHAPTER 4

1. Give examples of:
(a) abstract images
(b) fictitious images
(c) narrative images
(d) line signifiers
(e) shape signifiers

    (f) value signifiers
    (g) color signifiers
    (h) texture signifiers
    (i) synesthesia
    (j) aesthesia

2. Give examples of how to elicit images based on the following modalities:
    (a) visual
    (b) auditory
    (c) tactile
    (d) olfactory
    (e) gustatory

3. Draw a visual sign or text to represent the following, describing the visual signifiers you used and how you combined them:
    (a) a sad face
    (b) night
    (c) day
    (d) a cat
    (e) a right turn
    (f) a horizon
    (g) anger
    (h) love

4. Give the meanings of each of the following visual signs, discussing how each signifier represents its referent(s):
    (a) @
    (b) &
    (c) #
    (d) %
    (e) +
    (f) ©
    (g) 🗁

5. Draw a map of how to get from your home to your school or place of work, describing the visual signifiers you used and how you combined them.

6. What are the emotional connotations associated with the following colors (or their equivalents) in your culture? Can you explain why they probably evoke such connotations?
    (a) blue
    (b) red
    (c) green
    (d) yellow
    (e) black
    (f) orange
    (g) white
    (h) pink
    (i) brown
    (j) gray
    (k) purple

7. Compare a painting by Vincent van Gogh (1853–1890) with one by Andy Warhol in terms of what they mean and how they deliver their meanings.

QUESTIONS FOR DISCUSSION

1. Why do you think people doodle?

2. Using the example of maps, discuss the relation between representation, knowledge, and discovery.

3. Why do you think visual art is so intrinsic to human life?

4. Do you agree that cinema is the dominant art form of the contemporary world? Explain your answer.

CHAPTER 5

EXERCISES

1. Give examples of:
    (a) echoic words
    (b) sound symbolism in English

(c) alliteration

(d) lengthening sounds for emphasis

(e) the use of intonation for emphasis

(f) sound-modeling

(g) onomatopoeia

2. Give the meanings of each of the following words, discussing how each signifier represents its referent(s):

(a) ouch

(b) slow

(c) slide

(d) whack

(e) hi

(f) bow-wow

(g) ping-pong

(h) bang

(i) try

3. Draw up a list of the main sources of name-giving cited in this chapter, adding any others you may know of.

4. What is the source of your name? Why do you think you were given that name? What name would you give yourself? Why?

5. Give examples of each of Jakobson's functions, and of the mystical and economizing functions added to it in this book.

6. Do you think that these functions apply to nonverbal forms of communication? How so?

7. What words would you coin to refer to the following referents? Explain your verbal signifiers.

(a) people with longer torsos than legs

(b) a new device that, when attached to an earlobe, will allow a person to feel happy

(c) ideas that have not yet found expression

8. What does the following poem refer to? Explain your answer.
Slippery, smooth
sliding through
slimy, slick
Beware of its lick!

9. What names would you give to the following? Explain your reasons.
(a) a gray furry cat
(b) a male child
(c) a female child
(d) a new luxury car

10. Identify the source from which the following names are derived:
(a) John
(b) Mary
(c) Alexander
(d) Sarah
(e) Sonny
(f) Fanny
(g) Violet
(h) Blanche

11. Now, identify the source of the following surnames:
(a) Mark *Eastwood*
(b) Mary *Israel*
(c) Kate *Morrison*
(d) Frank *Cardinal*
(e) Bill *Brown*
(f) Jill *Carpenter*
(g) Emily *Dickenson*
(h) Nadia *Peachtree*
(i) Kate *O'Neill*

12. Design pictographs or ideographs (as the case may be) to represent the
following referents:
(a) a broken heart
(b) a headache
(c) a bright idea
(d) love

    (e) hate
    (f) need
    (g) joy

13. Compose a four-line poem for each of the following:
    (a) a forlorn dog
    (b) a dying bird
    (c) the sunrise
    (d) the sunset

QUESTIONS FOR DISCUSSION

1. Do you think that language shapes thought? Explain your answer with examples.

2. Why do you think that the transition from gesture to vocal language occurred in the human species?

3. Why do you think children respond to poetry like that of Dr. Seuss?

4. Discuss the idea that communication is potentially always a dangerous act. Do you agree or disagree?

5. Why do you think we associate writing with literacy and being educated?

CHAPTER 6

EXERCISES

1. Give 5–6 examples of each of the following conceptual metaphors and conceptual metonyms (i.e., actual sentences exemplifying them):
    (a) life is a stage
    (b) justice is blind
    (c) hope is breathing
    (d) love is a mental disease
    (e) friendship is a journey
    (f) the part for the whole
    (g) the producer for the product

(h)   the place for the institution
(i)   the institution for the people responsible
(j)   the object used for the user

2.   Give the meanings of each of the following metaphors, discussing how each one creates its meaning, and then identifying the conceptual metaphor that it exemplifies:
(a)   My life is a comedy.
(b)   Their marriage is a sitcom.
(c)   I have lost all hope.
(d)   You must weigh all the evidence.
(e)   That mistake cost me several hours.

3.   Identify the conceptual metaphors that the following utterances reveal about love, giving more examples for each one of your own, and then drawing an ICM of love:
(a)   There were sparks between us.
(b)   We are attracted to each other.
(c)   My life revolves around her.
(d)   I am magnetically drawn towards her.
(e)   Theirs is a sick relationship.
(f)   Their marriage is dead; it can't be revived.
(g)   Their relationship is in good shape.
(h)   I'm crazy about her.
(i)   I'm constantly raving about her.
(j)   He's gone mad over her.
(k)   I've lost my head over her.
(l)   She cast a spell over me.
(m) The magic is gone.
(n)   She has bewitched me.
(o)   I'm in a trance over her.

4.   Give 5–6 examples of concepts derived from each of the following image schemas:
(a)   orientational
(b)   ontological
(c)   structural

5. Discuss the connotative meanings of the following.
   Animal metaphors:
   (a) George is a *cat.*
   (b) George is a *bear.*
   (c) George is a *snail.*
   (d) George is a *tiger.*
   (e) George is a *lion.*
   (f) George is a *hippo.*
   (g) George is an *elephant.*

   Color metaphors:
   (h) Mary is feeling *blue.*
   (i) Mary is *green* with envy.
   (j) Mary is *red* with embarrassment.
   (k) Mary is a *yellow-livered* person.
   (l) Mary is *pink*, politically speaking.
   (m) Mary is *white* with fury.
   (n) Mary was born to the *purple.*

6. Make up metaphors describing people with the following vehicles, and
   then discuss what they mean:
   (a) square
   (b) worm
   (c) pie
   (d) hot dog
   (e) Ferrari
   (f) rocket
   (g) hurricane

7. Following are examples of the metonymic uses of body parts to represent
   people and brand names to stand for the entire product type. Explain what
   the meaning of the metonym is in each one.
   Body metonyms:
   (a) She's a real *brain.*
   (b) He's a *crew cut.*
   (c) She's a *flat foot.*
   (d) He's a daddy *long legs.*

   Brand metonyms:
   (e) Did you buy the *Scotch tape?*
   (f) I bought a new *Skidoo.*

(g) I need some *Aspirin*.

(h) I bought some *Playtex*.

8. Context plays a central role in determining whether a statement is ironic or not. Come up with appropriate contexts that would make each of the following statements ironic:

(a) Nice day!

(b) Great course!

(c) I love your car!

(d) What a great haircut!

(e) What a smile!

QUESTIONS FOR DISCUSSION

1. Discuss the notion that abstract thought is probably metaphorical in its origin. Explain your answer.

2. Do you think that all scientific knowledge is forged by metaphor? Defend your position.

3. The following metaphor was uttered by a four-year-old child, in referring to his father's baldness: "My father has a hole in his head." What do you think it reveals?

4. Explain the following as extended or conceptual metaphors:

(a) the meaning of a movie

(b) the meaning of a poem

(c) the meaning of life

CHAPTER 7

EXERCISES

1. Invent an appropriate story to explain each of the following to a two-year-old child:

(a) the death of a pet

(b) the mean actions of a playmate

2. What is your favorite novel? Explain in your own words:
    (a) what it means
    (b) how it delivers its meaning

3. What is your favorite comic strip? What are the similarities and differences between a comic strip and a novel?

4. What is your favorite myth? Now, comment on:
    (a) what the probable function of the myth was
    (b) what it attempts to explain (in modern scientific terms)
    (c) who the narrator probably is

5. What mythic themes (e.g., good vs. evil, life as a journey, etc.), if any, underlie the following modern spectacles?
    (a) the World Series of baseball
    (b) WWF matches
    (c) Thanksgiving celebrations
    (d) Halloween
    (e) sixteenth birthday parties

6. Provide a caption for each cartoon:

    (a)

    (b)

    (c)

    (d)

(e)

7. Carry out a narratological analysis of the plot, character, and setting of any novel, movie, or TV program. Why do you think that these cohere into a single meaning, or levels of connotative meanings?

8. Explain the use of myth in psychoanalysis. Do you think this is scientifically legitimate? Explain your answer.

9. Do you think mythologies influence social behavior? Discuss the influence on social life that the following mythologies may have had:
   (a) the mythology of gender
   (b) the mythology of adolescence
   (c) the mythology of fatherhood
   (d) the mythology of motherhood

10. Discuss a recent movie that was based on a novel. Which medium—the novel or the movie—was more artistically effective? Why?

QUESTIONS FOR DISCUSSION

1. Do you think the human species has a "narrative instinct"?

2. Why do you think myth has not disappeared from modern-day thinking? Explain your answer.

3. Referring to the case of the Cabbage Patch doll craze, discuss any other "toy crazes" that you know of.

4. Why do you think that certain novels become best-sellers?

5. Who determines what the meaning of a novel is?

CHAPTER 8

EXERCISES

1. What is your favorite piece of music? Explain:
   (a) what it means to you
   (b) why it "moves" you

2. What is the difference between a play performed by actors on a stage and a movie of the same play in terms of the following?
   (a) perspective
   (b) effect on the viewer

3. Which of the following arts do you think is the most popular today? Explain your answer.
   (a) theater
   (b) painting
   (c) cinema
   (d) photography
   (e) music

4. Read *Waiting for Godot* or watch a video/DVD of the play. Then discuss the following elements of the play:
   (a) its language
   (b) its characters
   (c) its costumes
   (d) its scenery
   (e) its plot
   (f) its symbols
   (g) the names of the characters

5. Discuss any current movie that you think displays postmodern techniques.

6. Give examples of current TV programs that might be characterized as postmodern. Justify your selections.

7. Give examples of current postmodern ads. Again, justify your selections.

8. Can you find examples of postmodern technique in the musical arts?

QUESTIONS FOR DISCUSSION

1. We often say that this or that work of art is "beautiful." What does this mean?

2. Why do you think some works of art remain across time, while others disappear into oblivion?

3. Some people characterize mathematics as an "art." Do you agree? Explain your answer.

CHAPTER 9

EXERCISES

1. How would an adult male and an adult female dress for the following situations? Can you give semiotic reasons why?
   (a) at a wedding
   (b) at a fast-food joint
   (c) at a high-class restaurant
   (d) while shopping in a mall
   (e) on a first date

2. Explain the difference between clothing and dress.

3. First, describe the clothing items that make up each of the following uniforms. Then, discuss what they might designate as individual signifiers:
   (a) uniform of a specific hockey team
   (b) military uniform of any kind
   (c) private school uniform
   (d) clothing worn by a religious cleric

4. Discuss the meanings of nudity in the following situations:
   (a) on a beach
   (b) in a sex club
   (c) in a nudist camp
   (d) in a crowded bus

5. Describe current fashion trends today, giving brief semiotic analyses of each one:

(a) current teen fashion

(b) current office fashion

(c) current formal attire for various kinds of ceremonies

(d) current fashion for "older" people

QUESTIONS FOR DISCUSSION

1. Discuss the notion that clothing is an extension of persona.

2. Why do you think fashion shows are so popular? Explain your answer.

3. Do you think that there is too much emphasis today on fashion? If so, what do you think it reveals about our society?

4. Why do you think we are so intrigued by representations of nude bodies? What makes some depiction or representation obscene? Explain your answer.

CHAPTER 10

EXERCISES

1. Explain Lévi-Strauss's distinction between "the raw" and "the cooked" in you own words. Does it still apply?

2. In the "Robinson Crusoe" vignette depicted in this chapter, what do you think would happen if the people in the vignette all spoke different languages?

3. List the various ways in which food and eating are interconnected with the other codes and sign systems of a culture.

4. What do the following food/drink items symbolize in your culture?

(a) apple

(b) lamb meat

(c) grapes

(d) bread

    (e) potatoes
    (f) wine
    (g) milk
    (h) peach

5. Describe how you would put together an *eating text* for each of the following situations:
    (a) birthday party of a parent
    (b) birthday party of a child
    (c) peer party
    (d) your own wedding
    (e) Thanksgiving
    (f) any traditional religious feast

6. Describe the table-manner code that applies to each of the following situations:
    (a) eating at home
    (b) eating at a fast-food joint
    (c) eating at a high-class restaurant

7. What kinds of food would you serve in the following situations? Why?
    (a) to an employer whom you have invited to dinner
    (b) to a date whom you have invited to dinner
    (c) to a child who has come to visit you

8. The following are generally considered to be nonedible in Western culture, but they are edible in others. Give probable reasons why they are categorized as nonedible:
    (a) earthworms
    (b) silkworms
    (c) cockroaches
    (d) termites
    (e) cats
    (f) dogs
    (g) snails
    (h) maggots
    (i) flowers

QUESTIONS FOR DISCUSSION

1. Why do you think people are judged on the basis of what they eat? Explain your answer.

2. Why do you think there is so much religious symbolism associated with food and eating? Explain your answer.

3. Why do you think we continue to indulge in fast food and junk food? Explain your answer.

4. Discuss the saying "We are what we eat."

CHAPTER 11

EXERCISES

1. Explain why artifacts allow archeologists to reconstruct a culture.

2. What do the following objects mean and why do you think they have these meanings?
   (a) a ring
   (b) high-heel shoes
   (c) a gold coin
   (d) a penny

3. What gift would you give to the following people on their birthdays? Why?
   (a) a five-year-old brother
   (b) a five-year-old sister
   (c) a fifteen-year-old brother
   (d) a fifteen-year-old sister

4. What do you think would happen to the human species today if each of the following were to be eliminated from human society permanently?
   (a) the automobile
   (b) electronic media (television, radio)
   (c) the computer

5. Comment on what the cultural meanings of the following toys are:
    (a) action figures
    (b) dolls
    (c) toy weapons
    (d) board games
    (e) electronic games
    (f) play mobiles
    (g) sports equipment

6. Take some examples of pop art to class. Then comment on:
    (a) what their messages might be
    (b) what emotions they evoke (if any) and how they do this
    (c) if they will still be appreciated 20 years from now

7. Give examples of "computerese" (i.e., of words that come from computer terminology but applied to humans) that indicate how extensive the influence of computers on human social life has become.

QUESTIONS FOR DISCUSSION

1. Do you agree with the notion that we now evolve as a species through our technology? Explain your answer.

2. Do you think that true artificial intelligence will ever come about: i.e., machines that are exactly like human beings? Explain your answer.

3. What kind of culture would emerge that was dependent in large part on robots? Explain your answer.

CHAPTER 12

EXERCISES

1. Describe the proxemic patterns, such as zone maintenance and orientation, involved in handshaking the following people:
    (a) a friend you haven't seen in a while
    (b) a stranger of the opposite sex
    (c) a prospective employer
    (d) a stranger from a foreign country

2. Give other examples of orientation patterns, in addition to the ones mentioned in this chapter.

3. List various ways in which buildings and places are interconnected with the other sign systems of a culture.

4. List the various meanings associated with:
   (a) the home
   (b) the rooms within the home
   (c) a sacred space
   (d) a mall

5. Explain how you feel in each of these places and why.
   (a) the classroom
   (b) a place of worship
   (d) one's bedroom
   (e) the school cafeteria
   (f) the office of someone in authority
   (g) a hall during a rock concert
   (h) a hall during a classical music concert

6. What are the tallest buildings in your city/town? Does this feature mean anything in terms of the social role they play?

7. Describe how you would build and decorate the following rooms, and why (including height of ceiling, number and type of windows, etc.):
   (a) a study room
   (b) a "workout" room
   (c) a meeting room (for a company)
   (d) a room for contemplating spiritual matters

QUESTIONS FOR DISCUSSION

1. Why do you think people go to malls? Explain your answer.

2. Do you think that someone's personality can be figured out from the type of home and/or rooms he or she lives in? Explain your answer.

3. Do you think that the structure of cities influence people's worldview?

4. What do you think makes a building "beautiful?" Explain your answer.

5. How do you think cities of the future will be designed? Explain your answer.

6. How do you think communities in space will be designed in the future (including city infrastructure, housing, etc.)?

7. How do you think worldview will be shaped in space communities?

CHAPTER 13

EXERCISES

1. Give concrete examples of what has been called in this book the mythologizing, history fabrication, and cognitive compression effects.

2. What is a social text? Give examples of different kinds of social texts.

3. Explain what a TV mythology is.

4. Can you give examples of other kinds of TV mythologies, in addition to the fatherhood one discussed in this chapter (motherhood, childhood, etc.), each accompanied with a specific TV programming analysis?

5. Describe the latest programs in terms of their meanings and textual functions:
 (a) a soap opera
 (b) a news and information program
 (c) a sitcom
 (d) an adventure drama
 (e) any other kind of drama
 (f) a documentary
 (g) a specialty program (sports, movies, etc.)

6. Summarize in your own words the notion of narrowcasting.

QUESTIONS FOR DISCUSSION

1. What do you think would happen if, all of a sudden, all TV transmission were to be shut down for a period of time? Explain your answer.

2. What do you think will replace TV as the next culture-wide social text?

3. If you had the power to transform TV, what would you do and why?

CHAPTER 14

EXERCISES

1. Bring to class an ad from a current magazine for a lifestyle product (perfume, clothes, etc.). Discuss:
   (a) what meanings (connotations) the ad elicits (if any);
   (b) how it achieves these;
   (c) the overall aesthetic effect of an ad;
   (d) how it is put together (visually and verbally);
   (e) to which audience the ad is directed;
   (f) the effectiveness of the brand name;
   (g) the effectiveness of product design;
   (h) the connotative chain the ad suggests.

2. Summarize the technique of semiotic ad analysis in your own words.

3. Find and bring in an example of each of the following ads, taking each one at random from a magazine. Then analyze each ad semiotically:
   (a) a men's cologne ad
   (b) a women's perfume ad
   (c) a watch ad
   (d) a cigarette ad
   (e) a men's clothing ad
   (f) a women's clothing ad
   (g) an automobile ad

4. Give examples from current advertising of:
   (a) jingles
   (b) slogans

    (c) the use of the imperative form

    (d) formulas

    (e) alliteration

    (f) intentional omission

    (g) the strategic use of tone of voice (in radio or TV commercials)

5. Give examples of current brand names for the following products discussing their semiotic significance:

    (a) a perfume

    (b) a soft drink

    (c) a record label

    (d) a luxury car

QUESTIONS FOR DISCUSSION

1. Why do you think advertising is so appealing?

2. Do you think that advertising is effective in enhancing desire for a product? Explain your answer.

3. Why do you think advertisers create subtexts in promoting products?

CHAPTER 15

EXERCISES

1. Give examples of the following media:

    (a) natural

    (b) artifactual

    (c) mechanical

2. What are the main differences between animal and human communication systems?

3. Use Hockett's typology to compare human language to cat and dog communication.

4. Indicate which aspects of media convergence are occurring at the present time.

5. If you have a household animal, explain how you communicate with each other.

QUESTIONS FOR DISCUSSION

1. Why do you think people are so dependent today on digital media for information and recreation?

2. Which medium do you think will become dominant in the twenty-first century? Explain your answer.

3. Discuss the idea that "communication is potentially always a dangerous act." Do you agree or disagree?

Biographical Sketches

Aristotle
(384–322 BC)

student of the ancient Greek philosopher Plato, Aristotle shared his teacher's reverence for human knowledge, revising many of Plato's ideas by emphasizing methods rooted in observation and experience. Aristotle surveyed and systematized nearly all the existing branches of knowledge and provided the first ordered accounts of biology, psychology, physics, and literary theory. In addition, Aristotle invented the field known as formal logic, pioneered zoology, and addressed virtually every major philosophical problem known during his time.

Augustine (Saint)
(354–430 AD)

philosopher and religious thinker who was among the first to distinguish clearly between natural and conventional signs and to espouse the view that there is an interpretive component to the whole process of representation.

Barthes, Roland
(1915–1980)

French semiotician who claimed that the largely unconscious mythological thinking of human beings manifests itself in all kinds of discourses, spectacles, performances, and symbols.

Benedict, Ruth
(1887–1948)

American anthropologist, student of Franz Boas, who pioneered ethnological research on Native American tribes during the 1920s and

1930s. Benedict maintained that every culture developed its own particular moral and lifestyle systems that largely determined the choices individuals reared and living in that culture made throughout their lives.

Boas, Franz
(1858–1942)

American anthropologist who claimed that culture largely determined the ways in which individuals developed their personalities and their worldviews.

Campbell, Joseph
(1904–1987)

American writer, editor, and teacher, known for his writings on myth. Influenced by the psychoanalytical ideas of Sigmund Freud and Carl Jung, and the novels of James Joyce and Thomas Mann, he formulated the theory that myths across the world are culture-specific manifestations of the universal need of the human psyche to explain social, cosmological, and spiritual realities.

Cassirer, Ernst
(1874–1945)

German philosopher and educator, whose works dealt mainly with the theory of knowledge, the history of epistemology, and the philosophy of science. He proposed that language and myth spring from the same unconscious creative force, and that the categories of myth underlie human symbols and human actions.

Chomsky, Noam
(1928–)

American linguist who claims that the human brain is especially constructed to detect and reproduce language. According to Chomsky, children instinctively apply innate grammatical rules to process the verbal input to which they are exposed.

Darwin, Charles
(1809–1882)

British zoologist who formulated the theory of "natural selection," which holds that reproductive success in organisms tends to promote adaptation that is necessary for survival.

Derrida, Jacques
(1930–)

French philosopher whose work originated a method of analysis—known as *deconstruction*—that has been applied to literature, linguistics, philosophy, law, and architecture, by which texts are seen to be infinitely interpretable.

Durkheim, Emile
(1858–1917)

French sociologist and philosopher who saw remarkable similarities among the world's myths, which he explained as being based in a "collective consciousness" that is a consequence of specific brain functions.

Eco, Umberto
(1932–)

Italian semiotician and novelist who has provided various theoretical frameworks for the study of signs and who claims that while the interpretation of a text may be influenced primarily by culture, there is, nevertheless, an authorial purpose inherent in the text that cannot be ignored.

Foucault, Michel
(1926–1984)

French semiotician and philosopher who attempted to show that the basic ideas that people normally take to be permanent truths about human nature and society are instead no more than the products of historical processes.

Freud, Sigmund
(1856–1939)

German psychologist and founder of psychoanalysis who suggested that the moral behavioral patterns that have ensured the survival of the human species are built into human genetic structure. He also formulated the theory of the "unconscious" as a region of the mind that stores wishes, memories, fears, feelings, and ideas that are prevented from expression in conscious awareness. These manifest themselves instead in symbolic and unusual ways, especially in dreams, neurotic syndromes, and artistic texts.

Greimas, Algirdas Julien
(1917–1992)

French semiotician who developed the branch of semiotics known as narratology, i.e., the study of how human beings in different cultures invent remarkably similar stories (myths, tales, etc.) with virtually the same stock of characters, motifs, themes, and actions.

Herodotus
(c. 484–425 BC)

Greek thinker and first historian who spent a large part of his life traveling in Asia, Egypt, and Greece, noting and recording for posterity differences in the dress, food, etiquette, and rituals of the people he encountered. His annotations have come to constitute some of the first analyses of cultural differences.

Hippocrates
(c. 460–377 BC)

Greek founder of medical science who established *semeiotics* as the study of symptoms.

Jakobson, Roman
(1896–1982)

Moscow-born linguist and semiotician who carried out most of his work in the United States. Among his contributions to semiotics, linguistics, and communication theory is a widely used model that identifies the main functions and components of human communication.

Jung, Carl Gustav
(1875–1961)

Swiss psychiatrist who believed that the unconscious mind consisted of two interacting dimensions: the personal unconscious, the repressed feelings and thoughts developed during an individual's life, and the collective unconscious, those inherited feelings, thoughts, and memories shared by all humanity. He coined the term *archetype* to refer to the latter. Archetypes manifest themselves as recurring symbols in cultures the world over.

Lévi-Strauss, Claude
(1908–)

Belgian-born anthropologist based in Paris who sees culture as an external manifestation of the nature of human sign systems.

Locke, John
(1632–1704)

English philosopher who was among the first to suggest the inclusion of semiotics in philosophical inquiry. In his *Essay Concerning Human Understanding* (1690), Locke defined semiotics as the "doctrine of signs."

Lorenz, Konrad
(1903–1989)

Austrian zoologist who was instrumental in the founding of *ethology*, the study of animals in their natural habitats. He is perhaps best known for his discovery that auditory and visual stimuli from an animal's parents are needed to induce the young to follow the parents, but that any object or human being could elicit the same response by presenting the same stimuli. He called this phenomenon *imprinting*.

Lotman, Jurij
(1922–1993)

Estonian semiotician whose writings on the semiosphere have become instrumental for the study of culture within semiotics. The central idea of the semiosphere is that culture is a system of signs allowing humans to cope with existence in the same way that the biosphere is a system of physical features that allows them to survive physically.

Malinowski, Bronislaw
(1884–1942)

founder of the structuralist-functionalist school of anthropology in Britain, Malinowski claimed that each sign, symbol, code, or ritual, even if it might seem strange at first, had structural properties that came about to solve a specific problem and, thus, to serve a specific human function.

Marx, Karl
(1818–1883)

German social theorist who claimed that new forms of a society emerged as a consequence of individuals struggling to gain control over the production, use, and ownership of material goods. In Marx's conception of utopia, there is no capitalism and no state, just a working society in which all give according to their means and take according to their needs.

McLuhan, Marshall
(1911–1980)

Canadian communication theorist who argued that electronic technology has transformed the world into a "global village," and that technological innovations are the factors in human evolution.

Mead, Margaret
(1901–1978)

American anthropologist, student of Franz Boas, widely known for her studies of primitive societies and her contributions to cultural anthropology. Mead spent many years studying how culture influences individual personality, maintaining that the specific child-rearing practices of a culture shaped the behavior and temperament of the maturing individual.

Morris, Charles
(1901–1979)

American semiotician who conceived of semiosis as a chain of observable phenomena. Morris divided semiotics into the study of (1) relations between a sign and other signs, which he called *syntactics*; (2) relations between signs and their denotative meanings, which he called *semantics*; (3) relations between signs and interpreters, which he called *pragmatics.*

Peirce, Charles Sanders
(1839–1914)

American logician and mathematician who, along with Ferdinand de Saussure, is considered to be the founder of the modern-day scientific study of signs.

Plato
(c. 428–347 BC)

one of the most famous philosophers of ancient Greece, Plato was the first to use the term *philosophy*, which meant "love of knowledge." Chief among his ideas was the theory of forms, by which he proposed that objects in the physical world merely resemble perfect forms in the ideal world, and that only the perfect forms should be the objective of philosophical inquiry.

Radcliffe-Brown, Alfred
(1881–1955)

British anthropologist who emphasized the social functional aspects of Bronislaw Malinowski's approach to the study of culture.

Richards, I. A.
(1893–1979)

English literary critic and educator who emphasized the cognitive importance of metaphor.

Rousseau, Jean-Jacques
(1712–1778)

French philosopher who linked a life of happiness to the attainment of a state of "natural life" similar to that of indigenous tribes and of children. As a consequence, he advocated the elimination of the corrupting influences of Western civilization.

Sapir, Edward
(1884–1939)

American anthropologist and linguist, student of Franz Boas, who investigated how language shaped the minds and behaviors of its users.

Saussure, Ferdinand de
(1857–1913)

Swiss linguist who became a modern-day founder of semiotic theory.

Sebeok, Thomas A.
(1920–2001)

leading American semiotician and linguist famous for his work on animal communication and sign theory, and for the establishment of the fields of *zoosemiotics* and *biosemiotics*.

Turing, Alan Mathison
(1912–1954)

British mathematician who envisioned a device, referred to as the "Turing machine," that could, in theory, perform any calculation. He also originated the "Turing test," a procedure designed to show that a computer might be judged to be intelligent.

Tylor, Edward B.
(1832–1917)

British founder of cultural anthropology who founded the first department of anthropology at Oxford University in 1884. Tylor's studies on the role of religion in cultures, along with his definition of culture, were important early contributions to the field of anthropology.

Vico, Giambattista
(1688–1744)

Italian philosopher who sought to unravel the origins of culture by analyzing the meanings of the first words. He also proposed a cyclical theory of history, according to which human societies progress through a series of stages from sensory barbarism to civilization and then return to barbarism, but of a reflective kind.

Whorf, Benjamin Lee
(1897–1941)

American linguist and anthropologist, student of Edward Sapir, who kindled widespread interest among culture theorists in the view that language, thought, and culture are interdependent systems.

Wilson, Edward Osborne
(1929–)

American evolutionary biologist who argues that many human behavioral characteristics (such as heroism, altruism, aggressiveness, and male dominance) should be understood as evolutionary outcomes, and that human behavior is genetically determined.

Glossary of Technical Terms

A

Abstract concept	concept that cannot be demonstrated or observed directly
Actant	unit of narration (a hero, an opponent) that surfaces in all kinds of stories
Addressee	receiver of a message
Addresser	sender of a message
Advertising	any type or form of public communication designed to indicate the availability or to promote the sale of specific commodities or services
Aesthesia	experience of sensation; in art appreciation it refers to the fact that the senses and feelings are stimulated holistically by art works
Aesthetics	branch of semiotics that studies the meaning and interpretation of art in general
Alliteration	repetition of the initial consonant sound over two or more words
Alphabet	graphic code whereby individual characters stand for individual sounds (or sound combinations)
Alphabetic writing	writing system consisting of conventional symbols known as characters that can be used singly and in combination to make up the words of a language

Analogy	structural relation whereby a form replaces another that is similar in form, function, or use
Animism	philosophical and religious view that objects possess a life force
Anthroposemiosis	human semiosis
Anticlimax	rhetorical technique by which ideas are sequenced in abruptly diminishing importance, generally for satirical effect
Antithesis	rhetorical technique by which two words, phrases, clauses, or sentences are opposed in meaning in such a way as to give emphasis to contrasting ideas
Antonymy	relation by which different words, phrases, sentences, etc., stand in a discernible oppositeness of meaning to each other
Apostrophe	rhetorical technique by which an actor turns from the audience, or a writer from his or her readers, to address a person who usually is absent or deceased, an inanimate object, or an abstract idea
Archaeology	field studying the material remains of past human cultures, so as to reconstruct the cultures
Archetype	term coined by psychoanalyst Carl Jung to designate any unconscious image that manifests itself in dreams, myths, art forms, and performances across cultures
Architecture	art and science of designing and erecting buildings
Art	disciplined expressive activity that provides the people who produce it and the community that observes it with a range of experiences that might be aesthetic, emotional, intellectual, or a combination of these
Artifact	object produced or shaped by human craft, especially a tool, a weapon, or an ornament that is of archaeological or historical interest
Artifactual transmission	transmission of messages through artifactual means such as books and letters

Artificial intelligence	branch of computer science concerned with the development of machines having the ability to perform human mental functions
Axiom	statement universally accepted as true, and therefore accepted without proof

B

Ballet	classical dance form characterized by grace and precision of movement and elaborate formal technique
Basic level concept	concept that has a typological (classificatory) function
Bauhaus School	a twentieth-century school of architectural design, the aesthetic of which was influenced by and derived from techniques and materials employed especially in industrial buildings (e.g., skyscrapers, high-rise apartment buildings, etc.)
Biography	an account of a person's life
Biosemiotics	branch of semiotics studying semiosis in all life forms
Birth and rebirth myth	myth informing people about how life can be renewed or about the coming of an ideal society or savior
Brand image	creation of a personality for a product through naming, packaging, and pricing

C

Channel	physical means by which a signal or message is transmitted
Character	person portrayed in an artistic piece, such as a drama or novel
Cinema	visual narrative art form that encompasses the utilization of verbal and nonverbal codes

Climax	rhetorical technique by which ideas are sequenced in abruptly increasing importance, from the least to the most forcible
Clothing	apparel to cover the body
Code	system in which signs are organized and which determines how they relate to each other
Cognitive compression effect	term used in this book to refer to the fact that TV presents personages, events, and information globally and instantly, leaving little time for reflection on the topics, implications, words, etc., contained in a TV message, thus leading to a state by which information is desired and understood mainly in a compressed form
Comics	narrative text put together by means of a series of drawings arranged in horizontal lines, strips, or rectangles called panels, and read from left to right
Communication	production and exchange of messages and meanings
Communication science	science studying all the technical aspects of communication
Conative function	effect of a message on the addressee
Conceit	elaborate, often extravagant, metaphor or simile that makes an association between things that are normally perceived to be totally dissimilar
Concept	general thought connection or pattern made by the human mind (within cultural contexts)
Conceptual metaphor	generalized metaphorical formula that defines a specific abstraction
Conceptual metonym	generalized metonymical formula that defines a specific abstraction
Concrete concept	concept that is demonstrable and observable in a direct way
Connotation	extended or secondary meaning of a sign
Connotative chain	sequence of connotations suggested by an ad text
Consumer advertising	advertising directed towards the promotion of some product

Contact	physical channel employed in communication and the psychological connections between addresser and addressee
Context	environment (physical and social) in which signs are produced and messages generated
Conventional sign	sign that has no apparent connection to any perceivable feature of its referent
Cosmogonic myth	myth explaining how the world came into being
Cro-Magnon	early genus of *Homo sapiens* who lived in western and southern Europe during the last glacial age
Cuisine	term meant to emphasize the difference between the biological and cultural orders in human life in the area of eating; food pertains to the biological order, cuisine to the cultural order
Cultural model	constant juxtaposition of conceptual metaphors that leads to a complex abstract model of a concept
Culture	interconnected system of daily living that is held together by signs, codes, texts, and other sign-based phenomena
Culture hero myth	myth describing beings who discover a cultural artifact or technological process that radically changes the course of history
Cuneiform writing	writing code consisting of wedge-shaped symbols used in ancient Sumerian, Akkadian, Assyrian, Babylonian, and Persian writing

D

Dance	art of moving rhythmically, usually to music, using prescribed or improvised steps and gestures
Decoding	process of deciphering the message formed in terms of a specific code
Denotation	primary, intensional meaning of a sign
Diachrony	study of change in signs and codes over time
Discourse	verbal communication involving an addresser and an addressee

Distance	space that people maintain between themselves during socially meaningful contact or interaction
Drama	verbal performing art involving actors on a stage or platform with the background support of setting and props
Dress	system of clothing (e.g., the dress code for weddings)

E

Echoism	phonic imitation of sounds heard in the environment
Emotive function	addresser's emotional intent in communicating something
Encoding	process of putting together a message in terms of a specific code
Entropy	term referring to anything that is unpredictable in a message or text
Eschatological myth	myth describing the end of the world or the coming of death into the world
Euphemism	rhetorical technique by which a term or phrase that has coarse, sordid, or other unpleasant associations is replaced by one that is perceived to be more delicate or inoffensive
Exclamation	rhetorical technique by which a sudden outcry expressing strong emotion, such as fright, grief, or hatred, is interpolated into a text

F

Fashion	prevailing dress style in a society
Feedback	information, signals, cues issuing from the receiver of a message as detected by the sender, thus allowing him or her to adjust the message to make it clearer, more meaningful, more effective
Fetish	object that is believed to have magical or spiritual powers, or that can cause sexual arousal

Fetishism	extreme devotion to objects and desires
Fiction	literary work whose content is produced by the imagination and is not necessarily based on fact
Firstness	in Peircean theory, the first level of meaning derived from bodily and sensory processes
Focal color	color category that is associated with a universal sequencing of colors
Foundation myth	myth recounting the founding of cities

G

Gender	sexual identity established in cultural terms
Gesticulant	gesture unit accompanying speech
Gesticulation	use of gestures to accompany speech
Gesture	semiosis and representation by means of the hand, arms, and, to a lesser extent, the head
Grammar	system of rules that characterize any code
Ground	meaning of a metaphor
Gutenberg Galaxy	McLuhan's term to describe social life after the invention of print technology

H

Haptics	study of touching patterns during social interaction
Hermeneutics	study and interpretation of texts
Hieroglyphic writing	ancient Egyptian system of writing, in which pictorial symbols were used to represent meaning or sounds or a combination of meaning and sound
History fabrication effect	term used in this book to refer to the fact that TV both makes and documents historical events
Holophrase	one-word utterance produced by infants
Homonymy	verbal coincidence by which two or more words with distinct meanings are pronounced and/or spelled in the same way

Hyperbole	rhetorical exaggeration for effect
Hypertextuality	system for linking different texts and images within a computer document or over a network
Hypoicon	Peirce's term for an icon that is shaped by cultural convention but that can nonetheless be figured out by those who are not members of the culture
Hyponymy	semantic relation whereby one concept embraces another

I

Icon	sign in which the signifier has a direct (nonarbitrary), simulative connection to its signified or referent
Iconicity	process of representing with iconic signs
Ideographic writing	type of writing system in which a character, known as an ideograph, may bear some resemblance to its referent, but is also in part a symbolic signifier
Image schema	term used by George Lakoff and Mark Johnson to refer to the recurring structures of, or in, our perceptual interactions, bodily experiences, and cognitive operations that portray locations, movements, shapes, etc., in the mind
Index	sign in which the signifier has an existential connection to its signified or referent (i.e., the sign indicates that something "exists" somewhere in time and/or space)
Indexicality	process of representing with indexical signs
Information	any fact or datum that can be stored and retrieved by humans or machines
Interconnectedness principle	view that all signs, texts, and codes in a culture are connected to each other in signifying ways
Interpretant	process of adapting a sign's meaning to personal and social experiences
Interpretation	process of deciphering what a sign or text means

Intertext	the allusion of a text to some other text
Intertextuality	allusion within a text to some other text of which the interpreter would normally have knowledge
Irony	use of words to express something different from and often opposite to their literal meaning; use of words in a humorous but often sarcastic way

J

Jingle	an easy rhythmic and simple repetition of sound, etc., as in poetry and music

K

Kinesics	study of bodily semiosis

L

Language	verbal semiosis and representation
Legend	story derived from folk history that differs from myth in that it tells what has happened in the world since the period of its creation
Legisign	in Peircean theory, a representamen (signifier) that designates something by convention
Lexical field	set of lexical items (words) related to each other thematically (weather vocabulary, geometrical terms, etc.)
Linguistic Relativity Hypothesis	claim that language, cognition, and culture are interdependent (also known as the Whorfian hypothesis)
Litotes	rhetorical technique involving understatement for enhancing the effect of the ideas expressed
Logo	a distinctive company or brand signature, trademark, colophon, motto, newspaper nameplate, etc.

Logograph	full symbol or character representing a word
Logographic writing	highly symbolic writing system in which a character, known as a logograph, resembles its referent only in small part

M

Map	textual representation of a culturally significant territory or space drawn with a combination of iconic, indexical, and symbolic modes of representation
Meaning	concept that anything in existence has a design or purpose beyond its mere occurrence
Mechanical transmission	transmission of messages through such means as radio, television, etc.
Medium	technical or physical means by which a message is transmitted
Message	meaning of a text
Metalingual function	communicative function by which the code being used is identified
Metaphor	signifying process by which two signifying domains (A, B) are connected (A is B)
Metonymy	signifying process by which an entity is used to refer to another that is related to it
Modernism	technique in architecture also known as the Bauhaus school
Myth of the culture hero	myth describing the actions and characters of beings who are responsible for the discovery of a particular cultural artifact or technological process
Myth	story of early cultures that aims to explain the origin of life or of the universe in terms of some metaphysical or deistic entity or entities
Mythologizing effect	term used in this book to refer to the fact that TV imbues its characters with a mythological aura
Mythology	use and/or evocation of mythic themes in contemporary behaviors and performances; study of myths

N

Name	sign that identifies a person or place
Naming	process by which names are assigned to persons, places, and things
Narrative	something told or written, such as an account, story, tale
Narrative structure	universal patterns of plot, character, and setting in storytelling
Narratology	branch of semiotics that studies narrativity
Narrator	teller of the narrative
Natural sign	sign that represents its referent by attempting to imitate in its make-up some perceivable property of the referent
Natural transmission	transmission of messages naturally (through the air channel, through chemical signals, etc.)
Noise	anything that interferes with the reception of a message
Novel	fictional prose narrative in which characters and situations are depicted within the framework of a plot

O

Object	what a sign refers to
Objectification	process by which interconnected meanings are projected into the objects of a culture, thus creating the perception that they form an integrated sign system
Objectivity	perception of knowledge as independent of knowledge making
Onomastics	study of names
Onomatopoeia	vocal iconicity
Ontogenesis	development of all semiosic abilities during childhood
Opposition	process by which signs are differentiated through a minimal change in their form
Othello effect	lying in order to emphasize the truth

Oxymoron	rhetorical technique by which two seemingly contradictory or incongruous words are combined

P

Paradigmatic	structural relation between signs that keeps them distinct and therefore recognizable
Paradox	statement that appears contradictory or inconsistent
Parallelism	repetition of linguistic patterns
Parameter	term used by linguists to designate the kinds of constraints imposed by culture on the universal principles of the speech faculty
Performance	representation and communication of some text, framed in a special way and put on display for an audience
Persona	Self that one presents in specific social situations
Personification	rhetorical technique whereby inanimate objects or abstract ideas are portrayed as living beings
Perspective	technique of representing three-dimensional objects and depth relationships on a two-dimensional surface
Phatic function	communicative function by which contact between addresser and addressee is established
Phoneme	minimal unit of sound in a language that allows its users to differentiate meanings
Phylogenesis	evolution of all semiosic abilities in the human species
Pictographic writing	type of writing system in which a character, known as a pictograph, bears pictorial resemblance to its referent
Plot	plan of events or main story in a narrative or drama
Poetic function	communicative function based on poetic language
Poetry	verbal art based on the acoustic, rhythmic, and imagistic properties of words

Pop art	art form that utilizes themes and images taken from mass technological culture
Positioning	placing or targeting of a product for the right people
Postmodernism	contemporary school of thought which posits that all knowledge is relative and human-made, and that there is no purpose to life beyond the immediate and the present
Propaganda	any systematic dissemination of doctrines, views, etc., reflecting specific interests and ideologies (political, social, and so on)
Proportionality	the meaning of words or forms on the basis of binary features or components that keep them distinct
Proxemics	branch of semiotics and anthropology that studies the symbolic structure of the physical space maintained between people in social contexts
Public relations	activities and techniques used by organizations and individuals to establish favorable attitudes and responses to them on the part of the general public or of special groups
Publicity	craft of disseminating any information that concerns a person, group, event, or product through some form of public media

Q

Qualisign	in Peircean theory, the representamen (signifier) that refers to a quality

R

Receiver	person to whom a message or text is directed
Redundancy	that which is predictable or conventional in a message or text, thus helping to counteract the potential interference effects of noise

Referent	what is referred to (any object, being, idea, or event)
Referential domain	specific range of meanings to which signs refer
Referential function	communicative act in which there is a straightforward connection between the act and what it refers to
Representamen	in Peircean theory, the physical part of a sign
Representation	process by which referents are captured by signs or texts
Rhetoric	branch of philosophy and semiotics studying the various verbal techniques used in all kinds of discourses, from common conversation to poetry
Rhetorical question	rhetorical technique whereby a question is asked not to gain information, but to assert more emphatically the obvious answer to what is asked

S

Secondness	in Peircean theory, the second level of meaning derived from verbal processes
Semantic differential	experimental technique developed by Osgood, Suci, and Tannenbaum that aims to assess the emotional connotations evoked by words
Semantics	study of meaning in language
Semiology	Saussure's term for the study of signs
Semiosis	comprehension and production of signs
Semiosphere	the world of signs and codes to be differentiated from the biosphere (the physical life-supporting environment)
Semiotics	science that studies signs and their uses in representation
Sender	transmitter of a message or text
Setting	place and conditions in which a narrative takes place
Sign	something that stands for something or someone else in some capacity

Sign language	language code based on gestures and grammatical rules that share some common points with spoken language
Signal	an emission or movement that naturally or conventionally triggers some reaction on the part of a receiver
Signification	process of generating meaning through the use of signs
Signified	that part of a sign that is referred to
Signifier	that part of a sign that does the referring; the physical part of a sign
Simile	rhetorical technique by which two ideas are compared explicitly with the word *like* or *as*
Sinsign	in Peircean theory, a representamen (signifier) that draws attention to, or singles out, a particular object in time-space
Social text	text that underlies a signifying order and thus regulates communal sense-making
Sound symbolism	process by which referents are represented through some form of vocal iconicity in speech
Source domain	class of vehicles that deliver a conceptual metaphor
Speech	vocalized or articulated language
Structure	any repeatable, systematic, patterned, or predictable aspect of signs, codes, texts
Subordinate level	level on which a concept has a detailing function
Subtext	text (message) hidden within a text
Superordinate level	level on which a concept has a highly general classificatory function
Syllabary	writing system based on characters representing syllables
Syllable	word or part of a word pronounced with a single, uninterrupted sounding of the voice (usually a vowel) and generally one or more sounds of lesser sonority (usually consonants)
Symbol	sign that represents a referent through cultural convention
Symbolism	process of representing something with symbols
Symptom	bodily sign that stands for some ailment, physical condition, disease

Synchrony	study of signs, codes, texts as they exist at a specific point in time
Synecdoche	signifying process by which a part stands for the whole, the whole for a part, the species for the genus, etc.
Synesthesia	juxtaposition of signs so as to evoke different sense modalities simultaneously
Synonymy	relation by which the meanings of different signs overlap
Syntagmatic	structural relation that combines signs in code-specific ways
Syntax	syntagmatic structure in language

T

Target domain	topic of a conceptual metaphor
Technology	system of objects made by humans
Tenor	subject of a metaphor (topic)
Territoriality	mechanism by which animals seek out territories or stake boundary zones around themselves for survival
Text	a message put together in terms of a specific code
Theater	reenactment of some event in nature, in life, in society in some carefully scripted way, involving actors and a spatial location, such as a raised stage, around which an audience can view and/or hear the performance
Thirdness	in Peircean theory, the third level of meaning derived from symbolic processes
Topic	subject of a metaphor (tenor)
Trade advertising	advertising that is directed towards dealers and professionals through appropriate trade publications and media
Transmission	physical process of sending messages or texts to a receiver
Trope	figure of speech
Turing machine	computer program

U

Universal grammar	Chomsky's notion that the brain has a set of innate principles that undergird the development of specific languages

V

Vehicle	part of a metaphor to which a tenor is connected

W

Whorfian hypothesis	view elaborated by Benjamin Lee Whorf that the language one speaks shapes his or her worldview
Writing	process of representing speech with characters

Z

Zoosemiosis	semiosis in animal species
Zoosemiotics	branch of semiotics studying semiosis in and across species

Cited Works and
General Bibliography

The works listed here include both those mentioned in this text, and others that elaborate upon its themes (but are not cited directly in it). This list can thus be considered to be a general bibliography for exploring semiotics further.

Abbott, E. A. (1884). *Flatland: A Romance of Many Dimensions*. London: Seeley.

Abercrombie, N. (1996). *Television and Society*. Cambridge: Polity Press.

Alpher, B. (1987). Feminine as the Unmarked Gender. *Australian Journal of Linguistics* 7: 169–187.

Anderson, W. T. (1992). *Reality Isn't What It Used to Be*. San Francisco: Harper Collins.

Andren, G. L., Ericsson, L., Ohlsson, R., and Tännsjö, T. (1978). *Rhetoric and Ideology in Advertising*. Stockholm: AB Grafiska.

Ardrey, R. (1966). *The Territorial Imperative*. New York: Atheneum.

Argyle, M. (1988). *Bodily Communication*. New York: Methuen.

Aristotle. (1952a). *Rhetoric*. In: W. D. Ross (ed.), *The Works of Aristotle*, Vol. 11. Oxford: Clarendon Press.

Aristotle. (1952b). *Poetics*. In: W. D. Ross (ed.), *The Works of Aristotle*, Vol. 11. Oxford: Clarendon Press.

Armstrong, D. F., Stokoe, W. C., and Wilcox, S. E. (1995). *Gesture and the Nature of Language*. Cambridge: Cambridge University Press.

Arnheim, R. (1969). *Visual Thinking*. Berkeley: University of California Press.

Asch, S. (1950). On the Use of Metaphor in the Description of Persons. In: H. Werner (ed.), *On Expressive Language*, 86–94. Worcester: Clark University Press.

Asch, S. (1958). The Metaphor: A Psychological Inquiry. In: R. Tagiuri and L. Petrullo (eds.), *Person Perception and Interpersonal Behavior*, 28–42. Stanford: Stanford University Press.

Ashley, L. R. N. (1984). *The History of the Short Story*. Washington, DC: US Information Agency.

Atwan, R. (1979). *Edsels, Luckies and Frigidaires: Advertising the American Way*. New York: Dell.

Austin, J. L. (1962). *How to Do Things with Words*. Cambridge, Mass.: Harvard University Press.

Axtell, R. E. (1991). *Gestures.* New York: John Wiley.

Bachand, D. (1992). The Art of (in) Advertising: From Poetry to Prophecy. *Marketing Signs* 13: 1–7.

Bal, M. (1985). *Narratology: Introduction to the Theory of the Narrative*. Toronto: University of Toronto Press.

Barbe, K. (1995). *Irony in Context.* Amsterdam: John Benjamins.

Baron, N. (1992). *Growing Up with Language: How Children Learn to Talk.* Reading, Mass.: Addison-Wesley.

Barrett, W. (1986). *The Death of the Soul: From Descartes to the Computer.* New York: Anchor.

Barthes, R. (1957). *Mythologies.* Paris: Seuil.

Barthes, R. (1964). *Éléments de sémiologie.* Paris: Seuil.

Barthes, R. (1967). *Système de la mode.* Paris: Seuil.

Barthes, R. (1968). *Elements of Semiology.* London: Cape.

Barthes, R. (1970). *S/Z*, trans. by R. Miller. New York: Hill and Wang.

Barthes, R. (1977). *Image-Music-Text*. London: Fontana.

Basso, K. H. (1976). *Meaning in Anthropology*. Albuquerque: University of New Mexico Press.

Basso, K. H. (1990). *Western Apache Language and Culture: Essays in Linguistic Anthropology.* Tucson: University of Arizona Press.

Bauman, R. (1992). Performance. In: R. Bauman (ed.), *Folklore, Cultural Performances, and Popular Entertainments*, 41–49. Oxford: Oxford University Press.

Baudrillard, J. (1987). *The Ecstasy of Communication*. St. Louis: Telos Press.

Bauman, Z. (1992). *Intimations of Postmodernity*. London: Routledge.

Beaken, M. (1996). *The Making of Language.* Edinburgh: Edinburgh University Press.

Bellack, L. and Baker, S. S. (1983). *Reading Faces.* New York: Bantam.

Benedict, R. (1934). *Patterns of Culture.* New York: New American Library.

Bennett, T. J. A. (1988). *Aspects of English Colour Collocations and Idioms.* Heidelberg: Winter.

Berger, A. A. (1996). *Manufacturing Desire: Media, Popular Culture, and Everyday Life.* New Brunswick, NJ: Transaction Publishers.

Berger, A. A. (2000). *Ads, Fads, and Consumer Culture: Advertising's Impact on American Character and Society*. Lanham: Rowman & Littlefield.

Berger, J. (1972). *Ways of Seeing*. Harmondsworth: Penguin.

Bergin, T. G. and Fisch, M. (1984 [1948]). *The New Science of Giambattista Vico*. Ithaca: Cornell University Press.

Berlin, B. and Berlin, E. A. (1975). Aguarana Color Categories. *American Ethnologist* 2: 61–87.

Berlin, B. and Kay, P. (1969). *Basic Color Terms*. Berkeley: University of California Press.

Bettelheim, B. (1989). *The Uses of Enchantment: The Meaning and Importance of Fairy Tales.* New York: Vintage.

Bickerton, D. (1969). Prolegomena to a Linguistic Theory of Metaphor. *Foundations of Language* 5: 34–52.

Birdwhistell, R. (1970). *Kinesics and Context: Essays on Body Motion Communication*. Harmondsworth: Penguin.

Black, M. (1962). *Models and Metaphors*. Ithaca: Cornell University Press.

Bloomfield, L. (1933). *Language*. New York: Holt.

Blumenberg, H. (1985). *Work on Myth*. Cambridge, Mass.: MIT Press.

Boas, F. (1940). *Race, Language, and Culture*. New York: Free Press.

Bonner, J. T. (1980). *The Evolution of Culture in Animals*. Princeton: Princeton University Press.

Boole, G. (1854). *An Investigation of the Laws of Thought*. New York: Dover.

Bouissac, P., Herzfeld, M., and Posner, R. (1986) (eds.). *Iconicity: Essays on the Nature of Culture. Festschrift for Thomas A. Sebeok on His 65th Birthday*. Tübingen: Stauffenburg.

Boysson-Bardies, B. de and Vihman, M. M. (1991). Adaptation to Language: Evidence from Babbling and First Words in Four Languages. *Language* 67: 297–319.

Brand, P. and Yancey, P. (1993). *Pain*. New York: Harper Collins.

Bremer, J. and Roodenburg, H. (1991) (eds.). *A Cultural History of Gesture*. Ithaca: Cornell University Press.

Brent, J. (1994). *Charles Sanders Peirce: A Life*. Bloomington: Indiana University Press.

Bronowski, J. (1977). *A Sense of the Future*. Cambridge, Mass.: MIT Press.

Bronowski, J. (1978). *The Origins of Knowledge and Imagination*. New Haven: Yale University Press.

Brown, R. W. (1958). *Words and Things: An Introduction to Language*. New York: The Free Press.

Brown, R. W. (1970). *Psycholinguistics*. New York: The Free Press.

Brown, R. W. (1973). *A First Language*. Cambridge, Mass.: Harvard University Press.

Brown, R. W., Leiter, R. A., and Hildum, D. C. (1957). Metaphors from Music Criticism. *Journal of Abnormal and Social Psychology* 54: 347–352.

Bruner, J. S. (1990). *Acts of Meaning*. Cambridge, Mass.: Harvard University Press.

Bühler, K. (1934). *Sprachtheorie: Die Darstellungsfunktion der Sprache*. Jena: Fischer.

Bühler, K. (1951 [1908]). On Thought Connection. In: D. Rapaport (ed.), *Organization and Pathology of Thought*, 81–92. New York: Columbia University Press.

Burton, G. (2000). *Talking Television: An Introduction to the Study of Television*. London: Arnold.

Campbell, J. (1949). *The Hero with a Thousand Faces*. New York: Pantheon.

Campbell, J. (1969). *Primitive Mythology*. Harmondsworth: Penguin.

Carlson, M. (1989). *Places of Performance: The Semiotics of Theatre Architecture*. Ithaca: Cornell University Press.

Casad, E. H. (1996) (ed.). *Cognitive Linguistics in the Redwoods: The Expansion of a New Paradigm in Linguistics*. Berlin: Mouton de Gruyter.

Cashmore, E. (1994). *And There Was Television*. London: Routledge.

Cassirer, E. A. (1944). *An Essay on Man*. New Haven: Yale University Press.

Cassirer, E. A. (1946). *Language and Myth*. New York: Dover.

Cassirer, E. A. (1957). *The Philosophy of Symbolic Forms*. New Haven: Yale University Press.

Chevalier-Skolnikoff, S. and Liska, J. (1993). Tool Use by Wild and Captive Elephants. *Animal Behavior* 46: 209–219.

Chomsky, N. (1957). *Syntactic Structures*. The Hague: Mouton.

Chomsky, N. (1986). *Knowledge of Language: Its Nature, Origin, and Use*. New York: Praeger.

Chomsky, N. (1990). Language and Mind. In: D. H. Mellor (ed.), *Ways of Communicating*, pp. 56–80. Cambridge: Cambridge University Press.

Chomsky, N. (1995). *The Minimalist Program*. Cambridge, Mass.: MIT Press.

Clark, E. V. (1993). *The Lexicon in Acquisition*. Cambridge: Cambridge University Press.

Clarke, D. S. (1987). *Principles of Semiotic*. London: Routledge and Kegan Paul.

Classen, C. (1993). *Worlds of Sense: Exploring the Senses in History and across Cultures*. London: Routledge.

Classen, C., Howes, D., and Synnott, A. (1994). *Aroma: The Cultural History of Smell*. London: Routledge.

Cobley, P. (ed.) (2001). *The Routledge Companion to Semiotics and Linguistics*. London: Routledge, 2001.

Cole, K. C. (1984). *Sympathetic Vibrations*. New York: Bantam.

Coulmas, F. (1989). *The Writing Systems of the World*. Oxford: Blackwell.

Cox, M. (1992). *Children's Drawings*. Harmondsworth: Penguin.

Craik, J. (1993). *The Face of Fashion: Cultural Studies in Fashion*. London: Routledge.

Crawford, M. (1995). *Talking Difference: On Gender and Language*. Thousand Oaks: Sage.

Crispin Miller, M. (1988). *Boxed In: The Culture of TV*. Evanston: Northwestern University Press.

Crystal, D. (1987). *The Cambridge Encyclopedia of Language*. Cambridge: Cambridge University Press.

D'Andrade, R. and Strauss, C. (1992) (eds.). *Human Motives and Cultural Models*. Cambridge: Cambridge University Press.

Dance, F. and Larson, C. (1976). *The Functions of Communication: A Theoretical Approach*. New York: Holt, Rinehart and Winston.

Danesi, M. (1993). *Vico, Metaphor, and the Origin of Language*. Bloomington: Indiana University Press.

Danesi, M. (2001). *Encyclopedic Dictionary of Semiotics, Media, and Communications*. Toronto: University of Toronto Press.

Daniels, P. T. and Bright, W. (1995) (eds.). *The World's Writing Systems*. Oxford: Oxford University Press.

Danna, S. R. (1992). *Advertising and Popular Culture: Studies in Variety and Versatility*. Bowling Green, Ohio: Bowling Green State University Popular Press.

Darley, A. (2000). *Visual Digital Culture: Surface Play and Spectacle in Media Genres*. London: Routledge.

Darwin, C. (1858). *The Origin of Species*. New York: Collier.

Darwin, C. (1871). *The Descent of Man*. New York: Modern Library.

Darwin, C. (1872). *The Expression of the Emotions in Man and Animals*. London: Murray.

Davidoff, J. (1991). *Cognition through Color*. Cambridge, Mass.: MIT Press.

Davies, R. (1989). *How to Read Faces*. Woolnough: Aquarian.

Davis, F. (1992). *Fashion, Culture, and Identity.* Chicago: University of Chicago Press.

Davis, P. J. and Hersh, R. (1986). *Descartes' Dream: The World According to Mathematics.* Boston: Houghton Mifflin.

Dawkins, R. (1976). *The Selfish Gene.* Oxford: Oxford University Press.

Dawkins, R. (1987). *The Blind Watchmaker.* Harlow: Longmans.

Dawkins, R. (1995). *River Out of Eden: A Darwinian View of Life.* New York: Basic.

De Toro, F. (1995). *Theatre Semiotics: Text and Staging in Modern Theatre.* Toronto: University of Toronto Press.

Deacon, T. W. (1997). *The Symbolic Species: The Co-Evolution of Language and the Brain.* New York: Norton.

Deely, J. (1990). *Basics of Semiotics.* Bloomington: Indiana University Press.

Deely, J. (2001). *Four Ages of Understanding: The First Postmodern Survey of Philosophy from Ancient Times to the Turn of the Twentieth Century.* Toronto: University of Toronto Press.

Dennett, D.C. (1991). *Consciousness Explained.* Boston: Little, Brown.

Dennett, D.C. (1995). *Darwin's Dangerous Idea: Evolution and the Meanings of Life.* New York: Simon and Schuster.

Deregowski, J. B. (1972). Pictorial Perception and Culture. *Scientific American* 227: 82–88.

Derrida, J. (1976). *Of Grammatology*, trans. by G. C. Spivak. Baltimore: Johns Hopkins Press.

Descartes, R. (1637). *Essaies philosophiques.* Leyden: L'imprimerie de Ian Maire.

Diamond, A. A. (1959). *The History and Origin of Language.* New York: Philosophical Library.

Dirven, R. and Verspoor, M. (1998). *Cognitive Exploration of Language and Linguistics.* Amsterdam: John Benjamins.

Dissanayake, E. (1992). *Homo Aestheticus: Where Art Comes from and Why.* New York: Free Press.

Docker, J. (1994). *Postmodernism and Popular Culture: A Cultural History.* Cambridge: Cambridge University Press.

Dondis, D. A. (1986). *A Primer of Visual Literacy.* Cambridge, Mass.: MIT Press.

Douglas, M. (1966). *Purity and Danger.* Harmondsworth: Penguin.

Douglas, M. (1992). *Objects and Objections.* Toronto: Toronto Semiotic Circle.

Douglas, S. J. (1994). *Where the Girls Are: Growing Up Female with the Mass Media.* New York: Times.

Dubin, L. S. (1987). *The History of Beads.* New York: Abrams.

Duchan, J. F., Bruder, G. A., and Hewitt, L. E. (1995) (eds.). *Deixis in Narrative: A Cognitive Science Perspective.* Hillsdale, NJ: Lawrence Erlbaum Associates.

Dunbar, R. (1997). *Grooming, Gossip, and the Evolution of Language.* Cambridge, Mass.: Harvard University Press.

Dundes, A. (1972). Seeing Is Believing. *Natural History* 81: 9–12.

Dunning, W. V. (1991). *Changing Images of Pictorial Space: A History of Visual Illusion in Painting.* Syracuse: Syracuse University Press.

Durkheim, E. (1912). *The Elementary Forms of Religious Life.* New York: Collier.

Dyer, G. (1982). *Advertising as Communication.* London: Routledge.

Eagleton, T. (1983). *Literary Theory: An Introduction*. Minneapolis: University of Minnesota Press.

Eccles, J. C. (1989). *Evolution of the Brain: Creation of the Self*. London: Routledge.

Eccles, J. C. (1992). *The Human Psyche*. London: Routledge.

Eco, U. (1976). *A Theory of Semiotics*. Bloomington: Indiana University Press.

Eco, U. (1979). *The Role of the Reader: Explorations in the Semiotics of Texts*. Bloomington: Indiana University Press.

Eco, U. (1984). *Semiotics and the Philosophy of Language*. Bloomington: Indiana University Press.

Eco, U. (1990). *The Limits of Interpretation*. Bloomington: Indiana University Press.

Edie, J. M. (1976). *Speaking and Meaning: The Phenomenology of Language*. Bloomington: Indiana University Press.

Ekman, P. (1976). Movements with Precise Meanings. *Journal of Communication* 26: 14–26.

Ekman, P. (1980). The Classes of Nonverbal Behavior. In: W. Raffler-Engel (ed.), *Aspects of Nonverbal Communication*, 89–102. Lisse: Swets and Zeitlinger.

Ekman, P. (1982). Methods for Measuring Facial Action. In: K. R. Scherer and P. Ekman (eds.), *Handbook of Methods in Nonverbal Behavior*, 45–90. Cambridge: Cambridge University Press.

Ekman, P. (1985). *Telling Lies*. New York: Norton.

Ekman, P. and Friesen, W. (1975). *Unmasking the Face*. Englewood Cliffs: Prentice-Hall.

Eliade, M. (1972). *A History of Religious Ideas*. Chicago: University of Chicago Press.

Emantian, M. (1995). Metaphor and the Expression of Emotion: The Value of Cross-Cultural Perspectives. *Metaphor and Symbolic Activity* 10: 163–182.

Emmorey, K. and Reilly, J. (1995) (eds.). *Language, Gesture, and Space*. Hillsdale, NJ: Lawrence Erlbaum Associates.

Engen, T. (1982). *The Perception of Odours*. New York: Academic.

Enninger, W. (1992). Clothing. In: R. Bauman (ed.), *Folklore, Cultural Performances, and Popular Entertainments*, 123–145. Oxford: Oxford University Press.

Epstein, D. (1999). *Twentieth Century Pop Culture*. New York: Quadrillion Publishing.

Espes Brown, J. (1992). Becoming Part of It. In: D. M. Dooling and P. Jordan-Smith (eds.), *I Become Part of It: Sacred Dimensions in Native American Life*, 1–15. New York: Harper Collins.

Everaert, M. *et al.* (1995). *Idioms: Structural and Psychological Perspectives*. Mahwah, NJ: Lawrence Erlbaum Associates.

Ewen, S. (1976). *Captains of Consciousness*. New York: McGraw-Hill.

Ewen, S. (1988). *All Consuming Images*. New York: Basic Books.

Farb, P. (1974). *Word Play*. New York: Bantam.

Fauconnier, G. (1997). *Mappings in Thought and Language*. Cambridge: Cambridge University Press.

Fauconnier, G. and Sweetser, E. (1996). *Spaces, Worlds, and Grammar*. Chicago: University of Chicago Press.

Fauconnier, G. and Turner, M. (2002). *The Way We Think: Conceptual Blending and the Mind's Hidden Complexities*. New York: Basic.

Feher, M., Naddaf, R., and Tazi, N. (1989) (eds.). *Fragments for a History of the Human Body*. New York: Zone.

Fernandez, J. W. (1991) (ed.). *Beyond Metaphor: The Theory of Tropes in Anthropology*. Stanford: Stanford University Press.

Fisch, M. H. (1978). Peirce's General Theory of Signs. In: Thomas A. Sebeok (ed.), *Sight, Sound, and Sense*, 31–70. Bloomington: Indiana University Press.

Fisher, H. E. (1992). *Anatomy of Love*. New York: Norton.

Fleming, D. (1996). *Powerplay: Toys as Popular Culture*. Manchester: Manchester University Press.

Forceville, C. (1996). *Pictorial Metaphor in Advertising*. London: Routledge.

Foucault, M. (1972). *The Archeology of Knowledge*, trans. by A. M. Sheridan Smith. New York: Pantheon.

Foucault, M. (1976). *The History of Sexuality*, Vol. 1. London: Allen Lane.

Frege, G. (1879). *Begiffsschrift eine der Aritmetischen nachgebildete Formelsprache des reinen Denkens*. Halle: Nebert.

Freud, S. (1913). *Totem and Taboo*. New York: Norton.

Fridlund, A. J. (1994). *Human Facial Expression: An Evolutionary View*. New York: Academic.

Friedberg, A. (1993). *Window Shopping: Cinema and the Postmodern*. Berkeley: University of California Press.

Frisch, K. von (1962). Dialects in the Language of Bees. *Scientific American* 207: 79–87.

Frisch, K. von (1967). *The Dance Language and Orientation of Bees*. Cambridge, Mass.: Harvard University Press.

Frutiger, A. (1989). *Signs and Symbols*. New York: Van Nostrand.

Frye, N. (1981). *The Great Code: The Bible and Literature*. Toronto: Academic Press.

Frye, N. (1990). *Words with Power*. Harmondsworth: Penguin.

Gallagher, W. (1993). *The Power of Place: How Our Surroundings Shape Our Thoughts, Emotions, and Actions*. New York: Harper Collins.

Gardner, B. T. and Gardner, R. A. (1975). Evidence for Sentence Constituents in the Early Utterances of Child and Chimpanzee. *Journal of Experimental Psychology* 104: 244–262.

Gardner, H. (1982). *Art, Mind, and Brain: A Cognitive Approach to Creativity*. New York: Basic.

Gardner, H. (1985). *The Mind's New Science: A History of the Cognitive Revolution*. New York: Basic Books.

Gardner, H., Winner, E., Bechofer, R., and Wolf, D. (1978). The Development of Figurative Language. In: K. Nelson (ed.), *Children's Language*, 1–38. New York: Garner Press.

Gardner, R. A. and Gardner, B. T. (1969). Teaching Sign Language to a Chimpanzee. *Science* 165: 664–672.

Gartman, D. (1994). *Auto-Opium: A Social History of American Automobile Design*. London: Routledge.

Garza-Cuarón, B. (1991). *Connotation and Meaning*. Berlin: Mouton de Gruyter.

Gaylin, W. (1990). *On Being and Becoming Human*. London: Penguin.

Geertz, C. (1973). *The Interpretation of Cultures*. New York: Harper Torch.

Gelb, I. J. (1963). *A Study of Writing*. Chicago: University of Chicago Press.

Genette, G. (1988). *Narrative Discourse Revisited*. Ithaca: Cornell University Press.

Gentner, D. (1982). Are Scientific Analogies Metaphors? In: D. S. Miall (ed.), *Metaphor: Problems and Perspectives*, 106–132. Atlantic Highlands, N. J.: Humanities Press.

Gibbs, R. W. (1994). *The Poetics of Mind: Figurative Thought, Language, and Understanding*. Cambridge: Cambridge University Press.

Gibson, K. R. and Ingold, T. (1993) (eds.). *Tools, Language and Cognition in Human Evolution*. Cambridge: Cambridge University Press.

Gill, A. (1994). *Rhetoric and Human Understanding*. Prospect Heights, Ill.: Waveland.

Goatley, A. (1997). *The Language of Metaphors*. London: Routledge.

Goffman, E. (1959). *The Presentation of Self in Everyday Life*. Garden City: Doubleday.

Goffman, E. (1978). Response Cries. *Language* 54: 787–815.

Goffman, E. (1979). *Gender Advertisements*. New York: Harper and Row.

Goldblatt, D. and Brown, L. B. (1997) (eds.). *Aesthetics: A Reader in the Philosophy of the Arts*. Upper Saddle River: Prentice-Hall.

Goldman, R. and Papson, R. (1996). *Sign Wars: The Cluttered Landscape of Advertising*. New York: Guilford.

Goldwasser, O. (1995). *From Icon to Metaphor: Studies in the Semiotics of the Hieroglyphs*. Freiburg: Universitätsverlag.

Goode, J. (1992). Food. In: R. Bauman (ed.), *Folklore, Cultural Performances, and Popular Entertainments*, 233–245. Oxford: Oxford University Press.

Goodwin, A. (1992). *Dancing in the Distraction Factory: Music Television and Popular Culture*. Minneapolis: University of Minnesota Press.

Goody, J. (1982). *Cooking, Cuisine and Class*. Cambridge: Cambridge University Press.

Goossens, L. *et al.* (1995). *By Word of Mouth: Metaphor, Metonymy and Linguistic Action in a Cognitive Perspective*. Berlin: Mouton de Gruyter.

Gordon, W. T. (1997). *Marshall McLuhan: Escape into Understanding: A Biography*. New York: Basic Books.

Gottdiener, M. (1995). *Postmodern Semiotics: Material Culture and the Forms of Postmodern Life*. London: Blackwell.

Greenbie, B. (1981). *Spaces: Dimensions of the Human Landscape*. New Haven: Yale University Press.

Gregory, B. (1988). *Inventing Reality: Physics as Language*. New York: John Wiley and Sons.

Greimas, A. J. (1987). *On Meaning: Selected Essays in Semiotic Theory*, trans. by P. Perron and F. Collins. Minneapolis: University of Minnesota Press.

Greimas, A. J. and Courtés, J. (1979). *Semiotics and Language*. Bloomington: Indiana University Press.

Grice, H. P. (1975). Logic and Conversation. In: P. Cole and J. Morgan (eds.), *Syntax and Semantics*, Vol. 3, 41–58. New York: Academic.

Griffin, D. R. (1981). *The Question of Animal Consciousness*. New York: Rockefeller University Press.

Griffin, D. R. (1992). *Animal Minds*. Chicago: University of Chicago Press.

Grossberg, L. (1992). *We Gotta Get Out of This Place: Popular Conservatism and Postmodern Culture*. London: Routledge.

Gumpel, L. (1984). *Metaphor Reexamined: A Non-Aristotelian Perspective*. Bloomington: Indiana University Press.

Haley, M. C. (1989). *The Semeiosis of Poetic Metaphor.* Bloomington: Indiana University Press.

Hall, E. T. (1966). *The Hidden Dimension*. New York: Doubleday.

Hall, E. T. (1973). *The Silent Language*. New York: Anchor.

Hall, K. and Bucholtz, M. (1996). *Gender Articulated: Language and the Socially Constructed Self.* London: Routledge.

Hall, M. B. (1992). *Color and Meaning*. Cambridge: Cambridge University Press.

Halliday, M. A. K. (1975). *Learning How to Mean: Explorations in the Development of Language*. London: Arnold.

Halliday, M. A. K. (1985). *Introduction to Functional Grammar*. London: Arnold.

Hallyn, F. (1990). *The Poetic Structure of the World: Copernicus and Kepler*. New York: Zone Books.

Hardin, C. L. and Maffi, L. (1997) (eds.). *Color Categories in Thought and Language*. Cambridge: Cambridge University Press.

Harnad, S. R., Steklis, H. B., and Lancaster, J. (1976) (eds.). *Origins and Evolution of Language and Speech*. New York: New York Academy of Sciences.

Harré, R. (1981). *Great Scientific Experiments*. Oxford: Phaidon Press.

Harris, R. (1986). *The Origin of Writing*. London: Duckworth.

Harvey, D. (1990). *The Condition of Postmodernity: An Enquiry into the Origins of Cultural Change*. Cambridge: Blackwell.

Harvey, K. and Shalom, C. (1997) (eds.). *Language and Desire: Encoding Sex, Romance, and Intimacy.* London: Routledge.

Hassan, I. (1987). *The Postmodern Turn: Essays in Postmodern Theory and Culture*. Columbus: Ohio State University Press.

Hatcher, E. P. (1974). *Visual Metaphors: A Methodological Study in Visual Communication*. Albuquerque: University of New Mexico Press.

Hauser, M. D. (1996). *The Evolution of Communication*. Cambridge, Mass.: MIT Press.

Hausman, C. R. (1989). *Metaphor and Art*. Cambridge: Cambridge University Press.

Hausman, C. R. (1993). *Charles S. Peirce's Evolutionary Philosophy.* Cambridge: Cambridge University Press.

Hawkes, T. (1977). *Structuralism and Semiotics*. Berkeley: University of California Press.

Hayakawa, S. I. (1991). *Language in Thought and Action*, 5th ed. New York: Harcourt Brace Jovanovich.

Heinberg, R. (1989). *Memories and Visions of Paradise*. Los Angeles: J. P. Tarcher.

Herman, A. and Swiss, T. (eds.) (2000). *The World Wide Web and Contemporary Cultural Theory*. London: Routledge

Hilbert, D. R. (1987). *Color and Color Perception: A Study in Anthropocentric Realism*. Stanford: Center for the Study of Language and Information.

Hinton, J., Nichols, J. and Ohala, J. J. (1994) (eds.). *Sound Symbolism*. Cambridge: Cambridge University Press.

Hobbes, T. (1656 [1839]). *Elements of Philosophy*, Vol. 1. London: Molesworth.

Hockett, C. F. (1960). The Origin of Speech. *Scientific American* 203: 88–96.

Hodge, R. and Kress, G. (1988). *Social Semiotics*. Ithaca: Cornell University Press.

Holbrook, M. B. and Hirschman, E. C. (1993). *The Semiotics of Consumption: Interpreting Symbolic Consumer Behavior in Popular Culture and Works of Art*. Berlin: Mouton de Gruyter.

Holland, D. and Quinn, N. (1987) (eds.). *Cultural Models in Language and Thought*. Cambridge: Cambridge University Press.

Holland, P. (2000). *The Television Handbook*. London: Routledge.

Hollander, A. (1988). *Seeing through Clothes*. Harmondsworth: Penguin.

Hollander, A. (1994). *Sex and Suits: The Evolution of Modern Dress*. New York: Knopf.

Horn, R. E. (1998). *Visual Language: Global Communication for the 21st Century*. Bainbridge Island: MacroVU.

Horrocks, C. (2000). *Marshall McLuhan and Virtuality*. Duxford: Icon Books.

Howes, D. (1991) (ed.). *The Varieties of Sensory Experience*. Toronto: University of Toronto Press.

Hudson, L. (1972). *The Cult of the Fact*. New York: Harper & Row.

Huizinga, J. (1924). *The Waning of the Medieval Ages*. Garden City: Doubleday.

Humboldt, W. von (1836 [1988]). *On Language: The Diversity of Human Language-Structure and Its Influence on the Mental Development of Mankind*, trans. by P. Heath. Cambridge: Cambridge University Press.

Hume, D. (1749 [1902]). *An Enquiry Concerning Human Understanding*. Oxford: Clarendon.

Hutcheon, L. (1995). *Irony's Edge: The Theory and Politics of Irony*. London: Routledge.

Hutchison, M. (1990). *The Anatomy of Sex and Power: An Investigation of Mind–Body Politics*. New York: Morrow.

Hymes, D. (1971). *On Communicative Competence*. Philadelphia: University of Pennsylvania Press.

Indurkhya, B. (1992). *Metaphor and Cognition*. Dordrecht: Kluwer.

Ingham, P. (1996). *The Language of Gender and Class*. London: Routledge.

Inhelder, B. and Piaget, J. (1958). *The Growth of Logical Thinking from Childhood through Adolescence*. New York: Basic.

Innis, R. E. (1994). *Consciousness and the Play of Signs*. Bloomington: Indiana University Press.

Jackendoff, R. (1994). *Patterns in the Mind: Language and Human Nature*. New York: Basic Books.

Jackendoff, R. (1997). *The Architecture of the Language Faculty*. Cambridge, Mass.: MIT Press.

Jackson, B. S. (1985). *Semiotics and Legal Theory*. London: Routledge and Kegan Paul.

Jackson, J. B. (1994). *A Sense of Place, A Sense of Time*. New Haven: Yale University Press.

Jacobson, M. F. and Mazur, L. A. (1995). *Marketing Madness*. Boulder: Westview.

Jakobson, R. (1960). Linguistics and Poetics. In: T. A. Sebeok (ed.), *Style and Language*, 34–45. Cambridge, Mass.: MIT Press.

Jakobson, R. (1978). *Six Lectures on Sound and Meaning*, trans. by John Mepham. Cambridge, Mass.: MIT Press.

Jameson, F. (1991). *Postmodernism or the Cultural Logic of Late Capitalism*. Durham: Duke University Press.

Jhally, S. (1987). *The Codes of Advertising*. New York: St. Martin's Press.

Johanson, D. and Edgar, B. (1995). *From Lucy to Language*. New York: Simon and Schuster.

Johnson, M. (1987). *The Body in the Mind: The Bodily Basis of Meaning, Imagination and Reason*. Chicago: University of Chicago Press.

Johnson-Laird, P. N. (1983). *Mental Models*. Cambridge, Mass.: Harvard University Press.

Jones, R. (1982). *Physics as Metaphor*. New York: New American Library.

Joos, M. (1967). *The Five Clocks*. New York: Harcourt, Brace and World.

Jung, C. G. (1921). *Psychological Types*. New York: Harcourt.

Jung, C. G. (1956). *Analytical Psychology*. New York: Meridian.

Jung, C. G. (1957). *The Undiscovered Self*. New York: Mentor.

Jung, C. G. (1965). *Memories, Dreams, Reflections*. New York: Vintage.

Kant, I. (1790). *Critique of Judgment*. New York: Hafner Press.

Kaplan, J. and Bernays, A. (1996). *The Language of Names: What We Call Ourselves and Why It Matters*. New York: Simon and Schuster.

Kay, P. (1997). *Words and the Grammar of Context*. Cambridge: Cambridge University Press.

Kellner, D. (1995). *Media Culture*. London: Routledge.

Kendon, A. (1984). *Sign Languages of Aboriginal Australia: Cultural, Semiotic and Communicative Perspectives*. Cambridge: Cambridge University Press.

Kennedy, J. M. (1993). *Drawing and the Blind: Pictures to Touch*. New Haven: Yale University Press.

Key, W. B. (1972). *Subliminal Seduction*. New York: Signet.

Key, W. B. (1976). *Media Sexploitation*. New York: Signet.

Key, W. B. (1980). *The Clam-Plate Orgy*. New York: Signet.

Key, W. B. (1989). *The Age of Manipulation*. New York: Henry Holt.

Kilbourne, J. (1999). *Can't Buy My Love: How Advertising Changes the Way I Feel*. New York: Simon & Schuster.

Kinder, J. J. (1991). Up and Down: Structure of a Metaphor. In: B. Merry (ed.), *Essays in Honour of Keith Val Sinclair: An Australian Collection of Modern Language Studies*, 283–296. Townsville: James Cook University of North Queensland.

Kittay, E. F. (1987). *Metaphor: Its Cognitive Force and Linguistic Structure*. Oxford: Clarendon Press.

Klein, N. (2000). *No Logo: Taking Aim at the Brand Bullies*. Toronto: Alfred A. Knopf.

Kline, M. (1985). *Mathematics and the Search for Knowledge*. Oxford: Oxford University Press.

Koch, W. A. (1986). *Evolutionary Cultural Semiotics*. Bochum: Brockmeyer.

Koch, W. A. (1989) (ed.). *Geneses of Language*. Bochum: Brockmeyer.

Köhler, W. (1925). *The Mentality of Apes*. London: Routledge and Kegan Paul.

Konner, M. (1987). On Human Nature: Love among the Robots. *The Sciences* 27: 14–23.

Konner, M. (1991). Human Nature and Culture: Biology and the Residue of Uniqueness. In: J. J. Sheehan and M. Sosna (eds.), *The Boundaries of Humanity*, 103–124. Berkeley: University of California Press.

Kosslyn, S. M. (1983). *Ghosts in the Mind's Machine: Creating and Using Images in the Brain*. New York: W. W. Norton.

Kosslyn, S. M. (1994). *Image and Brain*. Cambridge, Mass.: MIT Press.

Kövecses, Z. (1986). *Metaphors of Anger, Pride, and Love: A Lexical Approach to the Structure of Concepts*. Amsterdam: Benjamins.

Kövecses, Z. (1988). *The Language of Love: The Semantics of Passion in Conversational English*. London: Associated University Presses.

Kövecses, Z. (1990). *Emotion Concepts*. New York: Springer.

Krampen, M. (1991). *Children's Drawings: Iconic Coding of the Environment*. New York: Plenum.

Kroeber, A. L. and Kluckholn, C. (1963). *Culture: A Critical Review of Concepts and Definitions*. New York: Vintage.

Kubey, R. and Csikszentmihalyi, M. (1990). *Television and the Quality of Life*. Hillsdale, NJ: Lawrence Erlbaum Associates.

Kuhn, T. S. (1970). *The Structure of Scientific Revolutions*. Chicago: University of Chicago Press.

Laitman, J. T. (1990). Tracing the Origins of Human Speech. In: P. Whitten and D. E. K. Hunter (eds.), *Anthropology: Contemporary Perspectives*, 124–130. Glenview, Ill.: Scott, Foresman and Company.

Lakoff, G. (1987). *Women, Fire and Dangerous Things: What Categories Reveal about the Mind*. Chicago: University of Chicago Press.

Lakoff, G. and Johnson, L. (1980). *Metaphors We Live By*. Chicago: Chicago University Press.

Lakoff, G. and Johnson, M. (1999). *Philosophy in Flesh: The Embodied Mind and Its Challenge to Western Thought*. New York: Basic.

Lakoff, G. and Turner, M. (1989). *More than Cool Reason: A Field Guide to Poetic Metaphor*. Chicago: University of Chicago Press.

Lamb, T. and Bourriau, J. (1995) (eds.). *Colour: Art and Science*. Cambridge: Cambridge University Press.

Landau, T. (1989). *About Faces: The Evolution of the Human Face*. New York: Anchor.

Langacker, R. W. (1987). *Foundations of Cognitive Grammar*. Stanford: Stanford University Press.

Langacker, R. W. (1990). *Concept, Image, and Symbol: The Cognitive Basis of Grammar*. Berlin: Mouton de Gruyter.

Langacker, R. W. (1999). *Grammar and Conceptualization*. Berlin: Mouton de Gruyter.

Langer, S. (1948). *Philosophy in a New Key*. Cambridge, Mass.: Harvard University Press.

Langer, S. (1957). *Problems of Art*. New York: Scribner's.

Lanier, V. (1982). *The Arts We See*. New York: Teachers College Press.

Layton, R. (1991). *The Anthropology of Art*. Cambridge: Cambridge University Press.

Le Guérer, A. (1992). *Scent: The Essential and Mysterious Powers of Smell*. New York: Kodansha.

Leach, E. (1976). *Culture and Communication: The Logic by Which Symbols Are Connected*. Cambridge: Cambridge University Press.

Lee, P. (1996). *The Whorf Theory Complex: A Critical Reconstruction*. Amsterdam: John Benjamins.

Leeming, D. A. (1990). *The World of Myth: An Anthology*. Oxford: Oxford University Press.

Leezenberg, M. (2001). *Contexts of Metaphor*. Amsterdam: Elsevier.

Leiss, W., Kline, S. and Jhally, S. (1990). *Social Communication in Advertising: Persons, Products and Images of Well-Being*. Toronto: Nelson.

Leitch, T. M. (1986). *What Stories Are: Narrative Theory and Interpretation*. University Park: Pennsylvania State University Press.

Lenneberg, E. (1967). *The Biological Foundations of Language*. New York: John Wiley.

Leroy, M. (1997). *Some Girls Do: Why Women Do and Don't Make the First Move*. London: Harper Collins.

Levenstein, H. (1993). *Paradox of Plenty: A Social History of Eating in Modern America*. Oxford: Oxford University Press.

Levin, S. R. (1988). *Metaphoric Worlds*. New Haven: Yale University Press.

Levine, R. (1997). *A Geography of Time: The Temporal Misadventures of a Social Psychologist or How Every Culture Keeps Time Just a Little Bit Differently*. New York: Basic.

Lévi-Strauss, C. (1958). *Structural Anthropology*. New York: Basic Books.

Lévi-Strauss, C. (1962). *La pensée sauvage*. Paris: Plon.

Lévi-Strauss, C. (1964). *The Raw and the Cooked*. London: Cape.

Lévi-Strauss, C. (1978). *Myth and Meaning: Cracking the Code of Culture*. Toronto: University of Toronto Press.

Lewontin, R. C., Rose, S., and Kamin, L. (1984). *Not in Our Genes: Biology, Ideology, and Human Nature*. New York: Pantheon Books.

Leymore, V. (1975). *Hidden Myth: Structure and Symbolism in Advertising*. London: Heinemann.

Linden, E. (1986). *Silent Partners: The Legacy of the Ape Language Experiments*. New York: Signet.

Liszka, J. J. (1989). *The Semeiotic of Myth: A Critical Study of the Symbol*. Bloomington: Indiana University Press.

Locke, J. (1690). *An Essay Concerning Human Understanding*. London: Collins.

Logan, R. K. (1987). *The Alphabet Effect*. New York: St. Martin's Press.

Longhurst, B. (1995). *Popular Music and Society*. Cambridge: Polity Press.

Lorenz, K. (1952). *King Solomon's Ring*. New York: Crowell.

Lotman, Y. (1991). *Universe of the Mind: A Semiotic Theory of Culture*. Bloomington: Indiana University Press.

Luciano, L. (2000). *Looking Good: Male Body Image in Modern America*. New York: Hill & Wang.

Lucy, J. A. (1994). *Grammatical Categories and Cognition: A Case Study of the Linguistic Relativity Hypothesis*. Cambridge: Cambridge University Press.

Lyle, J. (1990). *Body Language*. London: Hamylin.

Lyotard, J.-F. (1984). *The Postmodern Condition: A Report on Knowledge*. Minneapolis: University of Minnesota Press.

MacCannell, D. and MacCannell, J. F. (1982). *The Time of the Sign: A Semiotic Interpretation of Modern Culture*. Bloomington: Indiana University Press.

MacCormac, E. (1976). *Metaphor and Myth in Science and Religion*. Durham, NC: Duke University Press.

MacCormac, E. (1985). *A Cognitive Theory of Metaphor*. Cambridge, Mass.: MIT Press.

MacLaury, R. E. (1997). *Color and Cognition in Mesoamerica: Constructing Categories as Vantages*. Austin: University of Texas Press.

Malinowski, B. (1922). *Argonauts of the Western Pacific*. New York: Dutton.

Malinowski, B. (1929). *The Sexual Life of Savages in North-Western Melanesia*. New York: Harcourt, Brace, and World.

Mallery, G. (1972). *Sign Language among North American Indians Compared with That among Other Peoples and Deaf-Mutes*. The Hague: Mouton.

Mallory, J. P. (1989). *In Search of the Indo-Europeans: Language, Archaeology and Myth*. London: Thames and Hudson.

Malotki, E. (1983). *Hopi Time: A Linguistic Analysis of the Temporal Concepts in the Hopi Language*. Berlin: Mouton de Gruyter.

Markel, N. (1997). *Semiotic Psychology: Speech as an Index of Emotions and Attitudes*. New York: Peter Lang.

Mathiot, M. (1979) (ed.). *Ethnolinguistics: Boas, Sapir and Whorf Revisited*. The Hague: Mouton.

McCracken, G. (1988). *Culture and Consumption*. Bloomington: Indiana University Press.

McCracken, G. (1995). *Big Hair: A Journey into the Transformation of Self*. Toronto: Penguin.

McLuhan, M. (1951). *The Mechanical Bride: Folklore of Industrial Man*. New York: Vanguard.

McLuhan, M. (1962). *The Gutenberg Galaxy*. Toronto: University of Toronto Press.

McLuhan, M. (1964). *Understanding Media*. London: Routledge and Kegan Paul.

McLuhan, M. and McLuhan, E. (1988). *Laws of Media: The New Science*. Toronto: University of Toronto Press.

McNeill, D. (1992). *Hand and Mind: What Gestures Reveal about Thought*. Chicago: University of Chicago Press.

McRobbie, A. (1988). *Zoot Suits and Second-Hand Dresses*. Boston: Unwin Hyman.

Mead, M. (1939). *From the South Seas: Studies of Adolescence and Sex in Primitive Societies*. New York: Morrow.

Mead, M. (1950). *Coming of Age in Samoa*. New York: North American Library.

Megarry, T. (1995). *Society in Prehistory: The Origins of Human Culture*. New York: New York University Press.

Meissner, M. and Philpott, S. B. (1975). The Sign Language of Sawmill Workers in British Columbia. *Sign Language Studies* 9: 291–308.

Melzack, R. (1972). The Perception of Pain. In: R. F. Thompson (ed.), *Physiological Psychology*, 223–231. San Francisco: Freeman.

Melzack, R. (1988). Pain. In: J. Kuper (ed.), *A Lexicon of Psychology, Psychiatry and Psychoanalysis*, 288–291. London: Routledge.

Merrell, F. (1995). *Peirce's Semiotics Now: A Primer*. Toronto: Canadian Scholars' Press.

Merrell, F. (1996). *Signs Grow: Semiosis and Life Processes*. Toronto: University of Toronto Press.

Merrell, F. (1997). *Peirce, Signs, and Meaning*. Toronto: University of Toronto Press.

Metz, C. (1974). *Film Language: A Semiotics of the Cinema*. Chicago: University of Chicago Press.

Miller, R. L. (1968). *The Linguistic Relativity Principle and Humboldtian Ethnolinguistics: A History and Appraisal*. The Hague: Mouton.

Mintz, S. W. (1996). *Tasting Food, Tasting Freedom: Excursions into Eating, Culture, and the Past.* Boston: Beacon.

Mithen, S. (1997). *The Prehistory of the Mind: The Cognitive Origins of Art, Religion and Science.* London: Thames and Hudson.

Money, J. (1986). *Lovemaps: Clinical Concepts of Sexual/Erotic Health and Pathology, Paraphilia, and Gender Identity from Conception to Maturity.* Baltimore: Johns Hopkins University Press.

Montagu, A. (1986). *Touching: The Human Significance of the Skin.* New York: Harper and Row.

Moog, C. (1990). *Are They Selling Her Lips? Advertising and Identity.* New York: Morrow.

Morris, C. W. (1938). *Foundations of the Theory of Signs.* Chicago: University of Chicago Press.

Morris, C. W. (1946). *Writings on the General Theory of Signs.* The Hague: Mouton.

Morris, D. (1969). *The Human Zoo.* London: Cape.

Morris, D. (1994). *The Human Animal.* London: BBC Books.

Morris, D. *et al.* (1979). *Gestures: Their Origins and Distributions.* London: Cape.

Mumford, L. S. (1995). *Love and Ideology in the Afternoon: Soap Opera, Women, and Television Genre.* Bloomington: Indiana University Press.

Nash, C. (1994). *Narrative in Culture.* London: Routledge.

Neumann, J. von (1958). *The Computer and the Brain.* New Haven: Yale University Press.

Newcomb, H. (1996) (ed.). *Encyclopedia of Television.* Chicago: Fitzroy Dearborn.

Nietzsche, F. (1873 [1979]). *Philosophy and Truth: Selections from Nietzsche's Notebooks of the Early 1870's.* Atlantic Heights, NJ: Humanities Press.

Noble, W. and Davidson, I. (1996). *Human Evolution, Language and Mind.* Cambridge: Cambridge University Press.

Nochimson, M. (1992). *No End to Her: Soap Opera and the Female Subject.* Berkeley: University of California Press.

Norris, C. (1991). *Deconstruction: Theory and Practice.* London: Routledge.

Nöth, W. (1990). *Handbook of Semiotics.* Bloomington: Indiana University Press.

Nöth, W.(1994) (ed.). *Origins of Semiosis: Sign Evolution in Nature and Culture.* Berlin: Mouton de Gruyter.

Nuessel, F. (1992). *The Study of Names: A Guide to the Principles and Topics.* Westport: Greenwood.

Nuyts, J. (2001). *Epistemic Modality, Language, and Conceptualization: A Cognitive-Pragmatic Perspective.* Amsterdam: John Benjamins.

O'Barr, W. M. (1994). *Culture and the Ad.* Boulder: Westview Press.

O'Toole, M. (1994). *The Language of Displayed Art.* London: Leicester University Press.

Ogden, C. K. and Richards, I. A. (1923). *The Meaning of Meaning.* London: Routledge and Kegan Paul.

Ong, W. J. (1977). *Interfaces of the Word: Studies in the Evolution of Consciousness and Culture.* Ithaca: Cornell University Press.

Opie, I. and Opie, P. (1959). *The Lore and Language of Schoolchildren.* Frogmore: Paladin.

Ormiston, G. L, and Sassower, R. (1989). *Narrative Experiments: The Discursive Authority of Science and Technology.* Minneapolis: University of Minnesota Press.

Ortony, A. (1979) (ed.). *Metaphor and Thought.* Cambridge: Cambridge University Press.

Osgood, C. E., Suci, G. J., and Tannenbaum, P. H. (1957). *The Measurement of Meaning.* Urbana: University of Illinois Press.

Packard, V. (1957). *The Hidden Persuaders.* New York: McKay.

Paget, R. (1930). *Human Speech.* London: Kegan Paul.

Palek, B. (1991). Semiotics and Cartography. In: T. A. Sebeok and J. Umiker-Sebeok (eds.), *Recent Developments in Theory and History*, 465–491. Berlin: Mouton de Gruyter.

Palmer, G. B. (1996). *Toward a Theory of Cultural Linguistics.* Austin: University of Texas Press.

Parmentier, R. J. (1994). *Signs in Society: Studies in Semiotic Anthropology.* Bloomington: Indiana University Press.

Patterson, F. G. (1978). The Gestures of a Gorilla: Language Acquisition in Another Pongid. *Brain and Language* 5: 72–97.

Patterson, F. G. and Linden, E. (1981). *The Education of Koko.* New York: Holt, Rinehart and Winston.

Pavlov, I. (1902). *The Work of Digestive Glands.* London: Griffin.

Peck, S. R. (1987). *Atlas of Facial Expression.* Oxford: Oxford University Press.

Pedersen, H. (1931). *The Discovery of Language.* Bloomington: Indiana University Press.

Peirce, C. S. (1931–1958). *Collected Papers of Charles Sanders Peirce*, Vols. 1–8, C. Hartshorne and P. Weiss (eds.). Cambridge, Mass.: Harvard University Press.

Penn, J. M. (1972). *Linguistic Relativity Versus Innate Ideas: The Origins of the Sapir-Whorf Hypothesis in German Thought.* The Hague: Mouton.

Pfeiffer, J. E. (1982). *The Creative Explosion: An Inquiry into the Origins of Art and Religion.* Ithaca: Cornell University Press.

Piaget J. (1969). *The Child's Conception of the World.* Totowa, NJ: Littlefield, Adams and Co.

Piaget, J. and Inhelder, J. (1969). *The Psychology of the Child.* New York: Basic Books.

Piattelli-Palmarini, M. (1980) (ed.). *Language and Learning: The Debate between Jean Piaget and Noam Chomsky.* Cambridge, Mass.: Harvard University Press.

Piattelli-Palmarini, M. (1994). *Inevitable Illusions: How Mistakes of Reason Rule Our Minds.* New York: John Wiley.

Pinker, S. (1994). *The Language Instinct: How the Mind Creates Language.* New York: William Morrow.

Pinker, S. (1997). *How the Mind Works.* New York: Norton.

Pollio, H. and Burns, B. (1977). The Anomaly of Anomaly. *Journal of Psycholinguistic Research* 6: 247–260.

Pollio, H. and Smith, M. (1979). Sense and Nonsense in Thinking about Anomaly and Metaphor. *Bulletin of the Psychonomic Society* 13: 323–326.

Pollio, H., Barlow, J., Fine, H. and Pollio, M. (1977). *The Poetics of Growth: Figurative Language in Psychology, Psychotherapy, and Education.* Hillsdale, NJ: Lawrence Erlbaum Associates.

Popper, K. (1972). *Objective Knowledge: An Evolutionary Approach.* Oxford: Clarendon.

Popper, K. (1976). *The Unending Quest.* Glasgow: Harper Collins.

Popper, K. and Eccles, J. (1977). *The Self and the Brain.* Berlin: Springer.

Preble, D. and Preble, S. (1989). *Artforms*. New York: Harper Collins.

Premack, A. J. (1976). *Why Chimps Can Read*. New York: Harper and Row.

Premack, D. and Premack, A. J. (1983). *The Mind of an Ape*. New York: Norton.

Preziosi, D. (1979). *The Semiotics of the Built Environment: An Introduction to Architectonic Analysis*. Bloomington: Indiana University Press.

Prince, G. (1982). *Narratology: The Form and Functioning of Narrative*. Berlin: Mouton.

Propp, V. J. (1928). *Morphology of the Folktale*. Austin: University of Texas Press.

Radcliffe-Brown, A. R. (1922). *The Andaman Islanders*. Cambridge: Cambridge University Press.

Randazzo, S. (1995). *The Myth Makers*. Chicago: Probus.

Rathje, W. and Murphy, C. (1992). *Rubbish! The Archeology of Garbage*. New York: Harper Collins.

Reynolds, R. (1992). *Super Heroes: A Modern Mythology*. Jackson: University of Mississippi Press.

Richards, B. (1994). *Disciplines of Delight: The Psychoanalysis of Popular Culture*. London: Free Association Books.

Richards, I. A. (1936). *The Philosophy of Rhetoric*. Oxford: Oxford University Press.

Ricoeur, P. (1983). *Time and Narrative*. Chicago: University of Chicago Press.

Ries, J. (1994). *The Origins of Religions*. Grand Rapids: Eerdmans.

Riggins, S. H. (1994) (ed.). *The Socialness of Things: Essays on the Socio-Semiotics of Objects*. Berlin: Mouton de Gruyter.

Robinson, A. (1995). *The Story of Writing*. London: Thames and Hudson.

Robinson, A. H. and Petchenik, B. B. (1976). *The Nature of Maps*. Chicago: University of Chicago Press.

Rosch, E. (1973). On the Internal Structure of Perceptual and Semantic Categories. In: T. E. Moore (ed.), *Cognitive Development and Acquisition of Language*, 111–144. New York: Academic.

Rosch, E. (1975). Cognitive Reference Points. *Cognitive Psychology* 7: 532–547.

Rosch, E. (1981). Prototype Classification and Logical Classification: The Two Systems. In: E. Scholnick (ed.), *New Trends in Cognitive Representation: Challenges to Piaget's Theory*, 73–86. Hillsdale, N. J.: Lawrence Erlbaum Associates.

Rosch, E. and Mervis, C. (1975). Family Resemblances. *Cognitive Psychology* 7: 573–605.

Rousseau, J. J. (1966). *Essay on the Origin of Language*, trans. by J. H. Moran and A. Gode. Chicago: University of Chicago Press.

Royce, A. P. (1977). *The Anthropology of Dance*. Bloomington: Indiana University Press.

Rubinstein, R. P. (1995). *Dress Codes: Meanings and Messages in American Culture*. Boulder: Westview.

Ruesch, J. (1972). *Semiotic Approaches to Human Relations*. The Hague: Mouton.

Rumbaugh, D. M. (1977). *Language Learning by a Chimpanzee: The Lana Project*. New York: Academic.

Russell, B. and Whitehead, A. N. (1913). *Principia Mathematica*. Cambridge: Cambridge University Press.

Ruthroff, H. (1997). *Semantics and the Body: Meaning from Frege to the Postmodern*. Toronto: University of Toronto Press.

Saint-Martin, F. (1990). *Semiotics of Visual Language*. Bloomington: Indiana University Press.

Sapir, E. (1921). *Language*. New York: Harcourt, Brace, and World.

Sardar, Z. and Cubitt, S. (eds.) (2000). *Aliens R Us: Cinema, Science Fiction and the Other*. London: Pluto Press.

Sassienie, P. (1994). *The Comic Book*. Toronto: Smithbooks.

Saussure, F. de (1916). *Cours de linguistique générale*. Paris: Payot.

Savage-Rumbaugh, E. S. (1986). *Ape Language: From Conditioned Response to Symbol*. New York: Columbia University Press.

Savage-Rumbaugh, E. S., Rumbaugh, D. M., and Boysen, S. L. (1978). Symbolic Communication between Two Chimpanzees. *Science* 201: 641–644.

Schlosser, E. (2000). *Fast Food Nation*. Boston: Houghton Mifflin.

Schmandt-Besserat, D. (1978). The Earliest Precursor of Writing. *Scientific American* 238: 50–59.

Schmandt-Besserat, D. (1992). *Before Writing*, 2 vols. Austin: University of Texas Press.

Schogt, H. (1988). *Linguistics, Literary Analysis, and Literary Translation*. Toronto: University of Toronto Press.

Scholes, R. (1982). *Semiotics and Interpretation*. New Haven: Yale University Press.

Schrag, R. (1990). *Taming the Wild Tube*. Chapel Hill: University of North Carolina Press.

Seabrook, J. (2000). *Nobrow: The Culture of Marketing—The Marketing of Culture*. New York: Knopf.

Searle, J. R. (1969). *Speech Acts: An Essay in the Philosophy of Language*. Cambridge: Cambridge University Press.

Searle, J. R. (1984). *Minds, Brain, and Science*. Cambridge, Mass.: Harvard University Press.

Searle, J. R. (1992). *The Rediscovery of the Mind*. Cambridge, Mass.: MIT Press.

Sebeok, T. A. (1976). *Contributions to the Doctrine of Signs*. Lanham: University Press of America.

Sebeok, T. A. (1979). *The Sign and Its Masters*. Austin: University of Texas Press.

Sebeok, T. A. (1981). *The Play of Musement*. Bloomington: Indiana University Press.

Sebeok, T. A. (1986). *I Think I Am a Verb: More Contributions to the Doctrine of Signs*. New York: Plenum.

Sebeok, T. A. (1990). *Essays in Zoosemiotics*. Toronto: Toronto Semiotic Circle.

Sebeok, T. A. (1991). *A Sign Is Just a Sign*. Bloomington: Indiana University Press.

Sebeok, T. A. (1994, 2001). *Signs: An Introduction to Semiotics*. Toronto: University of Toronto Press.

Sebeok, T. A. and Danesi, M. (2000). *The Forms of Meaning: Modeling Systems Theory and Semiotics*. Berlin: Mouton de Gruyter.

Sebeok, T. A. and Umiker-Sebeok, J. (1994) (eds.). *Advances in Visual Semiotics*. Berlin: Mouton de Gruyter.

Seiter, E. (1995). *Sold Separately: Parents and Children in Consumer Culture*. New Brunswick, NJ: Rutgers University Press.

Shannon, C. E. (1948). A Mathematical Theory of Communication. *Bell Systems Technical Journal* 27: 379–423.

Shuker, R. (1994). *Understanding Popular Culture*. London: Routledge.

Sinclair, J. (1987). *Images Incorporated: Advertising as Industry and Ideology*. Beckenham: Croom Helm.

Singer, B. (1986). *Advertising and Society*. Toronto: Addison-Wesley.

Singer, M. (1991). *Semiotics of Cities, Selves, and Cultures: Explorations in Semiotic Anthropology*. Berlin: Mouton de Gruyter.

Sontag, S. (1978). *Illness as Metaphor*. New York: Farrar, Straus & Giroux.

Sontag, S. (1989). *AIDS and Its Metaphors*. New York: Farrar, Straus & Giroux.

Sparshott, F. (1995). *A Measured Pace: Toward a Philosophical Understanding of the Arts of Dance*. Toronto: University of Toronto Press.

Sperber, D. (1996). *Explaining Culture: A Naturalistic Approach*. Oxford: Blackwell.

Sperber, D. and Wilson, D. (1986). *Relevance, Communication, and Cognition*. Cambridge, Mass.: Harvard University Press.

Spigel, L. and Mann, D. (1992) (eds.). *Private Screenings: Television and the Female Consumer*. Minneapolis: University of Minnesota Press.

Stahl, S. (1989). *Literary Folkloristics and the Personal Narrative*. Bloomington: Indiana University Press.

Stark, S. (1997). *Glued to the Set*. New York: Free Press.

Steele, V. (1995). *Fetish: Fashion, Sex, and Power*. Oxford: Oxford University Press.

Stern, J. and Stern, M. (1992). *Encyclopedia of Pop Culture*. New York: Harper.

Straubhaar, J. and LaRose, R. (2000). *Media Now: Communications Media in the Information Age*. Belmont: Wadsworth.

Strinati, D. (2000). *An Introduction to Studying Popular Culture*. London: Routledge.

Sutton-Smith, B. (1986). *Toys as Culture*. New York: Gardner.

Swadesh, M. (1971). *The Origins and Diversification of Language*. Chicago: Aldine-Atherton.

Swann, P. (2000). *TVdotCom: The Future of Interactive Television*. New York: TV Books.

Synnott, A. (1993). *The Body Social: Symbolism, Self and Society*. London: Routledge.

Tannen, D. (1994). *Gender and Discourse*. Oxford: Oxford University Press.

Taylor, J. R. (1995). *Linguistic Categorization: Prototypes in Linguistic Theory*. Oxford: Oxford University Press.

Terrace, H. S. (1979). *Nim*. New York: Knopf.

Thom, R. (1975). *Structural Stability and Morphogenesis: An Outline of a General Theory of Models*. Reading: W. A. Benjamin.

Thomas, O. (1969). *Metaphors and Related Subjects*. New York: Random House.

Thorndike, E. L. (1898). *Animal Intelligence*. New York: Psychological Monographs.

Thorpe, W. H. (1961). *Bird-song*. Cambridge: Cambridge University Press.

Tilley, C. (1999). *Metaphor and Material Culture*. Oxford: Blackwell.

Tinbergen, N. (1963). On the Aims and Methods of Ethology. *Zeitschrift für Tierpsychologie* 20: 410–433.

Todorov. T. (1977 [1982]). *Theories of the Symbol*. Ithaca: Cornell University Press.

Toolan, M. J. (1988). *Narrative: A Critical Linguistic Introduction*. London: Routledge.

Tufte, E. R. (1997). *Visual Explanations: Images and Quantities, Evidence and Narrative*. Cheshire: Graphics Press.

Turing, A. (1936). On Computable Numbers with an Application to the Entscheidungs Problem. *Proceedings of the London Mathematical Society* 41: 230–265.

Turing, A. (1963). Computing Machinery and Intelligence. In: E. A. Feigenbaum and J. Feldman (eds.), *Computers and Thought*, 123–134. New York: McGraw-Hill.

Turnbull, D. (1989). *Maps Are Territories*. Chicago: University of Chicago Press.

Twitchell, J. B. (2000). *Twenty Ads that Shook the World*. New York: Crown.

Tylor, E. B. (1865). *Researches into the Early History of Mankind and the Development of Civilization*. London: John Murray.

Tylor, E. B. (1871). *Primitive Culture*. London: Murray.

Uexküll, J. von (1909). *Umwelt und Innenwelt der Tierre*. Berlin: Springer.

Umiker-Sebeok, J. (1987) (ed.). *Marketing Signs: New Directions in the Study of Signs for Sale*. Berlin: Mouton.

Ungerer, F. and Schmid, H.-J. (1996). *An Introduction to Cognitive Linguistics*. Harlow: Longman.

Valentine, T., Brennen, T., and Brédart, S. (1996). *The Cognitive Psychology of Proper Names*. London: Routledge.

Vardar, N. (1992). *Global Advertising: Rhyme or Reason?* London: Chapman.

Verene, D. P. (1981). *Vico's Science of the Imagination*. Ithaca: Cornell University Press.

Vestergaard, T. and Schrøder, K. (1985). *The Language of Advertising*. London: Blackwell.

Vihman, M. M. (1996). *Phonological Development: The Origins of Language in the Child*. London: Blackwell.

Visser, M. (1991). *The Rituals of Dinner*. New York: Harper Collins.

Visser, M. (1994). *The Way We Are*. Toronto: Harper Collins.

Vroon, P. and Amerongen, A. van (1996). *Smell: The Secret Seducer*. New York: Farrar, Straus and Giroux.

Vygotsky, L. S. (1962). *Thought and Language*. Cambridge, Mass.: MIT Press.

Walker, C. B. F. (1987). *Cuneiform*. Berkeley: University of California Press.

Watson, J. B. (1925). *Behaviorism*. New York: Norton.

Watson, J. B. (1929). *Psychology from the Standpoint of a Behaviorist*. Philadelphia: Lippincott.

Way, E. C. (1991). *Knowledge Representation and Metaphor*. Dordrecht: Kluwer.

Weissenborn, J. and Klein, W. (1982) (eds.). *Here and There: Cross-Linguistic Studies on Deixis and Demonstration*. Amsterdam: John Benjamins.

Werner, H. and Kaplan, B. (1963). *Symbol Formation: An Organismic-Developmental Approach to the Psychology of Language and the Expression of Thought*. New York: John Wiley.

Wernick, A. (1991). *Promotional Culture: Advertising, Ideology, and Symbolic Expression*. London: Gage.

Wescott, R. (1980). *Sound and Sense*. Lake Bluff, Ill.: Jupiter Press.

Wescott, R. W. (1974) (ed.). *Language Origins*. Silver Spring, Md.: Linstok Press.

Wescott, R. W. (1978). Visualizing Vision. In: B. Rhandawa and W. Coffman (eds.), *Visual Learning, Thinking, and Communication*, 21–37. New York: Academic.

Westphal, J. (1987). *Color: Some Philosophical Problems from Wittgenstein*. Oxford: Basil Blackwell.

Wheelwright, P. (1954). *The Burning Fountain: A Study in the Language of Symbolism.* Bloomington: Indiana University Press.

Whiteside, R. L. (1975). *Face Language.* New York: Pocket.

Whorf, B. L. (1956). *Language, Thought, and Reality,* J. B. Carroll (ed.). Cambridge, Mass.: MIT Press.

Wiener, N. (1949). *Cybernetics, or Control and Communication in the Animal and the Machine.* Cambridge, Mass.: MIT Press.

Williamson, J. (1985). *Decoding Advertisements: Ideology and Meaning in Advertising.* London: Marion Boyars.

Willis, R. (1990) (ed.). *Signifying Animals: Human Meaning in the Natural World.* London: Routledge.

Wilson, E. O. (1975). *Sociobiology: The New Synthesis.* Cambridge, Mass.: Harvard University Press.

Wilson, E. O. (1979). *On Human Nature.* New York: Bantam.

Wilson, E. O. (1984). *Biophilia.* Cambridge, Mass.: Harvard University Press.

Wilson, E. O. and Harris, M. (1981). Heredity Versus Culture: A Debate. In: J. Guillemin (ed.), *Anthropological Realities: Reading in the Science of Culture,* 459–467. New Brunswick, N. J.: Transaction Books.

Wilson, F. R. (1998). *The Hand: How Its Use Shapes the Brain, Language, and Human Culture.* New York: Pantheon.

Winner, E. (1982). *Invented Worlds: The Psychology of the Arts.* Cambridge, Mass.: Harvard University Press.

Winner, E. (1988). *The Point of Words: Children's Understanding of Metaphor and Irony.* Cambridge, Mass.: Harvard University Press.

Wise, R. (2000). *Multimedia: A Critical Introduction.* London: Routledge.

Wolfe, T. (1981). *From Bauhaus to Our House.* New York: Farrar, Strauss and Giroux.

Wright, B. W. (2000). *Comic Book Nation.* Baltimore: Johns Hopkins.

Wundt, W. (1973). *The Language of Gestures.* The Hague: Mouton.

Yu, N. (1998). *The Contemporary Theory of Metaphor: A Perspective from Chinese.* Amsterdam: John Benjamins.

Index

A

aboriginal maps, 84
abstract concepts, 115–116, 118,
    120–127
abstract referent, 5
absurdist theater, 167–169
actant, 144
Action Comics, 158
ad agency, 258
adaptors, 60
addressee, 106
addresser, 106
Adventures of Ozzie and Harriet, 250
advertising
    advent of, 258–260
    analysis of, 266–268
    brand names, 261–263
    commercial, 259
    consumer advertising, 257
    counterculture, use of, 271–272
    culture, 270–272
    described, 256–257
    electronic media, 258–259
    exposure to, 256
    as general persuasion technique, 255
    handbill, 258
    image-creation, 259–260
    Internet, 259
    language of, 259, 268–270
    logos, 263–266

and marketing, 257
    metaphor in, 269
    metonymy, 269
    mythologization, 260
    neomania, 256–257
    and new technology, 260
    as persuasive social strategy,
        256–257
    political-social advertising, 257
    positioning, 259
    restrictions on, 260, 270–271
    trade advertising, 257
    verbal techniques, 268–270
Advertising Research Foundation, 257
Aeschylus, 166
aesthesia, 76–77
aesthetic experience, 76–77
aesthetics, 161
affect displays, 60
age of reason, 172
alchemists, 206
Alexanderson, Ernst F.W., 240
All in the Family, 251, 252
Allen, Woody, 90, 132
alliteration, 100, 269
alphabetic system, 112–113
Alpher, B., 99
Amadeus (Forman), 171–172
American Ballet Theater, 63
American Buffalo (Mamet), 169